T0393676

# "WHO IS SITTING ON WHICH BEAST?"
# INTERPRETATIVE ISSUES IN
# THE BOOK OF REVELATION

Judaïsme ancien et origines du christianisme

# "WHO IS SITTING ON WHICH BEAST?" INTERPRETATIVE ISSUES IN THE BOOK OF REVELATION

## Proceedings of the International Conference held at Loyola University, Chicago, March 30-31, 2017

Edited by

Edmondo LUPIERI and Louis PAINCHAUD

BREPOLS

2023

Cover image: The Whore of Babylon Dresses the Part, by Loyset Liédet,
WIKIMEDIA COMMONS (Pierpont Morgan Library)



ISBN 978-2-503-60258-5
E-ISBN 978-2-503-60259-2
DOI 10.1484/M.JAOC-EB.5.131890
ISSN 2565-8492
E-ISSN 2565-960X

Printed in the EU on acid-free paper.

D/2023/0095/7

# CONTENTS

# AVANT-PROPOS

**Edmondo Lupieri et Louis Painchaud**

L'Apocalypse de Jean n'a cessé d'exercer une grande fascination chez ses lecteurs, religieux ou non. Sa transmission et sa réception en contexte chrétien ont donné lieu aux interprétions les plus diverses et à de multiples controverses. Au cœur de cette diversité interprétative, se trouvent des figures énigmatiques de femmes, de cités et de bêtes. C'est d'abord une femme de Thyatire, apparemment bien réelle, qui, selon Jean, « se dit prophétesse mais ne l'est pas », qu'il accuse de prostitution et affuble du nom ignominieux de Jézabel (Ap 2,20-21) ; c'est ensuite une mère portant un fils qui apparaît dans le ciel, puis est poursuivie au désert par un dragon (Ap 12,1-18) ; ensuite une prostituée qui chevauche dans le désert une bête (Ap 17,1-6) ; enfin, la fiancée de l'Agneau, identifiée à la Jérusalem nouvelle (Ap 21,1-27). Parallèlement apparaît une grande cité appelée tour à tour Babylone, Sodome et Égypte, « là même où le Seigneur a été crucifié » (Ap 11,8). Indissociable de ces figures féminines et de ces cités, une bête venue de la mer (Ap 13,1-10.18) emprunte les traits et l'autorité du dragon qui poursuit la femme au désert. Cette bête a son double venu, lui, de la terre, qui est à son service (Ap 13,11-17). Cette deuxième bête est aussi un « faux prophète » (Ap 16,13), un écho rendu à cette prophétesse de Thyatire. Toutes ces figures énigmatiques de femmes, de cités et de bêtes se reflètent l'une dans l'autre comme dans un jeu de miroirs où les identités se fondent et se confondent.

Cités, bêtes et prostituée sont généralement interprétées comme des références à peine voilées à Rome et à son empire, et en particulier à l'empereur Néron, figure archétypale de la persécution des chrétiens, ainsi qu'aux institutions liées au culte impérial dans les cités d'Asie Mineure, que Jean opposerait à la fiancée de l'Agneau, à la Jérusalem nouvelle, symboles de l'Église chrétienne. Pourtant, cette lecture, ne laisse pas de susciter un certain nombre de problèmes d'interprétation concernant le rapport de ces figures féminines entre elles et leur relation à la bête, concernant également l'identité de la cité qui se cache sous le nom symbolique de Babylone, de même que l'identité de la deuxième bête et son rapport à quelque réalité contemporaine de la rédaction de l'Apocalypse.

Les 30 et 31 mars 2017, des professeurs et des étudiants chercheurs du Canada, d'Italie et des États-Unis se sont réunis à Chicago à l'invitation des professeurs Edmondo Lupieri, titulaire de la chaire de théologie John Cardinal Cody à Loyola University, et Louis Painchaud de l'Université Laval (Québec), pour un atelier intitulé « Who Is Sitting on Which Beast ? Interpretative Issues in the Book of Revelation ». Cet atelier était parrainé par le département de théologie et le College of Arts and Sciences de Loyola University, ainsi que par ItalCultura, l'Institut culturel italien de Chicago, et le Consulat général d'Italie. Comme l'indique son titre, l'atelier portait sur l'interaction et l'interprétation de l'imagerie apocalyptique des bêtes et des femmes dans l'Apocalypse.

Le présent volume réunit les textes présentés lors de cet atelier. Hormis les deux derniers qui leur ont été ajoutés et qui illustrent la fluidité de la transmission de l'Apocalypse et de ses énigmes dans la culture et dans la religion, tous ces textes ont en commun de chercher les réponses aux problèmes d'interprétation que pose l'Apocalypse de Jean dans le contexte juif de sa composition et à la lumière des Écritures. La plupart s'inscrivent dans un courant minoritaire de lecture de l'Apocalypse qui voit dans cette grande cité, Babylone, non pas la Rome impériale, mais la Jérusalem terrestre ; dans ces femmes apparaissant tout à tour mère dans le ciel, prostituée au désert et à nouveau dans le ciel, fiancée de l'Agneau, non pas plusieurs femmes, mais une seule et même femme, symbolisant Israël. Ils sont répartis en quatre sections dont le cœur reflète la double interrogation qui a inspiré la tenue de cet atelier : « Qui chevauche quelle bête ? ».

Dans la première section, « Contexte », Luca Arcari (Université de Naples), situe l'Apocalypse de Jean parmi les différents groupes et factions du judaïsme du I^er^ siècle. Selon sa lecture, ce que Jean dépeint dans les sept messages aux assemblées (Ap 2-3) est développé dans les visions subséquentes, notamment, les deux bêtes (Ap 13) qui représentent une dynamique socioculturelle découlant de la place occupée par la religion publique dans le réseau sociopolitique de l'Asie Mineure ; plus précisément, la deuxième bête apparaît comme une sorte de miroir dans lequel se reflètent les effets d'une telle relation du politique et du religieux chez certains Juifs.

La seconde section, « Les femmes et les cités » réunit cinq textes qui examinent les figures féminines de l'Apocalypse à la lumière des Écritures. Stéphanie Audet (doctorante, Université Laval) propose une lecture intertextuelle de l'épisode de la femme au désert à partir des allusions scripturaires qu'il contient ; Robert Di Vito (Loyola University) propose un survol de l'utilisation du motif de la prostitution dans les Écritures dans le contexte du Proche-Orient ancien pour montrer que l'association de la « prostitution sacrée » à Babylone est en réalité une invention historiographique du XIX^e^ siècle ; Edmondo Lupieri (Loyola University) cherche à situer l'image de la Femme-Cité-Prostituée-Babylone dans ses contextes apocalyptiques et bibliques juifs et judéo-chrétiens les plus probables ; Iain Provan (Regent College, Vancouver) soutient que la dépendance du chapitre 18 aux Écritures résiste à toute application à des réalités historiques particulières contemporaines ; enfin Daniele Tripaldi (Université de Bologne) démontre à partir d'auteurs juifs que le discours royal appliqué à la « grande cité » de l'Apocalypse n'implique pas nécessairement une allusion à la Rome impériale mais peut très bien s'appliquer à Jérusalem.

La troisième section, « Le dragon et les bêtes » réunit trois textes. Dans le premier, Sergei Orlov (Marquette University, Milwaukee) soutient que la représentation du dragon dans l'Apocalypse reprend les principaux éléments des derniers moments du rituel juif du bouc émissaire tels qu'ils ressortent des témoignages apocalyptiques, mishnaïques et patristiques. Dans les deux textes suivants, Louis Painchaud (Université Laval, Québec) propose du dragon, des deux bêtes et des énigmes que posent ces figures une interprétation à la lumière des Écritures. Dans un premier volet, il interprète la station du dragon sur le sable de la mer (Ap 12,18) comme une affirmation voilée de sa domination sur Israël, et la bête issue de la mer, comme la récapitulation de tous les empires qui ont dominé Israël, et non comme le seul empire romain, qui n'est que le dernier d'entre eux. Dans le deuxième volet consacré à la bête issue de la terre, il interprète celle-ci comme une figure symbolique de la royauté et du sacerdoce juifs anciens souillés par l'or des nations, un or impur auquel renvoie le chiffre de la bête, 666 (Ap 13,18) lu à la lumière de l'or de Salomon (1 R 10,13).

La dernière section, intitulée « La réception, d'Irénée de Lyon à William Blake », comporte deux chapitres. Scott Brevard (doctorant, Loyola University) passe en revue la transmission et la réception de la figure de Babylone la grande à travers les œuvres de quelques auteurs chrétiens anciens, cherchant à comprendre les dynamiques changeantes qui ont présidé à sa transmission et à sa réception. Quant à Megan Wines (doctorante, Loyola University), elle nous transporte dans l'Angleterre du début du XIXe siècle où les diverses figures féminines de l'Apocalypse de Jean deviennent sous la plume visionnaire de William Blake une seule et même femme.

*We would like to thank here individually all the students and candidates in the New Testament and Early Christianity PhD Program at Loyola University Chicago who, in different ways, helped first with the organization of the 2017 conference and then, over the years, with the preparation of this volume. They are, in chronological order, Wesley Dingman, Scott Brevard, Joshua King, Eric Zito, Zach Eberhart, Megan Wines, Shane Gormley, Jared Teschner, Fabio Caruso, and Julian Sieber. Without their enthusiastic collaboration, this book would not have seen the light of day.*

# First Part

# Context

# OF BEASTS AND WOMEN: PROGRESSIVE HISTORY, TALES, OR WHAT ELSE? THE REVELATION OF JOHN BETWEEN HEGEMONY AND RELIGIOUS COHABITATION(S)

**Luca Arcari**

*Università degli Studi di Napoli Federico II*

Résumé

Ce que Jean dépeint dans les sept lettres aux ἐκκλησίαι (Ap 2-3) est développé dans les visions subséquentes, qui en dépeignent et relocalisent les éléments dans une perspective plus structurée et re-contextualisée. Dans cet essai, je lis certaines des visions de l'Apocalypse à la lumière de la dynamique groupale reflétée par ces lettres. Selon ces visions, les deux bêtes (Ap 13) représentent une dynamique socioculturelle découlant de la place occupée par la religion publique dans le réseau sociopolitique de l'Asie Mineure; plus précisément, la deuxième bête apparaît comme une sorte de miroir dans lequel se reflètent les effets d'une telle relation du « politique » et du « religieux » chez certains Juifs. Alors que les deux bêtes (Ap 13) représentent par leur action des prototypes d'organismes culturels et religieux perçus et décrits par Jean comme déviants et non conformes au « vrai » judaïsme, la Babylone prostituée d'Apocalypse 17-18 apparaît comme le prototype d'une ville dans laquelle vivent et opèrent ces organismes déviants. Dans un tel cadre, je soutiens la position minoritaire de la recherche contemporaine, principalement italienne, qui identifie Babylone avec une réalité juive, en fournissant quelques éléments supplémentaires en faveur de cette interprétation.

Abstract

What John depicts in the seven letters to the ἐκκλησίαι (Rev 2-3) is further developed by the following visions of the text, which re-visualize and relocate elements reported in the first part with a more structured and re-contextualized meaning. In this essay, I read some of the visions of Revelation in light of the group dynamics reported in the opening seven letters. According to John's visions, the two beasts of Rev 13:1-18 represent a socio-cultural dynamic arising from the place occupied by public religion in the socio-political network of Asia Minor; more specifically, the second beast emerges as a kind of mirror in which the effects of such a relationship are reflected among some Jews. If the two beasts of Revelation 13 represent, in action, prototypes of cultural and religious agencies both perceived and depicted by John as deviant and

*"Who is Sitting on Which Beast?" Interpretative Issues in the Book of Revelation. Proceedings of the International Conference held at Loyola University, Chicago, March 30-31, 2017,* ed. by Edmondo Lupieri and Louis Painchaud, JAOC 29 (Turnhout, 2023), pp. 15–46

DOI 10.1484/M.JAOC-EB.5.131927

not in line with the "true" Judaism, the whore-Babylon of Revelation 17-18 emerges as the prototype of a city in which previous deviant agencies live and operate. In such a framework, I aim at supporting the contemporary minority position of Italian scholarship which identifies Babylon with a Jewish reality, providing some further elements in favor of such an interpretation.

## 1. Introduction

The role played by the Revelation of John in the past and contemporary research on relationships between the first followers of Jesus and the multifaceted aspects of the Roman imperial hegemony is very well known.[1] Despite the fact that the text does not offer definite elements to obtain a precise dating, its "apocalyptic" nature and a deeply pessimistic historical vision have led the majority of its interpreters to read this text not only as a firm and definite reaction against the Roman imperial power, but also as a general reflection about the demonic nature of this hostile and repressive force against the rising Christianity.[2] It is not difficult to understand such an interpretation. From an apologetic (or intra-Christian) point of view, which aims at defending the canonical status of a difficult and repelling text, Revelation has mainly been read as the first chapter of a long history, that of the relationships between State and Church, as well as one of the first testimonies about the interchange of tolerance and repression in the Roman Empire, and therefore as the earliest more or less explicit evidence for a very complex history, that of the Roman persecution(s) against Christianity.[3] Rather than just a polemic against imperial power as a theoreti-

1. See the *status quaestionis* by M. Naylor, "The Roman Imperial Cult and Revelation," *Currents in Biblical Research* 8/2 (2010) 207-239 and the book by C.E. Frilingos, *Spectacles of Empire: Monsters, Martyrs, and the Book of Revelation* (Philadelphia: University of Pennsylvania Press, 2004). See also C.R. Koester, "The Image of the Beast from the Land (Rev 13:11-18): A Study in Incongruity," and E. Rosenberg, "'As She Herself Has Rendered': Resituating Gender Perspectives on Revelation's 'Babylon,'" in A. Yarbro Collins, ed., *New Perspectives in the Book of Revelation* (Leuven: Peeters, 2017) resp. 333-352 and 545-560. This paper echoes some of my previously published or current works: see L. Arcari, "Coabitazioni e autodefinizioni collettive nelle *ekklesiai* dell'Asia Minore alla fine del I sec. d.C. L'Apocalisse di Giovanni come 'discorso' locale in contesti urbani," *La parola del passato* 71 (2016) 296-331; Id., "Social Currency, Embodiment and Resilience (and/or Resistance). Judaism(s) and the Revelation of John in the Communicative Urban Market of Imperial Asia Minor (1st-2nd cent. C.E.)," *Studi e materiali di Storia delle religioni* 88/2 (2022) 426-442.

2. For a critique under the perspective of imperial studies, see S.J. Wood, *The Alter-Imperial Paradigm: Empire Studies and the Book of Revelation* (Leiden: Brill, 2016).

3. On these topics, see L. Arcari, "The Revelation of John and the Roman Empire: Methodological Observations on Witulski's Studies concerning the Dating

cal entity—which could theologize and therefore spiritualize John's text as a general meditation about human power—this essay aims at considering the local background to which our seer was exposed, i.e., a complex and fragmented social and cultural universe where different groups of believers in Christ live and cohabit in a very stratified religious market. In my approach, Revelation emerges as an indirect critique of other followers of Jesus who live under a fragmented and complex hegemonic context.

In light of this framework, I will try to read the seven letters in chapters 2-3 as some sort of literary and actual starting point of the following two beasts and Babylon visions (Rev 13:1-18; 17-18). It is not necessary to mention the difficulty caused by the excessive rigidity that has often been applied to understand the literary structure of the text, according to which the so-called epistolary section (Rev 2-3) would be definitely separated from the visionary one (Rev 4-22). Rather than as a progressive narrative or a sort of linear drama, Revelation should be proclaimed and written as an account in which more than one level of narration overlap each other, starting from the introductory seer's experience of the glorified Christ (Rev 1:7,9-20) up to the following revelations from the other-world reported in the rest of the book. What Jesus says to the angels of the seven ἐκκλησίαι comes even more "true" in the following visions of the book, which re-visualize and relocate what is reported in the first section again with more structured and re-contextualized meanings. The set of connections between the inaugural letters and the following visions, as well as the internal links between the various visions depicted in the work, are inevitably influenced by the fact that, in the proclamation of the text, the seven messages precede the other visions of the book and inform the readers directly of actual groups of believers who live the gospel in light of various cultural and religious actions.

The study of dynamics related to cultural and religious cohabitations among human micro-groups in antiquity should not rely on general or omni-comprehensive criteria of classification. Therefore, it should also not rely on our usual categories of generalization as for what concerns ancient religious agents, as in the case of such categories as "Jewish," "Christian," "Greek-Hellenistic," "Pagan" or "Roman Empire," since they are borrowed from late Christian apologetics and are in many cases not appropriate to describe the complexity of everyday lived realities of the ancient world.[4] In

---

of Revelation," *Annali di Storia dell'Esegesi* 33/1 (2016) 224-229.

4. On these topics, see the methodological assumptions by L. Arcari, "Cultural and Religious Cohabitations in Alexandria and Egypt between the 1st and the 6th Cent. CE," in Id., ed., *Beyond Conflicts. Cultural and Religious Cohabitations in Alexandria and Egypt between the 1st and the 6th Century CE* (Tübingen: Mohr Siebeck, 2017) 1-21. See also W. Mayer – C.L. de Wet, eds., *Reconceiving Religious Conflict: New Views from the Formative Centuries of Christianity. I: Re-Theorizing*

this essay, the idea of a "local discourse" seems to be the most suitable one to address the historicity of John's visionary account and, as such, when I refer to such terminology, it goes without saying that it is my aim to relativize its general application.

A theoretical glance at the contextualization of my terminology—especially concerning the terms "hegemony" and "cohabitation(s)"—shows that in my approach, cohabitation represents a sort of living historical process determined by contextual political, social and cultural dynamics, always "fabricated" under a specific cultural and/or political hegemony. In this regard, it is important to recall that postcolonial studies and related fields of research pay great attention to the problem of hegemony as well as to its intrinsic ambivalence. The concept of "cultural hybridity," as introduced by Homi Bhabha,[5] is only understandable in the context of the ambivalence of hegemony and power. Whereas in past scholarly debate, ethnicity was a central category in the study of ancient and modern colonization, postcolonial criticism emphasizes the role of ethnicity as one category among others to define power relations. Inspired in one way or another by the work of Antonio Gramsci,[6] postcolonial scholars have started to shift the perspective toward cultural hegemony and subordination. Summarizing Gramsci's concept of hegemony, Timothy Mitchell has underlined its dimension of

> Non-violent form(s) of control exercised through the whole range of dominant cultural institutions and social practices, from schooling, museums, and political parties to religious practice, architectural forms, and the mass media.[7]

In the ancient world, hegemony was often a violent form of physical coercion exercised through enslavement, policing actions, murders, torture, etc.; but it also assumed the aspects of more subtle forms of control conveyed through cultural institutions, systems of patronage, social networks, as well as through structured practices of everyday life. Both forms deal with the imperial Roman power in first-century Asia Minor. While Mitchell has highlighted mechanisms of hegemony, Daniel Miller has emphasized its "cosmological dimension":[8] hegemony often emerges

---

*Religious Conflict. Early Christianity to Late Antiquity and Beyond* (London-New York: Routledge, 2018).

5. See H. Bhabha, *The Location of Culture* (London: Routledge, 1994).

6. See Q. Hoare – G.N. Smith, eds., *Selections from the Prison Notebooks* (London: Lawrence & Wishart, 1971) 7-8 and 9-10. For an application of Gramsci's concept of "cultural hegemony" to the Hellenistic period, see A.E. Portier-Young, *Apocalypse Against Empire: Theologies of Resistance in Early Judaism* (Grand Rapids: Eerdmans, 2011) 3-45.

7. T. Mitchell, "Everyday Metaphors of Power," *Theory and Society* 19 (1990) 545-577 (553).

8. See D. Miller, "The Limits of Dominance," in Id. – M. Rowlands – C. Tilley, eds., *Domination and Resistance* (London: Unwin Hyman, 1989) 63-79.

as a normative and universal pattern based entirely on assumptions constructed (or invented) as traditional and, as a consequence, monolithic. Hegemony deliberately obliterates what is particular and contingent, assuming a specific tradition as the unique way in both perceiving the world and mapping the universe (and the place of human beings in it). "Tradition" separates inside from outside, normal from aberrant, and its logic legitimizes claims about truth and authority. Pierre Bourdieu has named such an invisible logic *doxa*, "the sum total of the theses tacitly posited on the hither side of all inquiry."[9]

The many reinventions of "tradition" relocated and renegotiated in the cultural contexts of the Greco-Roman world are all perceived as non-arbitrary, as products of a self-evident and natural order, which goes unquestioned. The aspirations of agents work in the system of orientation created by the same hegemony under which they all cohabitate together. Experiences of forced or intensive cultural contact open up possibilities for mutual renegotiations of different traditions, not only in naming and thinking what was previously unnamed and unthinkable, but also in rethinking and redefining what was rejected by the elite, in order to react to hegemony with counter-discourses aiming at articulating new parameters, always under hegemonic forms of cultural activity. In a hegemonic context, marginal (or constructed as marginal) social actors are forced to dress counter-discourses—often condemned by elites—with acceptable robes. Thanks to such a methodological approach that considers religious groups as *loci* of cohabitation rather than emphasizing ideological and/or theological polarizations, the Revelation of John assumes its actual dimension of counter-discourse, implicitly or explicitly connected to a contextual hegemonic system. In this framework, structures of power take on the appearance of something ideal, transcendent, and metaphysical, and a counter-discourse emerges as a competitive creation, which shares, and often reuses, the same hegemonic constructions in order to create a counter-space for religious and cultural actions.

## 2. The Seven Letters of Revelation 2-3 and the Cultural Dynamics of First-Century Asian ΕΚΚΛΗΣΙΑΙ

In Revelation 2-3, as a common element for characterizing many of the agents stigmatized in the text, we find the statement that these people "claim to be ... but are not" (Rev 2:9,20 ; 3:9). When some of the stigmatized agents show practices similar to one another (Rev 2:6//15 ;

9. See P. Bourdieu, *Outline of a Theory of Practice*, trans. R. Nice (Cambridge, U.K.: Cambridge University Press, 1977) 168.

2:9//3:9; 2:14//20), the seer highlights this, more or less explicitly referring to various social agents that are all engaged in hegemonic system(s) of the Greco-Roman cities of Asia Minor (Rev 2:9; 3:9 *vs.* 3:14,15,20). Nevertheless, the "social logic" of every text is "pressured" by extra-textual forces, and this is also the case of the discursive dimension arranged by the seer of Patmos.[10] In regards to the Jews in the Greco-Roman cities, literary and archaeological materials reveal that in such multifaceted universes there were various Jewish self-definitions, from people who sought to live in adherence with an interpretation—that was from time to time reinvented as "traditional"—of their Scripture, to people who represented themselves as perfectly integrated within the hegemonic socio-cultural fabric of the imperial cities. Such extra-textual pressures also demonstrate a salience of the various contextual Jewish identities or self-definitions, that is, their probability of being activated or not in particular situations.[11]

Keeping in mind such a theoretical framework, it is clear how extra-textual pressures are at work within John's discourse, along with inter- and intra-textual forces: does the belief in Jesus actually imply a refusal of the norms prescribed in the Bible? In contraposition with forms of Judaism depicted as expressions of "false" Jews, the seer of Patmos provides *his* answer: it is not possible to believe in Jesus and implement forms of hegemonic agency at the same time. In this framework, I explain also the attack against forms of perceived, concurrent leadership that, in John's opinion, seem to justify "idolatry." Among these are the criticism of the consumption of meats sacrificed to idols (Rev 2:6,14-15,20) and the polemics against female forms of prophetic leadership (Rev 2:20-23). Both appear to be expressions of a corruption of the "true" Judaism.[12]

---

10. On the concepts of "extra-textual pressure" and "social logic of texts," see G. Spiegel, "History, Historicism, and the Social Logic of the Text in the Middle Ages," *Speculum* 65/1 (1990) 59-86 (84); E.A. Clark, *History, Theory, Text: Historians and the Linguistic Turn* (Cambridge, MA: Harvard University Press, 2004) 12-13. See also the methodological observations carried out by É. Rebillard, *Christians and Their Many Identities in Late Antiquity, North Africa, 200-450 CE* (Ithaca: Cornell University Press, 2012) 5-6.

11. See the materials discussed by P.R. Trebilco, *Jewish Communities in Asia Minor* (Cambridge, UK: Cambridge University Press, 1991). See also the discussion carried out by Id., *The Early Christians in Ephesus from Paul to Ignatius* (Tübingen: Mohr Siebeck, 2004).

12. See D. Frankfurter, "Jews or Not? Reconstructing the 'Other' in Rev 2.9 and Rev 3.9," *Harvard Theological Review* 94/4 (2001) 403-425. On the meats sacrificed to idols in Revelation, see R. Penna, "Il caso degli idolotiti. Un test sulla sorte del cristianesimo da Paolo all'Apocalisse," in E. Bosetti – A. Colacrai, eds., Apokalypsis. *Percorsi nell'Apocalisse di Giovanni in onore di Ugo Vanni* (Assisi: Cittadella Editrice, 2005) 225-244. On the Jews mentioned in Rev 2:9 and 3:9 see also L. Painchaud, "Assemblées de Smyrne et de Philadelphie et congrégation de Satan.

The so-called Balaamites[13] do not consider it a problem to feed on meat sacrificed to the idols and this tolerance pushes John to accuse them of prostitution (Rev 2:14); also the prophetess Jezebel seems to support a similar tendency (Rev 2:20), and she is accused of "prostitution" (with the same association that we find in Rev 2:14). Balaamites are considered close to Nicolaites (Rev 2:25), and here we have a further reference to the ἐκκλησία of Ephesus (Rev 2:6) for its hatred towards the "works of Nicolaites, which I also despise." These associations between groups based in different cities suggest a leveling will as a direct consequence of the seer's discursive attitude. Nevertheless, the common element stressed by John is the intrinsic fakeness of these others' prophetic and preaching activities, evidently referring to people who do not regard their religious self-definition as more significant than other identities. In this framework, the stigmatization against those who "say they are Jews, and are not, but are the synagogue of Satan" (Rev 2:9; 3:9), emerge as an explicit reference to those who claim their Jewish origin despite their refusal of the faith in Jesus as it is proclaimed by John.

As a whole, it emerges that the author of Revelation claims for himself a conservative Jewish identity—or a Jewish identity actually reinvented as conservative—that is contrary to any form of dialogue with surrounding hegemonic backgrounds; but such an explicit refusal does not immediately mean that the seer is not sensitive as regards the multifaceted Hellenistic-Roman world in which he lives. For this, it is important to set apart rigid schematizations.[14]

---

Vrais et faux Judéens dans l'Apocalypse de Jean," *Laval théologique et philosophique* 70/3 (2014) 475-492.

13. This is a symbolic reinterpretation of Numbers 22-24, Deut 34:4-5, Jos 13:22 and 24:9; see also Neh 13:2 and Pseudo-Philo, *Biblical Antiquities* 18:13-14: E.F. Lupieri, *A Commentary on the Apocalypse of John*, trans. M. Poggi Johnson – A. Kamesar (Grand Rapids: Eerdmans, 2006) 120-121.

14. An example for such a cultural dynamic is emphasized by C.M. Conway, *Behold the Man: Jesus and Greco-Roman Masculinity* (Oxford: Oxford University Press, 2008) 159-174, according to whom Revelation shows a strict connection between the representation of Jesus and Greco-Roman "masculinity," which implies power, honor, fame, and violence, and whose best example from the time of Jesus is the portrayal of the emperor in the public realm. Another example is that emphasized by D.E. Aune, *Revelation 1-5* (Waco: Word Book Press, 1997), esp. 126-129, who has suggested the influence of the royal and imperial edicts on the format of the seven letters of Rev 2-3: (1) the *praescriptio* (introduction); (2) the central section; and (3) the conclusion. Aune holds that the seven messages follow this threefold structure: (1) an introduction; (2) a central section introduced by "I know"; and (3) a double conclusion containing a call for vigilance and a victory saying. See also the more general study by G. Biguzzi, "Giovanni di Patmos e la cultura ellenistica," in E. Bosetti – A. Colacrai, eds., Apokalypsis. *Percorsi nell'Apocalisse di Giovanni in onore di Ugo Vanni* (Assisi: Cittadella Editrice, 2005) 93-126, according to which, in Revelation, an ambiguity emerges between

As a "local discourse,"[15] Revelation embodies an ideological program of self-definition for specific contexts. Hence, the necessity of representing elements of the dominant cultural context as an instrument of self-definition as well as in polemic keys, assumes an important role. In Rev 2:13, when the seer addresses the believers at Pergamum, he states "[I] know where you live–where Satan has his throne" and for this reason it is possible that there is a reference to a well-known building (despite the fact that there are several possible buildings that could be identified with it: i.e., the large altar of Zeus or the temple of Asclepius). If, on the one hand, we need to think about a building related to Roman imperial power and,

---

the explicit refusal of some elements deriving from the cultural hegemonic system and an acceptance of other categories of the same world. An example is that of the use of θρόνος. John often uses the expression, "one sitting upon the throne," which is one of the ways of identifying some positive otherworld agents. John links the description of the throne with the one who sits on it in Rev 4, and, after this connection, the phrase "one who sits on the throne" becomes a customary way of referring to supreme heavenly agents. In other passages of Revelation, the throne stands for God itself. The clearest example is Rev 7:9, which indicates people standing before the throne and the Lamb; there is no mention of God's name, but the statement of the description is clearly concerned with the worship to God and to the Lamb. Another example is Rev 14:3, in which it depicts singing before the throne, the four living creatures and the elders. In this descriptive framework, references to Satan's throne in 2:13, as well as to the beast's throne in 13:2 and 16:10, emerge as a typical counter-image modeled on one of the typical imperial symbols of power (as it is well-known, θρόνος is attested in official inscriptions from Asia Minor: e.g., see *Supplementum epigraphicum graecum* 26 [1976] 1272 = *IEph* 275 = P.A. HARLAND, *Greco-Roman Associations: Texts, Translations and Commentary. II. North Coast of the Black Sea, Asia Minor* [Berlin: De Gruyter, 2014] 276-279; it is an honorary inscription for Hadrian by μύσται of Dionysos from Ephesus, 119-129 CE). The ἐκκλησία in Pergamum is told that it lives where Satan's throne is, or where Satan dwells (Rev 2:13). The beast's throne is firstly mentioned when John refers to its power and authority (Rev 13:2), while other allusions allude to its destruction (16:10), and after this destruction the world falls into the darkness. The literary connection between the beast's throne and its kingdom implies that the image of the throne signifies "having a power" or a "kingdom" or at least a "right reign" in a kingdom. The imagery of the throne is often employed in Hebrew texts (see Isa 6:1; 9:6; 10:13; 14:13; 16:5; 22:23; 47:1; 66:1; Jer 1:15; 3:17; 13:13; 14:21; 17:12,25; 22:2,30; 29:16; 33:21; 36:30; 43:10; 49:38; 52:32; Ezek 1:26; 10:1; 17:16; 28:2; 43:7; Zech 6:13; Dan 3:54; 7:9; etc.), and this is a typical image of power modeled on the Near East construction of the figure of the king, a construction that was partially re-assumed also during the Hellenistic and the Roman periods; in this regard, it is interesting to note that the symbol of the throne has played an important representative role under Titus and Domitian. For the throne image in Revelation in its historical and cultural *scenario*, see L. GALLUSZ, *The Throne Motif in the Book of Revelation* (London: Bloomsbury, 2014).

15. On Revelation as a (local) discourse, see S. FRIESEN, *Imperial Cults and the Apocalypse of John* (Oxford: Oxford University Press, 2001) 16-19.

more specifically, to a temple,[16] on the other hand we must not forget that such a detail acquires its value exactly within the discursive context set up by John, which is at the same time a counter-product of the hegemonic symbolism concerning power and/or authority.

Going beyond the polemical elements of John's discourse, descriptions in Revelation confirm dynamics of cohabitation between various religious agents in a strongly urbanized space.[17] It is interesting to notice how the very aspect of urbanization is put to the service of the seer's discursive flow.

John is almost certainly an itinerant visionary agent: he seems to personally know the various ἐκκλησίαι of Asia to which he sent his letters, and he is on the island of Patmos when he has his experience of contact with the otherworld. The island of Patmos itself is not a deserted and uninhabited place as many interpreters have imagined it.[18] There has been very little archaeological exploration undertaken on this island, in contrast to the massive archaeological projects at Ephesus, Pergamum, or Sardis.[19] As Ian Boxall has remarked,[20] archaeological ruins on the Castle Moun-

---

16. Considering the close relationship established by John between the throne and temple in 7:15, 8:3-5, 11:19 and 15:2,5-6.

17. Research on phenomena of urbanization have emphasized the relationships between religious authority and political, social, and economic power(s) for many years. The control exercised by local and/or state cultic centers presupposes not only the development of new institutions but also processes of modification and/or differentiation of existing religious groups and practices, also when an agent or a group explicitly define themselves in light of an unchangeable cultural and religious resistance against a perceived oppression. Here, I consider "urbanism" like a function, not morphology: see the comparative perspective carried out by D.N. KEIGHTLEY ("Religion and the Rise of Urbanism," *Journal of the American Oriental Society* 93/4 [1973] 527-538), and the recent analysis by A. LEONE (*The End of the Pagan City. Religion, Economy, and Urbanism in Late Antique North Africa* [Oxford: Oxford University Press, 2013]). See also the project at the Humanities Centre for Advanced Studies/Kolleg-Forschungsgruppe (KFG) "Religion and Urbanity: Reciprocal Formations" (FOR 2779), University of Erfurt, Max-Weber-Kolleg: https://www.uni-erfurt.de/en/max-weber-kolleg/forschung/forschungsgruppen-und-stellen/research-groups/humanities-centre-for-advanced-studies-kolleg-forschungsgruppe-kfg-religion-and-urbanity-reciprocal-formations-for-2779. See also A. LÄTZER-LASAR – E.R. URCIUOLI, eds., *Urban Religion in Late Antiquity* (Berlin-Boston: De Gruyter, 2021); J. RÜPKE, *Urban Religion. A Historical Approach to Urban Growth and Religious Change* (Berlin-Boston: De Gruyter, 2020); E.R. URCIUOLI, *La religione urbana. Come la città ha prodotto il cristianesimo* (Bologna: EDB, 2021).

18. See the cases illustrated by I. BOXALL, *Patmos in the Reception History of the Apocalypse* (Oxford: Oxford University Press, 2013).

19. See the general assessment carried out by R.E. OSTER, *Seven Congregations in a Roman Crucible: A Commentary on Revelation 1-3* (Eugene, OR: Wipf & Stock, 2013).

20. I. BOXALL, "Reading the Apocalypse on the Island of Patmos," *Scripture Bulletin* 40/1 (2010) 22-33.

tain overlooking the port of Skala, and pottery sherds scattered around the area, attest that this part of Patmos was probably inhabited continuously from the Middle Bronze Age to the Roman period, with fortifications built in the Hellenistic period.[21] A surviving inscription, dated to the second century BCE, reveals that the island was large enough to support its own gymnasium, with an association of torch-runners and one for athletic oil users.[22] Two other epigraphs reveal that the cult of the goddess Artemis was strong on the island, the most extensive of which is dated to the second century CE (it is preserved in the Monastery of St John the Theologian) and refers to Bera, the priestess of Artemis, mentioning also a temple of Artemis Scythia; this inscription describes Patmos as "the most august island of the daughter of Leto."[23] Boxall has also stressed that another relevant inscription is an undated dedication on an altar to Artemis under her apparently local title of Artemis Patmia. This inscriptional evidence fits in with much later local traditions, which claim that St. Christodoulos, the eleventh-century founder of the monastery, constructed it on the site of the Temple of Artemis, and that he destroyed the great cult statue in the process.[24]

As Henri-Dominique Saffrey has further reminded us,[25] in the Hellenistic-Roman period, Patmos was a district of the port city of Miletus. Miletus was a strategically important seaport and Patmos was populated by Miletus's citizens and a commandant who was effectively resident governor.[26] Culturally and administratively, Patmos looked to Miletus, and "continued to do so into the Roman period, even if Miletus and its dependents came under the ultimate authority of the Roman governor of Asia."[27] Thus, the picture of the island itself is that of an urbanized space.

---

21. See T. STONE, *Patmos* (Athens: Lycabettus Press, 1981) 5.

22. See D.F. MCCABE – M.A. PLUNKETT, *Patmos Inscriptions: Texts and List* (Princeton: Institute for Advanced Study, 1985) no. 001. See also H.-D. SAFFREY, "Relire l'Apocalypse à Patmos," *Revue Biblique* 82 (1975) 385-417 (399-407).

23. This is the inscription no. 004 in D.F. MCCABE – M.A. PLUNKETT, *Patmos Inscriptions: Texts and List* (Princeton: Institute for Advanced Study, 1985). H.-D. SAFFREY, "Relire l'Apocalypse à Patmos," *Revue Biblique* 82 (1975) 385-417 proposes on the basis of this inscription that Patmos had its own local variant on the birth of Artemis, presenting itself as the birthplace of the goddess.

24. I. BOXALL, "Reading the Apocalypse on the Island of Patmos," *Scripture Bulletin* 40/1 (2010) 22-33 (25). This is the inscription no. 003 in D.F. MCCABE – M.A. PLUNKETT, *Patmos Inscriptions: Texts and List* (Princeton: Institute for Advanced Study, 1985).

25. H.-D. SAFFREY, "Relire l'Apocalypse à Patmos," *Revue Biblique* 82 (1975) 385-417.

26. See D.E. AUNE, *Revelation 1-5* (Dallas: Word Books Press, 1997) 77.

27. I. BOXALL, "Reading the Apocalypse on the Island of Patmos," *Scripture Bulletin* 40/1 (2010) 22-33 (26). The connection with Miletus implies a religious link with Artemis's brother Apollo and her mother Leto. The title "water-bearer"

If we leave aside the romantic picture of John as a solitary and exiled man because of Domitian persecution, we are confronted with the image of a prophet who goes to the island in order to perform his prophetic and/or visionary functions (we do not know whether he was paid or not).[28] The "interstitial"[29] nature of groups of believers in Jesus in the first century is clearly emphasized by the fact that Jesus's followers engage prophecy in various "non-predisposed" places. The multifaceted conflicts between John and the other groups located in the main cities of Asia Minor, some of which are composed by agents who negotiate specific "temporary" self-definitions (also suspending it or engaging it intermittently), reveal a case

---

given to the priestess of Patmian Artemis quoted in the inscription no. 004 (see supra, n. 23) is distinctive to the city. Artemis's brother Apollo is frequently represented on Miletus's coins and other coins of the imperial period depict the flight of the pregnant Leto from the dragon Python. In this context, it is also important to remember that, in the iconography of Ephesus, Artemis is associated with the moon and the stars, like the woman of Rev 12:1. As noted by S. FRIESEN, *Imperial Cults and the Apocalypse of John* (Oxford: Oxford University Press, 2001) 70 and 168, in the courtyard of Miletus's βουλευτήριον, there was an altar dedicated to the imperial cult which bore a sculptural relief of Leto seated on the throne with Apollos and Artemis, integrating the worship of the Emperor into local myths. On the possible influence of the myth of the flight of the pregnant Leto from the dragon in the construction of the combat myth narrated in Rev 12, see the classic work by A. YARBRO COLLINS, *The Combat Myth in the Book of Revelation* (Missoula: Scholars Press, 1976). A. KERKESLAGER, "Apollo, Greco-Roman Prophecy, and the Rider on the White Horse in Rev 6.2," *Journal of Biblical Literature* 112 (1993) 116-121 has also noted that the rider on the white horse carrying a bow of Rev 6:2 is a representation of Apollo's figure, a symbol not only of false Christs but also of false prophecy, a sort of subversion of the true prophecy symbolized by the other rider depicted in Rev 19:11-16. As observed by I. BOXALL, "Reading the Apocalypse on the Island of Patmos," *Scripture Bulletin* 40/1 (2010) 28: "To a person living in the territory of Miletus or its islands in the first century, one of the primary resonances of a figure carrying a bow would be the figure of Apollo. Moreover, the prominence of Didyma would associate Apollo first and foremost with prophetic utterance."

28. See Acts 9:3-12; 22:10; Hermas, *Shepherd*, *Visio* 3.1.1-5; *2 Baruch* 10.3; *4 Ezra* 9.24-26. In the territory of Miletus, prophetic activity was linked to the oracle of Apollo at Didyma, which was connected to the city by a sacred way. By the first century, Didyma's oracle was a rival to the more famous oracle at Delphi and for citizens of Miletus, including those living over the water on Patmos, Apollo was pre-eminently the god of prophecy. As I. Boxall has noted in "Reading the Apocalypse on the Island of Patmos," *Scripture Bulletin* 40/1 (2010) 27, it is also possible that the cult of Apollo was established on Patmos: the version of the *Acts of John* attributed to Prochorus recalls frequently a temple and priests of Apollo, and a number of modern visitors to Patmos have suggested that Apollo's temple was located on the acropolis (for example, see V. GUÉRIN, *Description de l'île de Patmos et de l'île de Samos* [Paris: Durand, 1856] 13).

29. On such a terminology, see A. DESTRO – M. PESCE, "Dal gruppo interstiziale di Gesù alla *ekklêsia*: mutamenti nel ruolo delle donne," *Annali di Storia dell'Esegesi* 28 (2011) 37-58.

of dissociation as sometimes results from urbanization: living where you would not like to. Despite such a dissociation, John and the other followers of Christ depicted positively (see Rev 2:1-3,6-7,9-10,12-13,19; 3:4-5,8,10-12) live and continue to live in that hegemonic context. And some reactions that John elicits from other neighboring religious agents seem intolerable to him.

In summary, John is located in Patmos for his preaching of a contextual gospel, and the island of Patmos seems an odd choice for a concerted campaign, as a seaport in Miletus's district. John was either impelled to go to the island with a view to receiving the "word of God" or was ordered by the "word of God" to retreat there for obtaining a direct contact with the otherworld. This would also explain the wider context of Rev 1:9, in which John presents himself as sharing in the "tribulation" (θλῖψις), where this term alludes to a particular aspect of the extraordinary experience of prophecy,[30] an experience lived together with other visionary agents included by John among his privileged audience (John defines himself as ἀδελφός and συγκοινωνός of an unspecified second-person plural; see Rev 1:9).

## 3. The Two Beasts of Revelation 13: Prototypes of Deviant Agency

What John depicts in the seven letters is further developed by the following visions of the text, which re-visualize and relocate elements reported in the first part with a more structured and re-contextualized meaning.

30. It is interesting to note that the term θλῖψις primarily alludes to a physical "pressure," like in Rufus Medicus in Oribasius, *Medical Collections* 8.24.61, and Galen, *On Differences of Fever* 1.9 (see TLG, *s.v.*). The metaphoric interpretation of the noun in the sense of "tribulation" emerges as a consequence of the physical and/or internal movements connected to a "dysphoric activity," and for this it does not seem necessary to interpret the phrase in Rev 1:9 (Ἐγὼ Ἰωάννης, ὁ ἀδελφὸς ὑμῶν καὶ συγκοινωνὸς ἐν τῇ θλίψει καὶ βασιλείᾳ καὶ ὑπομονῇ ἐν Ἰησοῦ, ἐγενόμην ἐν τῇ νήσῳ τῇ καλουμένῃ Πάτμῳ διὰ τὸν λόγον τοῦ θεοῦ καὶ τὴν μαρτυρίαν Ἰησοῦ) as an allusion to an experience of imprisonment or political and/or religious persecution. On the relationships between the so-called "dysphoric activities" and the phenomena of contact with the otherworld in many past and present cultural and social environments, see H. Whitehouse – B. McQuinn, "Divergent Modes of Religiosity and Armed Struggle," in M. Juergensmeyer – M. Kitts – M. Jerryson, eds., *The Oxford Handbook of Religion and Violence* (Oxford: Oxford University Press, 2013) 597-619. For a socio-literary interpretation of θλῖψις, see L.L. Thompson, "A Sociological Analysis of Tribulation in the Apocalypse of John," *Semeia* 36 (1986) 147-174; Id., *The Book of Revelation: Apocalypse and Empire* (Oxford: Oxford University Press, 1990) 188-191; L. Arcari, "'Ecco, faccio nuove tutte le cose' (Ap 21,5). Epistemologia visionaria e (ri-)costruzione del mondo nell'Apocalisse di Giovanni," *Ricerche storico-bibliche* 34/1-2 (2022) 95-114 (105-107).

For this reason, I believe it is useful to read some of the visions of Revelation in light of the group dynamics reported in the opening seven letters, and this is also the case of the vision of both beasts in Rev 13:1-18.

## 3.1 The First Beast as a Prototype of Imperial Local Agency

The first beast, that coming from the sea, is modeled on the description of the four reigns we find in Dan 7:2-7. The Johannine monster emerges as a sort of hybrid in which some traits of the various Danielic beasts are assumed and conflated into the same figure. This beast stands as a kingdom that has substituted and assumed previous demonic powers as well as many of their characteristics.[31] The symbolic connections between the first beast and the δράκων of Revelation 12[32] seem to suggest another level of analysis, although strictly connected with the first one. This beast works on the heels of the ancestral figure of the δράκων, who is contrasted with the woman clothed with the sun and has persecuted her and her offspring. In such a visionary framework, while the δράκων is identified with a primeval figure—that of Satan—the first beast is continuing its primeval deviant work.[33] In such a perspective, behind the beast stands Satan as the primeval δράκων.

The importance of the first beast as a kind of "Immoveable Mover" and, at the same time, as someone who has received this prerogative from another (the δράκων), emerges especially from its main activity: to speak or to proclaim something blasphemous against God and his followers (Rev 13:5-6):

> Καὶ ἐδόθη αὐτῷ στόμα λαλοῦν μεγάλα καὶ βλασφημίας, καὶ ἐδόθη αὐτῷ ἐξουσία ποιῆσαι μῆνας τεσσαράκοντα δύο. Καὶ ἤνοιξεν τὸ στόμα αὐτοῦ εἰς βλασφημίας πρὸς τὸν θεόν, βλασφημῆσαι τὸ ὄνομα αὐτοῦ καὶ τὴν σκηνὴν αὐτοῦ, τοὺς ἐν τῷ οὐρανῷ σκηνοῦντας.

> And a mouth was given to it to utter great things and blasphemies, and authority was given to it to act for forty-two months. And it opened its mouth in blasphemies toward God, to blaspheme his name and his abode, that is, those who abide in heaven.[34]

---

31. See D. Tripaldi, *Apocalisse di Giovanni* (Rome: Carocci, 2012) 174-175.

32. Both these figures have ten horns and seven heads: see 12:3//13:1; the power of the first beast comes directly from the δράκων: 13:2,4; like the first beast, the δράκων receives the worship of the world: 13:4.

33. See E.F. Lupieri, *A Commentary on the Apocalypse of John*, trans. M. Poggi Johnson – A. Kamesar (Grand Rapids: Eerdmans, 2006) 201-207. On the protological interpretation of Rev 12, see L. Arcari, *"Una donna avvolta nel sole..." (Apoc 12,1). Le raffigurazioni femminili nell'Apocalisse di Giovanni alla luce della letteratura apocalittica giudaica* (Padua: Messaggero, 2008) 321-430.

34. Text and translation in E.F. Lupieri, *A Commentary on the Apocalypse of John*, trans. M. Poggi Johnson – A. Kamesar (Grand Rapids: Eerdmans, 2006) 72-73.

The beast officially proclaims and acts. It works with power or authority in front of others. And in so doing, it assumes a typical trait of the imperial self-definition as this emerges from various local contexts. In this regard, four terms employed by John assume a key role: ἐξουσία, προσκυνέω, λαλέω, and ποιέω. According to the imperial inscriptions from Asia Minor, the first noun is often used as a synonym of *tribunicia potestas*.[35] Apart from this technical use, the term generally designates—as S. Dmitriev has suggested—"the content of an office without separating it from the office itself,"[36] or a "power that did not originally come with official responsibilities."[37] Although this situation developed further in the second and third century: a decree of Ephesian γερουσία from the reign of Commodus refers to the ἐξουσία not only of ἄρχοντες but of private individuals as well.[38] The verb προσκυνέω is used by John as a synonym of "make obeisance," or also "fall down in worship."[39] Nevertheless, the coinage minted by Emperors often depicts Roman standards and the dominated people, the latter in a clearly subservient, kneeling position. This

35. See the letter of the Emperor Claudius to the sacred victors and performers of Dionysus from Miletus: *IMiletos* 156 = *Greek Constitutions of Early Roman Emperors from Inscriptions and Papyri* (Philadelphia: American Philosophical Society, 1989) 29 = R.S. Ascough – P.A. Harland – J.S. Kloppenborg, *Associations in the Greco-Roman World: A Sourcebook* (Waco: Baylor University Press; Berlin: De Gruyter, 2012) no. 178. See also the letter of the Emperor Marcus Aurelius to the synod of Dionysus Breiseus from Smyrna: *Supplementum epigraphicum graecum* 34 (1984) no. 1191 = *ISmyrna* 600 = R.S. Ascough – P.A. Harland – J.S. Kloppenborg, *Associations in the Greco-Roman World: A Sourcebook* (Waco: Baylor University Press; Berlin: De Gruyter, 2012) no. 192 = P.A. Harland, *Greco-Roman Associations: Texts, Translations and Commentary. II. North Coast of the Black Sea, Asia Minor* (Berlin: De Gruyter, 2014) 305-306.

36. See S. Dmitriev, *City Government in Hellenistic and Roman Asia Minor* (Oxford: Oxford University Press, 2005) 238.

37. S. Dmitriev, *City Government in Hellenistic and Roman Asia Minor* (Oxford: Oxford University Press, 2005) 239.

38. *IEph* (Ia) 26.202. Sviatoslav Dmitriev observes: "The separation of power from the office is especially well demonstrated by several inscriptions from the second and third centuries A.D. that refer to the 'prytanic power' (*prytanike exousia*) but, significantly, not to the 'power of the prytaneis.' The use of the phrase 'prytanic power' is reminiscent of the Roman 'tribunician power,' after which it was probably modeled. Therefore, on the one hand, such evidence suggests that this practice was well established at that time. On the other hand, the idea of the tribunician power appeared only under Augustus and, for this reason, was quite new for the Romans as well" (*City Government in Hellenistic and Roman Asia Minor* [Oxford: Oxford University Press, 2005] 239).

39. See Herodotus, *Histories* 2.121; Sophocles, *Oedipus C.* 1654; Aeschylus, *Persians* 499, *Prometheus* 936; Aristophanes, *The Knights* 156; Plato, *Republic* 451a, etc. For the "Oriental" fashion of the term, see Herodotus, 1.119; 8.118; Aristoteles, *The History of Animals* 630b 20, etc.

was how the return of the standards was publicly represented—as an act of submission, capturing the moment of the handing over of the Roman standards.[40] The verb λαλέω in John's account generically states the act of articulating a speech, implying a process of communication like that which is implicit in the terms usually employed in royal or imperial epigraphs: λέγω,[41] κελεύω, verbs in various ways linked to writing activities,[42] as well as ἐφίημι[43] or φημί,[44] these are performative linguistic instruments by which authorities show themselves *via* the diffusion of their power. The effects of authorities' communicative action(s) are conflated in John's use of ποιέω, i.e., a kind of symbolic reproduction of a series of verbs by which activities fielded by hegemonic power(s) are indicated

---

40. The coinage minted by Augustus in 19-17 BCE in Rome, Asia Minor, Spain, Gaul, and Italy depicts the Roman standards and the Parthians, the latter in a clearly subservient position, "probably as a part of the well-known Eastern full prostration, the *proskynesis*, that the Parthians would have performed as an act of obeisance": G. VAN KOOTEN, "Matthew, the Parthians, and the Magi: A Contextualization of Matthew's Gospel in Roman-Parthian Relations of the First Centuries BCE and CE," in ID. – P. BARTHEL, eds., *The Star of Bethlehem and the Magi: Interdisciplinary Perspectives from Experts on the Ancient Near East, the Greco-Roman World, and Modern Astronomy* (Leiden: Brill, 2005) 496-645 (547).

41. E.g., the reconstruction of the letters by Vespasian and Domitian on Physicians and Instructors from Pergamum (74 CE and 93-94 CE): J.H. OLIVER, *Greek Constitutions of Early Roman Emperors from Inscriptions and Papyri* (Philadelphia: American Philosophical Society, 1989) no. 38. See also R. HERZOG, "Urkunden zur Hochschulpolitik der römischen Kaiser," *Sitzungsberichte der Preußischen Akademie der Wissenschaften, Philosophisch-Historische Klasse* 32 (1935) 965-1019.

42. As an example, the use of verbs connected to γράφω as key-lexemes of the promulgation of provincial or municipal wills that are "written" on epigraphs: see S. FRIESEN, *Imperial Cults and the Apocalypse of John* (Oxford: Oxford University Press, 2001) esp. 33 and 64.

43. For both verbs, see the letters of Hadrian to the synod of Dionysiac performers from Mysia and Troad (133-134 CE): *Supplementum epigraphicum graecum* 56 (2006) 1359. See also G. PETZL – E. SCHWERTHEIM, *Hadrian und die dionysischen Künstler. Drei in Alexandria Troas neugefundene Briefe des Kaisers an die Künstler-Vereinigung* (Bonn: Habelt, 2006); C.P. JONES, "Three New Letters of the Emperor Hadrian," *Zeitschrift für Papyrologie und Epigraphik* 161 (2007) 145-156 (Eng. translation). A well-attested expression is ἀναγορεύω τὸν στέφανον: e.g., see *IG* II$^2$ 1263.67, 43-45 (Piraeus, 300/299 BCE); *ITomis* 7 (late first century BCE, early first century CE); *IEph* 22.54-55 (Nysa, *c.* 142 CE) = P.A. HARLAND, *Greco-Roman Associations: Texts, Translations and Commentary. II. North Coast of the Black Sea, Asia Minor* (Berlin: De Gruyter, 2014) 351-360.

44. See the example of the letter of Hadrian concerning Erastus the shipper from Ephesos (128-129 CE); see C.T. NEWTON – E.L. HICKS – G. HIRSCHFELD, *The Collection of Ancient Greek Inscriptions in the British Museum. III/2: Ephesos* (Oxford: Clarendon, 1890) n. 487 = *IEph* 1487 = J.H. OLIVER, *Greek Constitutions of Early Roman Emperors from Inscriptions and Papyri* (Philadelphia: American Philosophical Society, 1989) no. 82 A-B = *Supplementum epigraphicum graecum* 44 (1994) no. 929.

in epigraphic materials.[45] For all these reasons, it is very hard to believe that John had firsthand experience of the imperial power in its central, or Roman, dimension. The first beast makes sense in a mediated bodily experience of that power or in the visible effects of that hegemony, as a perception grounded directly in local socio-cultural experiences.

The Danielic building blocks forming the image of the first beast suggest that this symbol conveys various prototypical characteristics. It makes its proper sense in and for a Jewish mental universe, the core of which is directly grounded in a particular perception, that of the effects of the Roman hegemony on *some* (and not on *all*!) first century Jews in Asia Minor. This is more or less clearly emphasized by John himself in Rev 13:3-4:

> καὶ ἐθαυμάσθη ὅλη ἡ γῆ ὀπίσω τοῦ θηρίου, καὶ προσεκύνησαν τῷ δράκοντι ὅτι ἔδωκεν τὴν ἐξουσίαν τῷ θηρίῳ, καὶ προσεκύνησαν τῷ θηρίῳ λέγοντες, Τίς ὅμοιος τῷ θηρίῳ, καὶ τίς δύναται πολεμῆσαι μετ' αὐτοῦ;
>
> And the entire earth marvelled after the beast. And they bowed down to the dragon because he gave the authority to the beast, and they bowed down to the beast, saying: "Who is similar to the beast, and who is able to fight against it?"[46]

The allusion to the earth in its holistic dimension reveals a discursive space of minority self-definition in contraposition with the whole world.[47] On the basis of such an implicit contrast, John describes membership in terms of categorization, accentuation, and stereotyping, showing that he is judging membership in light of a degree of distance to an enemy-prototype (the "best example of"). The relationships between the description of the first beast and the initial seven letters imply, namely, that the monster's prototypicality plays a key role in John's judgments about membership.

---

45. On this aspect of hegemonic power, see M. Foucault, *Surveiller et punir. Naissance de la prison* (Paris: Gallimard, 1975) 172: "Le pouvoir disciplinaire en effet est un pouvoir qui, au lieu de soutirer et de prélever, a pour fonction majeure de 'dresser'; ou sans doute, de dresser pour mieux prélever et soutirer davantage." On imperial offices in epigraphic materials from Roman Asia Minor, see S. Dmitriev, *City Government in Hellenistic and Roman Asia Minor* (Oxford: Oxford University Press, 2005) 189-216.

46. Text and translation in E.F. Lupieri, *A Commentary on the Apocalypse of John*, trans. M. Poggi Johnson – A. Kamesar (Grand Rapids: Eerdmans, 2006) 72-73.

47. On group and/or collective self-definitions and categorizations in Revelation, see J.W. Marshall, *Parables of War: Reading John's Jewish Apocalypse* (Waterloo, ONT: Wilfrid Laurier University Press, 2001); S. Pattemore, *The People of God in the Apocalypse: Discourse, Structure and Exegesis* (Cambridge: Cambridge University Press, 2004).

The first beast has on its head "a name of blasphemy" (Rev 13:1), and with its mouth it utters "great things and blasphemies" (Rev 13:5), opening its mouth "in blasphemies against God, to blaspheme his name" (Rev 13:6). In the same way, the letter to the Ephesian ἐκκλησία knows the tribulation and the poverty of these people, as well as "the blasphemy coming from those who say they are Jews and are not, but are a synagogue of Satan" (Rev 2:9). It is not by coincidence that the "prime motor" of the first beast's activities in Rev 13:2, Satan, is evoked as the dragon that gives "authority to the beast," as well as a being to which the inhabitants of the entire earth bow down (Rev 13:4). In the seven letters, Satan is referenced with his personal name, as the figure to whom both the "synagogues" of Smyrna and Philadelphia belong (Rev 2:9 ; 3:9), as well as one who sits and dwells in Pergamum—wherein Antipas was killed (Rev 2:13)—and the being to whom the depths belong (Rev 2:24). But this figure is also mentioned with the title διάβολος, as one who is throwing in prison some of the Ephesians (Rev 2:10).[48]

Some details of the seven letters offer a kind of counter-formulary to that used by official documents.[49] Apart from the case of Rev 2:17, wherein the white stone on which a new name is written recalls the message written by the proconsul and the decree of Asia engraved "on a stele of white marble, which shall be set up in the precinct of Roma[50] and Augustus,"[51] the four warnings of Rev 2:7, 17 and 3:13,22 ("He who has an ear, let him hear ...")—with the presence of imperative ἀκουσάτω—evokes the reading experiences of imperial communications in and for local contexts.[52] For this very reason, it is no coincidence that there is another warning in

48. In Rev 12:9 we find : καὶ ἐβλήθη ὁ δράκων ὁ μέγας, ὁ ὄφις ὁ ἀρχαῖος, ὁ καλούμενος Διάβολος καὶ ὁ Σατανᾶς, ὁ πλανῶν τὴν οἰκουμένην ὅλην – ἐβλήθη εἰς τὴν γῆν, καὶ οἱ ἄγγελοι αὐτοῦ μετ' αὐτοῦ ἐβλήθησαν : see E.F. Lupieri, *A Commentary on the Apocalypse of John*, trans. M. Poggi Johnson – A. Kamesar (Grand Rapids : Eerdmans, 2006) 70-71.

49. See also D.E. Aune, *Revelation 1-5* (Waco : Word Biblical Press, 1997) 126-129.

50. This is probably a reference to a cultic statue conserved in the precinct. The worship in honor of the goddess *Roma* is attested after the third century BCE. See R. Mellor, *ΘΕΑ ΡΩΜΗ : The Worship of the Goddess Roma in the Greek World* (Göttingen : Vandenhoeck & Ruprecht, 1975).

51. *IPriene* 105 = *Orientis graeci inscriptiones selectae* 458. English translation in R.H. Sherk, *Rome and the Greek East to the Death of Augustus* (Cambridge, UK : Cambridge University Press, 1984) no. 101, 124-127. This is a new calendar for the province of Asia in honor of Augustus (9 BCE) ; it contains various documents assembled from copies published in different cities of Asia. On relationships with Rev 2:17, see M. Wilson, *The Victor Sayings in the Book of Revelation* (Eugene, OR : Wipf & Stock, 2007) 123-124.

52. See B. Burrell, "Reading, Hearing, and Looking at Ephesos," in W.A. Johnson – H.N. Parker, eds., *Ancient Literacies. The Culture of Reading in Greece and Rome* (Oxford : Oxford University Press, 2009) 69-95.

Rev 13:9,[53] which is an internal link between the description of the first beast and the initial seven letters. In all the warnings of the text, a more or less similar counter-formulary seems to mimic expressions or verbs which are employed in previous and contemporary official documents.[54] Another connection between both sections under examination is the usage of a further key term concerning victorious athletes, νικάω.[55] While to the beast it is granted to make war on the holy ones and to defeat them (Rev 13:7), all the victors recalled in the seven letters will be fed from the tree of life and the hidden manna (Rev 2:7,17) and will obtain authority over all the nations (2:26), as well as they will be wrapped in white garments (Rev 3:5), or will be made like pillars in the temple of God (3:12), or will be seated on a throne (Rev 3:21).

### 3.2 The Second Beast as a Prototype of "False" Jewish Agency

Another beast is seen by John, a beast coming up out of the earth. This monster has two horns like a lamb and speaks like a dragon. As Lupieri has observed, the second beast

> completes the Satanic trinity. Satan is imitating God; the beast from the sea who undergoes a false resurrection is an imitation of Christ (note καὶ ἔζησεν in v. 14, which repeats the precise expression in 2:8), and the beast who here comes up out of the earth is an imitation of the prophetic and religious function of the Spirit. Although it is defined as a "false prophet" only in 16:13, the aspect of false spirituality is already apparent here, and in fact it is characterized by its deceptiveness (it is a "dragon" disguised as a "lamb"), by its power of speech, and by its priestly function.[56]

53. Εἴ τις ἔχει οὖς ἀκουσάτω. εἴ τις εἰς αἰχμαλωσίαν, εἰς αἰχμαλωσίαν ὑπάγει· εἴ τις ἐν μαχαίρῃ ἀποκτανθῆναι, αὐτὸν ἐν μαχαίρῃ ἀποκτανθῆναι (Rev 13:9).

54. For the presence of warnings in oath inscriptions, see *IG* II$^2$, 1369 and *Supplementum epigraphicum graecum* 31 (1981) 122 = J.S. Kloppenborg – R.S. Ascough, *Greco-Roman Associations: Texts, Translations and Commentary. I. Attica, Central Greece, Macedonia, Thrace* (Berlin: De Gruyter, 2011) nos 49 and 50. For the usage of the verb ἀκούω in inscriptions, see *IMagn* 79 + 80 = *Supplementum epigraphicum graecum* 4 (1927) 505 = http://epigraphy.packhum.org/text/260455?=759-766%2C1470-1481 (the decree of Antiocheia [of Pisidia? or Alabanda?] accepting invitation of Magnesia to the Leukophryena: third-second cent. BCE); *IMagn* 59 = *Supplementum epigraphicum graecum* 4, 503 = https://inscriptions.packhum.org/text/260501?bookid=509&location=1035 (Decree of δῆμος of Laodikeia accepting invitation of Magnesia to the Leukophryena and giving honors to both δῆμος and πρεσβευταί from the inviting city [third cent. BCE, found at Magnesia]).

55. See Z. Newby, *Greek Athletics in the Roman World: Victory and Virtue* (Oxford: Oxford University Press, 2005) 229-271.

56. E.F. Lupieri, *A Commentary on the Apocalypse of John*, trans. M. Poggi Johnson – A. Kamesar (Grand Rapids: Eerdmans, 2006) 209. On the "pseudo-priestly" dimension of the second beast, see D.E. Aune, *Revelation 6-16* (Waco: Word Biblical Press, 1998) esp. 758.

The textual-narrative blocks from which this image results are those from the Elijah cycle (1 Kgs 17-19, 21 ; 2 Kgs 1, 2:1-15). The second beast performs Elijah's cultic miracle where Elijah made fire come down from heaven to consume a sacrificial animal (see 1 Kgs 18:20-24) and other "great signs" that are not described by John. The second beast is also responsible for establishing the new cult for the first beast, persuading "those that dwell ... on the earth" to "make an image of the beast," recalling the sin of Aaron, who led the people to "idolatry" in the desert by making a golden calf and establishing it as an object of worship (Exod 32). As Lupieri has observed,

> This second beast is thus a religious power in the service of the political and military power represented by the first beast. It is primarily an allusion to the imperial cult that was celebrated throughout a large part of the Roman Empire, and was particularly important in the East (the "sea," inasmuch as it is the site of the "islands," that is, of pagan kingdoms, is a mythologized projection of the Mediterranean, the Great Sea in the West from which came Rome and its power). John's words, here as elsewhere, take on a more generalized meaning, just as the divinization of sovereigns was not a local phenomenon but a widely diffused practice even outside the empire.[57]

However, many elements of the description seem to suggest that with the second beast John alludes to false forms (in John's view) of Jewish prophecy. John echoes the traditional prophetic accusation that Israel has become corrupt and has devoted herself to "idolatry." As Lupieri himself has remarked, the idea of two beasts, one from the sea and one from the earth, appears elsewhere in first century Judaism. *4 Ezra* 6:49-52 reports, in a passage about God's deeds on the fifth day of creation:

> Then thou didst preserve two living creatures which you created; the name of one thou didst call Behemoth and the name of the other Leviathan. And thou didst separate one from the other, for the seventh part where the water had been gathered together could not hold them both. And thou didst give Behemoth one of the parts which had been dried up on the third day, to live in it, where there are a thousand mountains; but to Leviathan thou didst give the seventh part of the watery part; and thou hast kept them to be eaten by whom thou wilt, and when thou wilt.[58]

John seems to apply such a traditional view to the text of Daniel, according to which the beasts that rise out from the sea emerge as a descriptive pattern for other apocalyptic beasts. John divides the nature of the beasts

57. E.F. LUPIERI, *A Commentary on the Apocalypse of John*, trans. M. POGGI JOHNSON – A. KAMESAR (Grand Rapids: Eerdmans, 2006) 209.

58. M.E. STONE – M. HENZE, *4 Ezra and 2 Baruch. Translations, Introductions and Notes* (Minneapolis: Fortress Press, 2013) 38.

into two parts, of which the first is primarily political and the second primarily religious. In this framework "political" and "religious" recall local manifestations of hegemonic elements of the Roman Empire as they are perceived and filtered by John himself in his proper cultural and historical context (the local *facies* of both the Imperial structure of power and the Jewish and, consequently, proto-Christian "religious" involvement in such a system).

A little clarification is useful on the relationships between "power" and "religion" as they emerge from John's discourse. As Jörg Rüpke has remarked, "religious tradition(s)," "shared social meaning," "ritual precepts," and "public religion" are well-researched areas of religious practices and beliefs in the ancient circum-Mediterranean world.[59] Yet it is also now time to focus on "lived ancient religion(s)," i.e. on the individual appropriation of tradition(s) and on personal experiences and responses, as well as on the incoherencies of situational interpretation(s), the isolated performances, and the local and group-specific styles. John's representation of the second beast seems to allude to an individual appropriation and transformation, or of a creative reassembling and consequential selection, of elements of a (specific) Jewish tradition. According to John's description, the second beast is strictly subordinate to the first beast, and its mission is not to exalt itself or to demand worship for itself, but solely to make sure that the earth's inhabitants worship the first beast (Rev 13:14-15). The verb "to do" or "to make" is very conspicuous in John's vision: if the first beast is given authority to "do" (that is, to exercise its authority) for forty-two months (13:5) and (in most manuscripts) to "make" war against believers in Christ (Rev 13:7), the second beast "does" (that is, exercises) all the authority of the first beast on its behalf, and "makes" the earth and its inhabitants worship the first beast (Rev 13:12). It also "does" (that is, performs) great and miraculous signs, so as to "make" fire come down from the sky in full public view (Rev 13:13). The second beast is given power to "do" this and other signs in order to deceive the earth's inhabitants, telling them to "make" (or set up) an image in honor of the first beast (13:14). The second beast then gives this image life and speech, and "makes" (that is, causes) those who refused to worship the image to be killed (Rev 13:15). Finally, the second beast "makes" (that is, forces) everyone small and great, rich and poor, free and slave, to receive a mark on their right hands or on their foreheads, so that no one could buy or sell unless they have the mark, which is the name of the beast or the num-

59. Cf. J. RÜPKE – W. SPICKERMANN, eds., *Reflections on Religious Individuality: Greco-Roman and Judaeo-Christian Texts and Practices* (Berlin: De Gruyter, 2012); J. RÜPKE, ed., *The Individual in the Religions of the Ancient Mediterranean* (Oxford: Oxford University Press, 2013). See also ID., "Lived Ancient Religion: Questioning 'Cults' and 'Polis Religion,'" *Mythos* 5 (2012) 191-204.

ber of its name (Rev 13:16-17). All the verbs noted are forms of ποιέω, "to do," and for this the two beasts are indeed "doers," or also agents, in John's eyes. This means that the second beast emerges as a religious agent that is stereotypically represented with a strong accent on "idolatry," with a characteristically Jewish insistence that the worship of idols is based on deception. In this context, the relationship between the two beasts is like the one between the public local cult and specific local agents, viewed in their attempt to transfer and to adapt elements of this worship to their specific tradition, while recognizing and at the same time isolating the time-hallowed institutions of public religion.[60]

According to John's visions, the two beasts represent a socio-cultural dynamic arising from the place occupied by public religion in the socio-political network of Asia Minor. The second beast, in this discursive construction, is a kind of mirror in which the effects of such a relationship are reflected among some Jews. As a public cult, state religion is financed and organized by the common council and officials, and the financing of the cult is a thread that runs through the entire local social system. If public religion is defined in terms of great rituals, its precise content is left to the local elites and their financial resources, and this means that all endeavours on the part of local agents to establish a particular public *persona* have to make use of facilities symbolically linked with this centralized system of religious representation.[61] This seems to explain why a Jewish "synagogue" in Akmoneia honor with an inscription Julia Severa, daughter of Gaius, high-priestess and director of contests of the whole household of the Σεβαστοί gods, because of her virtue and benefaction towards the cultic association.[62]

60. On such a topic, see J. Rüpke, *From Jupiter to Christ: On the History of Religion in the Roman Imperial Period* (Oxford: Oxford University Press, 2014) 132-133.

61. See J. Rüpke, *From Jupiter to Christ: On the History of Religion in the Roman Imperial Period* (Oxford: Oxford University Press, 2014) 133.

62. See *Corpus inscriptionum judaicarum* 766 = *Inscriptiones Judaicae Orientis* II 168 = R.S. Ascough – P.A. Harland – J.S. Kloppenborg, *Associations in the Greco-Roman World: A Sourcebook* (Waco: Baylor University Press; Berlin: De Gruyter, 2012) no. 145 = *Monumenta Asiae Minoris Antiqua* VI 264 = P.A. Harland, *Greco-Roman Associations: Texts, Translations and Commentary. II. North Coast of the Black Sea, Asia Minor* (Berlin: De Gruyter, 2014) 150-156. This inscription (*c.* 100 CE) is a slab of white marble with a panel and traces of handles on the right and left, found re-used as a support for a veranda of a home (49 × 58 × 15 cm; letter height: 1.75-2.25 cm). Another honorary inscription set up by the elders' organization at Akmoneia shows that Julia Severa was a high priestess in the local imperial cult and director of games for the civic cult of the Augustan (Σεβαστοί) gods (cf. *Monumenta Asiae Minoris Antiqua* VI 263 and List 153*). The inscription mentions an οἶκος, which was built by Julia Severa and was renovated by P. Tyrronius Klados, head of the synagogue, Lucius son of Lucius, also

Nevertheless, speaking of a Jewish agent does not mean automatically guaranteeing accession to the local context of John's depiction of the second beast. In this respect, a first aid seems to come from the other mentions of the monster in the following sections of the text. In Rev 16:13-14, John sees three impure spirits that came out of the mouths of the dragon, the beast, and the false prophet (ψευδοπροφήτης).[63] The sequence of the beings seems to ensure the identification of the pseudoprophet with the second beast of chapter 13. Also in Rev 19:20, John mentions the first beast's capture and with it that of the false prophet who had performed the signs on its behalf. Both the mentions prove correct Lupieri's statements concerning the second beast as a being that "is in charge of the cult for the first one (and therefore has a priestly function)," as well as a representation that "defines the positions of adversaries who seem to be *intra muros* among the members of the followers of Jesus."[64]

An additional argument in support of Lupieri's analysis results from the comparison of the description of the second beast with some lexical elements in the seven letters of Revelation. The second beast exercises all the power of the first beast before (ἐνώπιον) it (Rev 13:12). And there are some in Pergamum who hold the teaching of Balaam, who taught Balak to put a stumbling block before (ἐνώπιον) the sons of Israel (Rev 3:14). In a similar way, the monster performs great signs in front of people as well as on behalf of the first beast (Rev 13:13-14). The second beast causes the earth and those who "dwell" therein to worship the first beast (καὶ ποιεῖ τὴν γῆν καὶ τοὺς ἐν αὐτῇ κατοικοῦντας ἵνα προσκυνήσουσιν τὸ θηρίον τὸ πρῶτον), and the *persona loquens* of the seven letters knows where the members of the group

---

head of the synagogue, and Popilius Zotikos. In the inscription it is also recalled that these individuals decorated the walls and ceiling, made the windows secure, and took care of all the rest of the decoration. In the last lines of the epigraph, it is emphasized that "the synagogue honored them with a gilded shield because of their virtuous disposition, goodwill, and diligence in relation to the synagogue" (trans. by P.A. HARLAND, *Greco-Roman Associations: Texts, Translations and Commentary. II. North Coast of the Black Sea, Asia Minor* [Berlin: De Gruyter, 2014] 151). On the "synagogue" of Akmoneia as a Jewish meeting place, see the bibliography quoted by P.A. HARLAND, *Greco-Roman Associations: Texts, Translations and Commentary. II. North Coast of the Black Sea, Asia Minor* (Berlin: De Gruyter, 2014) 155-156.

63. On ψευδοπροφήτης as a Jewish and proto-Christian technical term (and/or concept), see E. NORELLI, *L'Ascensione di Isaia. Studio su un apocrifo al crocevia dei cristianesimi* (Bologna: Dehoniane, 1994) 92-113; L. ARCARI, "L'Apocalisse di Giovanni nel quadro di alcune dinamiche gruppali proto-cristiane: elementi per una (ri-)contestualizzazione," *Annali di Storia dell'Esegesi* 28 (2011) 137-183 (esp. 150-152).

64. E.F. LUPIERI, "From Sodom and Balaam to Revelation: Transtextual Adventures of Biblical Sins," in S. ALKIER – TH. HIEKE – T. NICKLAS, eds., *Poetik und Intertextualität der Johannesapokalypse* (Tübingen: Mohr Siebeck, 2015) 300-318 (esp. 314-316).

in Pergamum "dwell"—where Satan has his throne (οἶδα ποῦ κατοικεῖς, ὅπου ὁ θρόνος τοῦ Σατανᾶ). The verb κατοικέω returns also in Rev 3:10, wherein Jesus reminds us that he will save people that have conserved his command from the hour of trial that is going to come on the world to test its inhabitants (κἀγώ σε τηρήσω ἐκ τῆς ὥρας τοῦ πειρασμοῦ τῆς μελλούσης ἔρχεσθαι ἐπὶ τῆς οἰκουμένης ὅλης πειράσαι τοὺς κατοικοῦντας ἐπὶ τῆς γῆς). As we have seen, in Rev 13:12 the second beast causes the world and those who dwell on the earth (τοὺς κατοικοῦντας ἐπὶ τῆς γῆς) to worship the first beast; the noun γῆ returns also in 3:10, when Jesus alludes to the hour of trial that is coming on the whole world to test the people who live on the earth (πειράσαι τοὺς κατοικοῦντας ἐπὶ τῆς γῆς). Like the second beast "deceives" those who live on the earth (Rev 13:14, πλανᾷ τοὺς κατοικοῦντας ἐπὶ τῆς γῆς) thanks to the signs it is permitted to perform on behalf of the first beast, so Jezebel "deceives" Jesus's servants into sexual immorality and eating food sacrificed to idols (Rev 2:20, πλανᾷ τοὺς ἐμοὺς δούλους πορνεῦσαι καὶ φαγεῖν εἰδωλόθυτα).

This last aspect leads us in what is the most relevant connection between both sections that are linked by their use of the so-called language of falsehood. The second beast tells those who live on the earth to make an image to the beast (Rev 13:14, λέγων τοῖς κατοικοῦσιν ἐπὶ τῆς γῆς ποιῆσαι εἰκόνα τῷ θηρίῳ). The term εἰκών here is not only used for alluding to the monarch's effigy or to his head on the coin (like in Matt. 22:20 and Mark 12:15) but, in a more general sense, as an allusion to a false image like that of a cultic statue (for this use in the Septuagint, see Deut 4:16; 2 Kgs 11:18; 2 Chr 33:7; Isa 40:19-20; Ezek 7:20; 16:17; 23:14; Dan 2:31-32,34-35; 3:1-3,5,7,11-12,14,15; Hos 13:2).[65] The cultic activity carried out by the second beast is not only the act of προσκύνησις in front of the first beast. The second beast is empowered to give life to the image of the first beast so that it could speak[66] and could cause all those who do not worship the εἰκών to be killed (see Rev 13:15). All these are stigmatizing efforts to describe cultic practices that in John's view have to be refused, and this seems to explain, for example, why the second beast is called "pseudoprophet" in Rev 16:13-14 and 19:20. This technical expression, in such a framework, emerges as a typical Jewish interpretation of cultic activities that are perceived as deviant or evaluated as not in line with the "true" practice of Judaism. This leads us to seriously consider the connections of this pseudo-prophecy with that attributed to the

65. On the relationships between the consideration of ancient statues as εἰκών and the formative process of "idolatry" as a stigmatizing concept in the history of Christianity, see D. Barbu, *Naissance de l'idolâtrie. Image, identité, religion* (Liège: Presses Universitaires de Liège, 2016).

66. On "speaking statues" in the Hellenistic-Roman period, see D. Tripaldi, *Apocalisse di Giovanni* (Rome: Carocci, 2012) 181-182.

prophetess Jezabel, "who calls herself a prophet" (Rev 2:20, ἡ λέγουσα ἑαυτὴν προφῆτιν), as well as with the activities carried out by the people in Smyrna "who say they are Jews and are not, but are a synagogue of Satan" (Rev 2:9, ἐκ τῶν λεγόντων Ἰουδαίους εἶναι ἑαυτούς, καὶ οὐκ εἰσὶν ἀλλὰ συναγωγὴ τοῦ Σατανᾶ).

## 4. Babylon as a Prototype of Urban Religious Cohabitations

If the two beasts of Revelation 13 represent, in action, prototypes of cultural and religious agencies both perceived and depicted by John as deviant and not in line with the "true" Judaism, the whore-Babylon of chapters 17-18 emerges as the prototype of a city in which previous deviant agencies live and operate. Like every other representation we find in Revelation, so also the whore-Babylon is a traditionally built character. In this case, John relies on the traditional biblical way of representing cities as women, a way of thinking and depicting actual realities that was still alive in the first century CE, as shown by *4 Ezra* 9:38-10:59. I cannot discuss all the exegetical and the historical questions raised by the complex vision of Revelation 17-18 here. I can only "show my hand," clearly emphasizing that with this section I aim at supporting the contemporary minority position of Italian scholarship which identifies Babylon with a Jewish reality, providing some further elements in favor of such an interpretation.[67]

The main arguments raised by such an interpretation are as follows: in Revelation, the phrase "the great city" (ἡ πόλις ἡ μεγάλη) is used throughout, and if the phrase is used consistently to refer to the same city throughout the text, it is more than likely that the phrase refers to the city of Jerusalem (see Rev 11:8; 16:19).[68] In addition to the previous obser-

67. After the works by E. Corsini, *Apocalisse prima e dopo* (Torino: SEI, 1980; Engl. Transl. *The Apocalypse: The Perennial Revelation of Jesus Christ* [Wilmington, DE: Glazier, 1983]), and *Apocalisse di Gesù Cristo secondo Giovanni* (Turin: SEI, 2002), see E.F. Lupieri, *A Commentary on the Apocalypse of John*, trans. M. Poggi Johnson – A. Kamesar (Grand Rapids: Eerdmans, 2006), and my book *"Una donna avvolta nel sole..." (Apoc 12,1). Le raffigurazioni femminili nell'Apocalisse di Giovanni alla luce della letteratura apocalittica giudaica* (Padua: Messaggero, 2008). On Corsini's interpretation of John's Revelation, see also E.F. Lupieri, "L'Apocalisse dopo Corsini: un'eredità in evoluzione" and C. Mazzucco, "La passione di Eugenio Corsini per l'Apocalisse," in C. Lombardi – L. Silvano, eds., *Apocalisse ieri oggi e domani. Atti della giornata di studio in memoria di Eugenio Corsini (Torino, 2 ottobre 2018)* (Alessandria: Edizioni dell'Orso, 2019) respectively 19-28 and 29-40.

68. Such arguments are drawn largely from: A.J. Beagley, *The "Sitz im Leben" of the Apocalypse with Particular Reference to the Role of the Church's Enemies* (Berlin: FRG/New York: De Gruyter, 1987) 93; E.F. Lupieri, *A Commentary on the Apocalypse of John*, trans. M. Poggi Johnson – A. Kamesar (Grand Rapids: Eerdmans, 2006), 275-293; see also I. Provan, "Foul Spirits, Fornication and Finance:

vation, the Book of Revelation, as has been noted by numerous scholars,[69] outlines in various ways an antithetical parallelism between the "Whore" (Rev 17-18) and the "Bride" (Rev 21-22). An example of this can be shown in Ranko Stefanović's extensive outlining of such an ironical antithesis,[70] who showed that the settings, the descriptions, as well as the fates of both

---

Revelation 18 From an Old Testament Perspective," *Journal for the Study of the New Testament* 19 (1997) 81-100 (esp. 95). On the relationships between Sodom, Egypt, and Jerusalem according to John's literary construction, see E.F. LUPIERI, "From Sodom and Balaam to Revelation: Transtextual Adventures of Biblical Sins," in S. ALKIER – TH. HIEKE – T. NICKLAS, eds., *Poetik und Intertextualität der Johannesapokalypse* (Tübingen: Mohr Siebeck, 2015) 300-318 (esp. 305-312). On Rev 11:8, see the circular argument carried out by R. BAUCKHAM, *The Theology of the Book of Revelation* (Cambridge, UK: Cambridge University Press, 1993) 85-86 and 127, according to whom the great city here "cannot be Jerusalem, in spite of the reference to Jesus' crucifixion there (11:8), but because of that reference nor can it be only Rome, to which, under the symbol of Babylon, 'the great city' refers elsewhere in Revelation (14:8; 18:16,18,19,21)." Likewise, Giancarlo Biguzzi argues, that the temple is filled with Christian worshippers and that the city of Rev 11:8 is "a symbol of the whole world" ("Is the Babylon of Revelation Rome or Jerusalem?" *Biblica* 87 [2006] 371-386 [378]). In line with this insistence that Rev 11:8 cannot refer to Jerusalem, John W. Marshall goes as far as arguing that it does indeed refer to the city of Rome, and that the Apocalypse is "the only literature in the Christian canon that places the blame for the crucifixion of Jesus squarely on Rome" (*Parables of War: Reading John's Jewish Apocalypse* [Waterloo, ONT: Wilfrid Laurier University Press, 2001] 171-172). On Rev 16:19, it is interesting to note that here "the great city" is made distinct from the category of "the cities of the nations," implying perhaps that the great city is itself not among "the cities of the nations." Thus "the great city" would probably not be Rome, but much more likely Jerusalem, if the "cities of the nations" are an equivalent to the "cities of the Gentiles." In addition, the punishment of "the great city" being split into three parts has a textual "echo" in Ezek 5:1-5, where the prophet in a symbolic and prophetic depiction of the destruction of Jerusalem splits his hair into three parts, symbolizing the breakup of Jerusalem into three parts. It could now be suggested that the phrase is either not used consistently, or, as G. Biguzzi has suggested ("Is the Babylon of Revelation Rome or Jerusalem?" *Biblica* 87 [2006] esp. 379-380), that the phrase is meant to be a broad "archetype" of evil for all cities, but such suggestions presume an allegorical, de-historicized reading of Revelation as a whole.

69. Among these, see E.J. GILCHREST, *Revelation 21-22 in Light of Jewish and Greco-Roman Utopianism* (Leiden: Brill, 2013) 215, n. 39; P. LEE, *The New Jerusalem in the Book of Revelation: A Study of Revelation 21-22 in the Light of its Background in Jewish Tradition* (Tübingen: Mohr Siebeck, 2001) 264; P.L. MAYO, *"Those Who Call Themselves Jews": The Church and Judaism in the Apocalypse of John* (Eugene, OR: Pickwick, 2006) 167; B.R. ROSSING, *The Choice Between Two Cities: Whore, Bride, and Empire in the Apocalypse* (Harrisburg: Trinity Press, 1999); N.T. WRIGHT, "Jerusalem in the New Testament," in P.W.L. WALKER, ed., *Jerusalem: Past and Present in the Purposes of God* (Grand Rapids: Eerdmans, 1994) 53-77.

70. See R. STEFANOVIĆ, *Revelation of Jesus Christ: Commentary on the Book of Revelation* (Berrien Springs, MI: Andrews University Press, 2002) 373-375.

cities suggest that the bride, whose name is "the new (καινή) Jerusalem" (Rev 21:2), is set in contrast to the whore, who is "the old Jerusalem." In addition to this antithetical parallelism, other proto-Christian texts provide an external parallel in conceptual terms, by contrasting the "earthly/old" Jerusalem with a "heavenly/new" Jerusalem (Gal 4:25-26; Heb 12:22).

This leads to another strong argument, as it is emphasized in particular by Beagley,[71] Corsini, and Lupieri,[72] which is linked to the fact that in Revelation a pervasive background to the imagery of the whore of chaps. 17-18 can be found throughout the Hebrew Bible, especially in describing Israel's failure in its covenantal relationship with YHWH as "whoring." The "biblical" prophetic literature is more than sufficient to illustrate this imagery found throughout the Hebrew Bible in relation to Israel as a nation, and quite often Jerusalem itself, such as in Isaiah, where Zion is lamented because of "How the faithful city has become a whore (*zōnāh*)" (Isa 1:21). Very similar indictments are found in Jeremiah (2:20; 3:1-10; 5:7), Ezekiel (16:15-41; 20:30; 23:3-44), Hosea (1:2; 2:5; 3:3; 4:10,12-15,18; 5:3; 9:1), and Micah (1:7). The "whoring" of Israel is a metaphorical instrument used to indict her idolatry, which is often brought about through various economic and political alliances perceived as "not in line" with those belonging to the "true" Israel. Israel's relationship with YHWH is often understood as a marriage contract as implied in the way various forms of idolatry are called "prostitution" such as worshipping Molech (Lev 20:5), necromancy (Lev 20:6), and idol worship (Num 14:33; 15:39; Deut 31:16; Judg 2:17; 8:27,33; 1 Chr 5:25; 2 Chr 21:11, 13; Ps 73:27). With this, then, as a prevalent theme in the Hebrew Bible, Lynn R. Huber rightly wonders, "it is hard to imagine that John sees Rome, imagined as Babylon-Rome, as having some relationship to the Divine that would make

71. It is important to recall Beagley's observations about connections between some proto-Christian self-definitions and particular reinventions of biblical traditions: "... the Hebrew prophets always denounce the contemporary, empirical, earthly Jerusalem because of her immorality, injustice, and apostasy. Because of these iniquities, she is threatened with destruction ... Unlike many of the Old Testament prophets, however, John prophesies no restoration of the earthly Jerusalem, but instead envisages a 'new Jerusalem' which comes down to earth from heaven. There are obvious similarities between this 'new Jerusalem' and the glorious temple/city of Ezekiel's vision, and it seems that Ezekiel's failure to make it clear that he is thinking of a restored earthly Jerusalem may well have opened the way for John to prophesy the replacement of the old earthly city by a heavenly one" (*The "Sitz im Leben" of the Apocalypse with Particular Reference to the Role of the Church's Enemies* [Berlin: FRG/New York: De Gruyter, 1987] 149-150).

72. See E. Corsini, *The Apocalypse: The Perennial Revelation of Jesus Christ* (Wilmington, DE: Glazier, 1983) 328-337; E.F. Lupieri, *A Commentary on the Apocalypse of John*, trans. M. Poggi Johnson – A. Kamesar (Grand Rapids: Eerdmans, 2006) 260-264.

'her' potentially unfaithful."[73] The logic of the text is quite clear: if Babylon in John's Revelation is depicted as a whore, that means, in adherence to biblical prophetic imagery, she has been unfaithful in her covenantal relationship with YHWH, but if Babylon's referent is Rome it is difficult to see how the metaphor would be apt given that Rome is not known for having any covenantal relationship with YHWH.

The fact that there are only two non-Israelite cities in the Hebrew Bible to whom the accusation of "whoring" is also attached, namely Tyre (Isa 23) and Nineveh (Nah 3), leads to my own contribution to an anti-Jerusalem interpretation of Revelation 17-18 as well as to my peculiar approach to such an interpretive hypothesis. Richard Bauckham, in particular, has argued that:

> This Old Testament sense of harlotry could strictly be applied only to the people of God, but it is very likely that John takes advantage of the traditional association of harlotry with idolatrous religion, when he refers to the corrupting influence of the harlot city (19:2).[74]

Bauckham's suggestion would imply that the reason for John's use of such imagery is mere prophetic "coloring" for the representation of a deviant world. If much has been discussed in the background of the fall of Tyre from Ezek 26-27, in the economic critique of Babylon in chapter 18 of Revelation,[75] what has often been underestimated is that Tyre and Nineveh seem to be the examples of a kind of exportation (and extension) in other geographical contexts of the intra-Jewish imagery of Jerusalem. Tyre, as is well known, is portrayed in the Hebrew Bible as itself having an economic and covenantal relationship with the people of Israel, presumably for the role of some Jewish people living there in helping build the first temple (1 Kgs 5:1-12; 9:13). For this, YHWH declares that the wall of the city will be destroyed by fire (Amos 1:9-10). Likewise, Nineveh (or, at least, Jewish people living there) is portrayed at least once in the Hebrew Bible as having repented and worshiped YHWH (Jon 3:5-10). If images such as the harlotry of Nineveh, as shown by some of the Dead Sea

73. L.R. HUBER, *Thinking and Seeing with Women in Revelation* (London: T&T Clark, 2013) 66-67.

74. R. BAUCKHAM, *The Climax of Prophecy: Studies on the Book of Revelation* (London: T&T Clark, 2000) 348.

75. For instance: D.E. AUNE, *Revelation 17-22* (Waco: Word Biblical Press, 1998) 930-931; R. BAUCKHAM, *The Climax of Prophecy: Studies on the Book of Revelation* (London: T&T Clark, 2000) 346; S. FRIESEN, *Imperial Cults and the Apocalypse of John* (Oxford: Oxford University Press, 2001) 139-140; J.N. KRAYBILL, *Imperial Cult and Commerce in John's Apocalypse* (Sheffield: Sheffield Academic Press, 1996) 152-161; I. PROVAN, "Foul Spirits, Fornication and Finance: Revelation 18 From an Old Testament Perspective," *Journal for the Study of the New Testament* 19 (1997) 81-100.

scrolls (4QPesher Nahum/4Q169), were readily applied to the situation of the perceived deviancy embodied by other Jews, it is not difficult to read the image of Babylon in the literary construction of Revelation as a reference to the Jewish people living in Asia Minor on the basis of a peculiar stereotyped view, the one that combines and conflates Jerusalem with Jewish people living in the imperial cities.

As I have stressed elsewhere, the whore in chapters 17-18 seems to stand as a kind of counterpart to the woman clothed with the sun of Revelation 12,[76] a character that flees in the desert (12:6) where John will, afterwards, see Babylon-the-whore. For this, it seems that such a last *figura* appears as a kind of peculiar reference to the collective symbol of chapter 12, where it is seen in its primordial dimension of "archetypal" priesthood from which an individual agent of liberation emerges. In chapter 12, the woman clothed with the sun stands as a kind of collective and exhaustive representation of primeval Israel as a prototypical priestly entity on which evil forces try to wage war. With the vision of chapters 17-18, John seems to see a possible effect of such primeval war: the transformation of the woman clothed with the sun into Babylon-the-whore. In both visions, the desert is a mythical space.

But if in the vision of chapter 12 the woman emerges as an archetypal-primeval priestly entity, in chapters 17-18 the visionary sees a possible actual manifestation of this collective archetype, i.e., Jewish groups who live in Jerusalem as well as in the other cities of the Roman empire. Such a descriptive tendency aims at defining, rationalizing, and making sense of the identities of conflicting groups by means of casting them back to the order of creation itself. The woman clothed with the sun is the primeval dimension of the priestly Judaism that is further characterized as a collectivity for its association with a female figure and mother begetting a child. The whore, on the other side, stands as a further allusion to such a prototypical and stereotyped characterization as a Judaism that has degraded itself.

In this literary framework, I consider the whore-Babylon as a representation of the believers in the God of Israel who had not accepted the message of Jesus as it is proclaimed by John the seer, the same people that are stigmatized in various ways in the seven letters of Revelation 2-3. I find this local interpretation of a collective and inclusive traditional symbol like Babylon to be supported by two elements. The first involves the presence of female personifications of subject peoples in imperial monuments (like at the *Sebasteion* of Aphrodisias), represented as statues that often allude symbolically to different relationships of subject(s) and provincial

76. See L. Arcari, *"Una donna avvolta nel sole..." (Apoc 12,1). Le raffigurazioni femminili nell'Apocalisse di Giovanni alla luce della letteratura apocalittica giudaica* (Padua: Messaggero, 2008) 324-365, where additional exegetical elements in favor of this interpretation are discussed.

peoples that seem to corroborate the local cultural contexts on which John may have based his collective depiction as a woman later identified in a representative city.[77] The other element is a direct consequence of the literary links between the visions of chapters 17-18 and much of what John reports in the seven letters of chapters 2-3. As we have seen, the great city of Revelation 17-18 is presented as a prostitute (Rev 17:1-2), conflating the negative feminine characteristics of Jezebel, who is also guilty of idolatry and prostitution (see Rev 2:20-22). The whore-Babylon is "guilty in front of God because, instead of using the promise and knowledge of salvation received by God" (the woman of chapter 12 is the same woman), she "accepted an idolatrous relationship with those whom she was supposed to save, even trying to sell for money the instrument of salvation she had received freely from God." The pseudo-prophecy of Jezebel "defines the positions of adversaries who seem to be *intra muros* among the members

77. On this topic, see R.R.R. SMITH, "*Simulacra Gentium*: The *Ethne* from the *Sebasteion* at Aphrodisias," *The Journal of Roman Studies* 78 (1988) 38-77. For other female collective representations, see A. LALLE, "Le raffigurazioni di *Gentes* e *Nationes* nel Foro di Nerva: segno di potere e di pacificazione," *Bollettino di Archeologia Online* 2008: http://www.bollettinodiarcheologiaonline.beniculturali.it/documenti//_LALLE.pdf. It is quite understandable the extensibility of Jerusalem as symbol for the various self-definitions of Jews living in the urban contexts of the Roman Empire as one of the results of the fall of the temple of Jerusalem after Titus's campaign in Judea. For a fresh approach to this topic, see the essays collected in D.R. SCHWARTZ – Z. WEISS, eds., *Was 70 CE a Watershed in Jewish History? On Jews and Judaism before and after the Destruction of the Second Temple* (Leiden: Brill, 2012). Another traditionally modeled city mentioned in Revelation seems to corroborate the interpretation of Babylon as an allusion to Jews living in urban contexts of Asia Minor. The name of "Sodom" appears in Rev 11:8 where, together with "Egypt," it "describes the 'spiritual' reality of 'the city, the great one ... where also their Lord was crucified.' Scores of passages, from canonical and non-canonical Jewish writings, can be brought to support the idea that Sodom (alone or with Gomorrah), its fate and its sin, could be used around the end of the first century to identify Jerusalem (or at times another Jewish reality), its destiny, and its sinful conduct" (E.F. LUPIERI, "From Sodom and Balaam to the Revelation of John. Transtextual Adventures of Biblical Sins," in S. ALKIER – TH. HIEKE – T. NICKLAS, eds., *Poetik und Intertextualität der Johannesapokalypse* [Tübingen: Mohr Siebeck, 2015] 300-318 [esp. 305-306]). Sodom's connections with Judaism, and the consequent allusion to cultural and cultic activities that are perceived as "not in line" with a particular belonging to Judaism, appear to be quite present among the early followers of Jesus. In Rom 9:29 Paul "quotes Isa 1:9 (LXX) emphasizing that only the mercy of God has allowed a remnant of Israel to survive up to that point and not end up like Sodom and Gomorrah. He thinks that Isaiah's words are a prophecy of what is happening at his time, with the Gentiles adhering to the message of the followers of Jesus, while other Jews are mostly unable to recognize God's provenance and accept the salvation announced by Paul and his companions" (E.F. LUPIERI, "From Sodom and Balaam to Revelation: Transtextual Adventures of Biblical Sins," in S. ALKIER – TH. HIEKE – T. NICKLAS, eds., *Poetik und Intertextualität der Johannesapokalypse* [Tübingen: Mohr Siebeck, 2015] 306).

of the followers of Jesus,"[78] and this seems to explain why Babylon is depicted as an antithesis of the new Jerusalem, a symbolic transfiguration of that collective that John considers "in line" with and belonging to the true Judaism. John considers himself and his followers to be the real Jews as opposed to the ones who "say they are Jews and are not" (Rev 2:9; 3:9), and similarly, he considers himself and his followers to be the real prophets as opposed to Jezebel who "calls herself a prophet and is teaching and beguiling my servants to practice fornication and to eat food sacrificed to idols" (Rev 2:20).

Babylon the whore, in John's literary construction, becomes the prototype of a Jewish reality that refuses to accept the "true" Jewish message. That is the message proclaimed by John the seer: a symbol of a city in which Jews live and cohabit with other people. But such a cohabitation appears, in the seer of Patmos's view, as an impossible way of belonging to his conception of "true" Judaism.

## 5. Concluding Remarks

The first conclusion concerns the consideration of Revelation as a visionary discourse, with regard to which it is difficult to find a consequent or developing structure (as is the case with other ancient typologies of narration).[79] As G. Stevenson has remarked clearly, every symbolic description we found in Revelation ought to be understood in light of that polarized *scenario*, as it results from John's account, globally considered:

> By exposing his audience's world to a transcendent perspective, John provides them with a new understanding of Christian existence: they are at war. John establishes a stark set of oppositions; on one side stands the dragon, the beast, the inhabitants and kings of the earth, while on the other side stands God, the Lamb, and their faithful followers. Between the two sides a war is raging. The dragon and his angels war against Michael and his angels in heaven (12:7). The dragon makes war against the Christians (12:17). The beast and the kings of the earth wage war against the Lamb, the rider on the white horse, and his followers (17:14; 19:19). The

78. Quotations are from E.F. Lupieri, "From Sodom and Balaam to Revelation: Transtextual Adventures of Biblical Sins," in S. Alkier – Th. Hieke – T. Nicklas, eds., *Poetik und Intertextualität der Johannesapokalypse* (Tübingen: Mohr Siebeck, 2015) 315.

79. For similar conclusions, see also my essay: L. Arcari, "Social Currency, Embodiment and Resilience (and/or Resistance). Judaism(s) and the Revelation of John in the Communicative Urban Market of Imperial Asia Minor (1st-2nd cent. C.E.), *Studi e materiali di Storia delle religioni* 88/2 (2022) 426-442.

beast makes war against and conquers the two witnesses and the saints (11:7; 13:7).[80]

I am not so inclined to think that John provides a new understanding of "Christian" existence, especially since it is very difficult to define what Christianity actually meant in the first century CE. More than a new paradigm of existence, the visions discussed in this essay seem to stage various prototypes of false Judaism (in John's eyes). Such a falsehood receives its historical materiality on a case-by-case basis, in light of what the seer clearly states in the seven opening letters. In Lakoff's words,[81] with the term "proto-typicality," in the case of Revelation, it is possible to designate a literary creation that does not intend to describe particular things or individuals in the world, but a further deepening depiction of activities that get their meaning via the correspondences with what the opening seven letters recall through the employment of a more proactive communicative tool: that of the letter.

This is not a mere objectivist interpretation of John's literary text. The symbolic beings discussed in this essay embody experiences that John *perceives* as deviant. These Johannine monsters are grounded in individual perception and, at the same time, are forged as symbols. They may also be actual motors for that agency which is viewed as not in line with a special collective religious self-definition. But these visionary constructions are also products of an imaginative thought. Like a mediating prototype that claims to sum up a system as a set, they also go beyond local experiences of hegemony employing metaphor, metonymy, and mental imagery in order to take the audience's mind beyond what they can see and feel. Nevertheless, this imaginative capacity is also embodied—indirectly—since "metaphors, metonymies, and images are based on experience, often bodily experience."[82] Always, according to Lakoff's words, products of John's experience of contact with the otherworld have "*gestalt* properties" as well as an "ecological structure."[83] Their symbolic efficacy depends on the overall structure of both conceptual and narrative systems emerging

80. G. STEVENSON, *Power and Place: Temple and Identity in the Book of Revelation* (Berlin: De Gruyter, 2001) 282. On "market mentality" in Revelation in the context of early Christianity, see E.F. LUPIERI, "'Businessmen and Merchants Will Not Enter the Places of My Father': Early Christianity and Market Mentality," in J. VON HAGEN – M. WELKER, eds., *Money as God? Monetization of the Market and the Impact on Religion, Politics, Law, and Ethics* (Cambridge, UK: Cambridge University Press, 2014) 379-413.

81. See G. LAKOFF, *Women, Fire, and Dangerous Things: What Categories Reveal about the Mind* (Chicago: The University of Chicago Press, 1987) xiii-xiv.

82. G. LAKOFF, *Women, Fire, and Dangerous Things: What Categories Reveal about the Mind* (Chicago: The University of Chicago Press, 1987) xiv.

83. G. LAKOFF, *Women, Fire, and Dangerous Things: What Categories Reveal about the Mind* (Chicago: The University of Chicago Press, 1987) xiv-xv.

from Revelation as a literary set which aims at translating in an understandable way what would not be communicable in itself.

The second conclusive remarks concern the *vexata quaestio* of what "Judaism" (and such connected terms as "Jew/Jews," "Jewish," "Proto-Christian[s]," and so on) meant in the first century CE in the various cultural and social contexts of the Roman Empire. What emerges in Revelation is an oppositional dualism between belonging to Judaism as it is under Roman colonial rule in the cities of Asia Minor (and thus corrupted in John's view) and a Jewish belonging transfigured in the eschatological heavenly New Jerusalem, as it appears in much of Jewish apocalyptic literature. Focusing on Revelation through the theoretical lens resulting from the study of religious cohabitations in the first century CE reveals an interesting case of "hybridity."[84] Claims of one's own belonging to the "true" Judaism is itself a construct of the colonized subject seeking to articulate its identity, an identity that stands as a rigid and essentialist entity that is unable to communicate with other integrated Jewish identities, at least in the urban spaces of the Empire. Nevertheless, the analysis carried out in this chapter shows that John's essentialist identity, and his consequent essentialist rereading of authoritative traditions as actual "building blocks" for this work of re-invention of tradition, are perfectly understandable in a continuum that seeks to appreciate Judaism "as an autonomous, changing, and diverse tradition."[85] In avoiding generalized and monolithic descriptions about Jewish tradition(s) or about "indigenous" cultures, what emerges is that what is so called as a "real" culture is always constructed, contested, forged through debate, negotiation, and sometimes confrontation. This suggests that we contextualize John's Revelation among the different groups and factions of first century Judaism(s) as they emerge in the stereotyped discourse carried out in the first part of John's work; at the same time placing it in the wider contexts of the Roman imperial cities as they emerge outside the literary construction of our text.

---

84. On the concept of "hybridity," see supra, note 5. For a study of early Christian texts in light of Bhabha's theoretical framework, see J.W. MARSHALL, "Hybridity and Reading Romans 13," *Journal for the Study of the New Testament* 31 (2008) 157-178; ID., "Gender and Empire: Sexualized Violence in John's Anti-Imperial Apocalypse," in A.-J. LEVINE – M.M. ROBBINS, eds., *A Feminist Companion to the Apocalypse of John* (London: T&T Clark, 2009) 23-24; S.D. MOORE, *Empire and Apocalypse: Postcolonialism and the New Testament* (Sheffield: Phoenix, 2006) 86-96, 109-115; ID., "The Revelation to John," in F.F. SEGOVIA – R.S. SUGIRTHARAJAH, eds., *A Postcolonial Commentary on the New Testament Writings* (London: T&T Clark, 2007) 436-454.

85. J. PLASKOW, "Anti-Judaism in Feminist Christian Interpretation," in E. SCHÜSSLER FIORENZA, ed., *Searching the Scriptures: A Feminist Introduction (Vol. 1)* (New York: Crossroad, 1993) 125.

# Second Part

# The Women and the Cities

# INTERTEXTUALITY IN THE APOCALYPSE: THE DESERT AND THE WOMAN*

**Stéphanie Audet**
*Université Laval, Québec*

Résumé

Cet article a pour objectif principal d'étudier les liens intertextuels qui existent entre l'Apocalypse de Jean et l'Exode afin d'éclairer la signification du texte apocalyptique et de mieux comprendre la présence du motif du désert et des représentations féminines. Une première partie révise la théorie et la méthodologie qui permettent de repérer les procédés littéraires utilisés par Jean et les possibles liens intertextuels entre ces deux textes. En deuxième partie, l'intertextualité entre l'Exode et l'Apocalypse, déjà mise en évidence par d'autres auteurs et autrices, est étudiée d'abord en mettant en parallèle trois groupes de fléaux: les trompettes et les coupes de l'Apocalypse et les fléaux d'Égypte dans le récit de l'Exode. Ensuite, d'autres parallèles entre l'Exode et les chapitres 12 à 17 de l'Apocalypse sont explorés. En troisième partie, les motifs du désert et de l'idolâtrie dans les deux textes sont analysés. Enfin, les représentations féminines sont abordées. Sur l'arrière-plan de la trame narrative de l'Exode, la personnification d'Israël et de Jérusalem comme femme et cité dans l'Apocalypse semble plausible.

Abstract

The main objective of this paper is to study the intertextual links between the Apocalypse of John and Exodus in order to shed light on the meaning of the apocalyptic text and to better understand the presence of the desert motif and the feminine representations therein. The first part reviews the theory and methodology that allow us to identify the literary devices used by John and the possible intertextual links between these two texts. In the second part, the intertextuality between Exodus and Revelation, already highlighted by other authors, is studied first by comparing three groups of plagues: the trumpets and the bowls of Revelation and the plagues of Egypt in the Exodus narrative. Then, other parallels between Exodus and chapters 12 to 17 of Revelation are explored. In the third part, the motifs of the desert and idolatry in both texts are analyzed. Finally, feminine represen-

* I would like to thank Professors Painchaud and Lupieri for their help in writing this chapter as well as the shared ideas that have been the inspiration for this research.

*"Who is Sitting on Which Beast?" Interpretative Issues in the Book of Revelation. Proceedings of the International Conference held at Loyola University, Chicago, March 30-31, 2017,* ed. by Edmondo Lupieri and Louis Painchaud, JAOC 29 (Turnhout, 2023), pp. 49–84

DOI 10.1484/M.JAOC-EB.5.131928

tations are discussed. Against the background of the narrative of Exodus, the personification of Israel and Jerusalem as woman and city in Revelation seems plausible.

## 1. Introduction

When it comes to interpretations of John of Patmos's text, the Book of Revelation, consensus is difficult to reach. Even the use of the appellation "John of Patmos" here is not unanimous.[1] Nevertheless, there are sometimes convergences. For example, more and more scholars recognize that this apocalyptic writing uses other stories, images, and themes from the Tanakh.[2] Many authors have commented on the links between excerpts in Revelation and other texts.[3] Beale, Ford and Moyise consider Revelation to be the book in the New Testament that contains the most references to the Tanakh.[4] However, because the author of this Apocalypse does not

1. Although, designations of "writer," "author" and "composer" are used here in the singular to facilitate the reading of the chapter, I am well aware of the many debates about composition (i.e., that some texts have a single author vs. multiple authors or contain later additions and/or layered composition); however, this is not the particular subject of this contribution, and so we will focus on other issues.

2. About the Old Testament in Revelation, see A. LANGELLOTTI, "L'Antico Testamento nell'Apocalisse," *Rivista Biblica* 14 (1966) 369-384; L.P. TRUDINGER, "Some Observations Concerning the Text of the Old Testament in the Book of Revelation," *The Journal of Theological Studies* 17/1 (1966) 82-88; G.K. BEALE, "Revelation," in D.A. CARSON – H.G.M. WILLIAMSON, eds., *It Is Written: Scripture Citing Scripture: Essays in Honour of Barnabas Lindars* (Cambridge: Cambridge University Press, 1988) 318-336; J. PAULIEN, "Elusive Allusions: The Problematic Use of the Old Testament in Revelation," *Biblical Research* 33 (1988) 37-53; S. MOYISE, *The Old Testament in the Book of Revelation* (Sheffield: Sheffield Academic Press 1995); I. PROVAN, "Foul Spirits, Fornication and Finance. Revelation 18 in an Old Testament Perspective," *Journal for the Study of New Testament* 64 (1996) 81-106; for the presence of Daniel, see G.K. BEALE, *The Use of Daniel in Jewish Apocalyptic Literature and in the Revelation of St John* (Lanham: University Press of America, 1984); for the link between Revelation and Isaiah, see B. MARCONCINI, "L'utilizzazione del T. M. nelle citazioni Isaiane dell'Apocalisse," *Rivista Biblica* 24 (1976) 113-136; about Ezekiel, see J.-P. RUIZ, *Ezekiel in the Apocalypse: The Transformation of Prophetic Language in Revelation 16,17-19,10* (Frankfurt am Main: Lang, 1989).

3. For a more complete list, G.K. BEALE, "Revelation," in D.A. CARSON – H.G.M. WILLIAMSON, eds., *It Is Written: Scripture Citing Scripture: Essays in Honour of Barnabas Lindars* (Cambridge, UK: Cambridge University Press, 1988) 325.

4. G.K. BEALE, "Revelation," in D.A. CARSON – H.G.M. WILLIAMSON, eds., *It Is Written: Scripture Citing Scripture: Essays in Honour of Barnabas Lindars* (Cambridge, UK: Cambridge University Press, 1988) 318; J. MASSYNGBERDE FORD, *Revelation* (Garden City: Doubleday, 1975) 27; S. MOYISE, *The Old Testament in the Book of Revelation* (Sheffield: Sheffield Academic Press, 1995) 14.

directly quote the Scriptures, the number of accepted references is problematic and diverges depending on the commentator.[5]

One major difficulty in determining intertextuality in Revelation is the frequent absence of theoretical and methodological definitions, creating what Paulien describes as a "chaos" among the references made by different researchers.[6] It is therefore appropriate to start with a methodological approach (the analysis of implicit intertextuality) that is too often dismissed and to define the terms used. Apocalyptic literature and its use of rhetoric must first be addressed before one can understand how it uses intertextuality. It uses literary devices such as allusion, which is particularly important in the literature that concerns us. Allusion, however, brings a lot of problems that I will try to solve by applying certain criteria.

After developing its methodology and definitions, this paper intends to apply a specific approach. Since some commentators call attention to elements that link Revelation to Exodus, this link appears to be a good object of study.[7] Indeed, by using the plagues of Exodus in the text by John of Patmos, "this confluence of evidence lends this direct allusion a high level of certainty that is rare in Rev."[8] In order to bring new elements of understanding to the text, I will look at John of Patmos's use of Exodus and how the images of this book appear in the apocalyptic visions. Some parallels have already been identified by other scholars, but it is necessary to give an overview of the text and to establish the relationship between Exodus and Revelation.

Once this overall picture is drawn up, it is then possible to shed light on other questions.[9] The last part of this chapter focuses on Exodus as a key to understanding Revelation, particularly through the use of the desert motif[10] and the golden calf narrative. It develops the hypothesis that

---

5. J. PAULIEN, "Elusive Allusions: The Problematic Use of the Old Testament in Revelation," *Biblical Research* 33 (1988) 37-39.

6. J. PAULIEN, "Elusive Allusions: The Problematic Use of the Old Testament in Revelation," *Biblical Research* 33 (1988) 38.

7. This is the case, among others, of L.A. VOS, *The Synoptic Traditions in the Apocalypse* (Kampen: J.H. Kok, 1965) 45-47; E. CORSINI, *The Apocalypse: The Perennial Revelation of Jesus Christ* (Wilmington: Glazier, 1983) 168-169; G.K. BEALE, "Revelation," in D.A. CARSON – H.G.M. WILLIAMSON, eds., *It Is Written: Scripture Citing Scripture: Essays in Honour of Barnabas Lindars* (Cambridge, UK: Cambridge University Press, 1988) 324. Beale notes that "there is a consensus that the plagues of the 'trumpets' in Rev 8:6-12 and those of the bowls in 16:1-9 follow the paradigm of the Exodus plagues (Exod 8:12), although creatively reworked and applied."

8. J. PAULIEN, "Elusive Allusions: The Problematic Use of the Old Testament in Revelation," *Biblical Research* 33 (1988) 46.

9. L. PAINCHAUD, "The Use of Scripture in Gnostic Literature," *Journal of Early Christian Studies* 4/2 (1996) 144.

10. I use Talmon's definition of motif: "A literary motif is a representative complex theme which recurs within the framework of the Old Testament in variable

certain passages use intertextuality as a device. I conclude with the issue of the identity of the woman in the desert, and I suggest a reading that differs from that of common historiography, in which the harlot is associated with Rome.

## 2. Theory and Methodology

### 2.1 Apocalyptic Rhetoric

John's Revelation is renowned as part of apocalyptic literature.[11] This category encompasses many religious texts,[12] both Jewish and Christian. As for the purpose of such literature, the rhetorical approach provides convincing answers. Apocalyptic texts, indeed, contain elements of persuasion in order to convert the audience to the writer's faith and ideas.[13] One of the typical elements of persuasion in rhetorical art is the call to

---

forms and connections. It is rooted in an actual situation of anthropological or historical nature. In its secondary literary setting, the motif gives expression to ideas and experiences inherent in the original situation and is employed to reactualize in the audience the reaction of the participants in that original situation." S. TALMON, "The 'Desert Motif' in the Bible and in Qumran Literature," in A. ALTMANN, ed., *Biblical Motifs: Origins and Transformations* (Cambridge, MA: Harvard University Press, 1966) 38.

11. Despite their diversity, apocalyptic texts typically describe a vision/dream/journey that transcends earthly reality both in space and time to experience otherworldly affairs and deliver an eschatological message, some elements of which are revealed by a supernatural intermediary. See J.J. COLLINS, "What Is Apocalyptic Literature?" in J.J. COLLINS, ed., *The Oxford Handbook of Apocalyptic Literature* (Oxford: Oxford University Press, 2014) 4-5. See, in the same book, G. CAREY, "Early Christian Apocalyptic Rhetoric," 218; M. HENZE, "Apocalypse and Torah in Ancient Judaism," 312; H. NAJMAN, "The Inheritance of Prophecy in Apocalypse," 36-37. Apocalyptic literature often uses paradigms and symbolic images from the mythologies of the target groups. On this subject, see J.J. COLLINS, "What Is Apocalyptic Literature?," in J.J. COLLINS, ed., *The Oxford Handbook of Apocalyptic Literature* (Oxford: Oxford University Press, 2014) 8 and, in the same book, F. FLANNERY, "Dreams and Visions in Early Jewish and Early Christian Apocalypses and Apocalypticism," 109.

12. There have been many attempts to define apocalyptic literature, along with debates which revolve around whether it should be included with prophetic literature. See J.J. COLLINS, ed., *The Oxford Handbook of Apocalyptic Literature* (Oxford: Oxford University Press, 2014); especially: J.J. COLLINS, "What Is Apocalyptic Literature?" 7; S.L. COOK, "Apocalyptic Prophecy," 19-35 and H. NAJMAN, "The Inheritance of Prophecy in Apocalypse," 36-51.

13. G. CAREY, "Early Christian Apocalyptic Rhetoric," in J.J. COLLINS, ed., *The Oxford Handbook of Apocalyptic Literature* (Oxford: Oxford University Press, 2014) 220. Carey writes that "the extant corpus of early Christian writing and copying reflects that ancient people almost always wrote with a purpose."

*pathos.*[14] For example, the author can encourage the readers/hearers to identify with, or discourage them from identifying with, certain characters. In the case of Revelation, the addressees should not want to identify with the fate of the harlot but should prefer to rise among the righteous with the author.[15] In order to arouse fear or respect, apocalyptic texts frequently employ the rhetoric of the sublime. Using striking images, the author associates himself with the mysteries of the afterlife and inspires the listener's admiration through descriptive visual experience.[16] These images contribute to the *ethos* of the author, and, therefore, to the authority of the text. That is how apocalyptic literature becomes rhetorical: "One of the core aspects of the rhetoric of the apocalyptic is the identification of the audience with the seer, the audience and the seer with the angels, and the angels with God."[17]

Another rhetorical method uses *Vaticinia ex eventu*, "predictions" of events that have already occurred.[18] The author, claiming to have received his vision before the events, will become more authoritative, since divine favor allowed him to see the future.[19] The author will be able to use this

14. In the case of Revelation, the text evokes the contradictory emotions of hope and fear in order to prompt quick action. To convince the audience to reach the author's point of view, the descriptive narrative arouses the fear of the last judgment if the message is defied, while also offering the hope of a reward if the message of the author is received. See D.A. DESILVA, "Final Topics: The Rhetorical Functions of Intertexture in Revelation 14:14-16:21," in D.F. WATSON, ed., *The Intertexture of Apocalyptic Discourse in the New Testament* (Atlanta: Society of Biblical Literature, 2002) 217.

15. G. CAREY, "Early Christian Apocalyptic Rhetoric," in J.J. COLLINS, ed., *The Oxford Handbook of Apocalyptic Literature* (Oxford: Oxford University Press, 2014) 229; C.A. NEWSOM, "The Rhetoric of Jewish Apocalyptic Literature," in J.J. COLLINS, ed., *The Oxford Handbook of Apocalyptic Literature* (Oxford: Oxford University Press, 2014) 202.

16. The elements that are part of the rhetoric of the sublime are associated with the sublimity of the divine: physical descriptions of God or celestial spokespersons, the vision of the throne, the heavenly Temple, to name a few. See C.A. NEWSOM, "The Rhetoric of Jewish Apocalyptic Literature," in J.J. COLLINS, ed., *The Oxford Handbook of Apocalyptic Literature* (Oxford: Oxford University Press, 2014) 206-207. This is the case in 1 Enoch 10-36; 2 Enoch 3-22; Apoc. Zephaniah; 3 Baruch; Daniel, etc.

17. C.A. NEWSOM, "The Rhetoric of Jewish Apocalyptic Literature," in J.J. COLLINS, ed., *The Oxford Handbook of Apocalyptic Literature* (Oxford: Oxford University Press, 2014) 207. Newsom applies this to Judean-type texts, but it is applicable to John's text since it testifies to a typically Hebraic worldview.

18. G. CAREY, "Early Christian Apocalyptic Rhetoric," in J.J. COLLINS, ed., *The Oxford Handbook of Apocalyptic Literature* (Oxford: Oxford University Press, 2014) 221; C.A. NEWSOM, "The Rhetoric of Jewish Apocalyptic Literature," in J.J. COLLINS, ed., *The Oxford Handbook of Apocalyptic Literature* (Oxford: Oxford University Press, 2014) 213.

19. C.A. NEWSOM, "The Rhetoric of Jewish Apocalyptic Literature," in J.J. COLLINS, ed., *The Oxford Handbook of Apocalyptic Literature* (Oxford: Oxford University-

narrative principle in the future to convince his audience. It is "the impression of plausibility" through the representations of the future in the text that persuades the audience.[20] In some cases, the author predicts a fall, uses his visions to explain the cause of this fall, and ends with the hope of restoration after judgment. As it explains the behavior that led to the inevitable fall and destruction, as though it had already occurred, the narrative outlines the actions necessary for the readers/listeners to be among the Chosen People, as is the author.

The apocalyptic style, then, becomes a tool of persuasion for authors, so that the hearer quickly adheres to a way of conceiving of the faith, as John does for the new faith in Jesus Christ.[21] This persuasive element in John can be seen from the first chapters in the letters to the ἐκκλησίαι, where the language emphasizes the urgency of joining the faith of Jesus and of rejecting behaviors that the author believes lead to damnation.[22]

## 2.2 Intertextuality

Another device in apocalyptic literature that must be increasingly taken into account is *intertextuality*. The very meaning of the word is complex and can be interpreted in different ways. To better define it, we must turn to literary analysts like Genette. This author uses the image of a palimpsest to define intertextuality: "a copresent relationship between two or more texts that is, eidetically and most often, the actual presence of a text into another text."[23] Here, intertextuality is considered as a relation between two texts, the source text being the *hypotext* and the subsequent composition being the *hypertext*. Though it never mentions the hypotext,

sity Press, 2014) 212.

20. D.A. deSilva, "Final Topics: The Rhetorical Functions of Intertexture in Revelation 14:14-16:21," in D.F. Watson, ed., *The Intertexture of Apocalyptic Discourse in the New Testament* (Atlanta: Society of Biblical Literature, 2002) 221. It is this technique that is used especially in the Apocalypse of Abraham, in reference to the pillage of Jerusalem by the Romans. This is what was also used in most texts referring to the first destruction of Jerusalem and the Exile in Babylon. See B.G. wold, "Revelation 16 and the Eschatological Use of Exodus Plagues," in *Eschatologie-Eschatology. The Sixth Durham-Tübingen Research Symposium: Eschatology in Old Testament, Ancient Judaism and Early Christianity (Tübingen, September, 2009)* (Tübingen: Mohr Siebeck, 2011) 262.

21. D.A. deSilva, "Final Topics: The Rhetorical Functions of Intertexture in Revelation 14:14-16:21," in D.F. Watson, ed., *The Intertexture of Apocalyptic Discourse in the New Testament* (Atlanta: Society of Biblical Literature, 2002) 216; and, in the same book, "Introduction" by D.F. Watson (1).

22. D.A. deSilva, "Final Topics: The Rhetorical Functions of Intertexture in Revelation 14:14-16:21," in D.F. Watson, ed., *The Intertexture of Apocalyptic Discourse in the New Testament* (Atlanta: Society of Biblical Literature, 2002) 219.

23. Free translation of G. Genette, *Palimpseste. La littérature au second degré* (Paris: Éditions du Seuil, 1982) 7.

the hypertext is unable to exist without it.[24] The hypotext is transformed in the hypertext in a number of ways, three of which are *imitation*, *borrowing*, and *echo*.[25]

Imitation mainly concerns the style and language that the author may have emulated from other texts, whereas borrowing concerns the themes and literary motifs taken from previous stories, more specifically. An example of imitation can be seen in John's Greek, which Charles describes by saying, "while he writes in Greek, he thinks in Hebrew."[26] The difficulties of the text's language indicate that John deliberately wrote in a Semitic idiom[27] using the Greek language that was more common and, thus, allowed for the spread of these writings in Asia Minor. According to Beale, "His purpose was deliberately to create a 'biblical' effect on the hearer and thus to demonstrate the solidarity of his work with that of the divinely inspired OT Scripture."[28] In doing so, John of Patmos uses a Hebrew style, an editorial model that imitates the Jewish scriptures,[29] and associates himself with the activity of a prophet:[30] "John chose a

---

24. G. GENETTE, *Palimpseste. La littérature au second degré* (Paris: Éditions du Seuil, 1982) 11-12; G.K. BEALE, "Revelation," in D.A. CARSON – H.G.M. WILLIAMSON, eds., *It Is Written: Scripture Citing Scripture: Essays in Honour of Barnabas Lindars* (Cambridge, UK: Cambridge University Press 1988) 326. Beale notes: "This use can be considered the most general description of OT usage in the Apocalypses, since the very act of referring to an OT text is to place it in some comparative relationship to something in the NT."

25. G. GENETTE, *Palimpseste. La littérature au second degré* (Paris: Éditions du Seuil, 1982) 8-14 and 81. Genette uses an example from ancient literature: the texts of the Aeneid and the Odyssey (the latter of which served as the hypotext that allowed for the writing of Virgil's text, even though Virgil never mentioned the Homeric text or quoted it directly).

26. R.H. CHARLES, *A Critical and Exegetical Commentary on the Revelation of St John* (Edinburgh: T&T Clark, 1920), cxliii.

27. G.B. CAIRD, *A Commentary on the Revelation of St John the Divine* (London: A&C Black, 1984) 5.

28. G.K. BEALE, "Revelation," in D.A. CARSON – H.G.M. WILLIAMSON, eds., *It Is Written: Scripture Citing Scripture: Essays in Honour of Barnabas Lindars* (Cambridge, UK: Cambridge University Press 1988) 332. Beale adds, "The Old Testament was indispensable to the understanding of the character and purpose of God, but it must be read in the light of the fullest illumination of Christ."

29. G. GENETTE, *Palimpseste. La littérature au second degré* (Paris: Éditions du Seuil, 1982) 81. Genette defines "hébraïsme" as a literary genre that uses imitations of expressions characteristic of OT, including, among others, the uses of superlatives and repetition.

30. D. DIMANT, "Use and Interpretation of Mikra in the Apocrypha and Pseudepigrapha," in M.J. MULDER – H. SYSLING, eds., *Mikra: Text, Translation, Reading, and Interpretation of the Hebrew Bible in Ancient Judaism and Early Christianity* (Assen: Van Gorcum, 1988) 418. Dimant wrote that "authors employing biblical elements in this way aim at re-creating the biblical models and atmosphere, and identify themselves with biblical authors."

rather special means, the apocalyptic literary genre, which he understood as a continuation of Hebrew prophetism, especially messianic prophecy."[31] This use of intertextuality helps the rhetorical construction of his *ethos*.

Borrowing activates motifs that are part of the collective imagination of its recipients. According to the symbolic convergence theory,[32] a group of people shares the same symbolic world. This is particularly the case in religious groups that have a common way of conceiving the world, their history, and their sacred texts.[33] This symbolic world makes it possible to create ancient religious bonds, even within new texts. To use one example: borrowing an image like the plagues directs the attention of the Jewish reader to the text of Exodus. The use of the desert motif similarly calls to mind the books of Exodus and Numbers and the themes they contain. The audience can, therefore, understand the meaning of John's text when he evokes these common symbols.[34] The echo, meanwhile, is a trace left in the lexicon that can recall what has already been said (like an echo in a cave). Using imitation, borrowing, and echo, the author can refer to another text without quoting it explicitly.[35]

---

31. E. CORSINI, *The Apocalypse: The Perennial Revelation of Jesus Christ* (Wilmington: Glazier, 1983) 388.

32. Regarding the symbolic convergence theory, see E.G. BORMANN, "Rhetorical vision," in T.O. SLOANE, ed., *Encyclopedia of Rhetoric (e-reference edition)* (Oxford University Press, 2006); S.L. COOK, "Apocalyptic Prophecy," in J.J. COLLINS, ed., *The Oxford Handbook of Apocalyptic Literature* (Oxford: Oxford University Press, 2014) 21-22 and C.A. NEWSOM, "The Rhetoric of Jewish Apocalyptic Literature," in J.J. COLLINS, ed., *The Oxford Handbook of Apocalyptic Literature* (Oxford: Oxford University Press, 2014).

33. E.G. BORMANN, "Rhetorical vision," in T.O. SLOANE, ed., *Encyclopedia of Rhetoric (e-reference edition)* (Oxford University Press, 2006).

34. D. DIMANT, "Use and Interpretation of Mikra in the Apocrypha and Pseudepigrapha," in M.J. MULDER – H. SYSLING, eds., *Mikra: Text, Translation, Reading, and Interpretation of the Hebrew Bible in Ancient Judaism and Early Christianity* (Assen: Van Gorcum, 1988) 400; J. PAULIEN, "Elusive Allusions: The Problematic Use of the Old Testament in Revelation," *Biblical Research* 33 (1988) 41. Paulien notes: "The author assumes that the source literature is familiar to the reader and that the reader can import from the context of the source insights which enhance his appreciation of the work he is reading." See also L. PAINCHAUD, "The Use of Scripture in Gnostic Literature," *Journal of Early Christian Studies* 4/2 (1996) 142-143. As Painchaud wrote: "In other words, it is only in its intertextual context where its full meaning appears."

35. G.K. BEALE, "Revelation," in D.A. CARSON – H.G.M. WILLIAMSON, eds., *It Is Written: Scripture Citing Scripture: Essays in Honour of Barnabas Lindars* (Cambridge, UK: Cambridge University Press 1988) 321-322; D. DIMANT, "Use and Interpretation of Mikra in the Apocrypha and Pseudepigrapha," in M.J. MULDER – H. SYSLING, eds., *Mikra: Text, Translation, Reading, and Interpretation of the Hebrew Bible in Ancient Judaism and Early Christianity* (Assen: Van Gorcum, 1988) 409-410: allusions are used for "the simultaneous activation of two texts, using a special signal referring to the independent external text. These sig-

Allusion is the implicit use of intertextuality (unlike quotation, which is explicit).[36] Imitation, borrowing, and echo, taken individually, are ways of recalling other texts, sometimes without necessarily referring to them intentionally. But when there is an intentional hint, this process uses the audience's intelligence to determine the origin of the reference and to go back to the original text in order to understand the hypertext.[37] There is, then, an implicit intertextual relation. The larger structures of a hypertext are built to recall specific images and themes with the help of a common imaginative language drawn from the hypotext.[38] In the case of Revelation, these images, triggered by a keyword or a theme, lead the reader

---

nals may consist of isolated terms, patterns and motifs taken from the independent text alluded to." See J. PAULIEN, "Elusive Allusions: The Problematic Use of the Old Testament in Revelation," *Biblical Research* 33 (1988) 40, who notes: "The author may use a source directly and consciously with its original context in mind. Such an allusion is 'willed into being.' The author is fully conscious of the source as well as of its relevance to his composition. He/she is assuming the reader's knowledge of the source and of his/her intention to refer to that source." See also S. MOYISE, *The Old Testament in the Book of Revelation* (Sheffield: Sheffield Academic Press, 1995) 18-19, 110 and L. PAINCHAUD, "The Use of Scripture in Gnostic Literature," *Journal of Early Christian Studies* 4/2 (1996) 130. Painchaud notes: "Allusions, although they are difficult to recognize, are no less relevant for an understanding of the use of Scripture than are explicit quotations. On the contrary, their identification as allusions is absolutely necessary for the understanding of a given text."

36. G. GENETTE, *Palimpseste. La littérature au second degré* (Paris: Éditions du Seuil, 1982) 8; J. HOLLANDER, *The Figure of Echo: A Mode of Allusion in Milton and After* (Berkeley: University of California Press, 1981) 88; S. MOYISE, *The Old Testament in the Book of Revelation* (Sheffield: Sheffield Academic Press, 1995) 109; J. PAULIEN, "Elusive Allusions: The Problematic Use of the Old Testament in Revelation," *Biblical Research* 33 (1988) 39.

37. D. DIMANT, "Use and Interpretation of Mikra in the Apocrypha and Pseudepigrapha," in M.J. MULDER – H. SYSLING, eds., *Mikra: Text, Translation, Reading, and Interpretation of the Hebrew Bible in Ancient Judaism and Early Christianity* (Assen: Van Gorcum, 1988) 400, 410; J. PAULIEN, "Elusive Allusions: The Problematic Use of the Old Testament in Revelation," *Biblical Research* 33 (1988) 39; S. MOYISE, *The Old Testament in the Book of Revelation* (Sheffield: Sheffield Academic Press, 1995) 18, 133-134. Moyise notes on p. 18, "Alluding to a past work set up a link or correspondence between the two contexts. The reader is asked to follow the current text while being mindful of a previous context." Moyise also states on pp. 133-134 that "two verses suggest that the author was not seeking to provide easy answers but wishes to force the reader to stop and think. It is possible that his use of the Old Testament is also meant to do the same." See also L. PAINCHAUD, "The Use of Scripture in Gnostic Literature," *Journal of Early Christian Studies* 4/2 (1996) 135.

38. J. PAULIEN, "Elusive Allusions: The Problematic Use of the Old Testament in Revelation," *Biblical Research* 33 (1988) 44.

towards a precise point of view, one of which the author is convinced:[39] "hearing Revelation's text in light of these other subtexts enhances its rhetorical impact."[40]

However, as Genette would say, there are no works that are not inspired by an earlier one or that do not evoke others. The problem of allusion lies in its subjectivity and the difficulty to determine the extent of its purposefulness.[41] Moreover, it is difficult to discern when the author only uses vocabulary that is familiar to him or if he really wants to evoke another text.[42] An author can refer to a text in a way that cannot be considered "conscious," without regard for the original text.[43]

---

39. E.G. Bormann, "Rhetorical vision," in T.O. Sloane, ed., *Encyclopedia of Rhetoric (e-reference edition)* (Oxford University Press, 2006): "Investigators called the new idea a rhetorical vision: 'rhetorical' because the larger symbolic structures were constructed by rhetorical imaginative language triggering shared fantasies".

40. D.A. deSilva, "Final Topics: The Rhetorical Functions of Intertexture in Revelation 14:14-16:21," in D.F. Watson, ed., *The Intertexture of Apocalyptic Discourse in the New Testament* (Atlanta: Society of Biblical Literature, 2002) 218; I. Provan, "Foul Spirits, Fornication and Finance: Revelation 18 in an Old Testament Perspective," *Journal for the Study of the New Testament* 64 (1996) 87. Provan provides here an example of understanding a text by referring to a hypotext, to possibly allude to Ezekiel: "It seems just as likely that he intends to direct us to Ezekiel 27 itself—not so much to comment on his contemporary situation as to say to his readers, 'read Ezekiel if you wish to understand what I am saying here.'"

41. G. Genette, *Palimpseste. La littérature au second degré* (Paris: Éditions du Seuil, 1982) 169; G.K. Beale, "Revelation," in D.A. Carson – H.G.M. Williamson, eds., *It Is Written: Scripture Citing Scripture: Essays in Honour of Barnabas Lindars* (Cambridge, UK: Cambridge University Press, 1988) 219.

42. G.K. Beale, "Revelation," in D.A. Carson – H.G.M. Williamson, eds., *It Is Written: Scripture Citing Scripture: Essays in Honour of Barnabas Lindars* (Cambridge, UK: Cambridge University Press, 1988) 323; L. Painchaud, "The Use of Scripture in Gnostic Literature," *Journal of Early Christian Studies* 4/2 (1996) 135, and E.F. Lupieri, "A Beast and a Woman in the Desert, or the Sin of Israel: A Typological Reflection," in E.F. Mason – E.F. Lupieri, eds., *Golden Calf Traditions in Early Judaism, Christianity, and Islam* (Leiden: Brill, 2018) 157.

43. S. Moyise, *The Old Testament in the Book of Revelation* (Sheffield: Sheffield Academic Press, 1995) 30; J. Hollander, *The Figure of Echo: A Mode of Allusion in Milton and After* (Berkeley: University of California Press, 1981) 64; L. Painchaud, "The Use of Scripture in Gnostic Literature," *Journal of Early Christian Studies* 4/2 (1996) 135; G.K. Beale, "A Reconsideration of the Text of Daniel in the Apocalypse," *Biblica* 67 (1986) 539-543. Beale uses the distinction between a "clear," "probable," and "possible" allusion. J. Paulien, "Elusive Allusions: The Problematic Use of the Old Testament in Revelation," *Biblical Research* 33 (1988) 40-41, first differentiates between allusion, direct allusion, and echo. Then, he redivides potential allusions into "certain allusions, probable, possible, non-allusive." He also notes that "an author may 'echo' ideas, the origin of which he/she is unaware. In an echo, the author does not point the reader to a particular background source but merely utilizes a 'live symbol' that would be generally understood in his original situation."

The Jewish and Christian texts bring another difficulty. Between the Apocalypse and Exodus, there are many possible hypotexts and hypertexts. We cannot know exactly which texts or which variants of these texts John used. Nevertheless, because of the importance of Exodus as a grand narrative, this book has been used in many religious texts, some of which originated in Second Temple Judaism (Hosea 8-10, *Wisdom of Solomon* 1-19, Isa 43-52, etc.).[44] In the case of Christian groups, the text of Exodus has been reinterpreted under the magnifying glass of messianic deliverance. This is the case in the Gospels of Matthew and John especially, but also in the Epistles.[45] Some passages of *4 Ezra* present the scribe as a new Moses (*4 Ezra* 14).[46] It is, therefore, not surprising that Revelation reappropriates this specific text in order to build its own narrative. Many of its passages can, therefore, relate to the text of a prophet, but prophetic texts relate directly or indirectly to Exodus. This work will not exhaust every potential intertextual resonance between Revelation and Exodus; rather, it will focus on the relationship between Exodus and the Johannine text.

### 2.3 Criteria of Implicit Intertextuality

To mitigate the possibility of subjectivity, criteria must be applied to determine whether an author intentionally alludes to another text. Some of these criteria are based on Paulien and Painchaud.[47] The first of these is the repetition of elements that can call a text prior to the hypertext to mind. These elements can take a lexical form (the echo), which in isolation cannot be considered voluntary, but its repetition increases the likelihood that the allusion is conscious. The repetition of a theme or a style in a text is also a factor in its identification. I repeat here the three sub-criteria as stated by Paulien : verbal parallels, thematic parallels, and structural paral-

44. G.K. BEALE, "Revelation," in D.A. CARSON – H.G.M. WILLIAMSON, eds., *It Is Written : Scripture Citing Scripture : Essays in Honour of Barnabas Lindars* (Cambridge, UK: Cambridge University Press 1988) 324; F.L. FISHER, "The New and Greater Exodus : The Exodus Pattern in the New Testament," *Southwestern Journal of Theology* 20/1 (1977) 70; B.W. ANDERSON, "Exodus Typology in Second Isaiah," in *Israel's Prophetic Heritage : Essays in Honor of James Muilenburg* (London : SCM, 1962) 177-195.

45. F.L. FISHER, "The New and Greater Exodus : The Exodus Pattern in the New Testament," *Southwestern Journal of Theology* 20/1 (1977) 71.

46. M. HENZE, "Apocalypse and Torah in Ancient Judaism," in J.J. COLLINS, ed., *The Oxford Handbook of Apocalyptic Literature* (Oxford : Oxford University Press, 2014) 319.

47. J. PAULIEN, "Elusive Allusions : The Problematic Use of the Old Testament in Revelation," *Biblical Research* 33 (1988) 38 ; L. PAINCHAUD, "The Use of Scripture in Gnostic Literature," *Journal of Early Christian Studies* 4/2 (1996) 136. I add one that I think is necessary, historical plausibility, because some authors tend to forget the socio-political context of writing.

lels.[48] A text repeatedly referring to another text in particular reinforces the possibility that an allusion is conscious and deliberate.[49] This is one of the most important criteria that can be applied internally to the text. In our case, I will apply this criterion to the text of Revelation to look for repeated references to Exodus.

Another criterion is external to the text: *historical plausibility*.[50] For this criterion, one must ask whether it is historically possible for an author to refer to a particular text. It is then necessary to question the possible spatial and temporal frameworks of composition, the anteriority of the hypotext, the cultural and religious traditions of the author, the social and political context in which he or she evolves, and the possibility that he or she had access to specific scriptures. In this case, it is likely that the author of Revelation had access to the texts of the Tanakh and other religious texts circulating in his time and in Asia Minor.[51] Moreover, according to Caird, John's use of the scriptures and their style seems to show that he is familiar with the language of the Tanakh, to the point of forming a "permanent furniture" on which he forms his text.[52] Carey even argues that the author must be a "profoundly scholarly" person engaged in Jewish scripture.[53]

Finally, two other criteria can then be used to validate the presence of implicit intertextuality. One that applies precisely to literature that frequently uses imagery (such as apocalyptic literature) is that of the strangeness of a specific passage. Even as we shed light onto the text and the sym-

---

48. J. PAULIEN, "Elusive Allusions: The Problematic Use of the Old Testament in Revelation," *Biblical Research* 33 (1988) 41-42.

49. L. PAINCHAUD, "The Use of Scripture in Gnostic Literature," *Journal of Early Christian Studies* 4/2 (1996) 136; G.K. BEALE, "Revelation," in D.A. CARSON – H.G.M. WILLIAMSON, eds., *It Is Written: Scripture Citing Scripture: Essays in Honour of Barnabas Lindars* (Cambridge, UK: Cambridge University Press 1988) 323; J. PAULIEN, "Elusive Allusions: The Problematic Use of the Old Testament in Revelation," *Biblical Research* 33 (1988) 41.

50. J. PAULIEN, "Elusive Allusions: The Problematic Use of the Old Testament in Revelation," *Biblical Research* 33 (1988) 41.

51. J. PAULIEN, "Elusive Allusions: The Problematic Use of the Old Testament in Revelation," *Biblical Research* 33 (1988) 46: "Where it can be determined that a strong literary parallel exists, the external evidence should be brought to bear. The external evidence supports the likelihood that John was familiar with the OT and, to a lesser extent, such previous Jewish works as 1 Enoch, Jubilees, Wisdom of Solomon, Psalms of Solomon, and portions of the Sibylline Oracle."

52. G.B. CAIRD, *A Commentary on the Revelation of St John the Divine* (London: A&C Black, 1984) 74.

53. G. CAREY, "Early Christian Apocalyptic Rhetoric," in J.J. COLLINS, ed., *The Oxford Handbook of Apocalyptic Literature* (Oxford: Oxford University Press, 2014) 224. See also L.P. TRUDINGER, "Some Observations Concerning the Text of the Old Testament in the Book of Revelation," *The Journal of Theological Studies* 17/1 (1966) 84.

bols it uses, we might come across parts of the text that remain incoherent or unintelligible. We must then suspect that a possible allusion to another text would bring about a better understanding of the hypertext. And this is precisely the way that the last criterion, the insight that a hypotext can bring to the hypertext, comes into play.[54] In places where the Apocalypse seems incoherent, one must ask whether the text of Exodus would help shed light on it.

These four criteria make it possible to determine whether there is an intentional intertextual relationship between two texts. Some criteria may admittedly not apply to the text at hand, but the accumulation of several elements under one or more criteria would nevertheless confer the allusive value of a passage which, in isolation, could not with certitude be considered as in intertextual relation with another text.[55] Combined with an analysis using the aforementioned processes, such as imitation, borrowing, and echo, the method presented so far suggests a way of determining with some degree of certainty that one text may intentionally allude to another text. As Paulien admits, "the confluence of evidence can lead to various levels of certainty."[56] In the following section, I will attempt to determine the extent to which the text of Revelation refers to Exodus.[57]

## 3. Exodus and Revelation

### 3.1 The Plagues

Among the divine manifestations of Exodus,[58] the plagues sent against Egypt while Pharaoh refuses to let the people of God leave with Moses are

54. L. Painchaud, "The Use of Scripture in Gnostic Literature," *Journal of Early Christian Studies* 4/2 (1996) 136.

55. J. Paulien, "Elusive Allusions: The Problematic Use of the Old Testament in Revelation," *Biblical Research* 33 (1988) 40-43.

56. J. Paulien, "Elusive Allusions: The Problematic Use of the Old Testament in Revelation," *Biblical Research* 33 (1988) 45.

57. For English translation, I use the Revised Standard Version of the Bible with some revision of my own. For the Greek version of Revelation, I use "Apocalypsis Joannis," K. Aland – M. Black – C.M. Martini – B.M. Metzger – A. Wikgren, *The Greek New Testament*, 26th ed. (Stuttgart, 1968) 836-895. For the Greek version of Exodus in the Septuagint, see A. Rahlfs, *Septuaginta*, vol. 1 (Stuttgart, 1971) 86-158.

58. I will not explain the debate surrounding this text's composition nor provide explication of the documentary theory. I understand the text of Exodus, and the Pentateuch more generally, to have had, by the first and second centuries, almost the form of the canonical Pentateuch, and that there is a great possibility that John had access to almost all of the text of Exodus. See E.F. Lupieri, "A Beast and a Woman in the Desert, or the Sin of Israel: A Typological Reflection," in

one of the most famous (Exod 7:8-13:16).[59] It has been acknowledged that the Apocalypse uses the same striking images and, especially, the same vocabulary as Exodus. However, it divides these events into two groups of seven plagues: one group associated with the trumpets' signal (Rev 8:1-9:21; 11:15-18) and another with bowls (Rev 16:2-21). Between these two septets, and between Revelation's plagues and those depicted in Exodus, certain elements are analogous. In what follows, I will assess the similarities between these three groups of plagues: those of the trumpets, of the bowls, and of the Exodus.[60]

In Rev 8:7, the first trumpet sounds and brings the plague of hail and fire mixed with blood, together with the annihilation of a third of the Earth and its vegetation. This trumpet can be compared to the fourth bowl, where there is also fire (Rev 16:8-9), but it is much more similar to the seventh bowl, where there is hail (Rev 16:17-21). The hailstone, a scourge described as fearsome, appears in Exodus as the seventh plague (Exod 9:22-26), accompanied by the fire of the first trumpet and the fourth bowl. Thunder and lightning are also present in both Exodus's seventh plague and Revelation's seventh bowl. Just as in the first trumpet of the Revelation, the seventh plague of the Exodus also brings about the annihilation of nature, trees and plants: "The hail struck down everything that was in the field throughout all the land of Egypt, both man and beast; and the hail struck down every plant of the field, and shattered every tree of the field" (Exod 9:25). The plague of the first trumpet and the seventh plague of Exodus both imply destruction.

The theme of the transformed waters dominates in the second and third trumpets (Rev 8:8-11), as it does in the second and third bowls (Rev 16:3-4). In the trumpets, one third of sea life is destroyed by a mountain thrown into the sea, followed by the poisoning of a third of the water by a star called Absinthe. The bowls, on the other hand, hint at the popular symbolism of the Exodus: the water transformed into blood with the first plague (Exod 7:20-21). In any case, the water becomes undrinkable and represents a divine manifestation.

Darkness strikes a third of the sun, the moon, the sky, and the stars in the fourth trumpet (Rev 8:12), whereas in the fifth bowl, darkness presides over the beast's kingdom (Rev 16:10). This is linked to the ninth plague of Exodus, the darkness over the Egyptians (Exod 10:21-22).

---

E.F. Mason – E.F. Lupieri, eds., *Golden Calf Traditions in Early Judaism, Christianity, and Islam* (Leiden: Brill, 2018) 160.

59. S. Moyise, *The Old Testament in the Book of Revelation* (Sheffield: Sheffield Academic Press, 1995) 120.

60. Similar to my analysis, see E. Corsini, *The Apocalypse: The Perennial Revelation of Jesus Christ* (Wilmington: Glazier, 1983); J. Massyngberde Ford, *Revelation* (Garden City: Doubleday, 1975) 270-275. See also the analysis of D.E. Aune, *Revelation 6-16* (Nashville: Thomas Nelson Publishers, 1998) 499-504.

I did not find an equivalent in the septet of the bowls for the fifth trumpet (Rev 9:1-12). However, the very descriptive and pained depiction of locusts in the trumpet raises a comparison to the eighth plague of Exodus (Exod 10:4-20).

The sixth trumpet (Rev 9:13-21) and the sixth bowl (Rev 16:12-14) are analogous in their reference to the Euphrates and in their less explicit reference to armies. The sixth bowl also contains impure spirits similar to frogs, which correspond to the second plague that falls on Egypt (Exod 8:1-3).

The seventh trumpet does not really have any resemblance to another plague. However, there is an interlude between the sixth and seventh trumpets (Rev 10:1-11:14), just as there is an interlude between the 9th and 10th plague in Exodus (Exod 12:1-28).

It must be mentioned that the first bowl (Rev 16:2), despite bearing no obvious resemblance with any of the trumpets, uses the image of the evil ulcer that attacks men who idolize the image and have the mark of the beast. It is akin to the sixth plague of Egypt (Exod 9:8-12), the sores against humans and animals.[61]

Another possible association between texts is the theme of unrepentance that is intertwined with plagues. After the sixth trumpet (Rev 9:20-21), humans do not repent for worshiping idols, nor do they regret their murders, sorcery, debauchery, and robberies. As for the bowls, men obstinately do not ask God for forgiveness and repeatedly blaspheme against him for the hardships they endure (Rev 16:9,11,21). Similarly to Pharaoh in many ways, their hearts harden, and they do not repent (Exod 7:13, 22-23; 8:15,32; 9:7,12,34-35; 10:20,27; 11:10; 14:4,8).[62]

### 3.2 Differences in the Plagues

While we can establish a clear pattern of repeated echoes from Exodus in Revelation, there are also some important differences between the two texts. John uses two septets for his plagues, rather than ten plagues, as in Exodus. Four of Exodus's plagues are not found in John's text: the midges (Exod 8:12-15), the vermin (Exod 8:16-20), the pestilence of animals (Exod 9:1-7), and the death of the firstborn (Exod 11:1-12:33).[63] This

---

61. Ford notes the same. See J. MASSYNGBERDE FORD, *Revelation* (Garden City: Doubleday, 1975) 270.

62. DeSilva also sees a link between the repentance of Revelation and that of Exodus. D.A. DESILVA, "Final Topics: The Rhetorical Functions of Intertexture in Revelation 14:14-16:21," in D.F. WATSON, ed., *The Intertexture of Apocalyptic Discourse in the New Testament* (Atlanta: Society of Biblical Literature, 2002) 233.

63. B.G. WOLD, "Revelation 16 and the Eschatological Use of Exodus Plagues," in *Eschatologie-Eschatology. The Sixth Durham-Tübingen Research Symposium: Eschatology in Old Testament, Ancient Judaism and Early Christianity (Tübingen,*

should not be disconcerting. The use of the number seven is in continuity with the numerology of the Johannine text; the number is present throughout the text (churches, candlesticks, stars, spirits, torches, seals, the Lamb's horns and eyes, angels, the dragon's heads and crowns, etc.). It should also be noted that the number ten, frequently applied to the plagues of Exodus, is only one tradition among others.[64] As Wold demonstrates, the plagues of Egypt are considered in different numbers in Psalms 78:44-51 and 105:28-36.[65] Interpreters of the scriptures have also sometimes come to the conclusion that there were more than ten plagues in Exodus (Pseudo-Philo, *Liber antiquitatum biblicarum* 10:1; Josephus, *Antiquitates judaicae* 2:293-314; 4Q422). It is also difficult to establish what plagues come from which tradition, and whether the author has decided to omit some voluntarily. He indeed used them in a disorderly manner, but the style of a revelation allows for a certain freedom of reuse. As Wold argues, "Therefore, John does not stand out as being abnormal, but rather the evidence suggests that he is following an interpretative trend."[66] Further, in the eschatological perspective of Revelation, the universalization of Egypt's plagues creates a kind of mirror image to the universalism of the new Faith, in which Jesus's covenant applies to all nations (Rev 5:9).[67]

Thus, despite these few differences, the repeated echoes between Revelation and Exodus, in the episodes of trumpets and bowls, as well as the

*September, 2009)* (Tübingen: Mohr Siebeck, 2011) 252. Nevertheless, Wold does not associate the locusts with the plagues of the bowl.

64. B.G. Wold, "Revelation 16 and the Eschatological Use of Exodus Plagues," in *Eschatologie-Eschatology. The Sixth Durham-Tübingen Research Symposium: Eschatology in Old Testament, Ancient Judaism and Early Christianity (Tübingen, September, 2009)* (Tübingen: Mohr Siebeck, 2011) 254.

65. B.G. Wold, "Revelation 16 and the Eschatological Use of Exodus Plagues," in *Eschatologie-Eschatology. The Sixth Durham-Tübingen Research Symposium: Eschatology in Old Testament, Ancient Judaism and Early Christianity (Tübingen, September, 2009)* (Tübingen: Mohr Siebeck, 2011) 253-263. See the summary table of Wold on p. 255.

66. B.G. Wold, "Revelation 16 and the Eschatological Use of Exodus Plagues," in *Eschatologie-Eschatology. The Sixth Durham-Tübingen Research Symposium: Eschatology in Old Testament, Ancient Judaism and Early Christianity (Tübingen, September, 2009)* (Tübingen: Mohr Siebeck, 2011) 257. Wold examines the *Book of Wisdom*, the *Book of Jubilees*, the *Testament of Dan*, the *Apocalypse of Abraham*, and *3 Baruch* to conclude that there is no uniformity in the use of the Exodus plagues.

67. G.K. Beale, "Revelation," in D.A. Carson – H.G.M. Williamson, eds., *It Is Written: Scripture Citing Scripture: Essays in Honour of Barnabas Lindars* (Cambridge, UK: Cambridge University Press 1988) 327; B.G. Wold, "Revelation 16 and the Eschatological Use of Exodus Plagues," in *Eschatologie-Eschatology. The Sixth Durham-Tübingen Research Symposium: Eschatology in Old Testament, Ancient Judaism and Early Christianity (Tübingen, September, 2009)* (Tübingen: Mohr Siebeck, 2011) 252.

borrowing of literary motifs such as the plagues, opens the door for an analysis of the intertextual relationship between these two texts. As Aune explains: "The parallels between Exodus 7:8-13:16 (the ten plagues) and Revelation 8:1-11:19 and 15:1-16:21 indicate that Exodus provided the model for the author's vision of the eschatological punishments inflicted by God on the unbelieving inhabitants of the world."[68] The Exodus is part of the universe of allusions in Revelation, and we can go further in this research to see how Exodus might be present in the text of Revelation and whether John's use of its echoes persists.

### 3.3 Other Manifestations from Chapter 12 to Chapter 17

Apart from the plagues, scholars seem to have missed another important lexical parallel: two instances of the wilderness, one at 12:6 and another at 17:3. I will therefore proceed with an assessment of this part of the text, between the point where the woman fled to the wilderness in chapter 12 and the moment when John is transported to the wilderness to have the mystery of the harlot revealed to him in chapter 17.

Chapter 12, which begins after the seventh trumpet, features a woman who flees into the desert: "and the woman fled into the wilderness (εἰς τὴν ἔρημον), where she has a place prepared by God, in which to be nourished for one thousand two hundred and sixty days" (Rev 12:6). This narration is reminiscent of Israel going out of Egypt into the wilderness (ἡ ἔρημος, in Hebrew, *midbār*) after the plagues of Egypt. A place is prepared in the desert for the woman, as it was for the people of Israel. The text also uses a strong image from the escape from Egypt, the eagle: "But the woman was given the two wings of the great eagle (αἱ δύο πτέρυγες τοῦ ἀετοῦ τοῦ μεγάλου) that she might fly from the serpent into the wilderness, to the place where she is to be nourished for a time, and times, and half a time" (Rev 12:14). This corresponds to the eagle's appearance in Exodus: "You have seen what I did to the Egyptians, and how I bore you on eagles' wings (ἐπὶ πτερύγων ἀετῶν) and brought you to myself" (Exod 19:4).[69]

---

68. D.E. Aune, *Revelation 6-16* (Nashville: Thomas Nelson Publishers, 1998) 546; see also the analysis of E. Corsini, *The Apocalypse: The Perennial Revelation of Jesus Christ* (Wilmington: Glazier, 1983) 164-210.

69. E. Corsini, *The Apocalypse: The Perennial Revelation of Jesus Christ* (Wilmington: Glazier, 1983) 168: "The image of the eagle is regular in the Old Testament and refers to the care, at the same time both powerful but loving [...] It is an important symbol when the Old Testament speaks of the liberation from Egypt (see Exod 19:4; Deut 32:11). This reference to the Exodus will be taken up by John again in ch. 12 when he will write of the second flight of the woman into the desert (12:14), another allegory on the Hebrew Exodus." See also J. Massyngberde Ford, *Revelation* (Garden City: Doubleday, 1975) 201: "Our writer is probably resuming the Exodus motif; the eagle is the symbol of God's providence in Exod 19:4, Deut 32:10-12, in which the wings of the eagle are explicitly mentioned."

In the above two passages in Revelation, the woman is nourished in the wilderness, as were the people of Israel, thanks to the miracle of the manna appearing during their journey (Exod 16). Ford sees this passage as having a direct link with Exodus: "To nourish also seems to have a religious connotation, similar to God's nourishing Israel with manna in the desert."[70] Manna is also mentioned in Rev 2:17: "To him who conquers I will give some of the hidden manna (τοῦ μάννα τοῦ κεκρυμμένου)." The parallel could not be clearer. In the same way, Wold considers the opening of the earth in Rev 12:15-16 that swallows (κατέπιεν) the red dragon's river as comparable to the opening of the Red Sea and the engulfment of Pharaoh's army.[71] Later in Exodus, a song refers to the land that swallows them: "Thou didst stretch out thy right hand, the earth swallowed (κατέπιεν) them" (Exod 15:12).

In chapter 13, lexical parallels appear with thematic borrowing. One of the themes of this passage is the veneration of the beast and its image. The worship of the beast or its image is present at several points in Revelation 13 (13:8,12,15), and also in 14:9,11; 16:2 and 20:4. The recurrence of this theme in the apocalypse could indicate a borrowing of the idolatry motif. Some words, like προσκυνέω, are used in the same way in Revelation 13 as in the episode of the golden calf in Exod 32. In Rev 13:4, while worshiping the beast, men say "Who is like the beast (Τίς ὅμοιος τῷ θηρίῳ)?" This seems to be a parody of a phrase often used in the Tanakh (Exod 15:11; Ps 18:31; Isa 40:25; etc.), and Aune takes it as a precise reference to the first speech of "Who is like thee, O Lord, among the gods (τίς ὅμοιός σοι ἐν θεοῖς, κύριε)?" (Exod 15:11).[72] Rev 13:8 refers to the Book of Life, a reference that recurs several times (3:5; 17:8; 20:12; 20:15; 21:27). With these references, John recalls the book mentioned during the apostasy of the people in Exod 32:32, "But now, if thou wilt forgive their sin—and if not, blot me, I pray thee, out of thy book which thou hast written."[73] A

70. J. MASSYNGBERDE FORD, *Revelation* (Garden City: Doubleday, 1975) 202. See also B.G. WOLD, "Revelation 16 and the Eschatological Use of Exodus Plagues," in *Eschatologie-Eschatology. The Sixth Durham-Tübingen Research Symposium: Eschatology in Old Testament, Ancient Judaism and Early Christianity (Tübingen, September, 2009)* (Tübingen: Mohr Siebeck, 2011) 251: "Being fed in the wilderness is reminiscent more of God's provision of quail and manna for Israel than anything else."

71. B.G. WOLD, "Revelation 16 and the Eschatological Use of Exodus Plagues," in *Eschatologie-Eschatology. The Sixth Durham-Tübingen Research Symposium: Eschatology in Old Testament, Ancient Judaism and Early Christianity (Tübingen, September, 2009)* (Tübingen: Mohr Siebeck, 2011) 251.

72. D.E. AUNE, *Revelation 6-16* (Nashville: Thomas Nelson Publishers, 1998) 741.

73. Exodus 32:32-33 is the first reference that the Ecumenical Translation of the Bible makes to this passage of Revelation. Nevertheless, the Book of Life or the Book of the Living is more prominent in *1 Enoch* 47:3; 103:3; 108:3. The theme

little further in the chapter, the themes of captivity and the sword appear (Rev 13:10). These themes find parallels in Exodus, first in the captivity in Egypt, and again in Exod 32:26-35, the episode of the golden calf, with the death of idolatrous people by the swords of the Levites.

Between chapters 12 and 17, we find an almost explicit echo back to the time when the people crossed the wilderness with Moses: "Those who had conquered the beast and its image and the number of its name, standing beside the sea of glass (ἐπὶ τὴν θάλασσαν τὴν ὑαλίνην) with harps of God in their hands. And they sing the song of Moses (καὶ ᾄδουσιν τὴν ᾠδὴν Μωϋσέως), the servant of God, and the song of the Lamb ..." (Rev 15:2-3). The song is either a direct echo of Exod 15, after the passage of the sea where "Israel saw the Egyptians dead upon the seashore (τῆς θαλάσσης)" (Exod 14:30), or to Deut 31:30-32:43, where Moses delivered his speech from the rock to all Israel. Exodus 15 is the more likely referent because of the many elements that bind them: the presence of the sea, the singing, the presence of musical instruments, the presence of Moses and the notion of victory over the enemy of God.[74]

The tent of testimony and the ark of the covenant serve as an important intertextual link. The tent of testimony appears in Rev 15:5: "After this I looked, and the temple of the tent of witness (τῆς σκηνῆς τοῦ μαρτυρίου) in heaven was opened." "The ark of his covenant (ἡ κιβωτὸς τῆς διαθήκης)" appears in Rev 11:19. The theme of διαθήκη comes back frequently in Exodus, as does that of the "tent" ("τῆς σκηνῆς τοῦ μαρτυρίου" in 29:4, but also 29:10,11,32; 30:16, 18; 35:21; 37:5, etc.) as well as that of the "ark" ("τὴν κιβωτὸν τοῦ μαρτυρίου" in 26:33, but also 26:34; 30:26; 35:12; 40:3,21). In addition, the Johannine text often mentions the testimony of Jesus, in the same way that Exodus mentions the testimony of God given to the people.

Chapter 16 has already been analyzed for its relation to the plagues of Egypt, but there is one more interesting element: the use of ὁ ὤν (Rev 16:5 but also 1:4,8; 11:17) in the context of prayer. According to Aune, this is

---

of the Book of Life, or a book from which names are subtracted, is recurrent: Dan 7:9-10; Phil 4:3; Luke 10:20; Heb 12:23; Isa 4:3; 65:6; Ps 56:9; 87:6.

74. G.B. CAIRD, *A Commentary on the Revelation of St John the Divine* (London: A&C Black, 1984) 198; D.A. DESILVA, "Final Topics: The Rhetorical Functions of Intertexture in Revelation 14:14-16:21," in D.F. WATSON, ed., *The Intertexture of Apocalyptic Discourse in the New Testament* (Atlanta: Society of Biblical Literature, 2002) 225. DeSilva notes that "'conquerors' singing the 'Song of Moses and of the Lamb' while standing 'beside the Sea' recalls in a rather obvious way the Exodus setting," adding, "even though the content of the 'Song of Moses' in Deut 32 appears to be more in view here." I agree instead with D.E. AUNE, *Revelation 6-16* (Nashville: Thomas Nelson Publishers, 1998) 872-873 and J. MASSYNGBERDE FORD, *Revelation* (Garden City: Doubleday, 1975) 265. Ford notes on p. 66: "The whole chapter must be understood against the background of the Exodus."

the first occurrence of this (relatively rare) divine name in early Christian writings.[75] John's imitation of the language of the Tanakh affirms, right from the outset, the links between Moses and John as well as his function as a prophet: "Just as Moses was told by God to accredit his message by telling the people that ὁ ὤν had sent him, so John appears to be authenticating his prophetic book by claiming that its actual source is none other than ὁ ὤν."[76] In chapter 17, an angel proposes to show John the judgment of the great harlot who is "seated upon many waters" (Rev 17:1); however, John is actually brought in spirit "into a wilderness (εἰς ἔρημον)" to see a woman (γυναῖκα) sitting on a scarlet beast (Rev 17:3). Despite the problems caused by this passage, it appears to be a resonance of chapter 12 where a woman fled to the wilderness.[77]

In sum, there are lexical, thematic, and stylistic parallels between the Apocalypse and Exodus. The Johannine text thus uses three literary processes, imitation, borrowing and echo, which recall a founding text of Judaism. Many times, it is possible to *feel* the text of Exodus in Revelation. The repetition of these references is a hint of a real allusion and a palimpsest where the text of the Exodus acts as a prototype narrative. Intertextuality is at work in the text of John, especially since the historical likelihood of the use of Exodus can be established. As mentioned above, John is familiar with the Tanakh corpus. It is not surprising that Exodus was reused by John of Patmos, because of the importance of the book as a grand narrative in Jewish and Christian groups. It is therefore not surprising that the Apocalypse reappropriates this specific text and some of the themes it contains in order to build its narrative.

## 4. Exodus as Key to Understanding the Text

In the case of Revelation, intertextuality also assists in narrative comprehension. It is here that the last criterion is applied: the light that the hypotext can bring to the hypertext. The activation of a specific subject within a founding text assures that some of the hearers/readers will find the allusion and sense of purpose in the Johannine text. We must therefore

75. D.E. Aune, *Revelation 1-5* (Dallas: Word, 1997) 30 and 40.

76. D.E. Aune, *Revelation 1-5* (Dallas: Word, 1997) 30.

77. In addition to these references, other chapters add elements of divine manifestations in the same way that they are used in Exodus: "Kingdom and priest" (Rev 1:6 and Exod 19:6); Sinai theophany (Rev 1:10; 4:5 and Exod 19:16; 20:18); "the sealed" (Rev 7:3-4 and Exod 12:23); the way God manifests himself in the cloud (Rev 14:14 and Exod 13:21); "God with them" (Rev 21:3 and Exod 3:12); Temple wall (Rev 21:10-22:5 and Exod 28:17); Lamb and washing dress (Rev 7:14; 22:14 and Exod 12:3-13; 19:10).

return to the text of Exodus to understand the other text being read. This is called the *simultaneous activation* of two texts. Many of the allusive elements give the impression that the space-time of the apocalyptic narrative is in that pivotal moment in Israel's religious history of wandering in the desert. The sum total of these images leads to a symbolic convergence of two motifs in particular: the desert motif and, at its center, the golden calf episode. Through these motifs, it is possible to better understand a particularly mysterious part of the narrative schema of Revelation, the symbolic presence of female representations.

### 4.1 Desert Motif and Idolatry

The *midbār* is a motif to which several works continuously return in the history of Jewish-Christian religious literature, including non-canonical texts such as those of Qumran.[78] The wilderness corresponds to that 40-year period between the escape from Egypt and the people's arrival to the promised land. Many of the occurrences of *midbār* refer to two books. The first, Exodus, begins with the story of Moses and the plagues sent to Egypt. In this book, the experience of the wilderness is limited to two years, from deliverance by crossing the Red Sea (Exod 14-16) to the covenant and the ritual prescriptions (Exod 34-40), passing by the Sinai theophany and the golden calf (Exod 31-33). The second book is Numbers. It tells the story of the remaining 38 years in the wilderness, recounting Israel's constant apostasy as the reason for its wandering and the sacrifice of the first generation before they are finally brought to the promised land.[79]

In both the Exodus and Numbers accounts, the story of the wandering in the wilderness sets a group of God's people who keep faith and those who have sinned against God in opposition. Within the Chosen People, only a small group serve as a model for salvation.[80] Exodus and Numbers show the Chosen People in the wilderness, from which only a part comes out of the desert saved and pure and reaches the promised land. In Exodus, while Moses seals the covenant on Mount Sinai, the

---

78. S. Talmon, "The 'Desert Motif' in the Bible and in Qumram Literature," in A. Altmann, ed., *Biblical Motifs: Origins and Transformations* (Cambridge, MA: Harvard University Press, 1966) 38.

79. S. Talmon, "The 'Desert Motif' in the Bible and in Qumram Literature," in A. Altmann, ed., *Biblical Motifs: Origins and Transformations* (Cambridge, MA: Harvard University Press, 1966) 46.

80. A.J. Beagley, *The "Sitz Im Leben" of the Apocalypse with Particular Reference to the Role of the Church's Enemies* (Berlin: FRG/New York: De Gruyter, 1987) 4: "This view of misfortune as the punishment for sin was also maintained strongly by the pre-Exilic prophets, and was confirmed in the mind of the people through the fall, first of the Northern Kingdom, and then of the Southern Kingdom."

priest Aaron offers the golden calf to the group that becomes apostate by no longer respecting the laws of God. In the story, Moses breaks the tablets of the covenant and three thousand of the Chosen People die at the hands of the Levites for committing idolatry in the wilderness (Exod 31-33).

For its part, the book of Numbers, whose Hebrew name *bemidbar* means "In the desert," is called "The Book of Israel's Falling"[81] by Talmon because it recounts the many failings of the Chosen People before God's commandments. On several occasions, many of the people are cut down by the wrath of God (Num 11:1-2,4-32; 12; 14; 15:32-36; 16; 17; 20; 21; 25; 30:17-19). The wilderness then represents a transitional state of purge and chaos, effected so that Israel is worthy to reach the divine promise: "The 'desert motif' that occurs in the Old Testament expresses the idea of an unavoidable transition period in which Israel recurrently is prepared for the ultimate transfer from social and spiritual chaos to an integrated social and spiritual order."[82]

The episode of the wilderness and Mount Sinai in Exodus is a key moment in the history of Israel because of its repeated use as a symbol in the Jewish cognitive world.[83] Besides the fact that the desert episode plays an important role as a founding narrative, it is also a constant reminder of the sin of idolatry.[84] In Exodus, the covenant with God, when it is barely sealed with Moses on Mount Sinai, is already broken by the idolatry of the

---

81. S. TALMON, "The 'Desert Motif' in the Bible and in Qumram Literature," in A. ALTMANN, ed., *Biblical Motifs: Origins and Transformations* (Cambridge, MA: Harvard University Press, 1966) 46.

82. S. TALMON, "The 'Desert Motif' in the Bible and in Qumram Literature," in A. ALTMANN, ed., *Biblical Motifs: Origins and Transformations* (Cambridge, MA: Harvard University Press, 1966) 37.

83. E.F. LUPIERI, "From Sodom and Balaam to Revelation: Transtextual Adventures of Biblical Sins," in S. ALKIER – TH. HIEKE – T. NICKLAS, eds., *Poetik und Intertextualität der Johannesapokalypse* (Tübingen: Mohr Siebeck, 2015), 301-318; E.F. LUPIERI "A Beast and a Woman in the Desert, or the Sin of Israel: A Typological Reflection," in E.F. MASON – E.F. LUPIERI, eds., *Golden Calf Traditions in Early Judaism, Christianity, and Islam* (Leiden: Brill, 2018) 157-160, 172: "During its centuries-old life and afterlife, the scriptural imagery related to the (golden) calf incident became a generative and constitutive element of a broader imagery, expression of which, at a certain point in its development, seems to appear in Revelation." See also E. CORSINI, *The Apocalypse: The Perennial Revelation of Jesus Christ* (Wilmington: Glazier, 1983) 214-217.

84. E.F. LUPIERI, "A Beast and a Woman in the Desert, or the Sin of Israel: A Typological Reflection," in E.F. MASON – E.F. LUPIERI, eds., *Golden Calf Traditions in Early Judaism, Christianity, and Islam* (Leiden: Brill, 2018) 159: "The trend we are detecting is that transgression of any covenant with God becomes analogous or at least comparable to the making of the calf." See also E. CORSINI, *The Apocalypse: The Perennial Revelation of Jesus Christ* (Wilmington: Glazier, 1983) 214-217.

people in the episode of the golden calf. In this desert scene, the motif of the golden calf evokes the idolatry and infidelity of Israel.[85] It represents the paradigm of idolatry, since it is the first example of such in the Bible and is countlessly repeated afterwards.[86] As MacDonald notes, "As the inaugural act of rebellion the incident with the golden calf has a paradigmatic role for the wilderness period ... the post-calf stories are always acts of rebellion that deserve punishment."[87] Another use of this motif can be found in Numbers 25, during the episode of Peor's sin. This instance is, with the golden calf, the only act of idolatry in the wilderness. The story of Peor's Baal follows the same narrative as the golden calf: a form of idolatry is followed by a plague sent by God and the subsequent intervention of the Levites.[88]

The wilderness, then, assumes a continual duality. It is simultaneously a place of tests of faith and a place of miracles; it is the place of religious prostitution and that of the covenant with the people. It represents violent punishment, but also possible redemption.[89] This motif of possible redemption, appearing later in many prophetic texts, is only allowed to a portion of the people. Thus, the wilderness motif present in Exodus and Numbers has some similarities with apocalyptic literature, where only a small number of the redeemed is worthy of God's designs and shares in eschatological hope.[90] The Exodus would become a literary paradigm, as some texts reproduce the plot: elections/deliverance - wandering - apostasy/idolatry - purge/destruction - promised restoration. Jews and then

85. L. Smolar – M. Aberbach, "The Golden Calf Episode in Postbiblical Literature," *Hebrew Union College Annual* 39 (1968) 91-116.

86. E.F. Lupieri, "A Beast and a Woman in the Desert, or the Sin of Israel: A Typological Reflection," in E.F. Mason – E.F. Lupieri, eds., *Golden Calf Traditions in Early Judaism, Christianity, and Islam* (Leiden: Brill, 2018) 157-160, 168-172

87. N. MacDonald, "Recasting the Golden Calf: The Imaginative Potential of the Old Testament Portrayal of Idolatry," in S.C. Barton, ed., *Idolatry: False Worship in the Bible, Early Judaism, and Christianity* (New York: T&T Clark, 2007) 29.

88. N. MacDonald, "Recasting the Golden Calf: The Imaginative Potential of the Old Testament Portrayal of Idolatry," in S.C. Barton, ed., *Idolatry: False Worship in the Bible, Early Judaism, and Christianity* (New York: T&T Clark, 2007) 35-37.

89. E. Corsini, *The Apocalypse: The Perennial Revelation of Jesus Christ* (Wilmington: Glazier, 1983) 216. He notes: "The desert has a profound and clear biblical background, even if ambivalent: it is a place of refuge, but also of difficult trials, of encounter with God, but also of diabolic temptation."

90. See the interpretation of E. Corsini, *The Apocalypse: The Perennial Revelation of Jesus Christ* (Wilmington: Glazier, 1983) 62-64: "It [Revelation] is a story of sin and redemption, of suffering and hope, told four times."

Christian groups use the desert motif to rewrite historical events.[91] We only have to think of the narratives attempting to explain the destruction of Jerusalem and the Exile of Babylon to find similarities,[92] because "To this day the narrative of the Exodus inspires those who recount the disasters and salvation of Israel, ancient or modern, secular or spiritual."[93] In a critical situation and religious hesitation, a text that mentions the desert motif invites the listeners to believe that they live a "wilderness-like situation — an ongoing state of exile," as does the *Book of Jubilees*.[94] The text of Revelation borrows the wilderness motif in order to bring its audience into a wilderness-type religious experience, as was the case in Exodus and Numbers.

The use of the plagues of Exodus and the instance of the desert in chapter 12 of Revelation creates a symbolic convergence which, firstly, brings us specifically back to Exodus, and not to Numbers. Secondly, it identifies the woman in chapter 12 as a representation of Israel taking refuge in the desert. Then, many other elements continue to maintain the desert motif in the narrative and make us feel that we are still in the desert in the company of Israel : the manna, the eagle, the cloud, the hymn of Moses, etc. This part of the text corresponds to the election/deliverance of the people of Israel and their wandering in the narrative thread of Exodus.

As I have already argued in the first part of the text, apocalyptic literature wants to be persuasive. In the case of John's Apocalypse, the hearers ("blessed is he who reads aloud the words of the prophecy, and blessed are those who hear" : Rev 1:3) must receive some persuasive message from John, as in this exhortation : "Come out of her, my people, lest you take part in her sins, lest you share in her plagues" (Rev 18:4). But what are these sins ? In addition to those already mentioned, below is a survey of the various transgressions that can be found in the text of John of Patmos :

---

91. G.J. Brooke – H. Najman – L.T. Stuckenbruck, eds., *The Significance of Sinai : Traditions about Sinai and Divine Revelation in Judaism and Christianity* (Leiden : Brill, 2008) ix. I follow Lupieri's hypothesis with my own addition : E.F. Lupieri, "A Beast and a Woman in the Desert, or the Sin of Israel : A Typological Reflection," in E.F. Mason – E.F. Lupieri, eds., *Golden Calf Traditions in Early Judaism, Christianity, and Islam* (Leiden : Brill, 2018) 170-171.

92. S.L. Cook, "Apocalyptic Prophecy," in J.J. Collins, ed., *The Oxford Handbook of Apocalyptic Literature* (Oxford : Oxford University Press, 2014) 30.

93. D. Daube, *The Exodus Pattern in the Bible* (London : Faber and Faber, 1963) 11.

94. B.G. Wold, "Revelation 16 and the Eschatological Use of Exodus Plagues," in *Eschatologie-Eschatology. The Sixth Durham-Tübingen Research Symposium : Eschatology in Old Testament, Ancient Judaism and Early Christianity (Tübingen, September, 2009)* (Tübingen : Mohr Siebeck, 2011) 259.

| Sins | Revelation |
|---|---|
| Lying<br>ψεῦδος | 2:2 those who call themselves apostles but are not (καὶ οὐκ εἰσίν), and have been found to be false (ψευδεῖς)<br>2:9 the blasphemy (τὴν βλασφημίαν) of those who say that they are Jews and are not (καὶ οὐκ εἰσίν)<br>3:9 who say that they are Jews and are not (καὶ οὐκ εἰσίν), but lie (ψεύδονται)<br>14:5 and in their mouth no lie was found (οὐχ εὑρέθη ψεῦδος) |
| Idolatry<br>τὸ εἴδωλον<br>πορνεύω<br>μοιχεύω<br>τὰ ἔργα τῶν χειρῶν αὐτῶν<br>προσκυνέω<br>ἡ εἰκών | 2:14 the sons of Israel, that they might eat food sacrificed to idols (φαγεῖν εἰδωλόθυτα) and practice prostitution (πορνεῦσαι)<br>2:20 who calls herself a prophetess and is teaching and beguiling my servants to practice prostitution (πορνεῦσαι) and to eat food sacrificed to idols (φαγεῖν εἰδωλόθυτα)<br>2:22 and those who worship idolatrously with her (καὶ τοὺς μοιχεύοντας: Lidell – Scott – Jones: metaph.)<br>9:20 did not repent of the works of their hands (τῶν ἔργων τῶν χειρῶν αὐτῶν) nor give up worshiping demons and idols (προσκυνήσουσιν τὰ δαιμόνια καὶ τὰ εἴδωλα) of gold and silver and bronze and stone and wood, which cannot either see or hear or walk<br>13:4 Men worshiped (προσεκύνησαν) the dragon, for he had given his authority to the beast, and they worshiped the beast (προσεκύνησαν)<br>13:8 and all who dwell on earth will worship (προσκυνήσουσιν) it<br>13:12 makes the earth and its inhabitants worship (προσκυνήσουσιν) the first beast<br>13:14 bidding them make an image (ποιῆσαι εἰκόνα) for the beast<br>14:9 If anyone worships (προσκυνεῖ) the beast and its image, and receives a mark on his forehead or on his hand<br>14:11 these worshipers of the beast and its image (οἱ προσκυνοῦντες τὸ θηρίον καὶ τὴν εἰκόνα αὐτοῦ)<br>16:2 upon the people who bore the mark of the beast and worshiped its image (προσκυνοῦντας τῇ εἰκόνι αὐτοῦ)<br>19:20 those who worshiped its image (τοὺς προσκυνοῦντας τῇ εἰκόνι) |

| | |
|---|---|
| Prostitution<br>ἡ πορνεία | 2:21 I gave her time to repent, but she refuses to repent of her prostitution (τῆς πορνείας αὐτῆς)<br>14:8 Fallen, fallen is Babylon the great, she who made all nations drink the wine of her prostitution (πορνείας)<br>17:2 with whom the kings of the earth have committed fornication (ἐπόρνευσαν), and with the wine of whose prostitution (τῆς πορνείας αὐτῆς) the dwellers on earth have become drunk<br>17:4 a golden cup full of abominations and the impurities of her prostitution (τῆς πορνείας αὐτῆς)<br>18:3 for all nations have drunk the wine of her prostitution (τῆς πορνείας αὐτῆς), and the kings of the earth have committed fornication (ἐπόρνευσαν) with her<br>18:9 And the kings of the earth, who committed fornication (πορνεύσαντες) and were wanton with her<br>19:2 he has judged the great harlot who corrupted the earth with her prostitution (τῇ πορνείᾳ αὐτῆς) |
| Blasphemy<br>ἡ βλασφημία | 13:1 and a blasphemous name (ὄνομα βλασφημίας) upon its heads<br>13:5 the beast was given a mouth uttering haughty and blasphemous (βλασφημίας) words<br>13:6 to utter blasphemies (βλασφημίας) against God, blaspheming (βλασφημῆσαι) his name and his dwelling<br>16:9 and they blasphemed the name of God (ἐβλασφήμησαν τὸ ὄνομα τοῦ θεοῦ)<br>16:11 and blasphemed God (καὶ ἐβλασφήμησαν τὸν θεόν)<br>16:21 till people blasphemed God (καὶ ἐβλασφήμησαν οἱ ἄνθρωποι τὸν θεόν)<br>17:3 a scarlet beast which was full of blasphemous names (ὀνόματα βλασφημίας) |
| Other transgressions | 9:21 nor did they repent of their murders (τῶν φόνων) or their sorceries (τῶν φαρμάκων) or their prostitution (τῆς πορνείας) or their thefts (τῶν κλεμμάτων)<br>21:8 But as for the cowardly (δειλοῖς), the faithless (ἀπίστοις), the polluted (ἐβδελυγμένοις), as for murderers (φονεῦσιν), prostitutes (πόρνοις), sorcerers (φαρμάκοις), idolaters (εἰδωλολάτραις), and all lies (ψευδέσιν)<br>22:15 Outside are the dogs (κύνες) and sorcerers (φάρμακοι) and prostitutes (πόρνοι) and murderers (φονεῖς) and idolaters (εἰδωλολάτραι), and everyone who loves and practices lies (ψεῦδος) |

Looking at this picture, it is obvious that John insists against different forms of idolatry and prostitution. This last vice is related to idolatry.[95] It implies a lack of respect for the covenant that the Chosen People received from God upon leaving Egypt, where they were slaves. It takes on the meaning of religious corruption, often in relation to idolatry or mixing with nations. Thus, John uses apocalyptic language to warn his audience about practices he deems sinful.[96] It seems that by the apocalyptic style and the call to *pathos*, John tries to persuade the contemporary religious groups to practice the new faith in Jesus of Nazareth in accordance with Jewish laws.[97] In three excerpts from the seven letters, he condemns the act of lying, but particularly those "who say that they are Jews and are not, but lie" (Rev 3:9), for they practice idolatry, eat sacrificial meat and prostitute themselves. The sin of lying is related to other sins, especially that of idolatry, because liars are those who call themselves Jews but do not respect the Law.

These vices are thus mentioned repeatedly, increasing the probability that the author was a follower of the Jewish Law. Among the vices, the idolatrous paroxysm holds a special place between the two instances of the wilderness. Just after the woman fled to the wilderness in chapter 12, the idolatry of the beast and its image became analogous to that of the golden calf in the desert narrative. The text of the Apocalypse seems to reproduce the episode of the golden calf not only with the idolatry of the beast but also by other subtle and repeated analogies. In chapter 14, besides the presence of the cloud, the appearance of the Lamb on Mount Zion recalls Moses on Mount Sinai (Exod 31:18-32:19). The redeemed who stayed with the Lamb and upheld the commandments are associates with the Levites who had not taken part in the worship of the golden calf (Exod 32:26).[98] Then comes the announcement of the judgment (Rev 14:6-20) that can be paralleled with the sentence that the Israelites had to undergo in Exodus (Exod 32:28-29). Those who have resisted the beast and overcome it will

---

95. J. MASSYNGBERDE FORD, *Revelation* (Garden City: Doubleday, 1975) 277: "In prophetic language prostitution or adultery equals idolatry."

96. E. CORSINI, *The Apocalypse: The Perennial Revelation of Jesus Christ* (Wilmington: Glazier, 1983) 332: "The symbol of the prostitute, like the beast from the land/false prophet, also points towards Judaism. The symbol signifies Judaism's perversion, through the metaphor of prostitution. Prostitution means idolatry and Judaism has become idolatrous because it adores the beast and its statue ..."

97. Rev 12:17: "Those who keep the commandments of God and bear testimony to Jesus"; 14:12: "Here is a call for the endurance of the saints, those who keep the commandments of God and the faith of Jesus."

98. J. MASSYNGBERDE FORD, *Revelation* (Garden City: Doubleday, 1975) 54: "Revelation 14 shows those who resisted the temptations to idolatry and blasphemy. They are the companions of the Lamb, the one hundred and forty-four thousand 'virgins,' that is, those who have not adulterated their religion."

sing the old and new song (Rev 15). The two states (old and new) coexist in the faith of John.

The desert motif allows us to study the literary composition of the Apocalypse. It seems that, following the narrative thread of Exodus in Revelation, the episode of the golden calf is implied in the Johannine text as a reminder of the sin of Israel, as a reminder of its apostasy. The author tries to bring us back to this episode in which the Chosen People are saved by God, but only after they undergo the test and the miracles of the desert, prostitute themselves by idolatry, undergo a judgment, and still receive the grace of the covenant with the Lord.

### 4.2 The Light on the Woman

Symbolically, the woman in chapter 12 would correspond to Israel in the desert, but what about the woman in chapter 17 ? John uses the metaphor of Babylon the Great to condemn prostitution and reveal what can lead to divine chastisement. She represents "The Great City," a clear entity that is falling to judgment. In continuity with the plot of the wilderness motif, would it be possible that this harlot is the representation of the corruption of the people of Israel in the wilderness and the destruction of the impure part of the community ?

The expression "great city" is used for the first time in Rev 11:8 (τῆς πόλεως τῆς μεγάλης). Up to chapter 21, where it is clearly about the New Jerusalem, the word "city" is used to characterize the harlot, the Great Babylon, the city that is punished and destroyed. The first occurrence in chapter 11 is important because it has singularities. The passage is about the "holy city" (τὴν πόλιν τὴν ἁγίαν) (Rev 11:2) which will be trodden by the nations. At the same time, it is about "the street of the great city, which is spiritually called Sodom and Egypt, where their Lord was crucified" (Rev 11:8). In this passage, in addition to using the adverb "spiritually," while implicitly asking the audience to be wise in the face of an enigma, John points out that this is the place where Jesus Christ suffered his martyrdom : Jerusalem. The latter, however sacred, is then put into relation with one city and one nation which the Jewish people had to run away from in the past. The holy city cannot be any other than Jerusalem, since it is the one that houses the Temple. In combination with the *spiritual* nation of Egypt, the city can *spiritually* represent the people of Israel.

When it comes to his Temple, whose forecourt "is given over to the nations, and they will trample over the holy city" (Rev 11:2),[99] the lexi-

---

99. Here the verb tenses are very important to understand the full meaning of the text. The author voluntarily uses both the past and the future of the original text : καὶ τὴν αὐλὴν τὴν ἔξωθεν τοῦ ναοῦ ἔκβαλε ἔξωθεν καὶ μὴ αὐτὴν μετρήσῃς,

con used by John recalls that of the prophet Isaiah when it comes to the destruction of the Temple by the Babylonian Empire (Isa 64:9-11). Jerusalem, already handed over to the Babylonians in the past, will be trodden again in the near future. Only as Jerusalem can the great city be Sodom and Egypt. As Aune recognizes: "this phrase clearly identifies 'the great city' as Jerusalem ... However, Rev 11:1-2 clearly sets the scene in Jerusalem, and nothing in 11:3-13 suggests a change in scene."

In chapter 14, we find a first reference to the fall of the city: "Fallen, fallen is Babylon the great, she who made all nations drink the wine of her prostitution" (Rev 14:8). This theme returns in chapter 18: "Fallen, fallen is Babylon the great! It has become a dwelling place of demons, a haunt of every foul spirit, a haunt of every foul and hateful bird; for all nations have drunk the wine of her impure passion, and the kings of the earth have committed fornication with her" (Rev 18:2-3). The phrase "Fallen is" appears in the book of Amos. The prophet receives the mission to warn the Chosen People of their perversion and the imminence of the judgment, announcing the destruction of Jerusalem in the sixth century BCE. Thus, in an era of economic prosperity, he is the bearer of a dark message: "Fallen, no more to rise, is the virgin Israel; forsaken on her land, with none to raise her up" (Am 5:2). This passage in Amos is about Israel and its accommodations with the Gentiles. It is quite possible that John reused the association between the fall and Israel already present in another prophet's book, especially since this is consistent with Exodus and the idolatry of the Chosen People.[100]

In chapter 17, as in chapter 11, there are peculiarities in the text. An angel offers to show John "the judgment of the great harlot who is seated upon many waters" (Rev 17:1). But strangely, instead of being in the sea or at least by some large river, the angel carries John in spirit to a desert. In this wilderness, there is a prostitute sitting on a scarlet beast. Babylon, the great harlot, is in the same place where Israel fled to. It is called, from the end of chapter 16 to chapter 18, "the great city" (Rev 16:19; 17:18; 18:10,16,18,19,21), as was the case for the "holy city" likened to Sodom and Egypt in chapter 11. Throughout chapters 17 and 18, the prostitute reproduces the vices for which those who call themselves Jews are reproached.

---

ὅτι ἐδόθη τοῖς ἔθνεσιν, καὶ τὴν πόλιν τὴν ἁγίαν πατήσουσιν μῆνας τεσσαράκοντα δύο.

100. J. MASSYNGBERDE FORD, *Revelation* (Garden City: Doubleday, 1975) 54-55: "The seer then receives a warning from an angel that Babylon has fallen. The past tense is used although the event has not yet occurred; see Amos 5:2. 'Babylon' is the adulterous generation in Jerusalem against whom both John the Baptist and Jesus spoke; in the OT only twice is a non-Israelite nation called a harlot."

All these elements are unique. It is at this point that intertextuality can shed light on our understanding of Revelation. The hypotext can help us to find some coherence among this confusion. If we follow the narrative thread of Exodus that I explained earlier (election/deliverance - wandering - apostasy/idolatry - purge/destruction - promised restoration), it is possible to understand the clues embedded by John in Revelation. The return to the desert is not trivial but is mentioned despite its strangeness to put the plot of Exodus in perspective and remind readers that we are still in the desert. And what do we find in the wilderness at this stage of the narrative? We find the apostate people after the worship of the beast/golden calf. The term "great city" is used both for the "holy city," assimilated to Sodom and Egypt, and for Babylon the prostitute. The two women are both in the desert but at different moments. The reason for this is that it is the same entity: cities as Jerusalem and women as Israel are allegorically connected.[101] The apocalyptic text condemns the vices perpetrated in the Jewish community by those who lied, predicting the fall of Jerusalem in chapter 17 because of the prostitution of its principal inhabitants. By repeating the words of Amos, Revelation could bring the reader back to the theme of that book, the fall of Jerusalem, while at the same time proposing a wilderness reading. In an eschatological way, John arouses a sense of urgency, given the socio-political context. This would correspond to the crisis experienced by the Judeans contemporary to John: the capture of Jerusalem and the destruction of the Temple in the first century.[102] The author explains Jerusalem's fall by using echoes from Amos as well as the technique of *vaticinia ex eventu*. He condemns Israel's corruption by allusions to Exodus's narrative plot, in particular the golden calf motif.

Despite its strangeness, the text is not incomprehensible when we consider that the great city remains the same until the end, that the feminine representations are one entity, and that the wilderness is the one of Exodus. According to the intertextual clues of the author, the city that falls

---

101. J. Massyngberde Ford, *Revelation* (Garden City: Doubleday, 1975) 195. Ford writes: "Although the woman may be an individual, a study of the OT background suggests that she is a collective figure, like the two witnesses. In the OT the image of a woman is a classical symbol for Zion, Jerusalem, and Israel, e.g. Zion whose husband is Yahweh (Isa 54:1,5,6, Jer 3:20, Ezek 16:8-14, Hos 2:19-20); Who is a mother (Isa 49:21; 50:1, 66:7-11, Hos 4:5, Bar 4:8-23); who is in the throes of birth (Mic 4:9-10, see Isa 26:16-18, Jer 4:31, 13:21)." See note 102.

102. E. Corsini, *The Apocalypse: The Perennial Revelation of Jesus Christ* (Wilmington: Glazier, 1983) 329: "Therefore, if the destruction to which the passage alludes is to be understood in a literal and material sense, it can only refer to the destruction of Jerusalem by the Romans in 70 A.D." For the context of the first century, see L. Smolar – M. Aberbach, "The Golden Calf Episode in Postbiblical Literature," *Hebrew Union College Annual* 39 (1968) 91-116 and P.B. Duff, *Who Rides the Beast? Prophetic Rivalry and the Rhetoric of Crisis in the Churches of the Apocalypse* (Oxford: Oxford University Press, 2001).

under the judgment of God would not be the imperial city of Rome, but Jerusalem and its Temple, because of the idolatry of its people. The reading key is provided by Exodus, which enlightens us regarding the presence of two instances of the desert and insists on a narrative reenactment of the wilderness and the idolatry motif. The woman protected by God in chapter 12, Israel, is going to the wilderness where religious prostitution takes place. When John is transported to the desert to have the mysteries of the prostitute revealed to him, it is this same Israel that we find in the desert in chapter 17, an Israel corrupted and prostituted by vices. Corsini writes: "The parallel (antithetic though it may be) is certainly not casual. The reference to the desert is not for effect, but a clear reference, in chapter 17, to a situation already described in 12. The prostitute of chapter 17 takes up that symbol once more, especially in its second aspect: the representation of the Chosen People of Israel. The fact that the woman is here presented under the aspect of a prostitute indicates that, evidently, her spiritual attitude has changed."[103] This spiritual change is caused by the vices which John warns the communities about (Rev 2 and 3). What John notes is the sin of Israel, which is corrupted by the worship of other gods and by not following the covenant and the Law of the Lord.

## 5. Conclusion

Now that the narrative chain has been clarified, I argue that there is only one woman in Revelation, who embodies different moments in Israel's religious life.[104] This is confirmed by the third woman, who is the divine spouse (Rev 21:2). Israel is often portrayed as the bride of God; thus, following other gods is considered an act of adultery.[105] This divine spouse

103. E. Corsini, *The Apocalypse: The Perennial Revelation of Jesus Christ* (Wilmington: Glazier, 1983) 331.

104. See E. Corsini, *The Apocalypse: The Perennial Revelation of Jesus Christ* (Wilmington: Glazier, 1983) 41. In the introduction, Corsini writes: "As well as this, she is found in close contact with other symbols: a woman 'in heaven'; a woman 'in the wilderness'; a woman 'who comes down from heaven.' Even though it may appear to be a paradox, it is clear that the basic meaning of the symbol never changes. The only thing that changes is its contact with other symbols and different contexts." See also Arcari's book, which has considerably increased the reflection on female representations in Revelation: L. Arcari, *"Una donna avvolta nel sole..." (Apoc 12,1): Le raffigurazioni femminili nell'Apocalisse di Giovanni alla luce della letteratura apocalittica giudaica* (Padoua: EMP, 2008).

105. E. Corsini, *The Apocalypse: The Perennial Revelation of Jesus Christ* (Wilmington: Glazier, 1983) 332; N. MacDonald, "Recasting the Golden Calf: The Imaginative Potential of the Old Testament Portrayal of Idolatry," in S.C. Barton, ed., *Idolatry: False Worship in the Bible, Early Judaism, and Christianity* (New York: T&T Clark, 2007) 35-36.

is associated with the holy city, the New Jerusalem (Rev 21:2). Once purified of the earthly vices from which she has repented, the heavenly city opens to believers who respect the Law. As in other parts of Revelation, the woman is the representation of Israel, associated with a city, which is Jerusalem. As Ford notes: "It is the covenant which makes the bride, the breaking of it which makes the adulteress."[106]

The allusions to Exodus and especially to the episode of the wilderness are intended to enlighten the readers of John's text: "The broader context of Exodus plagues in the Apocalypse coupled together with the application of Exodus plagues in other literature suggests that they function as judgments that occur before the restoration of the saints/Israel."[107] Thus, there is only one woman in the Apocalypse of John who represents Israel (the people) and one city that represents Jerusalem, and both are interconnected. Therefore, we can see Israel at the birth of the Chosen People (Rev 12) as a stiff-necked people prostituting themselves (Rev 17) and as the purified Israel entering through the new covenant of Jesus Christ in the heavenly Jerusalem (Rev 21). Jerusalem is the holy city that was and will be destroyed by an enemy (Rev 11:2), the city that is corrupted by prostitution (Rev 17), and the heavenly city.[108]

This accusation of Israel's corruption is not impossible, nor is it confusing. The people of Israel have been accused of religious corruption by their own prophets, and the city of Jerusalem is often used as a symbol of prostitution. Some prophetic books, including the books of Jeremiah, Isaiah, and Hosea, focus on the condemnation of the ways of Jerusalem or other important cities of the Chosen People, who are called "harlots."[109]

---

106. J. MASSYNGBERDE FORD, *Revelation* (Garden City: Doubleday, 1975) 285.

107. B.G. WOLD, "Revelation 16 and the Eschatological Use of Exodus Plagues," in *Eschatologie-Eschatology. The Sixth Durham-Tübingen Research Symposium: Eschatology in Old Testament, Ancient Judaism and Early Christianity (Tübingen, September, 2009)* (Tübingen: Mohr Siebeck, 2011) 249.

108. E.F. LUPIERI, "A Beast and a Woman in the Desert, or the Sin of Israel: A Typological Reflection," in E.F. MASON – E.F. LUPIERI, eds., *Golden Calf Traditions in Early Judaism, Christianity, and Islam* (Leiden: Brill, 2018) 170-171: "First, she descends from the old heaven to the old earth and to the desert (12:1-6). Then she stays in the desert, where her mystery as 'Babylon, the great' is revealed (17:3-5) so that she can be at the same time the great city where their Lord was crucified and whose spiritual (not historical) meaning is Egypt and Sodom (11:8). Lastly, she descends anew from a new heaven to a new earth (21:2,9-10). The trajectory is one of election, betrayal, fall, physical corruption and destruction, followed by redemption and salvation at a new, spiritual level."

109. See E. CORSINI, *The Apocalypse: The Perennial Revelation of Jesus Christ* (Wilmington: Glazier, 1983) 330-333. Ford herself noticed the tendency to use harlot in reference to Israel: "A study of the metaphorical use of 'harlot' in the OT shows a marked tendency to depict faithless Israel thus." J. MASSYNGBERDE FORD, *Revelation* (Garden City: Doubleday, 1975) 283.

Provan notes "the way in which the harlot in the Old Testament is predominantly faithless Israel, the bride who has broken her covenant promise to her husband (Hos 2:5 ; 3:3 ; 4:15 ; Isa 1:4, 9,21, where Israel is named Sodom and Gomorrah ; Jer 2:20 ; 5:7 ; Mic 1:7 ; Ezek 23, noting the cup in 23:31-34; and especially Ezek 16)."[110] Indeed, John takes up a theme that is present in other prophets' books who strongly condemn the religious corruption inside the community of Israel while referring to the golden calf.[111] By taking us back to the wilderness a second time, he recalls that, even if Israel is chosen by God, disruptive elements reside within the people.[112]

Having been redacted towards the end of the first century, the writing of the text could have a link with the crisis situation of its time, the siege and sack of Jerusalem, the holy city, and the burning of the

---

110. I. PROVAN, "Foul Spirits, Fornication and Finance. Revelation 18 in an Old Testament Perspective," *Journal for the Study of the New Testament* 64 (1966) 92.

111. In the book of Jeremiah, it is about the kingdom of Judah as a prostitute because it compromised itself with idols : "But where are your gods that you made for yourself ? Let them arise, if they can save you, in your time of trouble ; for as many as your cities are your gods, O Judah" (Jer 3:8-9). Wood and stone are in Judaic literature the symbol of false gods, idols. As it is mentioned in Deuteronomy : "You know how we dwelt in the land of Egypt, and how we came through the midst of the nations through which you passed ; and you have seen their detestable things, their idols of wood and stone, of silver and gold, which were among them" (Deut 29:16-17). In the text of Hosea, emphasis is placed on "handmade" objects when Israel recognizes its idolatry : "we will say no more, 'Our God,' to the work of our hands" (Hos 14:4). The author in chapter 8 refers to Israel in this way : "With their silver and gold they made idols for their own destruction. I have spurned your calf, O Samaria" (Hos 8:4-5). It is quite possible to see here how literary reappropriation is current among the prophets concerning the condemnation of idolatry and its characteristic elements. In addition, the book of Isaiah contains the idea of compromise with nations while associating it with idolatry : "For thou hast rejected thy people, the house of Jacob, because they are full of diviners from the east and of soothsayers like the Philistines, and they strike hands with foreigners. Their land is filled with silver and gold, and there is no end to their treasures ; their land is filled with horses, and there is no end to their chariots. Their land is filled with idols ; they bow down to the work of their hands, to what their own fingers have made" (Is 2:6-8). See my work about Israel's prostitution in the Old Testament in S. AUDET, "Israël comme antécédent à la grande cité de l'Apocalypse," *Actes du 173 colloque international étudiant du département des sciences historiques de l'Université Laval* (Québec : Artefact, 2018) 69-81.

112. E.F. LUPIERI, "A Beast and a Woman in the Desert, or the Sin of Israel : A Typological Reflection," in E.F. MASON – E.F. LUPIERI, eds., *Golden Calf Traditions in Early Judaism, Christianity, and Islam* (Leiden : Brill, 2018) 157-158 : "The (golden) calf incident was an object of attention for Second Temple Jewish thinkers because it offered an answer to the question : what was the sin that the Jews committed to deserve God's punishment(s) ? ... reflections on various elements of the (golden) calf narrative were quite common and became attested as a locus communis in Jewish and Christian contexts."

Temple in 70 CE. Referring to the previous destructions, especially the one that brought with it the exile to Babylon, Revelation could direct the people to understand the reasons for the misfortune that afflicts them, in an attempt to convert them to the new faith.[113] The golden calf motif provides an explanation for the events that have occurred, as well as their causes.[114] The author offers hope to his audience if they accept his religious ideas. In the context of the destruction of the temple and the period of religious instability that followed, the questions of religious identity and the rules that ought to be followed were important preoccupations. In such a context, John only had to imitate the previous authors and use an *ex eventu* prophecy to convince the hearers/readers.[115] This is one of the important arguments for identifying the great city as Jerusalem. It is the sack of Jerusalem and its fall that can be most recognized by the reader according to lived historical events and those described in the imagery. It is this technique that is used especially in the Apocalypse of Abraham, which refers to the sack of Jerusalem by the Romans.[116] John certainly uses this process since his generation endured a tragic shared experience, whose "evocative power"[117] is a source of persuasion. As a result, it would proceed somewhat like the text of *4 Ezra* or *2 Baruch*: the authors use the capture of Jerusalem by the Babylonians in the sixth century BCE as a metaphor to provide an interpretation of the events that have just occurred: the destruction of Jerusalem by the Romans.[118] The fact remains that the text is a reflection of its his-

---

113. J. MASSYNGBERDE FORD, *Revelation* (Garden City: Doubleday, 1975) 54: "Jewish literature from the first century B.C. to the first century A.D. shows that some Jews were faithless and fell in with the Roman customs. They defiled the sanctuary, made a mockery of their religion, amassed unlawful wealth and fell prey to blasphemy and idolatry."

114. E.F. LUPIERI, "A Beast and a Woman in the Desert, or the Sin of Israel: A Typological Reflection," in E.F. MASON – E.F. LUPIERI, eds., *Golden Calf Traditions in Early Judaism, Christianity, and Islam* (Leiden: Brill, 2018) 157-158.

115. C.A. NEWSOM, "The Rhetoric of Jewish Apocalyptic Literature," in J.J. COLLINS, ed., *The Oxford Handbook of Apocalyptic Literature* (Oxford: Oxford University Press, 2014) 213.

116. B.G. WOLD, "Revelation 16 and the Eschatological Use of Exodus Plagues," in *Eschatologie-Eschatology. The Sixth Durham-Tübingen Research Symposium: Eschatology in Old Testament, Ancient Judaism and Early Christianity (Tübingen, September, 2009)* (Tübingen: Mohr Siebeck, 2011) 262.

117. D.A. DESILVA, "Final Topics: The Rhetorical Functions of Intertexture in Revelation 14:14-16:21," in D.F. WATSON, ed., *The Intertexture of Apocalyptic Discourse in the New Testament* (Atlanta: Society of Biblical Literature, 2002) 216; S. MOYISE, *The Old Testament in the Book of Revelation* (Sheffield: Sheffield Academic Press, 1995) 125.

118. P.F. ESLER, "Social-Scientific Approaches to Apocalyptic Literature," in J.J. COLLINS, ed., *The Oxford Handbook of Apocalyptic Literature* (Oxford: Oxford University Press, 2014) 128; M. HENZE, "Torah and Eschatology in the Syriac

torical context, the defeat of the Jews. By using the image of the woman and her journey through the wilderness, John wants to instruct the new believers about his faith and the importance of following it.[119]

---

Apocalypse of Baruch," in G.J. Brooke – H. Najman – L.T. Stuckenbruck, eds., *The Significance of Sinai: Traditions about Sinai and Divine Revelation in Judaism and Christianity* (Leiden: Brill, 2008) 201.

119. M. Henze, "Apocalypse and Torah in Ancient Judaism," in J.J. Collins, ed., *The Oxford Handbook of Apocalyptic Literature* (Oxford: Oxford University Press, 2014) 317.

# "I WILL TELL YOU THE MYSTERY OF THE WOMAN" (REV 17:7)

**Edmondo Lupieri**

*Loyola University Chicago*

Résumé

Ce chapitre tente de recadrer l'image de la Femme-Cité-Prostituée-Babylone dans ses contextes apocalyptique et biblique juif et judéo-chrétien les plus probables. La relation avec la bête sur laquelle la femme est assise, son lien étroit, dans la structure littéraire du livre, avec la « deuxième bête » (celle qui vient de la terre/pays), et ses attributs royaux, sacerdotaux et prophétiques sont tous expliqués comme des marqueurs que Jean utilise pour enseigner aux fidèles qui est cette figure. Dans la réalité à plusieurs niveaux de la vision apocalyptique du monde, Babylone, comme Sodome et l'Égypte, représente la seule et unique ville où le Seigneur a été crucifié.

Sa « prostitution », une manière traditionnelle de décrire la corruption idolâtre d'Israël et de ses villes, ne lui rapporte rien, car ses anciens amants la détruiront, montrant non seulement qu'elle a les mêmes ennemis que l'Agneau, mais aussi que c'est précisément de cette manière que la volonté de Dieu s'accomplira et que sa condamnation annoncera prophétiquement la condamnation de Jérusalem. La féminité de la prostituée souligne la dégénérescence des autorités royale et sacerdotale juives.

Ce n'est peut-être pas, néanmoins, l'ultime niveau de la réalité mystique que Jean révèle. Comme les Israélites dans le désert, comme les dirigeants politiques et religieux juifs qui ont corrompu leur fonction sainte dans l'histoire salvatrice que Dieu avait planifiée, au point de livrer le Sauveur aux païens, Babylone-Jérusalem peut très bien, comme Jézabel ou les anges déchus, être un avertissement prophétique pour les disciples de Jésus qui ont aussi trahi leur statut saint en mangeant les idolothytes des païens. Un résultat non négligeable de cette étude est que—si la discussion tient la route—, il n'y a qu'une seule femme dans l'Apocalypse, qui apparaît sous différents aspects, marquant les différents points de sa trajectoire dans l'histoire générale du salut.

Abstract

This chapter tries to frame the picture of the Woman-City-Prostitute-Babylon in its most probable Jewish and Jewish-Christian apocalyptic and biblical contexts. The relationship with the beast on whom/which the woman is seated, her deep connection, in the literary structure of the book, with the "second beast" (the one coming from the earth/land), and her royal, priestly,

*"Who is Sitting on Which Beast?" Interpretative Issues in the Book of Revelation. Proceedings of the International Conference held at Loyola University, Chicago, March 30-31, 2017*, ed. by Edmondo Lupieri and Louis Painchaud, JAOC 29 (Turnhout, 2023), pp. 85–100
 DOI 10.1484/M.JAOC-EB.5.131929

and prophetic attributes are all explained as markers John uses to teach the faithful who this figure is. In the multi-layered reality of the apocalyptic worldview, Babylon, like Sodom and Egypt, represents a city, the only City where the Lord was crucified.

Her "prostitution," a traditional way to describe the idolatrous corruption of Israel and its cities, does not pay her back, because her former lovers will destroy her, showing not only that she has the same enemies the Lamb has, but also that precisely in this way the will of God will be accomplished and that her condemnation will announce prophetically the condemnation of Jerusalem. The femininity of the prostitute underlines the degeneration of the Jewish royal and priestly authorities.

This may not be, nevertheless, the last level of the mystical reality John is revealing. Like the Israelites in the desert, like the Jewish political and religious leadership that corrupted its holy function in the salvific history God had planned, to the point of handing down the Savior to the heathens, Babylon-Jerusalem may very well, like Jezebel or the fallen angels, be a prophetic admonition for those followers of Jesus who also betrayed their holy status by eating the idolothytes of the pagans. A non-secondary result of this study is that—if the discussion holds water—there is only one woman in Revelation, who appears under different aspects, marking the different points of her trajectory in the general history of salvation.

## 1. Introduction

The *angelus interpres* promises to tell John "the mystery of the woman," but the sentence sounds ironic after almost two millennia of discussion and conflicting explanations regarding who or what that famous woman is supposed to represent. Indeed, the words of the angel in this verse promise more: "Why do you marvel? I will tell you the mystery of the woman and of the beast who bears her, the one that has the seven heads and the ten horns" (Rev 17:7).[1] Had the "mystery" been explained in a satisfactory way, the present book would have no reason to exist.

## 2. Main Text(s)

To be fair to John, he started talking about the woman at the beginning of the chapter, when "one of the seven angels ... who have the seven bowls" tells him: "Come here, I will show you the condemnation of the prosti-

1. Unless otherwise noted, all translations of Greek originals are by the author. Texts and translations from Revelation are from E.F. Lupieri, *A Commentary on the Apocalypse of John*, trans. M. Poggi Johnson – A. Kamesar (Grand Rapids: Eerdmans, 2006); trans. of *L'Apocalisse di Giovanni* (Milan: Mondadori – Lorenzo Valla, 1999).

tute, the great one, the one who is seated on many waters, with whom the kings of the earth fornicated and those who inhabit the earth became drunk with the wine of her prostitution" (Rev 17:1-2). As happens quite often in Revelation, what John is first told does not correspond to what he then sees. Here, he is carried "in spirit into a desert," where there are no "waters," and the "woman" he sees is "sitting on a scarlet beast" and does not seem to be suffering from any sort of condemnation. On the contrary, she is very richly dressed, holds "a golden cup in her hand, full of abominations—the impurities of her prostitution," and is even "drunk," not with wine but "with the blood" of "the holy ones and ... the witnesses of Jesus" (Rev 17:3-6a), with whom John wants us to empathize. Her sin, therefore, is one of the most polluting; drinking (human) blood was the sin of the monstrous giants born to the sinful angels (*1 Enoch* 7:5), a sin deserving the greatest punishment.[2] It is no marvel, then, that by "seeing her" sitting ("as a queen," as confirmed in Rev 18:7) on a scarlet beast instead of many waters, John is very surprised "with great wonder" (Rev 17:6b).[3]

With respect to apocalyptic literary conventions and following John's own narrative style, the "reality" of what John hears and sees is a multilayered one. We are immersed in the "in-between world," which is typical of apocalyptic experiences.[4] As in a great theater outside of space and time,[5] various angels and angelomorphic figures[6] represent a level of reality usually unreachable to the seer, through words, sounds, and images, as in a dramatic performance. It is a mystical, spiritual reality that is defined as

2. "Partaking of blood," even animal blood, involves being "cut off" (Lev 17; cf. Gen 9:4-6; Deut 12:16 and passim). In the canonical Old Testament, drinking human blood is mentioned by David as a metaphor for an atrocious sin in 2 Sam 23:17 // 1 Chr 11:19.

3. I do not believe John's "wonder" has anything to do with sexual desire and/or repressed Oedipal pulsion, as notoriously hypothesized by T. Pippin, *Death and Desire: The Rhetoric of Gender in the Apocalypse of John* (Louisville: Westminster/John Knox, 1992). Against this, see E.F. Lupieri, "Sex and Blood: Some New Approaches to the Apocalypse of John," *Folia Orientalia* 35 (1999) 85-92, and E.F. Lupieri, "'E stupii vedendola con grande stupore' (Ap. 17,6). Noterelle semiserie ed a tratti lamentose in onore di Piero Boitani," in E. Di Rocco, ed., *Astonishment: Essays on Wonder for Piero Boitani* (Rome: Edizioni di storia e letteratura, 2019) 115-127.

4. For this terminology, see the "mondo di mezzo" of P. Sacchi, *L'apocalittica giudaica e la sua storia* (Brescia: Paideia, 1990) 55-61: *Jewish Apocalyptic and its History*, trans. W.J. Short (Sheffield: Sheffield Academic Press, 1996).

5. In a dimension which is often described as "being in spirit" (cf. Rev 1:10).

6. For lack of a better term, "angelomorphic figures" describes whatever appears to the seer when "in spirit": voices, thunders, composite beasts, humanlike characters, etc. For its meaning, see L.T. Stuckenbruck, *Angel Veneration and Christology: A Study in Early Judaism and in the Christology of the Apocalypse of John* (Tübingen: Mohr Siebeck, 1995); C.A. Gieschen, "Angelomorphic Christology" (PhD diss., University of Michigan, 1995).

a "mystery." This level of reality is not God's level, which no living human can truly experience, but a level between the human and the divine. It is partially understandable to humans, but it requires explanation, so that the seer can later report its meaning to his[7] fellow humans, without assuming that he has seen the true reality of God and God's supercelestial world.[8] The mystical representation does not seem to be what it truly is—or not even what is announced to the seer. A typical example is Rev 5:5-6, where "the lion ... of the tribe of Judah" is announced as having "won" (ἐνίκησεν), but then "a lamb ... as if slaughtered" appears. The slaughtered lamb is the victorious lion, according to the Christian theological oxymoron, and is particularly stressed in the Johannine corpus. Typical humans need explanations to understand it.[9]

A similar scene takes place now with the woman, whose first "mystery" is her "name ... written ... on her forehead": "Babylon the great, the mother of the prostitutes and of the abominations of the earth" (Rev 17:5).

The mystical name of the woman, "Babylon," is followed by the equally mystical description of her obscene motherhood. Leaving aside other questions for now, the first thing to note is this: if Babylon is a mystical, spiritual name, then it is not her historical name. It is not a symbol either, because it is real, but this reality is not what it would be for us, i.e., "real" in a physical way. For John, "Babylon"—as everything he hears and sees—is a degree beyond the physical reality of things, towards the real and deeper spiritual reality, which only God really knows. It is mystery.

The communication of the mystical name is the first step towards comprehending the deeper truth, which is in the process of being revealed by the apocalyptic writing. It is not a riddle, but the first step of an explanation. The "mystery" of the woman is going to be told immediately after. The angel's subsequent revelatory explanation proceeds chiastically. Having first announced "the mystery of the woman" and then the one "of the beast" (Rev 17:7), the angel begins to explain the mystical reality of the beast and its parts. It is only gradually, and particularly at the end of the

---

7. In most ancient mainstream Jewish and Christian Apocalypses, the seer is a man. In Gnostic and heterodox traditions, and also later in Christian orthodox texts, the recipient of a revelation can be a woman, either some biblical figure (such as Mary Magdalene or Mary the Mother) or some other historical prophetess. For the Montanist prophetesses and similar figures, see M. DELL'ISOLA, *L'ultima profezia. La crisi montanista nel cristianesimo antico* (Trapani: Di Girolamo, 2020).

8. As Dante Alighieri explains very well in his *Divina Commedia* (which can rightly be considered a late medieval apocalypse), especially in *Paradiso* IV, 37-47 (where he also justifies biblical anthropomorphisms for God).

9. The pattern is present right from the opening vision, when John turns around "to see the voice that was speaking" to him (Rev 1:12), but, instead of a simple "voice" (possibly a member of an angelic category, as in Rev 11:15-19; 16:18), he sees a complex scene, a "mystery" whose details are explained afterward (Rev 1:20).

long explanation, that he tells John what the woman is: "And the woman that you saw is the city, the great one, the one that has rule over the kings of the earth" (Rev 17:18).[10]

While the fall of the woman-city-Babylon—the expected and announced "condemnation"—is narrated from different points of view in the following chapter (Rev 18), we already find elements that explain—or, at least, prepare the explanation of—the woman in the description of the mystery of the beast (Rev 17:8-17). Two chapters of the present book, both by Louis Painchaud, are dedicated to the two beasts of Revelation, their functions, and their intertextual meanings, including the probable, biblical origin of "the number" at Rev 13:18. Therefore, I will only talk about the beast upon whom/which the woman sits when it is necessary to explain the relationship between the two figures and when it helps us better understand the function and the probable meaning of the woman. One element that is important for our discussion is this: this beast is almost identical or at least very similar to the "beast coming up from the sea" (Rev 13:1). The two overlapping descriptions convince me that the beast of Revelation 17 is a manifestation, a new level of reality, of the beast of Revelation 13,[11] and represents the world's political and military power through time, since it is the conflation of the four beasts/empires of Dan 7:3-7. Therefore, we can expect it to be "embodied" in the last universal power at the time of John, the Roman empire. This may or may not then be the fifth (and final) empire. In any case, three ferocious external aspects of the composite Johannine beast of Revelation 13 (the "lion," the "leopard," and the "bear") correspond to three of the four Danielic animals, as well as the seven heads and the ten horns are the totality of the heads and horns in Daniel's passage.[12] While the number and characteristics of the beasts in Daniel 7 reflect the author's "historical experience," John derives his description from Daniel, and any possible connection with his contemporary reality is only secondary. A strong connection between this beast and contemporary Roman power seems to be required

10. As it is typical in apocalyptic literature, the adjective "great" does not mean that the reality so described is particularly "large," but that it transcends the human dimension. Among humans, indeed, kings are usually the ones who have rule over cities, not vice-versa, as in the case of this "great city."

11. Inside John's narrative, the dragon is the model of the beast: see following footnote.

12. See E.F. LUPIERI, *A Commentary on the Apocalypse of John*, trans. M. POGGI JOHNSON – A. KAMESAR (Grand Rapids: Eerdmans, 2006) 201. Given the same number of heads and horns, the beast of Revelation 13 shows itself to be a first manifestation of the dragon/Satan of Rev 12:3; the passage of the diadems from the seven heads of the dragon to the ten horns of the beast from the sea probably indicates the passage from the cosmic power of Satan to the historical power of the beast. The ten horns/kings are the historical manifestation of one of the seven Satanic heads/kings/mountains at the time of John (see footnote 19).

by the text, but the heads are seven and the horns are ten because those numbers are traditional and not because John was consulting some lists of more or less ephemeral Roman rulers.

During the detailed description-explanation of the beast, the angel mentions Babylon twice, once as "the woman" and once as "the prostitute." The first context is probably the heart of the angel's revelation, since it is introduced by the sentence: "Here is the intellect that has wisdom" (Rev 17:9a).[13] The mystical explanation that follows is centered on the relationship between the beast and the woman: "The seven heads are seven mountains, where the woman sits upon them. And they are seven kings" (Rev 17:9b). I want to stress that the seven heads described as kings are not hills, but mountains. This situates our text into a precise Jewish apocalyptic tradition of thinking, since the "seven mountains," who are also "stars" and whose real nature is that of "angels," appear numerous times, particularly in apocalyptic texts of Enochic tradition.[14] This beast, as it is presented by John, can also be considered a mystical "angelomorphic" figure, the number of whose heads could connect it to the flowing of time, like the "heads of the times" that the Lord can "summon," so that they "stand before" him, in *2 Baruch* 48:2.[15]

## 3. Main Context(s)

The woman, who in v. 2 was said to be sitting on "many waters" and in v. 3 was seen on "a scarlet beast" (who "bears her" in v. 7), is now said to be seated upon the beast's seven heads, which are mountains and kings. Therefore, the relationship between the woman and the beast is one of being seated upon or being borne/carried by, but the reality of the beast

13. While one's attention was attracted to the uses of "ear" and "hearing" in the opening letters (Rev 2:7,11,17,29; 3:6,13,22), now the use of "wisdom" stresses the most important passages in the revelatory process (cf. Rev 13:18).

14. See E.F. Lupieri, "Esegesi e simbologie apocalittiche," *Annali di Storia dell'Esegesi* 7/2 (1990) 379-396, and E.F. Lupieri, "Apocalisse di Giovanni e tradizione enochica," in R. Penna, ed., *Apocalittica e Origini Cristiane* (Bologna: EDB, 1995) 137-150. Gods for the Greeks, angels for the Jews, the spiritual nature of the heavenly bodies was usually recognized at the time of John (see Paul in 1 Cor 15:40 f.). Mountains, then, appear to be the earthly correspondents to stars in the apocalyptic literature, esp. in *1 Enoch* (please see passages discussed in the quoted articles).

15. These "heads of the times," which can be "hastened" by God according to *2 Baruch* 54:1, seem to be individual angelic or angelomorphic figures, who can be co-present before the Lord; A.F.J. Klijn, in J.H. Charlesworth, ed., *The Old Testament Pseudepigrapha, Vol. I: Apocalyptic Literature and Testaments* (New York: Doubleday, 1983) 635 and 639, translates the phrase as "the coming of the times" and "the beginnings of the times," respectively.

appears increasingly complex. This is confirmed towards the end of the explanation of the beast, when the angel talks again about the prostitute and we read: "The waters that you saw, where the prostitute is seated, are peoples and throngs and nations and tongues" (Rev 17:15). Needless to say, John has seen no waters at all under the seated woman, but one beast and seven heads that are also seven kings, which are now explained as "peoples and throngs and nations and tongues." The explanation then continues with something that we can suppose is or will be the condemnation announced from the beginning: "And the ten horns that you saw and the beast, these will hate the prostitute and will make her desolate and naked and will eat her flesh and will burn her with fire" (Rev 17:16). Since the angel has already explained that the ten horns are "ten [future] kings" (Rev 17:12), whose only "purpose" appears to be able to give "their own power and authority" to the beast and to "battle with the Lamb" and be defeated (Rev 17:13 f.), he can now further explain his own words by saying that whatever happens will be according to God's purpose, not theirs: "For God has put into their hearts to do his purpose, a single purpose, and to give their kingdom to the beast, until the words of God should be fulfilled" (Rev 17:17). Therefore, John can be reassured that the grim destiny of the woman-prostitute-city will fulfil not only the purpose of God, but explicitly his "words." This means that we can expect some prophecy to be realized in John's historical reality (presented as an immediate future from the time of the revelation), so that the Scripture be fulfilled.

Therefore, does the prostitute have a prophetic function?

She does not talk, but her prophetic function may be implicit in her actions and characteristics, as happens with many prophets in the Old Testament who used their bodies and lives to represent the future destiny of Israel,[16] or with Anna, another prophetess, whose words are not reproduced in Luke 2:36-38, but whose life, name, patronymic, tribe, age, and actions in the temple are all prophetic and meaningful.[17] On the other side, it has been noted that when the woman/prostitute is present in

16. Even Jewish pseudoprophets, like Zedekiah son of Kenaanah, could make "iron horns" for themselves to symbolically describe the hoped-for victory against the Arameans (who will instead triumph over Israel, as prophesized by Micah; see 1 Kgs 22, esp. v. 11). However, Ezekiel's whole life has prophetic meaning, including the death of his beloved (and innocent) wife (Ezekiel 24), his consumption of impure and contaminated food (Ezekiel 4), and the shaving of his own head and beard in three parts (with some little rest) to show the destiny of the Israelites, who are symbolized by the individual hairs (Ezekiel 5). Most impressive for us, though, is the behavior of Hosea, obliged by God to buy and marry a prostitute, with whom he had three children, to show everyone the relationship of love and betrayal between God (him) and Israel (the prostitute: Hosea 1-3). Various figures, then, can act prophetically, with their own lives being representations of Israel's future.

17. See E.F. Lupieri, "Dodici, sette, undici, ventiquattro: numeri, chiese e fine del mondo," *Annali di Storia dell'Esegesi* 22/2 (2005) 357-371.

John's narrative, the second beast, the one coming from the earth/Land, is not on the scene—and likewise, when the second beast is not there, the prostitute appears. Apparently, the prostitute has a narrative function that is parallel and complementary to the one of the second beast in its relationship to the first beast.[18] However, John identifies the second beast with the pseudoprophet, a figure who not only has prophetic attributes and functions, but also priestly ones, since it organizes the cult for the first beast. If the woman/prostitute has a function similar to the pseudoprophet, then the beast upon which/whom she is seated corresponds (with many identical details) to the first beast, the one coming from the sea.

If the beast and the woman of Revelation 17-18 have narrative functions in the structure of the book that are similar to those of the two beasts of Rev 13 (and of the beast and the pseudoprophet in the final chapters), this does not mean that they are identical. The multi-layered mystical reality in John's apocalyptical reflections allows for any level to mirror elements and aspects of the others. The two beasts of Revelation 13 are the expressions, some sort of emanation of the Satanic power in the whole of the world history (in an antitypical imitation of Christ and the Spirit). The beast and the woman of Revelation 17-18, then, should be their "incarnation" at the time of John.[19] If the woman is Jerusalem, then she is at the same time the first victim and the main instrument of the second beast. She has power of doing evil (she can corrupt "the nations" with "the wine ... of her prostitution" [Rev 18:3] and she is responsible for the "blood of prophets and holy ones and of all those slaughtered upon the earth/Land" which was found in her [Rev 18:24]) and therefore she will be punished, but her punishment will be different from that of the pseudoprophet.

If we read the descriptions of the two beasts of Revelation 13 with Jewish, prophetic-apocalyptic eyes, and if we assume the geographical perspective of Jerusalem and the Holy Land in the first century CE, then the "sea" is the Mediterranean Sea and the beast from the sea becomes the mystical dimension of the most recent Western power, the Roman empire, expressed with scriptural language, as happens at Qumran with the *Kittim*, their island(s), and their ships.[20] If this is the "sea," then the earth is the Land, and its beast, which is also the pseudoprophet, is none other

18. This aspect was particularly developed by E. CORSINI, *Apocalisse prima e dopo* (Torino: Società Editrice Internazionale, 1980) 358, 453-456.

19. This is willingly ambiguous, meaning both the time of the "historical John" and the fictitious time of the narrative, so that the beast and the woman can be a visual prophecy (*ex eventu*) of the war with Rome and the fall of Jerusalem.

20. People from the [western] "Islands" (meaning Greece and Italy); see esp. Dan 11:30, but also Jer 2:10, Ezek 27:6 and 23:1,12. See H. ESHEL, "The Kittim in the War Scroll and in the Pesharim," in D. GOODBLATT – A. PINNICK – D.R. SCHWARTZ, eds., *Historical Perspectives: From the Hasmoneans to Bar Kokhba in Light of the Dead Sea Scrolls: Proceedings of the Fourth International Symposium*

than the corrupt Jewish religious authority that also had political (and, under the Hasmoneans, royal) power during the whole Second Temple period.[21] It is particularly important for this reading that the beast from the earth/Land is the one who organizes the cult for the beast of the sea; this would be the way John chose to describe the corruption of the Jewish royal and priestly leadership that was reproducing the sin of Aaron, Solomon, and Manasseh.[22]

If all this makes sense, and if the woman has the same literary function as the pseudoprophet, then we should expect to find royal, priestly, and prophetic attributes in her. She would, indeed, represent the historical embodiment of the Satanic power described by the second beast. As Jerusalem, she would represent all the sinful human dimension of Israel, and the City, and the part of its people deceived by their corrupt leaders (kings and priests).

As for her royal dimension, apart from the fact that (as we mentioned above) she is explicitly presented "as a queen" in Rev 18:7, all the scholars who believe that the woman represents Rome also believe that her "sitting upon" the beast and its heads/kings symbolizes her imperial power. The idea of "sitting" (on a throne or in absolute) is indeed very often connected with figures of power, from God[23] to earthly kings, princes, and the like. This should be the case here.[24]

For her priestly and prophetic dimensions, it is worth noting that the connection between priestly and prophetic functions was quite strong in the Jewish traditions of the first century CE. Josephus stresses it on various occasions, particularly for John Hyrcanus (*Jewish War* 1.68-69) and for himself (3.152). In the New Testament, the famous passage in John 11:50 regarding Caiaphas's prophecy seems to imply that priesthood *per se* offers

---

*of the Orion Center for the Study of the Dead Sea Scrolls and Associated Literature, 27-31 January, 1999* (Leiden: Brill, 2002) 29-44.

21. E. CORSINI, *Apocalisse prima e dopo* (Torino: Società Editrice Internazionale, 1980) 358-365; see Painchaud in this volume.

22. See on this subject the second contribution by Louis Painchaud (L. PAINCHAUD, "The Dragon, the Beasts, and the Gold: The Number of the Beast in Revelation 13:18. Part 2: 'Its Number is Six Hundred and Sixty-Six' [Rev 13:18]: The Priest, the King, and the Gold of the Nations") in this volume. Also the use of προσκυνεῖν, as he rightly stresses, should be indicative of the double, royal and religious, dimension of this leadership (see esp. his footnote 126 and its context).

23. I want to quickly recall here the rabbinic discussion about Metatron (Enoch) and his punishment for having allowed himself to be seen sitting near God, so that R. Ishmael, the traveler of the Merkabah, could think of a "second principle" in Heaven (*3 Enoch* 16).

24. It is this context that gives the full meaning to the act, since "sitting" *per se* could also be a sign of the change in fortune of a formerly powerful person, particularly Jerusalem. According to Lam 1:1,3, she who used to be a queen or princess (LXX: ἄρχουσα) is now "sitting alone."

a prophetic charisma to the priest, even if the person is unaware of it.[25] It is also possible that this connection plays some role in Luke's Infancy Gospel, where, apart from John the Baptist and his parents (who all prophesy since they are all, like Mary, of priestly stock), we find the previously mentioned Anna, who was a prophetess and, even if not of priestly family, is described as worshiping in the temple night and day. The choice of words is quite strong, since it was usually priests who did "worship" and only priests could stay on the premises of the temple "at night."[26]

Similar connections also appear earlier in Revelation, though already with strong negative markers. The first female figure we meet in the narrative is Jezebel, in the *ekklesia* of Thyatira (Rev 2:18-25). Her name may be fictional, since it was also the name of the queen of Israel, the pagan wife of Achab, the main reason for the cult of Baal in Samaria, the enemy of the prophet Elijah, the one responsible for the death of Naboth (see 1 Kgs 16-22), and whose gruesome end is described in 2 Kings 9:30-37.[27] "Jezebel," therefore, could be a name John chose to put his own adversary

---

25. "[Caiaphas] did not say this on his own, but, since he was high priest that year, he prophesied that Jesus was going to die for the nation [of the Jews] – and not for the nation only, but also so that he could gather into one the children of God who had been dispersed" (John 11:51-52). On the connection between priesthood and prophecy, see F. Adinolfi, *Giovanni Battista. Profilo storico del maestro di Gesù* (Rome: Carocci, 2021), who underlines the priesthood of John the Baptist in Luke 1-2 as a logical background for his prophetic activity.

26. "She did not go away from the temple, worshiping with fasting and prayers night and day" (Luke 2:37). It is possible that Luke, by omitting sacrifice, wants to stress the new, eschatological worship; it is worth noting, though, that he uses the character of a woman, albeit a widow, for this narrative function and therefore apparently connects female prophetism with sexual abstinence (as possibly represented also by the daughters of Philip, all four of whom are prophetesses and virgins, in Acts 21:9). This last element might be a sign of a persistent discomfort with female prophetism in Pauline or post-Pauline communities in Luke and in Acts, which could represent a successive phase of the one notoriously described in 1 Corinthians 14 (esp. 14:33b-36). If women have to prophesy in the churches, at least their life must be one of absolute sexual purity; Tertullian, *De ieiunio* 8.11. See E. Giannarelli, "Fra profezia ignorata e profezia nascosta. La storia esegetica di Anna," in A. Valerio, ed., *Donna, potere e profezia* (Napoli: D'Auria, 1995) 74-75, and J.C. Poirier – J. Franković, "Celibacy and Charism in 1 Cor 7:5-7," *Harvard Theological Review* 89/1 (1996) 1-18.

27. Louis Painchaud draws my attention to the fact that Jezebel was the daughter of the (new) prince of Tyre, "Ethbaal, king of the Sidonians" (1 Kgs 16:31). Ethbaal was a priest of Astarte and, like Omri, Achab's father and the founder of Samaria, became king with a coup, as Josephus narrates (*Contra Apionem* I,18). It is more than logical to think that the two usurpers wanted to strengthen their political positions, arranging the marriage of their offspring, which also explains the wise openness of both Omri and Achab to the cult of Canaanite divinities, in spite of the Yahwist absolutism of the biblical authors. The traditional alliance between Chiram and Solomon was therefore revived under the new souverains.

in the right polemical perspective. Further, John could use her figure to represent not a particular leader, but the whole group against whose message he is polemicizing.[28] Even if she was completely fictional (as possibly was the case with Anna), the character of Jezebel shows that it is thinkable for a woman to be a leader of a group of followers of Jesus.[29] John stresses that she is a "woman,"[30] that any relationship with her is "prostitution," that she is a "teacher" and a "prophet," and that she has two kinds of followers, her "children," for whom the punishment will be death, and the "adulterers," for whom there will be a "great tribulation." In spite of John's criticism, she seems to lead (or at least represent) the majority of the followers of Jesus in Thyatira, while the faithful ones—the ones who recognize John's authority—are a "rest," whose non-theological but sociological weight is difficult to hypothesize. The connection, at least rhetorical if not historical, between female leadership among (some) followers of Jesus, prophetism, and prostitution seems to be strongly supported by John: femininity and prostitution in this case help to define the falsity and negativity of prophetism (and teaching) originating from a competing group of believers.

A similar literary and mental attitude should be supposed behind the woman prostitute who appears in ch. 17. Both she and the second beast, or pseudoprophet, have priestly functions and attributes, in a scenario reminiscent of the Exodus narrative of the Golden Calf.[31]

---

28. Apparently, at least one text in Qumran uses a female figure to represent a competing Jewish group of believers (4Q184; see S.W. CRAWFORD, "Lady Wisdom and Dame Folly at Qumran," *Dead Sea Discoveries* 5/3 [1998] 355-366).

29. I refrain from using the word "Christian(s)" in the context of Revelation, since John avoids or ignores it: for him, both his followers and his adversaries are "Jews," either true (his own) or false (the others).

30. The only one explicitly mentioned as such in the first 11 chapters of the book. (Before the "woman" of chapter 12, the only other time John mentions "women" earlier is when he describes the hair of the composite monsters "similar to grasshoppers" which have human faces, lion's teeth, scorpion's tails and women's hair; Rev 9:7-8). On the real or presumed misogyny in John's Apocalypse, see the classical feminist analysis by T. PIPPIN, *Death and Desire: The Rhetoric of Gender in the Apocalypse of John* (Louisville: Westminster/John Knox, 1992).

31. On the importance of the facts that the prostitute appears in the desert and the pseudoprophet, like Aaron, organizes the cult for an image of a beast, see E.F. LUPIERI, "A Beast and a Woman in the Desert, or the Sin of Israel: A Typological Reflection," in E.F. MASON – E.F. LUPIERI, eds., *Golden Calf Traditions in Early Judaism, Christianity, and Islam* (Leiden: Brill, 2018) 157-175, and S. AUDET, "Intertextuality in the Apocalypse: The Desert and the Woman," in the present volume. A further connection could be seen again with the prostitute/prophetess of Thyatira, whose name (nickname?), Jezebel, relates her to corrupted kingship in Jerusalem.

Together with a growing minority of scholars, I believe that Revelation's great prostitute does not represent Rome (or a Roman reality that was already present in the first beast, the one coming from the sea, and in its equivalent, the beast on which the woman is sitting), but, at the first level of its mystical allegory, Jerusalem and its corrupt leadership.[32] Indeed, the image of "prostitution" is traditionally used in prophetic language to depict the idolatrous betrayal of Yahweh by his beloved spouse, either a city of Israel or the nation as a whole.[33] Jerusalem in particular was depicted as an adulteress and a prostitute whose corruption with the political and religious power of the Gentiles dated to the very construction of the temple under king Solomon.[34] If this is true with Revelation, then the book would show the same "woman" twice, first in Rev 12 as the recipient of God's salvific promise who is "pregnant" with the eschatological Messiah/Christ and saved and protected "in the desert" for a given time, but later in Revelation 17 as sinfully seduced by the idolatrous "beast" in that same desert, like Israel in the Exodus. Both Aaron and Solomon are perpetrators and victims of idolatrous behavior, and so too is the whole Jewish leadership over the centuries. Therefore, it makes sense that the prostitute has royal and especially Jewish priestly attributes. Vest-

32. For this scholarly position in relatively recent years, see E. CORSINI, *Apocalisse prima e dopo* (Torino: Società Editrice Internazionale, 1980) (Eng. trans. *The Apocalypse: The Perennial Revelation of Jesus Christ*, trans. F.J. MOLONEY [Wilmington, DE: Glazier, 1983]; Fr. trans. *L'Apocalypse maintenant*, trans. R. ARRIGHI [Paris: Éditions du Seuil, 1984]); E. CORSINI, *Apocalisse di Gesù Cristo secondo Giovanni* (Torino: Società Editrice Internazionale, 2002); E.F. LUPIERI, *L'Apocalisse di Giovanni* (Milan: Mondadori – Lorenzo Valla, 1999) (Eng. trans. *A Commentary on the Apocalypse of John*, trans. M. POGGI JOHNSON – A. KAMESAR [Grand Rapids: Eerdmans, 2006]); L. ARCARI, *"Una donna avvolta nel sole ..." (Apoc 12,1). Le raffigurazioni femminili nell'Apocalisse di Giovanni alla luce della letteratura apocalittica giudaica* (Padova: Edizioni Messaggero, 2008); F.J. MOLONEY, *The Apocalypse of John:* A *Commentary* (Grand Rapids: Baker, 2020).

33. To have a "betrayal," you first need a pact, which, in Jerusalem/Israel's case, is the covenant with God that was constantly broken by Israel since its first constitution on Sinai, when even the first tables of the Law were destroyed by Moses in the face of the idolatry of the Golden Calf. It is worth noting that, even if we (as most ancient Christian commentators) stress the fact that all of Israel is represented in the Scripture as the adulterous betrayer of the spousal covenant with her God, some scholars rightly underline the fact that the rebellious female figures in the Old Testament are usually the individual cities of Israel (especially Jerusalem), while the people is usually described as a rebellious "son" (see J.J. SCHMITT, "Israel as Son of God in Torah," *Biblical Theology Bulletin* 34 [2004] 69-79).

34. On this and on the 666 gold talents of Solomon, see L. PAINCHAUD, "The Dragon, the Beasts, and the Gold: The Number of the Beast in Revelation 13:18. Part 2: 'Its Number is Six Hundred and Sixty-Six' (Rev 13:18): The Priest, the King, and the Gold of the Nations," in the present volume. And recently K. BODNER – B.A. STRAWN, "Solomon and 666 (Revelation 13.18)," *New Testament Studies* 66 (2020) 299-312.

ments of the high priests and ornaments of the temple are connected with her three times: in the description of her dress (Rev 17:4), in the list of the loved and desired cargo for the fallen city (Rev 18:12),[35] and in the dress of that fallen city (Rev 18:16), with whom[36] she had just been identified (Rev 17:18). Besides purple, scarlet, silk, and precious stones, which we find in the Old Testament in contexts describing priestly dresses or temple ornaments, "fine linen" (or white byssus) and real gold (not "similar to gold" as in Rev 9:7) are particularly important.[37] In the other occurrences in Revelation, they always characterize positive characters in John's visionary narrative (even the heavenly Jerusalem, eschatological city-bride of the Lamb; see esp. Rev 19:8-14 and 21:18-21). Pearls are ignored in the Old Testament and do not appear in any ancient description of the temple, but in the first century CE, according to logia attributed to Jesus, they were not only so precious that they could be compared to the kingdom of God (Matt 13:45-46), but they also could be put in parallel with the "holy thing," the sacred food reserved for the priests that derived from the offerings in the temple (Matt 7:6).

We have seen how the prostitute, whom John overloaded with priestly attributes, probably represents Jerusalem and its corrupt leadership. Nevertheless, as a second level of interpretation, this does not exclude the possibility that, like the ancient Jezebel, she also refers mystically and symbolically to John's opponents among other followers of Jesus and not, or not only, to other Jews.[38] This would explain John's insistence on the almost eucharistic symbology of the golden cup[39] in the hands of the prostitute, which is full not with the wine/blood of Christ,[40] but with "the wine of

---

35. See on this I. PROVAN, "Foul Spirits, Fornication and Finance: Revelation 18 from an Old Testament Perspective," *Journal for the Study of New Testament* 64 (1996) 87-88.

36. I will be using feminine pronouns, since she is constantly considered a woman.

37. Esp. Exod 28:2-43; see R.E. WINKLE, "'You Are What You Wear': The Dress and Identity of Jesus as High Priest in John's Apocalypse," in H.L. WILEY – C.A. EBERHART, eds., *Sacrifice, Cult, and Atonement in Early Judaism and Christianity* (Atlanta: SBL Press, 2017) 327-346, esp. 343.

38. On this, see D. TRIPALDI, *Apocalisse di Giovanni* (Roma: Carocci, 2012). In the following centuries among orthodox as well as Gnostic or heretical groups, it will become almost customary to depict one's Christian adversaries as "Jews"; already in *Gospel of Thomas* 39 and 102, the "Pharisees" probably represent ecclesiastical Christians.

39. Please note that it is real gold too.

40. This should not be equated with the blood of the victims offered in the temple, which no one would have dreamt of drinking. The fact that she "drinks" that blood could signify the full degeneration of Jewish priesthood (see n. 2 above) or the spiritual depravity of the eucharistic ritual celebrated by John's adversaries. The accusation of ritually drinking blood, also directed against Christians by Pagan polemicists, will soon become traditional in polemical Christian texts against both

her prostitution" (Rev 17:2), which is "abominations (see Dan 12:11 in Mark 13:14)—the impurity of her prostitution" (Rev 17:4), but is also "the blood of the holy ones ... the witnesses of Jesus" (Rev 17:6). The betrayal/prostitution of the false Jews among the followers of Jesus (Rev 2:9 ; 3:9) parallels the ancient sin of Israel with the Gentiles (Rev 18:3).

Finally, while the consumption of idolothytes, characteristic of idolatrous prostitution for Jezebel, could certainly be interpreted and understood as a polemical element in discussions with Pauline or post-Pauline traditions and communities, it could also be connected to the ancient sin of the Jews in the desert. Indeed, according to Exod 32:5-6, Aaron and the Jews not only built an altar to the Golden Calf, but also offered sacrifices (and not only holocausts, but also a "sacrifice of salvation" [LXX: θυσία σωτηρίου]), and then were able to "eat," "drink," and "frolic." What did they eat, in the "celebration of the[ir] Lord" (LXX: ἑορτὴ τοῦ κυρίου), if not their offering to the molten idol ?

We can also ask ourselves if the sinful behavior of the woman-prostitute, particularly her apparent triumphal attitude, does not imply or even already constitute the beginning of her punishment. According to Rev 16:6, drinking blood is a punishment for those who "poured the blood of saints and prophets," the very sin of the prostitute, as well as, in a logion attributed to Jesus, that of Jewish authorities and the personified Jerusalem (Matt 23:29-39 ; esp. 30 f., 35 and 37). And if drinking blood as punishment is a memory of one of the plagues of Egypt (Exod 7:14-25), two more textual details are worth mentioning.

Firstly, in Rev 11:8, John says that "the city, the great one ... where also their Lord was crucified," which seems to be one of the few historical details in the whole book and which I find quite difficult to apply to any other city but Jerusalem,[41] "spiritually is called Sodom and Egypt." Sodom and Egypt, therefore, should describe the spiritual, degenerated reality of Jerusalem, and we should feel authorized to apply the sinful attributes and (prophetically ?) the biblical destiny of both Sodom and Egypt to that of Jerusalem. If Babylon is Jerusalem, and Jerusalem is Sodom and Egypt, this would explain both her punishment with fire and the connection with the plagues, as particularly underlined in Rev 18:4-5 : "Go out, O my people, from her, so as not to have a share in her sins, and not receive of her plagues, because her sins have been piled up to heaven." The passage opens with an echo of Jesus's exhortation to abandon Judaea (Mark 13:14-18 and Matt 24:15-20) or Jerusalem itself (Luke 21:20-22), followed by the

---

Jews and heretics. The fact that a woman is connected with blood does not seem to me particularly meaningful in John's context.

41. Even if some scholars think that by extension the persecuting Rome could have taken over the attributes of Jerusalem (e.g., U. VANNI, *La struttura letteraria dell'Apocalisse* [Brescia: Morcelliana, 1980] 69).

mention of the "plagues" and the "piling up" of sins, which recalls Sodom in Gen 18:20. Both the Old Testament Sodom and the New Testament Jerusalem are going to be soon destroyed.

Secondly, then, it has long been noted that, while the Bible and the Jewish tradition expect that the enemies of Israel have to be "paid back" with a punishment corresponding to their offenses against the Jews (e.g., the "Daughter of Babylon" in Ps 137 [136] :8), Israel and Jerusalem will receive a punishment twice as heavy.[42] This idea is quite common in various layers of the Old Testament (Isa 40:2 ; Jer 16:18 ; Job 42:10) and is echoed in a Qumran commentary on Isaiah (4QTanḥumim [4Q176] frag. 1-2, end of col. 1). Indeed, all of *4 Ezra* is centered on the fact that God is punishing Israel too much ! If Babylon were Rome, and not Jerusalem or a Jewish reality, we should suppose that John was writing against his own tradition, without giving his followers the scriptural keys to understand what he was talking about.[43]

That Babylon is Jerusalem can also be confirmed by the nature of her enemies. She is not destroyed by the Lamb and his army, but by her own former lovers, those kings who will battle against the Lamb and will be in turn defeated by him. The prostitute and the Lamb, then, have the same enemies.

If the sin of the woman is the traditionally Jewish idolatrous prostitution with the kings of the Gentiles, then the prophetic dimension of the prostitute is her end, which should be interpreted as an *ex eventu* announcement of the fall of Jerusalem. In this way, like the roughly contemporary *4 Ezra* and *2 Baruch*, John's Revelation is also an explanation to the Jewish and Christian faithful of the most traumatic (for them) historical event of that century : the destruction of the Holy City and the burning of its temple.[44] But not only that. If the connections we noticed above with priestly characteristics and eucharistic symbology are to be taken into consideration, then the prostitute, with her grim destiny, is also a prophetic admonition for groups of self-styled followers of Jesus who are considered deviant by

42. A.J. Beagley, *The 'Sitz im Leben' of the Apocalypse : With Particular Reference to the Role of the Church's Enemies* (Berlin : De Gruyter, 1987) 98.

43. An obstacle to our reading of Babylon in Revelation is the fictional statement of 1 Pet 5:13 to be a letter written "in Babylon," an expression that is often considered a euphemism for Rome. However, Troy Martin has convincingly shown that "Babylon" in that context probably refers to the eastern Jewish (and Christian) diaspora (now see esp. his "Faith : Its Qualities, Attributes, and Legitimization in 1 Peter," *Biblical Research* 61 [2016] 46-61, but also *Metaphor and Composition in First Peter* [Atlanta : Scholars Press, 1992] 144-148).

44. For the reciprocal relationships of Revelation, *4 Ezra* and *2 Baruch*, see E.F. Lupieri, "The Seventh Night : Visions of History in the Revelation of John and Contemporary Apocalyptic," *Henoch* 14 (1992) 113-132 ; E.F. Lupieri, "Dalla storia al mito. La distruzione di Gerusalemme in alcune apocalissi degli anni 70-135," in P. Sacchi, ed., *Il Giudaismo palestinese : dal I secolo A.C. al I secolo d.C.* (Bologna : AISG, 1993) 137-155.

John. There will be, for sure, an eschatological reversal of fortune, but for now the end of the old Jerusalem, the punishment planned by God for her idolatrous prostitution and biblically executed by the hand of the heathens, is the dreadful example of the future destiny of those who will not adhere to the teaching of the prophecy that John has received directly from the angel of Jesus, who had received it from God (Rev 1:1).[45]

## 4. Concluding Remarks

Many of the various conceptual elements and textual details I have collected here have already largely been discussed in the scholarly literature, and their interpretations have been brought to support opposing positions.[46] The royal dimension of the prostitute has been variously analyzed and, in our reading, it does support the idea that she represents the final stage of the corruption of Jewish political leadership and its consequences on the Jewish people. What I think is relatively new and hope I showed with this contribution, is that attributing particularly priestly and prophetic characteristics and functions to a female character, as well as Eucharistic imaging, should be the way John chose to represent the prostitution of prophetic and cultic leadership among his religious adversaries. The corruption of Jewish and/or early "Christian" religious leadership is visually and vividly represented by its transformation into a "prostitute." It is not that the prostitute becomes a priest, but that the male priesthood, because of its corruption, participates in prostitution and becomes symbolically and mystically a woman, with an imagery already largely adopted by Old Testament prophetic traditions.

All this has little or nothing to do with Rome and its emperors.

45. Using exempla from the Scriptures is also part of John's *modus operandi* to describe the present and possible future situation of the religious groups with whom he is interacting, including those of other followers of Jesus. I find the fact that he decides to address his letters to seven angels of seven churches, some of whom must "hold fast" (Rev 2:25; 3:11), but others of whom already "have fallen" (Rev 2:4), and that all are at risk of falling if they do not repent, to be particularly meaningful. The negative model, then, should be the fallen angels of the Enochic tradition, whose attempt to find mercy in the eyes of God through the intercession in writing by a human intermediary (Enoch) was rejected (*1 Enoch* 12:4-14:7; *2 Enoch* 7:4-5). John is a new Enoch who brings a message of hope in the name of Jesus to angels on the verge of becoming the new victims of Satan (cp. Rev 12:4 and 9). On this, see E.F. Lupieri, "Apocalisse di Giovanni e tradizione enochica," in R. Penna, ed., *Apocalittica e Origini Cristiane* (Bologna: EDB, 1995) 137-150.

46. I have already collected many of them in E.F. Lupieri, *A Commentary on the Apocalypse of John*, trans. M. Poggi Johnson – A. Kamesar (Grand Rapids: Eerdmans, 2006); trans. of *L'Apocalisse di Giovanni* (Milan: Mondadori – Lorenzo Valla, 1999).

# SAMARIA, JERUSALEM, AND OTHER PROSTITUTES: A FICTIVE HISTORY FOR THE ETIOLOGY OF A DISASTER

**Robert A. Di Vito**

*Loyola University Chicago*

Résumé

Étant donné l'importance générale de l'Ancien Testament pour l'identification de la femme insaisissable qui chevauche la bête dans Apocalypse de Jean (17,5-6), l'intention fondamentale de ce chapitre est de fournir un aperçu de la façon dont le motif de la prostituée est utilisé dans l'Ancien Testament, dans le contexte du Proche-Orient ancien. Les trois principaux usages du terme hébreu pour « prostituée » sont explorés : comme désignation d'un phénomène quotidien et séculier, comme métaphore (religieuse), et enfin comme désignation d'une fonction cultuelle dans un rite religieux supposé avoir été populaire dans le Proche-Orient ancien et en Israël. Une attention particulière est accordée à ce dernier usage et à des textes tels que Dt 23,18-19, qui sont censés fournir des preuves de l'existence de la prostitution sacrée. Bien que toute tentative d'identification positive de la femme chevauchant la bête de l'Apocalypse dépasse le cadre de ce chapitre, le caractère purement littéraire de la prostitution sacrée dans l'Ancien Testament et l'intention de la fiction tendent à corroborer l'identification juive de cette femme qui chevauche la bête.

Abstract

Given the importance generally of the Old Testament to the identification of the elusive figure atop the beast in Rev 17:3-6, the basic intent of the chapter is to provide an overview of how the motif of the prostitute figures in the Old Testament, in the context of the ancient Near East. The three primary uses of the Hebrew term for "prostitute" are explored: as a designation for the everyday, secular phenomenon; as a (religious) metaphor; and finally, as the designation of a cultic functionary in a religious rite alleged to have been popular in the ancient Near East and Israel. Special attention is given to the latter usage and such texts as Deut 23:18-19 that are alleged to provide evidence for the existence of sacred prostitution. While any attempt at a positive identification of the figure atop Revelation's beast is beyond the scope of the chapter, the purely literary character of sacred prostitution in the Old Testament and the intent of the fiction provide further corroboration for a Jewish identification of the figure atop the beast.

*"Who is Sitting on Which Beast?" Interpretative Issues in the Book of Revelation. Proceedings of the International Conference held at Loyola University, Chicago, March 30-31, 2017*, ed. by Edmondo Lupieri and Louis Painchaud, JAOC 29 (Turnhout, 2023), pp. 101–128
 DOI 10.1484/M.JAOC-EB.5.131930

## 1. "Babylon the great, the mother of harlots" (Rev 17:5, NABRE)

The identity of the Harlot of Babylon has occupied the attention of scholars and curious readers alike from the time John put pen to paper. Disputed though the referent may be, nothing suggests more strongly the importance of the Old Testament to the identification of Babylon than this gendered personification of the city as a harlot—indeed "the mother of harlots." It represents one of the key motifs utilized by the author of Revelation; and the Old Testament is clearly his source for the motif, providing much of the figure's linguistic adornment and definition. Given the importance of this background, therefore, the intent of this chapter is simply to provide an overview of how the motif of the harlot, or prostitute,[1] figures in the Old Testament. It proceeds on the assumption that the discussion is best served by distinguishing in the material we have in the Old Testament three primary uses of the term: viz., 1) the prostitute as a social phenomenon and purely mundane "secular" figure; 2) the prostitute as metaphor; and 3) the prostitute as a religious functionary in a cultic institution deemed to have been popular in ancient Israel (even if at variance with the kind of worship demanded by her god Yahweh) and, more generally, at home in the ancient Near East.[2] In view of our concern with the personification of the city Babylon in the Book of Revelation, the everyday, "secular" phenomenon will be treated below in cursory fashion to focus on the demonstrably more significant metaphoric usage found in the Bible. That discussion in turn lays the foundation, in a perhaps unexpected way, for the argument that will be made below regarding the presence in ancient Israel of an historical institution referred to as cultic, or sacred, prostitution, carried out within the context of an alleged

1. While used interchangeably, the former term is in current usage gendered for women and bears a somewhat derogatory connotation, having come into vogue specifically in sixteenth century English translations of the Bible. Although it is still recognizable to English speakers in non-technical writing, *Oxford English Dictionary* assigns it to frequency band 4 on an 8-point scale, with band 8 comprised by words of very high frequency and band 1 with those of very low frequency (see "harlot, n." *Oxford English Dictionary Online*. June 2019. Oxford University Press. https://www-oed-com.flagship.luc.edu/view/Entry/84255?rskey=ivYUQw&result=1 (accessed July 21, 2019). "Prostitute," however, is assigned to frequency band 5. It may be used both of women and men "who engage in sexual activity in return for payment" (with men, especially homosexual activity and frequently used in conjunction with the qualifier "male"); see "prostitute, n." *Oxford English Dictionary Online*. June 2019. Oxford University Press. https://www-oed-com.flagship.luc.edu/view/Entry/153082 (accessed July 21, 2019).

2. I borrow this sensible categorization of the biblical material from Elaine Adler Goodfriend's and Karel van der Toorn's treatment of prostitution in D.N. Freedman, ed., *Anchor Bible Dictionary* V (New York: Doubleday, 1992) 505-513.

regular fertility ritual and rite. Although it is clearly beyond the scope of this chapter to provide a positive answer to the identity of the enduringly enigmatic figure sitting on Revelation's beast, this latter argument offers nonetheless further corroboration, we believe, for a Jewish identification. Not only does this argument remove, definitively, any literal application of the sobriquet "the mother of harlots" to the city Babylon based on an historical recollection of the practice of cultic prostitution; but the argument to be made below for the institution's purely *literary* character in ancient Israel also supports at the same time the one candidate for the identification of Babylon that emerges most clearly in the discussion of the metaphoric use of prostitution in the Old Testament. In short, once any historical justification for the moniker's application to Babylon itself is removed, based on the supposed existence of the practice of cultic prostitution, a survey of the metaphor's usage underscores the significance of Babylon as a cipher for another entity and decisively puts the spotlight on one candidate in the Bible for the title "harlot" par excellence.

## 2. Prostitution in Ancient Israel

It is said, usually in jest, that common prostitution is among the oldest of professions; but it—and here we are speaking of female prostitution[3]—is in fact neither universal nor necessary. Ancient though it may be, it is, as P. Bird has noted,[4] basically characteristic of urban patriarchal society, where it emerges as the natural outcome of the conflicting demands men make for exclusive control over their wives' sexuality, on the one hand, and for free access to other women, on the other. Indeed, the greater the inaccessibility of women, the greater is the need for an institutionally legitimized "other" woman—one who may not be honored or esteemed but one who, nonetheless, is tolerated and may even be accepted. Put differently, ambivalence attends the institution wherever it exists as a characteristic feature of the institution itself.

That ambivalence is certainly evident in biblical Israel, where stringent norms govern the sexual relations of men and women in the Old Testament (with the possible exception of Song of Songs); and it is evidently

3. The phenomenon of *male*, same-sex prostitution appears to be comparatively rare, insofar at least as it is poorly attested, according to P.A. Bird ("The Harlot as Heroine: Narrative Art and Social Presupposition in Three Old Testament Texts," *Semeia* 46 [1989] 119-139 [121], who cites on this issue P.H. Gebhard, "Prostitution," in *The New Encyclopedia Britannica* 15 [15th ed.; Chicago: University of Chicago, 1974] 75-81). As such its lack is symptomatic of the unequal power relations and statuses that pertain to the relations that determine men and women in the ancient world and a patriarchal society.

4. P.A. Bird, "The Harlot as Heroine: Narrative Art and Social Presupposition in Three Old Testament Texts," *Semeia* 46 (1989) 119-139 (121).

more pronounced than what is generally seen elsewhere in the literary deposit of the ancient Near East, especially the literary texts emerging from ancient Mesopotamia.[5] The extent of this ambivalence comes through in multiple prohibitions of legal bearing, of course, but also in numerous other indications of societal disapproval, whether implicit or explicit. So, to begin with the prohibitions, when Priestly legislation explicitly prohibits the *defilement* of a daughter by having her become a prostitute, it is out of no less than a fear that the very land would in effect prostitute itself and be *filled* with wickedness (Lev 19:29). And naturally a priest, presumably unlike a layman, is also then explicitly forbidden to marry a woman *defiled* through prostitution (Lev 21:7,14); but even the daughter of a priest *defiles* her father by her prostitution, the magnitude of the offense underscored by the prescription that she is to be punished by being burnt with fire (Lev 21:9). In fact, so grievous is the defilement occasioned by prostitution in matters of holiness that it extends even to a prostitute's earnings, which on no account could come into the temple, though they were for the precise purpose of paying off a vow (Deut 23:19).

Indications of societal disdain for the prostitute are not limited to Priestly concerns, and other pointers, implicit or explicit, abound, so only a couple of illustrations are necessary to make the point. For example, so horrific is the prostitute's degradation in Israel that the prophet Amos can think of no worse fate than to begin his litany of the punishments to befall the king's priest at the royal sanctuary in Bethel with the doom of his wife: while his children shall die by the sword and his land divided up, his wife will be reduced to prostitution (Amos 7:17).[6] And certainly the whole point of the Old Testament's metaphorical equation of apostasy

5. See, for example, the comments of J. ASSANTE ("The kar.kid / *ḫarimtu*, Prostitute or Single Woman? A Reconsideration of the Evidence," *Ugarit-Forschungen* 30 [1998] 5-97 [50-53]) on "street life" in ancient Mesopotamia suggesting a more relaxed attitude to public expressions of sexuality, at least in earlier periods. Her concluding comment on this discussion is striking: "If we believe both law and literature, sex seems to have occurred in every conceivable non-residential locale. Besides the street, Mesopotamians found the main thoroughfare, the city square, the inn, the granary, the sheep hut, the storehouse, the canebrake, the city wall and the garden convenient places to copulate outside the home." In fact, Assante, among others, has even argued that Mesopotamia lacks a specific word for "prostitution" or "prostitute," suggesting perhaps it found prostitution "more consonant with cultural practice" or "less exotic" than we do (86). For her part, E.A. Goodfriend suggests a connection between Israel having a relatively greater abhorrence of unknown paternity than Mesopotamia and her scorn of the prostitute, because of the importance of the patrilineal bloodline for purposes of inheritance (E.A. GOODFRIEND, "Prostitution," in D.N. FREEDMAN, ed., *Anchor Bible Dictionary* V [New York: Doubleday, 1992] 506).

6. Compare the ignominy attaching to Ahab's death by having dogs lap up his blood washing into the pool of Samaria, where prostitutes bathed in it (1 Kgs 22:38).

with prostitution (see below) is just to exploit such underlying, value-laden negative judgments regarding prostitution and trade on Israel's abhorrence at the prostitute's degradation. Through the vehicle supplied by prostitution, and in a world suffused with divine powers, Israel cast apostasy as not just a consequential change of allegiance but the act of a prostitute. Thereby she rendered, as Goodfriend suggests, any deviation in divine allegiance all the more vile and contemptible, all the more repulsive and abhorrent.[7] In fact, so thorough-going and pervasive is the censure of prostitution in biblical Israel that even texts apparently crediting a prostitute with deeds of extraordinary courage or heroic virtue at the same time subtly subvert the honor; for it is precisely her marginalized social location in the narrative that heightens the heroism, as it does in the prostitute Rahab's befriending of two Israelite spies (Joshua 2) on the eve of Jericho's conquest.[8] Good deeds will not change her status. As Prov 23:37 has it, a prostitute is, all the same, a "deep pit."

Yet even if prostitutes are not held in high regard generally, in ordinary practice prostitution seems, nevertheless, to have been largely tolerated. Just as the narrator makes nothing of those two spies in Joshua 2 going immediately to the house of a prostitute after entering Jericho, "where they lay," Judges 16:1 reports unproblematically that upon sighting a prostitute in Gaza, Samson "went in" to her and subsequently lay in bed until midnight (v. 3). Nor are two prostitutes prevented from bringing their lawsuit directly before the great King Solomon himself, their "occupation" of no apparent consequence (or at least not worthy of comment), although it might account for how they found themselves alone in a house with two newborn infants (1 Kgs 3:16-28). As Goodfriend notes,[9] prostitutes apparently could be seen everywhere in the public space: the street, the square, the corner (Prov 7:12; comp. Ezek 16:24f), and even the site of sacrifice (Hos 4:14; comp. Mic 1:7).

In sharp contrast to Mesopotamia (and Egypt?), if one accepts the more recent view of some Assyriologists that Mesopotamia lacks a specific word to designate a prostitute or prostitution,[10] in biblical Hebrew there is a lexeme—and only one— usually employed for the agent or the practice.[11] It is

---

7. E.A. GOODFRIEND, "Prostitution," in D.N. FREEDMAN, ed., *Anchor Bible Dictionary* V (New York: Doubleday, 1992) 506.

8. E.A. GOODFRIEND, "Prostitution," in D.N. FREEDMAN, ed., *Anchor Bible Dictionary* V (New York: Doubleday, 1992) 505. She also notes Simeon and Levi's put down in responding to Jacob's rebuke of their vengeance upon Shechem for the rape of their sister Dinah: "Shall our sister be treated like a prostitute" (Gen 34:31).

9. E.A. GOODFRIEND, "Prostitution," in D.N. FREEDMAN, ed., *Anchor Bible Dictionary* V (New York: Doubleday, 1992) 507.

10. J. ASSANTE, "The kar.kid / *ḫarimtu*, Prostitute or Single Woman? A Reconsideration of the Evidence," *Ugarit-Forschungen* 30 (1998) 86; for Egypt, n. 238.

11. S. ERLANDSSON, "*zānāh*," in G.J. BOTTERWECK – H. RINGGREN – H.-J. FABRY, eds., *Theological Dictionary of the Old Testament* IV (Grand Rapids: Eerdmans, 1998) 99.

the root *z-n-y/w* represented in a number of cognate lexical entries, such as the verb *zānāh*, "to prostitute oneself" or the participle used as a noun *zōnāh*, "prostitute," harlot."[12] In fact, only rarely does this root *z-n-y/w* designate anything like fornication (sexual intercourse outside of the framework of a formal union such as marriage) as opposed to prostitution.[13] What is more, if one leaves aside other terms that have been identified as designations of cultic prostitution, as opposed to ordinary prostitution, the only other term that is used, rarely in my reckoning—and possibly only once—is the root *n-ʾ-p*, which more commonly means "to commit adultery," and is a term that needs to be distinguished both from prostitution and fornication. Where a prostitute will be paid for her services (Prov 6:26 says for "scarcely a loaf of bread" NABRE), and the fornicator seeks a liaison outside of marriage—the adulterer (married or unmarried) in the Old Testament is one who has sexual intercourse with another man's wife, and the adulteress is one having sexual intercourse with anyone besides her husband. Of course, as Freedman and Willoughby note further, the terms are not necessarily mutually exclusive, since a prostitute may be married (see Hosea's wife Gomer, Hos 1:2).[14] All the same, it remains that only a woman is the proper subject of the verb *zānāh* with the meaning "to prostitute oneself." The only exception occurs possibly in the theologically (and metaphorically) charged introduction to the narrative recounting apostasy involving the Baal of Peor in Num 25:1, where it is the people (*hāʿām*). Equally interesting, and certainly symptomatic of woman's overall subordination to a man,[15] the *zōnāh*, "prostitute," is only found in biblical Hebrew gendered for feminine.

## 3. The Prostitute as Metaphor

Of more significance in the Old Testament than the mundane phenomenon of prostitution is the metaphoric use of the word "prostitute" or "prostitution." According to *the Dictionary of Classical Hebrew*, occurrences of

---

12. *The Dictionary of Classical Hebrew* III (D.J.A. Clines, ed.; Sheffield: Sheffield Academic Press, 1996) 121-122.

13. *The Dictionary of Classical Hebrew* III (D.J.A. Clines, ed.; Sheffield: Sheffield Academic Press, 1996) 121 cites above all Gen 38:24; Deut 22:21; Isa 57:3 and Hos 4:13f, where both passages have *z-n-y/w // n-ʾ-p*, "to commit adultery"; and Num 25:1, where the use of the root *z-n-y/w* probably also plays with the metaphorical usage to be treated below.

14. D.N. Freedman – B.E. Willoughby, "*naʾap*," in G.J. Botterweck – H. Ringgren – H.J. Fabry, eds., *Theological Dictionary of the Old Testament* IX (Grand Rapids: Eerdmans, 1998) 113-115.

15. So S. Erlandson, "*zānāh*," in G.J. Botterweck – H. Ringgren – H.-J. Fabry, eds., *Theological Dictionary of the Old Testament* IV (Grand Rapids: Eerdmans, 1998) 100.

words employing the root *z-n-y/w* in the Masoretic Text number 101, 41 of which represent a noun formation,[16] not including the participle *zōnāh*, "prostitute." The remainder of the occurrences are some forms of the verb "to prostitute." What is noteworthy, however, is the fact that most occurrences of the root behind the verb *zānāh* and its cognate nominal forms do not refer to the mundane phenomenon of prostitution but bear a metaphorical, or figurative, meaning.[17] In this they refer primarily to Israel's apostasy or infidelity towards God in some related fashion, "prostitution" being, in Goodfriend's language, the "dominant term" in any depiction of Israel's betrayal of YHWH as an illegitimate sexual act (e.g., Deut 31:16; Hos 1:2; 2:4; 5:3-4):

> Do you see what rebellious Israel has done? She has gone up every high mountain, and under every green tree she has played the prostitute. (Jer 3:6 NABRE)

The dominance of the Hebrew root *zny/w* "to prostitute" in depictions of apostasy is not exactly what one might expect, given the importance of ancient Israel's covenantal theology (e.g., Exod 19:3-8; 34:14; Deut 6:4; Ezek 16:8) and the closely allied marriage metaphor (Hos 1:3-9), which aptly highlights the exclusivity of the relationship normative Yahwism demands, with YHWH as husband and Israel his spouse. In the context of marriage, one might well expect to find a term such as "adultery" (*nʾp*) to be more prevalent or, at least, to vie with "prostitution" in a more equal distribution; but it just does not. Goodfriend's explanation of this oddity may well be right. To start with, because the subject of the root *zny/w* when referencing illicit sexual intercourse is almost exclusively reserved for a woman, unlike the Hebrew word "adultery" (*nʾp*), Goodfriend suggests that the use of cognates built on the root *zny/w* is also rhetorically more appropriate for Israel, who in a covenantal context is personified as a woman. What is more, owing to the use of Hebrew *zōnāh* to designate specifically a professional prostitute, the use of words with root *zny/w* also strongly suggests repetitive and habitually problematic behavior that the term "adultery" does not—in fact, multiple "partners selected indiscriminately and without forethought."[18] The "wages of prostitution," then, pro-

16. The lemma *znh*, "prostitute oneself," 60 times, *zĕnût*, "prostitution," 9 times, and *zĕnûnîm*, "prostitution," 12 times (*The Dictionary of Classical Hebrew* III [D.J.A. Clines, ed; Sheffield: Sheffield Academic Press, 1996] 34-35); *taznût*, "prostitution," 20 times (*The Dictionary of Classical Hebrew* VIII [D.J.A. Clines, ed; Sheffield: Sheffield Phoenix Press, 1996] 92).

17. So also S. Erlandson, "*zānāh*," in G.J. Botterweck – H. Ringgren – H.-J. Fabry, eds., *Theological Dictionary of the Old Testament* IV (Grand Rapids: Eerdmans, 1998) 99.

18. E.A. Goodfriend, "Prostitution," in D.N. Freedman, ed., *Anchor Bible Dictionary* V (New York; Doubleday, 1992) 509.

vides the motive, one which the prophets see through as Israel's "folly" in thinking gods other than YHWH provide for her prosperity (Hos 2:10-15; Jer 2:28). And finally, as the *zōnāh* came to be typified as a hardened woman, in Jeremiah's words one with a "prostitute's brow," who will on no account be ashamed of her conduct, so too has Israel been over the course of her history, refusing to heed the message of the prophets and repent until it was too late. In sum, all this suggests that, despite the term "adultery" being perhaps the more appropriate choice "legally," rhetorically "prostitute" was the more effective[19] in its capacity to depict in savage terms Israel's infidelity to YHWH. No term of contempt or abuse was too ugly or vile somehow for the woman whose exercise of her sexuality flouted the norms imposed by patriarchal authority, even as it revealed the thoroughly ambivalent and morally suspect character of that same authority over her sexuality. No longer simply a human being in the construction of an elaborate metaphor, she becomes in its deepest dimensions the expressive vehicle or representation in fact for the self-loathing and anger patriarchal authority as the tenor has for itself.[20]

Again, the primary subject of this figurative meaning for "prostitute" is Israel's apostasy and infidelity to YHWH, as when God speaks to Moses of Israel's destiny in the land they are to enter:

> This people will go on to prostitute itself after the foreign gods in their midst belonging to the land which they are entering; and they will forsake me and break my covenant which I made with them. (Deut 31:16b [my translation])

The occurrence here of the metaphoric meaning "to prostitute oneself" in conjunction with the preposition *ʾaḥrê*, "after," is very common, especially with Israel as the subject and with the object of the preposition variable (Molech, Lev 20:5; the Baals, Judg 8:33; goat-demons, Lev 17:7; abominations, Ezek 20:30).[21] Indeed the construction even goes so far as to extend to the worship of these "other gods" by their own peoples (Exod 34:14-16). Yet while the worship of other gods is perhaps the most typical subject of this prostitution-language in a metaphorical sense, it is by no means the only such figurative usage. So, for example, not being mindful of the commandments is identified as "playing the harlot after your heart and eyes" (Num 15:39); turning to mediums and soothsayers is "to play the harlot after them" (Lev 20:6); to offer sacrifice in the open field is "to

---

19. E.A. Goodfriend, "Prostitution," in D.N. Freedman, ed., *Anchor Bible Dictionary* V (New York; Doubleday, 1992) 509.

20. For metaphor as a construction consisting of two parts (*tenor* and *vehicle*), see I.A. Richards, *The Philosophy of Rhetoric* (Oxford: Oxford University Press, 1936) 77-93 (86).

21. *The Dictionary of Classical Hebrew* III (D.J.A. Clines, ed.; Sheffield: Sheffield Academic Press, 1996) 121.

play the harlot after satyrs" (Lev 17:5-7); and even the Israelites lack of trust in God's promise to give them the land of Canaan is deemed harlotry / prostitution, for which their children will wander forty years in the wilderness (Num 14:33).[22]

Well-known, too, is the framing in times of national crises of Israel's alliances with other nations as the behavior of a prostitute. In this context the allies then can be designated as Israel's paramours and "lovers" (Jer 3:1; Lam 1:3, 19; Ezek 23:9), while the doomed of Zion, desperately trying to find someone to rescue them in her final hours, are likened to a woman rejected by her paramours: senselessly dressing herself in crimson, putting on her gold jewelry, and enlarging her eyes with antimony (Jer 4:29-31). And while the boundary between a political referent for the metaphor and a specifically religious use is not always sharply delineated,[23] it is Jerusalem's alliances with foreign nations, especially Egypt, Assyria, and Chaldea, that come to the fore in Ezek 16:14-15,26-34 and the companion piece to Ezekiel 16 in Ezekiel 23. In the latter, under the figure of two wanton sisters (Oholah and Oholibah) who betrayed the One to whom they belonged, Jerusalem is put on notice that she shall face the same fate that her sister Samaria has already suffered, for her even worse harlotry (*taznûnîm*) with foreign nations. The contrast is drawn even more sharply in Ezekiel 16's depiction (explicit in vv. 44-52), where Jerusalem's "prostitution" is regarded again the more appalling of the two and even to an extent unparalleled among *all* other women who prostitute themselves. For unlike these other women, Jerusalem would actually solicit her clients instead of being solicited by them; and she would give them payments rather than get payments from them (Ezek 16:34)! So, in the end she was in point of fact worse than her elder sister Samaria, who had not committed half her sins, and worse even than her notorious younger sister Sodom, whose only crime was her arrogant lack of support for the poor and the needy. Indeed, so abominably has Jerusalem acted that Samaria and Sodom even appear righteous in comparison:

> Did you not walk in their ways and do their abominations? In a very little time you became more corrupt than they were in all your ways. As I live, says the LORD, your sister Sodom and her daughters did not act like you and your daughters ... Samaria did not commit something like half your sins. You committed more abominations than they did and by all the abominations you committed you made your sisters look righteous! (Ezek 16:47-48,51 [my translation])

---

22. For these and other examples of a figurative use, see S. ERLANDSON, "*zānāh*," in G.J. BOTTERWECK – H. RINGGREN – H.-J. FABRY, eds., *Theological Dictionary of the Old Testament* IV (Grand Rapids: Eerdmans, 1998) 101-102.

23. N.B. the mention in Ezekiel 23 of Jerusalem's idolatry in vv. 7 and 30 in conjunction with her "prostitution" with Assyria and the nations, respectively.

As Walter Zimmerli notes in his commentary on the book of Ezekiel,[24] a marked progression is observable in the severity of the imagery between Jeremiah 3, where divorce is the punishment for rebellious Israel, to Ezekiel 23, where the killing of Oholah and Oholibah ensues at the hands of their lovers, the nations (v. 30). They strip Jerusalem of her garments and her "splendid jewels" (v. 26) to leave her "naked and bare"; expose "the nakedness of her prostitution," her lewdness, and her "harlotry" (v. 29); and force her to drink till she is drunk "the cup of desolation and woe," whose broken pieces she will gnaw until in the end she tears out in desperation her own breasts (v. 33). Clearly, the harsh judgment Ezekiel envisions for Jerusalem achieves its rhetorical impact in these depictions in no small degree, as here, by the repeated reference throughout these chapters to "harlotry" (*zny/w*) and the way it simply dominates the accusations of Ezekiel 16 and 23.[25] In these chapters the verb *zānāh*, in fact, occurs no less than 12 times in chap. 16 and 7 times in chap. 23; the noun *znwt* in 23:27; *znwnym* in 23:11, 29; *tznwt* 11 times in chap. 16 and another 11 times in chap. 23. Surely, that Jerusalem occupies the perhaps unenviable position of being designated in the Hebrew Bible the worst of harlots, leaving not only Samaria but even Sodom to look righteous in comparison (comp. Jer 3:11), is not without significance for deciphering the referent in Rev 17:1, "the great harlot who lives upon many waters."[26] And no less significant is the causal nexus drawn in Ezekiel 16 and especially Ezekiel 23 between the ultimate fall of Jerusalem in 587 and her "harlotry."

Even so, not all figurative uses of "prostitution" in the Old Testament concern directly fidelity to Israel's God. Thus in Isa 1:21 personified Jerusalem, "the faithful city," is accused of having become a "prostitute"; but, as the context makes clear with its referencing of murders, thieves, and the neglect of the widow and the orphan, the "prostitution" envisioned in this context is all about social injustice. And that may also be

---

24. W. Zimmerli, *Ezekiel 1: A Commentary on the Book of the Prophet Ezekiel, Chapters 1-24* (Minneapolis: Fortress Press, 1979) 482 f.

25. W. Zimmerli, *Ezekiel 1: A Commentary on the Book of the Prophet Ezekiel, Chapters 1-24* (Minneapolis: Fortress Press, 1979) 335. The numbers given for the attestation of words based on the root *zny/w* are Zimmerli's. He remarks further that since outside of these chapters this usage is rare in the book of Ezekiel (it occurs twice in 6:9 in a metaphorical sense with regard to the heart and the eye; and other than that in 20:30 and 43:7,9 [*znwt*]), it "clearly does not belong to the widely used vocabulary of the prophet, but is wholly dependent on the simile of the unfaithful wife, which reached Ezekiel from Hosea and Jeremiah."

26. Note that in Jer 51:13 Babylon dwells by the "many waters" (*mayim rabbîm*), argued by H.G. May (*Journal of Biblical Literature* 74 [1955] 9-21) among many others to be the fructifying waters of the primordial deep, imagery also to be associated with Jerusalem (Ezek 47:1-6 [waters flow from the temple]; Joel 4:18; Zech 14:8). See also the discussion by L.E. Stager, "Jerusalem as Eden," *Biblical Archaeology Review* 36/3 (2000) 36-47.

the case in Isa 23:15-17 for the Phoenician city of Tyre, which was something of a "commercial emporium" in the ancient Near East,[27] whose far-flung commerce with the world's kingdoms is labelled "harlotry" in Isaiah, and the profit derived therefrom named her *ʾetnan*, the same term applied to the hire of the prostitute (Hos 9:1; Deut 23:19; Ezek 16:31 passim).[28] Although Erlandsson regards this usage as essentially religious in its reference, based on the possibility that Israel's commercial dealings would bring Israel into contact with foreign deities, that does not seem a necessary inference. One might enlist here in support Nahum 3, in which the feared city of Nineveh is condemned for the "abundance of a harlot's harlotries," one who as "mistress of sorceries" apparently "sells nations (= slaves? Cf. Gen 37:27,28,36; 45:4,5; Exod 21:16; Deut 21:14) through her prostitution" (v. 4) and had more traders (v. 16) than the stars of the sky."

A final consideration with regard to the figurative meaning of "prostitution" in the Old Testament focuses on the entities associated with metaphorical meaning. As regards specifically the nations and cities personified and specified as the agents in a figurative "prostitution," a near exhaustive accounting would include:

a) the land (Lev 19:29; Hos 1:3, of Israel presumably; Jer 3:1ff, of Judah presumably);
b) the people (Num 25:1; Deut 31:16; Hos 4:12; see 1QPesher Habakkuk 5:7);
c) Ephraim (Hos 5:3,4 [Ephraim/Israel]; 6:10);
d) the half-tribe of Manasseh (1 Chr 5:25);
e) all Israel (Judges 8:27); Israel (Hos 4:15; 9:1; Jer 2:20, implicitly: cf. 2:3,14); rebel, *měšubāh*, Israel (Jer 3:6,8,11,12); house of Israel (Ezek 20:30; 43:7,9 + their kings);
f) faithless, *bāgôdāh* (adj.) / *bōgēdāh* (ptc.), Judah (Jer 3:7, 8,11);
g) the inhabitants (= the 7 original nations) of the land (= Canaan) (Exod 34:15-16 their daughters).

Of these, in other words, the only non-Jewish entity attested as the subject of "harlotry" (i.e., "to play the harlot after their gods") is this latter reference in Exod 34:15 concerning the original inhabitants of Canaan driven out by the Israelite conquest.

27. E.A. GOODFRIEND, "Prostitution," in D.N. FREEDMAN, ed., *Anchor Bible Dictionary* V (New York; Doubleday, 1992) 509.

28. Comp. S. ERLANDSON, "*zānāh*," in G.J. BOTTERWECK – H. RINGGREN – H.-J. FABRY, eds., *Theological Dictionary of the Old Testament* IV (Grand Rapids: Eerdmans, 1998) 104.

As for cities specifically associated with this metaphorical usage of "prostitution," there are apparently only four; but, interestingly, two of them turn out to be non-Jewish cities. The non-Jewish cities are Tyre, whose "prostitution" in Isa 23:17, as seen above, has been identified with commercial activity, and, seemingly in the same vein, Nineveh, in Nahum 3:4, the "mistress of sorceries," also above, accused there apparently of "selling nations" into slavery "through her prostitution." Given its prominence in the Book of Revelation, striking is the absence of Babylon from this pair. Not surprising, however, is the fact that the only two Jewish cities cited for "prostitution" are Jerusalem and Samaria, whom we have seen above both "play the harlot" in Ezekiel 23 under the guise of the two sisters Oholah and Oholibah (23:4), even if, as we saw, Jerusalem's "lust was more perverse" than her sister's and "her harlotry than the harlotry of her sister" (23:11). Along with Ezekiel 16's more pointed accusation that Jerusalem's abominations so outpace those of her sisters Samaria and Sodom that they look righteous in comparison (16:51-52), these two texts highlight, in other words, the unique status Jerusalem attains among the handful of cities actually named for their "prostitution."

All the same, as suggested above (n. 23), the accusation of "prostitution" directed at Jerusalem is not confined simply to the author of Ezekiel. Noteworthy in this context is the label of "harlot," *zōnāh*, applied to the so-called "faithful city," a.k.a. Jerusalem, of Isa 1:21 (= Zion in 1:3) in an oracle given in a vision concerning Judah and Jerusalem (Isa 1:1); and relevant too is the charge of Jer 13:27, where Jerusalem is explicitly accused of "lewd prostitutions" on the hills in the open field (see also 5:7 where the "children" of Jerusalem [5:1] are accused of adultery and banding together to go to the "prostitute's house"). If Zimmerli is correct in his surmise referenced above (n. 23) that the language of "prostitute" (using the root *zny/w*) is not of Ezekiel's own making but "is wholly dependent upon the simile of the unfaithful wife, which reached Ezekiel from Hosea and Jeremiah,"[29] one might further extrapolate from these references. Simply put, the designation of Jerusalem as a figurative "harlot" represents in fact traditional material apparently culminating in the hyperbolic and intensified diction of Ezekiel 16 and 23. In the Old Testament, then, it is Jerusalem—and only Jerusalem—who can be credited the "mother of harlots and of the abominations of the earth" (Rev 17:5) even as Babylon fails to be counted among the cities to get the tag *zōnāh* even once.[30]

---

29. W. Zimmerli, *Ezekiel 1: A Commentary on the Book of the Prophet Ezekiel, Chapters 1-24* (Minneapolis: Fortress Press, 1979) 335.

30. The closest perhaps we get is the apparent reference to Herodotus's (*Histories* 1.199) description of Babylonian women offering themselves to passers-by in the precincts of the goddess Ishtar in the Epistle of Jeremiah 42-44 LXX (= Baruch 6:42-44 Vulg.). See below.

## 4. Cultic Prostitution : Fact or Polemical Construct ?

That Jerusalem, and not "virgin daughter" Babylon (Isa 47:1), should bear this dubious distinction finds its rationale, as indicated earlier, in the causal relationship established in Ezekiel 16 and especially Ezekiel 23 between the ultimate fall of Jerusalem in 587 and her "harlotry." As will become clear, it is from this vantage point that the much-discussed phenomenon of cultic, or sacred, prostitution in the ancient Near East and in the Old Testament in particular becomes relevant—a theme that permeates to this day the scholarly literature and frequently is simply taken for granted in handbooks of religion on the Old Testament.[31] While the cultic institution frequently goes undefined, the following represents fairly well the common understanding:

> The practice of prostitution in the ancient Near East seems to have been under no moral censure whatever and was common. A peculiar feature of the Mesopotamian and Canaanite culture was ritual prostitution. To the temples of the goddesses of fertility (Inanna, Ishtar, Astarte) were attached bordellos served by consecrated women who represented the goddess, the female principle of fertility. The existence of sacred prostitution shows that the individual worshippers received in this way communion with the divine principle of life and a renewal of their vital forces.[32]

On this understanding, the ritual prostitution spoken of was simply a form of imitative magic presuming a kind of mythic worldview wherein the fecundity of nature is the consequence of sexual relations between gods and goddesses. Since intercourse among the gods promoted good harvests and flourishing livestock, the ritual was evidently a way of cajoling the gods to act accordingly and ensure the fertility of the land.

Heretofore the focus of discussion has been almost entirely upon the use of the Hebrew root *zny/w*, which is the standard term for prostitution in the Old Testament. But two other terms found in the Hebrew bible are also typically understood as implicated in prostitution while also providing textual support for the practice of the foregoing ritualized sexual performance in ancient Israel. They are the masculine noun *qādēš* and the feminine *qĕdēšāh*, customarily translated approximately "(male)

31. Such was already the judgment of E.J. Fisher, "Cultic Prostitution in the Ancient Near East? A Reassessment," *Biblical Theology Bulletin* 6 (1976) 225-236, esp. 225.

32. The definition, cited by E.J. Fisher ("Cultic Prostitution in the Ancient Near East? A Reassessment," *Biblical Theology Bulletin* 6 [1976] 225) is that of J.L. McKenzie, S.J., *Dictionary of the Bible* (Milwaukee: Bruce Publishing Co., 1965) 700-701.

cult prostitute" and "(female) cult prostitute," respectively.[33] Etymologically speaking, these Hebrew terms, if narrowly translated, might suggest only the sacred or consecrated status of the person so designated,[34] being noun formations based on the Hebrew root *qdš*, "holy" or "sacred."[35] Even so, the translation "sacred prostitute" seemed warranted enough, especially against the backdrop of what was perceived to be a religious practice widespread in Mesopotamian and Canaanite religion, and the evident parallelism observed in several Old Testament texts such as Deut 23:18-19:

> There shall be no temple harlot among the Israelite women, nor a temple prostitute among the Israelite men. You shall not offer a harlot's fee or a dog's price as any kind of votive offering in the house of the LORD, your God; both these things are an abomination to the LORD, your God. (Deut 23:18-19 NAB)

The RSV and NRSV offer substantially the same translation, the only difference being their gender-neutral "cult prostitute" for what the NAB translates as "temple harlot" and "temple prostitute" to reflect the two Hebrew terms *qĕdēšāh* and *qādēš*. In any case, what is decisive for all these translations is an interpretation in these two verses that relies on the rather evident pairing of the "temple harlot" and her male counterpart in v. 18 with the (ordinary) harlot and what is assumed to be a reference to a male prostitute in v. 19. The latter is derisively designated, here and only here, by the Hebrew word for "dog," *keleb*. While in the Old Testament *keleb* certainly may be used figuratively as a term of contempt (1 Sam 17:43; 2 Sam 9:8; 16:9),[36] all the same it must be emphasized that apart from the figurative usage proposed for Deut 23:19 no other word in Hebrew for the male equivalent of the professional female prostitute preceding it in the text, the *zōnāh*, is attested in the Old Testament. That said, the evident pairing in this passage of the ordinary female prostitute *zōnāh* with the female *qĕdēšāh*, or consecrated one, seems specifically calculated to identify the *qĕdēšāh*, like her male counterpart the *qādēš*, as a species of prostitute, distinguished from the professional only by her consecration to the deity and/or the temple. Thus, the traditional translation of the *qĕdēšāh*, or consecrated one, as "sacred, or temple prostitute" results.

33. See here, for example, at Deut 23:18 the Revised Standard Version (RSV) and Jewish Publication Society of America (JPS); New American Bible (NAB) "temple harlot" and "temple prostitute," respectively.

34. With P.A. BIRD, "The End of the Male Cult Prostitute: A Literary-Historical and Sociological Analysis of Hebrew *QĀDĒŠ-QĔDĒŠĪM*" (Brill: Leiden, 1995) 38.

35. "*qdš*," in W. GENESIUS, ed., *A Hebrew and English Lexicon of the Old Testament* (trans. E. ROBINSON; Oxford: Clarendon Press, 1907) 871-874.

36. "*keleb*," in W. GENESIUS, ed., *A Hebrew and English Lexicon of the Old Testament* (trans. E. ROBINSON; Oxford: Clarendon Press, 1907) 476-477.

This interpretation appears to be corroborated by both of the other instances of the term *qĕdēšāh* in the Hebrew Bible. The story of the patriarch Judah's inadvertent intercourse with his widowed daughter-in-law Tamar in Genesis 38 is a case in point. Although he himself had initially identified her, without knowing better, as an ordinary prostitute, *zōnāh*, subsequently in the same chapter Judah's Canaanite friend refers to her as a *qĕdēšāh*, the same word in Deut 23:18 translated "temple prostitute."[37] And it is this same pairing of *qĕdēšāh* and *zōnāh* that comes to the fore also in the third occurrence of the term, in Hos 4:13-14, which quite clearly associates sex with cultic practices:

> They sacrifice on the tops of the mountains, and make offerings upon the hills, under oak, poplar, and terebinth, because their shade is good. Therefore your daughters play the whore, and your daughters-in-law commit adultery. I will not punish your daughters when they play the whore, nor your daughters-in-law when they commit adultery; for the men themselves go aside with whores, and sacrifice with temple prostitutes; thus a people without understanding comes to ruin. (Hos 4:13-14 NRSV)

Thus it turns out that in all three attestations of the term *qĕdēšāh* in the Old Testament, it is always paired one way or another with the ordinary word in Hebrew for "prostitute," *zōnāh*. So whatever else may be going on, at the very least, the writers of these texts consciously associate the consecrated woman designated *qĕdēšāh* with prostitution. And by extension, we might assume the same of the male *qādēš*, to whom reference is also made in the books of Kings (1 Kgs 14:24; 15:12; 22:47; 2 Kgs 23:7). It is by extension, of course, because no information is given about his activity in the latter texts, only the report of his elimination from the land. But even so the reference to his rooms in the temple being destroyed in connection with the reforms of Josiah (2 Kgs 23:7) has been taken by more than one scholar as an indication of his having a role in prostitution, if not sacred prostitution,[38] as the NAB translation makes clear. That reference to Josiah reads in the NAB:

---

37. Note, however, alternative interpretations are available, such as that of J. Goodnick Westenholz ("Tamar, *Qĕdēšā, Qadištu*, and Sacred Prostitution in Mesopotamia," *Harvard Theological Review* 82/3 [1989] 245-265 [248]) who advances some earlier interpretations (e.g., E.A. Speiser, *Genesis. Anchor Bible I* [Garden City: Doubleday, 1964] 300) by arguing that Hirah is attempting to "cover" for his friend Judah by asking for the whereabouts of the *qĕdēšāh* rather than the prostitute, in effect denying the tryst took place and pretending that the kid-goat he carries for the *qĕdēšāh* from Judah is not a payment but for sacrifice, with reference to Hos 4:14. There Israel is rebuked for "sacrificing with the *qĕdēšôt*."

38. K. Van der Toorn takes the reference to rooms in 2 Kgs 23:7 in fact as an indication of the role the *qādēš* had in prostitution at least in some periods of the monarchy, without further justification, even while acknowledging especially the Ugaritic references to *qdšm* designate simply the class of non-priestly temple per-

> He tore down the apartments of the cult prostitutes which were in the temple of the LORD, and in which the women wove garments for the Asherah. (2 Kgs 23:7 NAB)

All this, however, hardly amounts to a compelling argument for the actual existence of sacred prostitution as an institution in ancient Israel. Outside the Bible, in the ancient Near East more generally, both the male *qādēš*, and his female counterpart, are also known figures, albeit not as well-known as one might wish. In thirteenth century-Ugaritic texts from Phoenicia, for example, the male *qādēš* is attested in mostly administrative texts, typically listed immediately after priests, *khnm*, or alongside them; but the only explicit notice of function occurs in one ritual text, where the *qdšm* are designated as cantors. On this basis, as Joan Westenholz notes, von Soden came to the conclusion that *qdšm* is simply a collective term for non-priestly temple personnel consecrated to the service of the temple's deity. However, on the basis of a text granting a tax exemption and new title to one of these functionaries and his progeny, she herself maintains that both the title and the status would be acquired through inheritance rather than through consecration to the god, inheritance confirming that the *qdšm* could both marry and have children. She ventures the thought that perhaps the bearers of the title performed a function in the cult similar to the levites.[39] But that is the limit of what can be said from the Ugaritic evidence—evidence from an area geographically, culturally, ethnically, and linguistically closest to ancient Israel and Canaan—and there is no evidence from this quarter of the *qdšm* having any role in something like sacred prostitution. That there was also a class of females at Ugarit corresponding to the *qdšm* is not at all evident. Although there are two occurrences of the corresponding feminine noun *qdšt*, both attestations are in contexts difficult to interpret and apparently occur as elements of names, perhaps merely theophoric designations.[40]

---

sonnel who have been consecrated to the deity, free to marry and have children and who could be released from temple service by royal decree (K. VAN DER TOORN, "Cultic (Prostitution)," in D.N. FREEDMAN, ed., *Anchor Bible Dictionary* V (New York; Doubleday, 1992) 511). But in van der Toorn's view the prostitution referenced was simply a source income for the temple—common, everyday prostitution. Sacred prostitution, as an element of a fertility rite he regards as a speculative assumption. If so, one must wonder who these male prostitutes are serving? Other males? "Liberated" women? There is precious little data in the Old Testament to suggest a large market for the latter, while the strictures against same-sex sexual relations in the Old Testament (Lev 18:22; 20:13), unlike those in the ancient Near East, are absolute and categorical.

39. J. GOODNICK WESTENHOLZ, "Tamar, *Qĕdēšā*, *Qadištu*, and Sacred Prostitution in Mesopotamia," *Harvard Theological Review* 82/3 (1989) 249-250.

40. P.A. BIRD, "The End of the Male Cult Prostitute: A Literary-Historical and Sociological Analysis of Hebrew *QĀDĒŠ-QĔDĒŠÎM*" (Brill: Leiden, 1995) 44, n. 26.

Conversely, in Mesopotamian texts no male figures are found with this designation; but women who bear the designation *qadištu*, the Akkadian etymological equivalent of the Hebrew *qĕdēšāh*, are well-attested, even if their specific role in the cult in various periods remains somewhat vague. Joan Westenholz, for one, has examined the scattered references stretching from third millennium sources well into the first millennium BCE; and she has shown conclusively that on no account do these include a role in anything like prostitution.[41] What emerges from Old Babylonian legal texts is that the *qadištu* could own property, enter into marriage, have children of her own, and apparently is associated in this period with nursing the children of others. In a literary text, the Babylonian story of the Flood *Atra-hasis*, she is further connected with the midwife, where she may be presiding over childbirth,[42] and this is an association that perdues into later periods as well as being attested also in Assyrian sources.[43] But that is not the only function attributed in the long timespan covered by the Mesopotamian sources, and the *qadištu* in Middle Assyrian ritual texts, for example, appears as an officiant performing a variety of liturgical roles alongside a male priest in the cult of the storm-god Adad in Assur. According to Julia Assante, this cultic role for the *qadištu* continues in fact well into the Neo-Assyrian period, even if in a number of texts she also appears as a midwife and a wet nurse.[44] Sumerian sources from earlier periods (e.g., third millennium), where the Sumerian lexical equivalent for the *qadištu* is the nu.gig and someone who has a high social status, largely concur with the Akkadian sources: the nu.gig also can marry and have children and seems to have a role in fertility and childbirth as well.[45] What is not explicitly attested again is any involvement in prostitution, sacred or otherwise.[46]

---

41. J. Goodnick Westenholz, "Tamar, *Qĕdēšā, Qadištu*, and Sacred Prostitution in Mesopotamia," *Harvard Theological Review* 82/3 (1989) 251-260.

42. J. Goodnick Westenholz ("Tamar, *Qĕdēšā, Qadištu*, and Sacred Prostitution in Mesopotamia," *Harvard Theological Review* 82/3 [1989] 252) citing W.G. Lambert -A.R. Millard, *Atra-ḫasīs, the Babylonian Story of the Flood* (Oxford: Clarendon, 1969) 62.

43. J. Goodnick Westenholz, "Tamar, *Qĕdēšā, Qadištu*, and Sacred Prostitution in Mesopotamia," *Harvard Theological Review* 82/3 (1989) 254.

44. J. Assante, "The kar.kid / *ḫarimtu*, Prostitute or Single Woman? A Reconsideration of the Evidence," *Ugarit-Forschungen* 30 (1998) 44.

45. J. Goodnick Westenholz, "Tamar, *Qĕdēšā, Qadištu*, and Sacred Prostitution in Mesopotamia," *Harvard Theological Review* 82/3 (1989) 258-260.

46. J. Assante (The kar.kid / *ḫarimtu*, Prostitute or Single Woman? A Reconsideration of the Evidence," *Ugarit-Forschungen* 30 [1998] 44) thoroughly agrees with Westenholz's assessment of this Mesopotamian evidence, mentioning also the 1986 study of M. Gruber, "Hebrew *Qĕdēšā* and her Canaanite and Akkadian Cognates," *Ugarit-Forschungen* 18 (1986) 133-148.

Nonetheless, the association was made and continues to this day,[47] demonstrating the validity of Julia Assante's label for the *qadištu* in traditional scholarship as "the quintessential sacred prostitute."[48] And it is an identification driven to a large extent by the documented association of the *qadištu* with the terms *ḫarimtu* in Akkadian and kar.kid in Sumerian, both traditionally translated "prostitute" and the primary definition provided by the *Chicago Assyrian Dictionary*.[49] To be sure, as Assante herself indicates, this is an identification that at first blush might appear irrefutable, insofar as it seems to be supported by lexical lists that make the equation of the *qadištu* with the *ḫarimtu* (who in one Old Babylonian list apparently also seems to be a *qadištu*) as well as with the *šamḫatu*. The latter is another figure also taken for a "prostitute," as in the famous encounter of the savage Enkidu with the "harlot" Shamhat in the Epic of Gilgamesh (Old Babylonian, Pennsylvania Tablet, lines 46-55).[50] That the term *ḫarimtu*, furthermore, in turn functions as an epithet of the goddess Ishtar/Inanna, who as the goddess of sexuality is known not only for her unbridled expressions of passion but also reckoned by scholars traditionally as the patron goddess of prostitutes,[51] only seems to provide additional corroboration of the linkage with sacred prostitution. This is true if for no other reason than the Sumerian equivalent of *qadištu*, i.e., nu.gig, is used not only as a designation of a religious office for mortal women but also serves as an epithet of the goddess Ishtar/Inanna, who, along with several other deities, is described in texts as the "*qadištu* of the gods."[52]

These equations inevitably call to mind again the story of Tamar in Genesis 38, where the terms for "prostitute" and *qĕdēšāh* alike are used of Tamar in the narrative,[53] and where another association of the *ḫarimtu*

47. See, for instance, M. STOL, *Women in the Ancient Near East* (trans. H. RICHARDSON – M. RICHARDSON; Berlin: De Gruyter, 2016) 399-418, esp. 399, 417-418.

48. J. ASSANTE, "The kar.kid / *ḫarimtu*, Prostitute or Single Woman? A Reconsideration of the Evidence," *Ugarit-Forschungen* 30 (1998) 44.

49. "*ḫarīmtu*," in A.L. OPPENHEIM, ed., *The Assyrian Dictionary of the Oriental Institute of the University of Chicago*, *Ḫ* (Oriental Institute: Chicago/Verlag J.J. Augustin: Glückstadt, 1956) 101-102.

50. J.B. PRITCHARD, ed., *Ancient Near Eastern Texts Relating to the Old Testament* (Princeton: Princeton University Press, 1969) 76-77 (trans. E.A. SPEISER).

51. J. ASSANTE, "Bad Girls and Kinky Boys? The Modern Prostituting of Ishtar, Her Clergy and Her Cults," in T.S. SCHEER, ed., *Tempelprostitution im Altertum: Fakten und Fiktionen* (Berlin: Verlag Antike, 2009) 31.

52. This is a point made by W. KORNFELD ("Prostitution sacrée," in H. CAZELLES – A. FEUILLET, eds., *Dictionnaire de la Bible. Supplément*, Tome VIII [Paris: Letouzey & Ané, 1972] 1360) whose full quotation in French is cited in J. GOODNICK WESTENHOLZ, "Tamar, *Qĕdēšā*, *Qadištu*, and Sacred Prostitution in Mesopotamia," *Harvard Theological Review* 82/3 (1989) 255.

53. It appears to be explicitly in the mind of Kornfeld, cited in the previous note.

and *qĕdēšāh* also surfaces, viz., her localization "in the street." Unavoidably, biblicists will recall at this point that in Genesis 38 Judah apparently had determined Tamar is a prostitute from her positioning herself "on the road to Timnah" (v. 14), the location reinforced later in the story by his friend Hirah's query about her of the townspeople, "Where is the *qĕdēšāh* in Ennaim *by the road*?" (v. 21). This is, to be sure, specifically the kind of association with ordinary prostitution that has reinforced in scholars' minds the connection of the *qĕdēšāh* generally with some form of prostitution, sacred or otherwise,[54] and of course the term *ḫarimtu*. But, as Joan Westenholz and others have shown, the point is not simply that the street / road is where the prostitute goes out to ply her trade (see Prov 7:6-10) but that in Mesopotamia this localization is determinative of certain women's social and legal status. Thus, when in an eighteenth-century BCE bilingual Sumerian-Akkadian compilation of various legal material known as *ana ittišu*, a man is said out of his love for a *qadištu* to take her "from the street," the point is less what he might presume to know of her profession from this localization (e.g., that she must be a prostitute) than it is her legal status within Mesopotamian society: viz., that she is not the wife of another man. She and other women sharing the same socio-legal status were figuratively, if not oftentimes literally, "in the street." This is simply to reference the "place where people not belonging to organized households congregated" and which was outside of the normative patriarchal system.[55] In other words, key here is the recognition that in Mesopotamian society a residence, especially for women, functions as the decisive factor in determining one's identity and that residence effectively establishes for a woman, if not a man, her socio-legal definition. How else but in explicit reference to one's place of residence could one establish a person's identity and legal status in a society where people did not bear other means of identification? And so the law collections in all periods inevitably placed great emphasis on the residential entities or organizations to which various categories of women belonged, because only a father's or husband's residence was recognized by law as a site of legally constituted authority, if not responsibility and accountability; and therefore only within the patriarchal household could a woman enjoy the full protection of the law.[56]

---

54. J. Goodnick Westenholz, "Tamar, *Qĕdēšā, Qadištu*, and Sacred Prostitution in Mesopotamia," *Harvard Theological Review* 82/3 (1989) 247.

55. J. Goodnick Westenholz, "Tamar, *Qĕdēšā, Qadištu*, and Sacred Prostitution in Mesopotamia," *Harvard Theological Review* 82/3 (1989) 251.

56. J. Assante, "The kar.kid / *ḫarimtu*, Prostitute or Single Woman? A Reconsideration of the Evidence," *Ugarit-Forschungen* 30 (1998) 45.

But if "the street"[57] says more finally about the legal status of a woman than her profession, this conclusion also opens the door somewhat to the reinterpretation of the *ḫarimtu*, whom numerous textual sources in Mesopotamia place "in the street." Quite apart from any association with the *qadištu*, it has been of course the linkage of the term *ḫarimtu* with any number of women's occupations or clerical religious titles, like the *qadištu*, that, as Assante asserts, "gave scholars false license to flood the Land Between the Two Rivers with professional fornicators,"[58] whose associations mutually reinforced the often-enough flimsy identifications. In an exhaustive review of all the attestations of the terms kar.kid and *ḫarimtu*—in legal, administrative, economic, and lexical texts, marriage and adoption contracts, wisdom literature, incantations and magical texts, as well as popular sayings and literary textual references over the long course of Mesopotamian history—the conclusion that Assante, for one,[59] comes to is simply that both terms have been egregiously mistranslated. The two terms do not mean "prostitute"; indeed she does not believe that in Mesopotamia prostitution was even recognized as a distinct profession but rather fell simply to those belonging legally to the class of "slaves."[60] What kar.kid and *ḫarimtu* do designate, then, is a woman who is neither "the daughter of a man" nor "the wife of a man"—which is to say, a woman outside of patriarchal authority, as the etymology from Akkadian *ḫarāmu*, "to separate," might suggest. "In short the *ḫarimtu* was a woman without patriarchal status, unmarried, and living outside the protection of a legitimate house." She was free to remain a virgin or have a lover—even a series of lovers. She might (have to) live off of

57. "*sūqu*," in E. Reiner, ed., *The Assyrian Dictionary of the Oriental Institute of the University of Chicago, S* (Oriental Institute: Chicago/Verlag J.J. Augustin: Glückstadt, 1956) 401-406.

58. J. Assante, "Bad Girls and Kinky Boys? The Modern Prostituting of Ishtar, Her Clergy and Her Cults," in T.S. Scheer, ed., *Tempelprostitution im Altertum: Fakten und Fiktionen* (Berlin: Verlag Antike, 2009) 31.

59. See here also I.M. Diakonoff, "Women in Old Babylonia not under patriarchal authority," *Journal of the Economic and Social History of the Orient* 29 (1986) 225-238.

60. M.T. Roth does not go so far in denying any place for prostitution in Mesopotamia, while granting the contested nature of the question, referring explicitly to Assante (M.T. Roth, "Marriage, Divorce, and the Prostitute in Ancient Mesopotamia," in C.A. Faraone – L. McClure, eds., *Prostitutes and Courtesans in the Ancient World* [Madison, WI: University of Madison, 2006] 21-39). All the same, she points out that in the millions of cuneiform texts from Mesopotamia, there is only one passage in a song addressed to the goddess Inanna (as Nanaya) known in a number of copies from the Old Babylonian period that makes explicit mention of sex being exchanged for money—which is to say, prostitution in the strict sense (24-25).

handouts but need not; she was for good and bad her own woman, an independent woman, whose sexuality was not regulated by patriarchal authority. That would only happen if she changed her legal status, for example, through marriage, or sold herself into slavery. The daughter of a man, the wife of a man, the slave, and the *ḫarimtu*—these all were mutually exclusive legal categories.[61]

That the *ḫarimtu* is in control of her own sexuality in a way that also sets her apart from the *qadištu* is one of the arguments, in fact, that Joan Westenholz adduces in support of her case against the latter's identification with "sacred prostitute."[62] That is to say in the Old Babylonian legal system the *qadištu* appears alongside other categories of women (the *nadītu*, *kulmašītu*, and *ugbabtu*) who are organized into distinct groups, with a special relationship to a male deity, and have their sexuality regulated by the codes (e.g., by celibacy or marriage). As such, she stood, in other words, over against other classes of women whose sexuality was *not* regulated in the codes, such as the *ḫarimtu*, whose status has just been defined. So once again all the evidence points to the conclusion that nowhere in Mesopotamian is there any indication of a role in prostitution for the *qadištu*, especially within the cult.

That might not preclude, as scholars such as van der Toorn have argued, lower-level personnel of the temples being employed in prostitution as a source of income for the temples, particularly those designated legally as "slaves"; and New Babylonian texts in the first millennium attest to the fact that such temple personnel could be lent out to wealthy gentlemen as concubines for their amusement.[63] Indeed, on the basis of Deut 23:18-19 and a rather vague allusion in Mic 1:7 to Samaria's collection of idols as the "wages of a prostitute," van der Toorn believes that even in Israel ordinary prostitution could be a source of temple income; and this, along with the reference in Prov 7:14 to a "foreign woman" apparently prostituting herself in order to earn what she needed to fulfill a vow, is enough for him to narrow the definition of cultic prostitution to prostitution carried out as an income-producing activity of the temple. However, that only serves to "muddy the waters." That temples might on occasion, or in certain peri-

61. J. ASSANTE, "Bad Girls and Kinky Boys? The Modern Prostituting of Ishtar, Her Clergy and Her Cults," in T.S. SCHEER, ed., *Tempelprostitution im Altertum: Fakten und Fiktionen* (Berlin: Verlag Antike, 2009) 31-32; "The kar.kid / *ḫarimtu*, Prostitute or Single Woman? A Reconsideration of the Evidence," *Ugarit-Forschungen* 30 (1998) esp. 10, 26. In the former, Assante summarizes nicely her earlier work on this issue, which is the basis for the argument here.

62. J. GOODNICK WESTENHOLZ, "Tamar, *Qĕdēšā*, *Qadištu*, and Sacred Prostitution in Mesopotamia," *Harvard Theological Review* 82/3 (1989) 251.

63. K. VAN DER TOORN, "Cultic (Prostitution)," in D.N. FREEDMAN, ed., *Anchor Bible Dictionary* V (New York; Doubleday, 1992) 510-513, esp. 512.

ods, deploy some portion of their sometimes vast human resources in an income-producing activity such as prostitution, is not necessarily implausible, given the complex economic function temples served in the ancient world. But the goal then is economic and not religious; and none of this activity is linked specifically to a fertility rite, for which again there simply is no real evidence.[64]

In light of the preceding, it yet needs to be said that if an institution such as sacred prostitution were as central to the temple cult as scholars have traditionally averred it to be, should one not expect to find among the thousands of cuneiform tablets recovered from Mesopotamia at least *one* reference to the practice in the copious administrative records and documents listing temple personnel, at least from Ishtar's (Inanna's) own precincts? Yet out of 2000 clay tablets and fragments recovered just from the temple of Inanna herself in the city of Nippur, of which no less than 1163 are economic documents from the Ur III period alone, not a single shred of documentary evidence has emerged.[65] Again, unambiguous evidence for the institution of sacred prostitution in Mesopotamia is simply hard to come by, making the accusation that female or male cultic personnel engaged as prostitutes in a sexual ritual strangely baseless and without foundation.[66]

---

64. Note, further, in a somewhat similar vein, that what little we can actually say of the institution of the Sacred Marriage between the goddess Inanna and the god Dumuzi in third millennium Ur as part of the Sumerian royal cult cannot remotely be characterized as sacred *prostitution*, even if it were to involve ritualized sexual intercourse. And as J. Assante, for one, notes, while in the relevant royal hymns depicting the marriage, the human representative of the god can be identified (the king, e.g., Shulgi), the human female surrogate of the goddess has yet to be established with the same level of definiteness or specificity (J. ASSANTE, "Bad Girls and Kinky Boys? The Modern Prostituting of Ishtar, Her Clergy and Her Cults," in T.S. SCHEER, ed., *Tempelprostitution im Altertum*: *Fakten und Fiktionen* [Berlin: Verlag Antike, 2009] 25 and n. 5). Even so, it is not at all clear that the participants would have actually engaged in sexual intercourse; Piotr Steinkeller, for one, regards the marriage between the gods (the divine statues?) as purely symbolic (P. STEINKELLER, "On Rulers, Priests and Sacred Marriage: Tracing the Evolution of Early Sumerian Kingship," in K. WATANABE, ed., *Priests and Officials in the Ancient Near East: Papers of the Second Colloquium on the Ancient Near East, The Middle Eastern Culture Center in Japan* [Heidelberg: Universitätsverlag C. Winter, 1999] 103-137).

65. J. ASSANTE, "The kar.kid / *ḫarimtu*, Prostitute or Single Woman? A Reconsideration of the Evidence," *Ugarit-Forschungen* 30 (1998) 8, n. 9; "Bad Girls and Kinky Boys? The Modern Prostituting of Ishtar, Her Clergy and Her Cults," in T.S. SCHEER, ed., *Tempelprostitution im Altertum: Fakten und Fiktionen* (Berlin: Verlag Antike, 2009) 25, n. 6: in the former citation she is explicitly citing with approval a point made previously by others, including D. ARNAUD ("La prostitution sacrée en Mésopotamie, un mythe historiographique," *Bulletin de la Société Ernest-Renan* 21 [1972] 111-115).

66. See M.T. ROTH, "Marriage, Divorce, and the Prostitute in Ancient Mesopotamia," in C.A. FARAONE – L. MCCLURE, eds., *Prostitutes and Courtesans in the*

That we largely owe both the popularity of the idea and the term "sacred prostitution" to Sir James George Frazer has already been reviewed by several scholars,[67] though the debt he owes to the work of Robertson Smith in the late nineteenth century is also clear. In the course of arguing for the superiority of ancient Israelite religion to that of her ancient Near Eastern neighbors, Smith had already been able to bolster this argument with the claim that "the temples of the Semitic deities were thronged with sacred prostitutes." Supporting evidence, Robert Oden notes, was unnecessary because it just seemed so obvious.[68] But Phyllis Bird makes the further point that what made Frazer's account polemically powerful and influential, in a way his predecessors had not been, was his insistence on the fundamentally religious character of the sexual activity of women with strangers that is reported in classical sources as prostitution at various temples. It was in point of fact *sacred* "prostitution" because this sexual activity was central to a ritual that could be found—or so Frazer believed—throughout the ancient world, one that was identifiable precisely as a fertility cult essential to the productivity of the herd and the field.[69] Of the reports Frazer collected, key of course was that of fifth-century Herodotus in the *Histories* (1.199), wherein presumably he titillated his cultivated Greek readers with his description of what he calls "the most shameful of the practices of the Babylonians," wherein he claims that every Babylonian woman once in her lifetime had to have sexual relations with a stranger in the precincts of Ishtar, the goddess of love, to whom her payment went. Yet given that Herodotus's relatively late report of what is portrayed as pre-Israelite practice seems, on the one hand, to be the source of the roughly fifteen or so other reports from antiquity (up to

---

*Ancient World* (Madison, WI: University of Madison, 2006) 24-25, among others, on the absence of documentary evidence supporting such a use of male or female Temple personnel.

67. e.g., R.A. ODEN JR., *The Bible without Theology: The Theological Tradition and Alternatives to It* (Harper & Row: San Francisco, 1987) 131-162, esp. 135-140; P.A. BIRD, *The End of the Male Cult Prostitute: A Literary-Historical and Sociological Analysis of Hebrew* QĀDĒŠ-QĔDĒŠĪM (Brill: Leiden, 1995) 39-40; J. ASSANTE, "The kar.kid / *ḫarimtu*, Prostitute or Single Woman? A Reconsideration of the Evidence," *Ugarit-Forschungen* 30 (1998) 7-8; "Bad Girls and Kinky Boys? The Modern Prostituting of Ishtar, Her Clergy and Her Cults," in T.S. SCHEER, ed., *Tempelprostitution im Altertum: Fakten und Fiktionen* (Berlin: Verlag Antike, 2009) 26-29.

68. R.A. ODEN JR., *The Bible without Theology: The Theological Tradition and Alternatives to It* (Harper & Row: San Francisco, 1987) 135, n. 12, citing W. ROBERTSON SMITH, *Religion of the Semites* (New York: Schocken, 1972 [1889]) 455.

69. P.A. BIRD, *The End of the Male Cult Prostitute: A Literary-Historical and Sociological Analysis of Hebrew* QĀDĒŠ-QĔDĒŠĪM (Brill: Leiden, 1995) 39. See also, R.A. ODEN JR., *The Bible without Theology: The Theological Tradition and Alternatives to It* (Harper & Row: San Francisco, 1987) 137-138 for his description of the larger interpretive construct underlying Frazer's argument.

the fifth-century CE), and, on the other hand, the unreliability if not biased nature of Herodotus's information about Mesopotamian culture,[70] the basis for claiming a fertility rite underlies the several Old Testament texts featuring a *qādēš* or *qĕdēšāh* is truly slender.

Even as there is no credible evidence of a sexual function in the cult for these presumed personnel, curiously the Chronicler systematically omits any reference to them in his rendition of the relevant material in Kings at the same time the LXX translators appear unsure how to translate the two appellatives *qādēš* and *qĕdēšāh* (outside of Gen 38:21, Deut 23:18-19, and Hos 4:14, where the context apparently dictates for them the translation *pornē*, "prostitute," or a compound of *teleō*, "to initiate to mysteries").[71] Dion concludes in his study that while cultic prostitution may have been little known among Jewish translators of the LXX in the last two centuries BCE, the Chronicler's omission requires a more nuanced explanation. Although a deliberate suppression of "abhorrent memories" of a depraved practice in earlier times might be one, if not "the most attractive" interpretation of his omissions, his concurrent multiplication of the equally heterodox *ʾăšērôt* beyond what he found in his sources suggests to Dion another explanation is necessary: viz., their lack of contemporary relevance even in his day.[72] Nevertheless, might not the irrelevance of the *qādēš* or *qĕdēšāh* in the Chronicler's day actually point to a deeper issue concerning the historical veracity of the Deuteronomic literature's reports in their regard?

If the truth be told, when it comes to the question of whether sacred prostitution ever was a feature of religious life in ancient Israel—or elsewhere in the ancient Near East, for that matter—there is good reason to think that what seemed so obvious a conclusion on the basis of texts such as Deut 23:17-18 is far less than that after all. To begin with, beyond etymological arguments and any lack of documentary evidence outside of the Old Testament, there is just something deeply incoherent, if not implausible, about the whole phenomenon as reconstructed by its proponents. Bird, for one, has observed how it is widely assumed that the *qādēš*, "(male)

70. R.A. ODEN JR., *The Bible without Theology: The Theological Tradition and Alternatives to It* (Harper & Row: San Francisco, 1987) 140-147.

71. P.E. DION, O.P., "Did Cultic Prostitution Fall into Oblivion during the Postexilic Era? Some Evidence from Chronicles and the Septuagint," *Catholic Biblical Quarterly* 43/1 (1981) 41-48, esp. 44-48. Dion also cites the Epistle of Jeremiah 42-44 LXX (Baruch 6:42-44 Vulg.) as indirect confirmation of their ignorance insofar as, in polemicizing against idol worship, reference is made to the Babylonian practice of cultic prostitution as an institution utterly foreign to Judah (47, n. 22).

72. P.E. DION, "Did Cultic Prostitution Fall into Oblivion during the Postexilic Era? Some Evidence from Chronicles and the Septuagint," *Catholic Biblical Quarterly* 43/1 (1981) 47-48. This leaves only an obscure if not doubtful passage in Job 36:14 (the Elihu speeches) as a possible attestation of the *qādēš* and *qĕdēšāh* in a biblical text later than the sixth century BCE (44).

temple prostitute," is a *homosexual* prostitute on account of the asymmetry between the sexes in Israel's patriarchal society with respect to status and power. The very idea of male prostitutes serving women worshippers at the sanctuary in a fashion analogous to the service of the female prostitutes is simply untenable. Not only are, as Bird points out, social norms governing sexual relations focused primarily, if not exclusively, on ensuring the satisfaction of men—note the lack in Hebrew of a masculine secular counterpart to the to the feminine *zōnāh*, "(female) prostitute," or any evidence of such a practice even at the margins of society—but so is the Temple cult equally dominated by male interests. Yet if the *qādēš*, "(male) temple prostitute," must be in this understanding a *homosexual* prostitute, one can only wonder then how homosexual intercourse supports the symbolism of a fertility ritual or otherwise finds a coherent place in an ancient fertility cult.[73] Of course, homosexual intercourse has no place in a fertility cult, at the heart of which is obviously the sexual union of male and female. But at the same time the asymmetry between men's and women's power relations also precludes the interpretation of the *qādēš*, "(male) temple prostitute," as a heterosexual prostitute. Furthermore, if the *qĕdēšāh*, "(female) temple prostitute," represents the goddess who partners with the priest or the male worshippers, who then exactly partners with the *qādēš*? Again, that the latter should exist to serve the needs of the female worshippers—presuming husbands and fathers would even be willing to let their women have sex with strangers—is simply implausible. And just what *male* fertility deity would a male temple prostitute represent?

The ritualized sexual intercourse presumed to function as part of an ancient fertility rite clearly does not add up; and the resulting incoherence on multiple levels renders Deut 23:18-19's construction of male and female sacred prostitutes thoroughly suspect—Deut 23:18-19 one of only three passages in the entire Hebrew Bible to mention the *qĕdēšāh*, the only text in which we get both the male and the female cult prostitute alongside their secular counterparts, and the only attestation of a derogatory appellative for a (secular) male prostitute, viz., *keleb*, "dog." Close textual analysis of Deut 23:18-19, however, only serves to underscore doubts.[74] Along with the thoroughgoing lack of specificity in the verse generally, the verbal precedence given to the female over the male in v. 18's prohibition of the female *qĕdēšāh* before the male *qādēš* is, as Bird remarks, "highly unusual." Suspicious, too, is the lack of real parallelism in the structure and content of these two verses, which obviously function as a self-contained unit com-

73. P.A. BIRD, *The End of the Male Cult Prostitute: A Literary-Historical and Sociological Analysis of Hebrew* QĀDĒŠ-QĔDĒŠĪM (Brill: Leiden, 1995) 41-42.

74. I follow here generally the detailed analysis of P.A. BIRD, *The End of the Male Cult Prostitute: A Literary-Historical and Sociological Analysis of Hebrew* QĀDĒŠ-QĔDĒŠĪM (Brill: Leiden, 1995) 47-49.

prised by parallel prohibitions focused on the cult. In other words, while v. 18 proscribes the very *existence* of a particular class of religious professionals in Israel, v. 19 actually proscribes an *action*, viz., the acceptance into the Temple of the proceeds of ordinary prostitution. Moreover, where the first prohibition is cast in an impersonal, third-person style; the second is framed in the apodictic "You shall not ..."—style more characteristic of this section of the chapter. In other words, these considerations, along with the fact that the following verses deal with the subject of money, lead Bird to conclude, rightly in my view, that v. 18's prohibition of the *qĕdēšāh* and the *qādēš*, like the mention of the male prostitute in v. 19, are secondary editorial creations of the book's author expanding older law. That older law simply forbade, as something abhorrent to the LORD, the dedication to the temple of income from prostitution. The interpretive thrust of the author's additions, however, had another purpose: viz., to heighten "the distinctiveness of Israel" over against "the other nations" (Bird).[75] In Deuteronomy's own words regarding her election and unique status, Israel was "to be a people specially his own out of all the peoples on the face of the earth" (7:6), even "a people *holy* (*qādôš*) to the LORD"—the appellative of course displaying the selfsame lexeme as that which underlies the proscribed cultic offices in Deuteronomy 23.

On this view, then, Deuteronomy's author has to some extent fabricated out of whole cloth for his contemporaries Deut 23:18's prohibition of a class of sacred personnel in Israel whom he regards as leftovers of long-gone Canaanite institutions. As a proscribed class of religious "outsiders," they functioned as projections of religious and social practice over against which Deuteronomy's author could define Jewish identity in his day. Apparently, he did this in dependence upon earlier biblical traditions aligned closely with Deuteronomic literature, such as Hos 4:13-14, where he could find the *qĕdēšāh*, at least—though not the *qādēš*, for which there is no biblical precedent—already used in parallel with the word for an ordinary prostitute, *zōnāh*. The actual cultic function of the *qĕdēšāh* in Hosea's day is unknown, but what is evident today is that "harlotry" in Hosea is simply the prophet's preferred metaphor for Israel's apostasy, with Yahweh as Israel's "husband" whom faithless Israel has rejected in favor of other divine "lovers" (Hos 2). If Deuteronomy's author knows the *qĕdēšāh* apart from Hosea, the text of Deut 23:18 does not display any independent understanding of her role, leading one to the conclude the *qĕdēšāh* might have been simply taken over from Hosea's text. But in the process, she also seems to have been "literalized," insofar as Hosea's *metaphor* of prostitution for Israel's religious infidelity becomes in her regard Deuteronomy 23's reality: a female cultic *prostitute* (probably, as Bird has it, with a male counterpart fabricated to

75. P.A. Bird, *The End of the Male Cult Prostitute: A Literary-Historical and Sociological Analysis of Hebrew* QĀDĒŠ-QĔDĒŠĪM (Brill: Leiden, 1995) 49.

complement her in the verse). Having once belonged to a class of religious women in Israel designated *qĕdēšôt*, "consecrated women," she takes on a polemical identification with (literal) prostitutes.

So on this account, proponents of the view that sacred prostitution was a functioning institution in ancient Israel get things partially correct. They get things partially correct because they grasp in fact what Deuteronomy's polemics intends them to get: how this religious institution and what it typifies is incompatible with genuine Yahwism in those days. Indeed it is a particularly depraved case of the danger posed to authentic Yahwism by the abominable practices precisely of *other* peoples. But again, the imputation of illicit sexual promiscuity in the cult—where it can only appear as especially abhorrent—betrays, as we have already indicated, not a little the suggestion of an effort on the part of Deuteronomy to establish a national identity, as Oden has put it, specifically by the "degradation" of an "other."[76] Alone among the nations, Israel is *qādôš*, "holy," to the LORD (Deut 7:6); and accomplishing this entailed the construction of an "other" that most likely never existed. The fiction was necessary; and the literary fiction became fact.

## 5. Conclusion

The utility of this polemical construct for the promotion of certain forms of identity at the expense of others did not end with Deuteronomy's original audience. If Deut 23:18-19 represents in whole or in part a polemical symbolic construct highlighting ritualized cultic prostitution that on closer inspection at points may even appear absurd or incoherent, this construction nevertheless allowed Deuteronomic writers to assert that some such depravity was, in fact, a recurrent problem throughout the monarchical period. It reasserts itself already during the reign of Rehoboam when Judah in 1 Kgs 14:24 "did the likeness of all the abominations of the nations which the LORD drove out before Israel" and the *qādēš* (sg., coll.), "the (male) temple prostitutes," appear in the land, only to see Asa of Judah then expelling the temple prostitutes (*haqqĕdēšîm*), presumably male and female here (comp. 2 Kgs 23:7),[77] in 1 Kgs 15:12. Nevertheless, it remains yet for Jehoshaphat in 1 Kgs 22:47 to eliminate the (male)

76. R.A. Oden Jr., *The Bible without Theology: The Theological Tradition and Alternatives to It* (Harper & Row: San Francisco, 1987) 132.

77. P.A. Bird, *The End of the Male Cult Prostitute: A Literary-Historical and Sociological Analysis of Hebrew* QĀDĒŠ-QĔDĒŠÎM (Brill: Leiden, 1995) 59. In fact, Bird sees the use of the masculine singular noun in 1 Kgs 14:24, in contrast to the plural in 1 Kgs 15:12 and 2 Kgs 23:7, as in fact a sharpening of the polemic against the nations' abominations insofar as the depravity of homosexual prostitution is presumed to exceed that of heterosexual prostitution.

temple prostitutes left over from the purge of his father Asa. Thereby, for the Deuteronomic authors, Jehoshaphat's reform of the cultus in the mid-ninth century BCE marks apparently the definitive end of this foreign religious institution. But even so, according to 2 Kgs 23:7, the apartments of the temple prostitutes were still to be found in the Temple at the time of Josiah's reform efforts, over two centuries later and on the eve of the Babylonian Exile; and while the Deuteronomic author here speaks only of their apartments' destruction and nothing explicitly, at least, of the temple prostitutes themselves to whom they belong, his very mention of them is surely no accident within the literary orbit of Deut 23:18's proscription of these selfsame religious personnel. On the eve of Judah's destruction, the author has intentionally evoked here the image of their abhorrent practice within Israel's cultus precisely for its "shock value," as Bird puts it,[78] even if technically they were no longer a factor, specifically to suggest such abhorrent practices were still going on in Josiah's day. That he should seek to conjure up images of temple prostitution, therefore, has less to do with a need to document scrupulously the history of a practice whose personnel were supposedly eliminated already under Jehoshaphat before 587 than an effort to rationalize Judah's end and Israel's loss of the land. As Israel had been able to dispossess the Canaanites on account of their "wickedness" and "abominations" (Deut 9:5; 1 Kgs 14:24), so by the same logic would others now dispossess Israel for their wickedness and depravity.

What the linkage of Israel's loss of land to the Deuteronomic construction of temple prostitution accomplishes, of course, is to intensify the feelings of horror, if not revulsion, that are occasioned by the practice on account of the dire consequences it entails. And the worse the practice the worse in turn is the burden of guilt to be borne by the parties responsible for its practice—here Judah / Jerusalem and its denigrated cultus. The Deuteronomic construction of sacred prostitution represents, in some respects, a further development or evolution of the metaphoric usage of prostitution to depict religious apostasy in the Old Testament, a literalization of the metaphor inspired by Hos 4:13-14. Along with the prophet Ezekiel's depiction of Jerusalem in chapters 16 and 23 as the most depraved of all prostitutes for all the abominations committed within her, the Deuteronomic creation of a literary reality for sacred prostitution within Judah and the Temple thus sharpens the Hebrew Bible's own stinging characterization of Jerusalem, and thereby Judah, as "the worst of all harlots" relative to other cities and peoples. With respect to the identity of that enigmatic figure seated upon Revelation's beast, in terms of the Old Testament, at least, the only possible candidate that has the required religious standing, negatively speaking, can be a Jewish one.

78. P.A. Bird, *The End of the Male Cult Prostitute: A Literary-Historical and Sociological Analysis of Hebrew* QĀDĒŠ-QĔDĒŠĪM (Brill: Leiden, 1995) 72.

# JERUSALEM, BABYLON, AND ROME : A TALE OF THREE CITIES (AND MORE)

**Iain Provan**

*Regent College, Vancouver*

Résumé

Quelles sont les implications de la dépendance totale du livre de l'Apocalypse à l'égard de passages bibliques plus anciens ? En prenant Apocalypse 18 comme étude de cas, cet essai soutient que le type de matériel que nous trouvons dans l'Apocalypse résiste largement aux questions particulières et historiques et ouvre plutôt sur des questions générales et universelles. En effet, les questions particulières et historiques nous détournent de ce dont parle réellement l'Apocalypse : la bataille permanente et longuement disputée, tout au long de la Bible chrétienne, entre Dieu et les puissances politiques et religieuses qui s'opposent à lui, même si elles semblent parfois le servir. Ce dont parle fondamentalement l'Apocalypse, c'est de la résolution de ce conflit dans l'avènement du royaume de Dieu et de la nouvelle Jérusalem, dont l'ancienne « Babylone » n'est qu'une façade. Ce sont les généralités, plutôt que les particularités, du livre qui sont les plus importantes. C'est aussi bien ainsi, puisque la nature même de cette littérature limite si manifestement notre accès à toute autre chose. Pourtant, ce à quoi nous avons accès est suffisant pour permettre à Jean d'atteindre son objectif général.

Abstract

What are the implications of the book of Revelation's thoroughgoing dependence on older biblical passages ? Taking Revelation 18 as its case-study, this essay argues that the kind of material that we find in Revelation largely resists particular and historical rather than general and universal questions about the book. Indeed, such questions distract us from what Revelation is really about : the ongoing, long-fought battle, spanning the length of the Christian Bible, between God (on the one side) and those political and religious powers (on the other) that oppose even while sometimes appearing to serve God. What Revelation is fundamentally about is the resolution of this conflict in the coming of the kingdom of God and of the New Jerusalem—to which old "Babylon" is simply a foil. It is the generalities, rather than the particularities, of the book that are most important. This is just as well, when the very nature of the literature so evidently limits our access to anything else. Yet what we *can* access is sufficient to allow the fulfillment of John's overall purpose.

*"Who is Sitting on Which Beast ?" Interpretative Issues in the Book of Revelation. Proceedings of the International Conference held at Loyola University, Chicago, March 30-31, 2017,* ed. by Edmondo Lupieri and Louis Painchaud, JAOC 29 (Turnhout, 2023), pp. 129–142

DOI 10.1484/M.JAOC-EB.5.131931

## 1. Introduction

It is important that I acknowledge at the outset of this modest contribution to our joint volume of essays on the book of Revelation that I come to the topic as something of an outsider. That is, my expertise lies in the area of Hebrew Bible/Old Testament studies, and not New Testament studies. Yet it has seemed to me for some time that when we are dealing with a text like Revelation, which was evidently composed in intimate conversation with the Old Testament and can scarcely be understood at all without constant reference to those prior texts to which it constantly and variously alludes, the Old Testament specialist has something valuable to add to discussions about its right interpretation. The focus of my own prior, published work (now over twenty years old) in seeking to add such value has been Revelation chapter 18[1]—the language and imagery of which, throughout, is fundamentally that of the Hebrew Scriptures, whether in their original forms or in their Greek translations.[2] It is especially the language and imagery of the prophetic passages that are cited or alluded to in the chapter—in particular, the prophecies concerning Babylon in Isaiah 13 and Jeremiah 51, Tyre in Ezekiel 26-27, Edom in Isaiah 34, and Nineveh in Nahum 3. My continuing interest, as a scholar who has spent a considerable amount of time thinking about Hebrew laments and dirges, lies in the *implications* of this thorough dependence in Revelation on such older biblical passages. Specifically, what is the implication when it comes to any attempt to read *history* out of a text like chapter 18? It is this question that I wish to keep in front of the reader of this present volume of essays about the whole book of Revelation, rehearsing once again and refining the arguments of my original paper, but also interacting with published research touching on chapter 18 that has appeared since that time.

## 2. Revelation and Roman Economics

I begin where the original essay more or less began: with an essay published in 1991 by Richard Bauckham, for whose scholarly work I generally have great admiration.[3] Bauckham finds in Rev 18, among other

1. I. Provan, "Foul Spirits, Fornication and Finance: Revelation 18 from an Old Testament Perspective," *Journal for the Study of the New Testament* 64 (1996) 81-100.

2. "... it is a veritable tapestry of interwoven threads from a range of Old Testament passages." I. Boxall, *The Revelation of Saint John* (Peabody, MA: Hendrickson, 2006) 254.

3. R. Bauckham, "The Economic Critique of Rome in Revelation 18," in L. Alexander, ed., *Images of Empire* (Sheffield: Sheffield Academic Press, 1991) 47-90.

criticisms, an economic critique of Rome. The presence of prostitution-language in the chapter is important to this analysis: the benefits of the *Pax Romana* are like the favors of a prostitute, purchased at a high price. For the *Pax Romana* is in reality all about economic exploitation—Rome's imperial subjects give to her much more than she gives to them, although they are too "intoxicated" to understand this. Important, too, is the list of cargoes in Rev 18:12-13—cargoes generally portrayed in contemporary sources as representative of the newly conspicuous wealth and extravagance of the rich elites in Rome. Moreover, the very structure of Rev 18 gives special prominence to imported wealth in general. For Bauckham, then, John clearly wished his description of the fall of "Babylon" (i.e., Rome) to highlight specifically the wealth that would perish along with the city. This kind of view is also reflected in further commentary on the chapter since 1991. Grant Osborne writes, for example, that "[t]he overarching theme" of Revelation 18 "is the judgment on Babylon/Rome for its economic oppression."[4] Ian Boxall believes that "Rome's crime is not simply that of political dominance supported by worship of Dea Roma and the deified emperors ... ; it is also one of economic dominance and exploitation, necessary to support the extravagant lifestyles of a tiny minority of her population."[5] For Gordon Fee, it is precisely Rome's economic policies, "through which the leading families in Rome in particular had become fabulously wealthy during the years in which John was writing," that John denounces in Rev 18.[6] Finally, by way of example, Craig Koester provides his readers with an extensive account of the commodities listed in Rev 18:12-13 and their roles in Roman economic life, in pursuit of the argument that John seeks to help his readers "see how Rome used the benefits of trade to make people accept a social and religious system that was at odds with the reign of God and the Lamb."[7]

A striking consensus exists among many New Testament scholars, then, that Roman economics lie at the heart of John's concern in Revelation 18. For my own part, however, I remain unconvinced that one can safely conclude that this is so. We may begin to illustrate the difficulty with the proposal by noting George Beasley-Murray's perspective on Revelation 18. Like Bauckham and others, Beasley-Murray notes the prominence of merchants in our chapter, but he draws a very different conclusion about its significance: "The merchants of the earth are given more space than the kings (vv. 11-17), doubtless through the precedent of Ezekiel's song, whose

---

4. G.R. Osborne, *Revelation* (Grand Rapids: Baker Academic, 2002) 631.

5. I. Boxall, *The Revelation of Saint John* (Peabody, MA: Hendrickson, 2006) 256.

6. G.D. Fee, *Revelation* (Eugene, OR: Cascade Books, 2011) 243.

7. C.R. Koester, *Revelation: A New Translation with Introduction and Commentary* (New Haven: Yale University Press, 2014) 702-706, 717-722 (713).

longer list of wares in which Tyre traded inspired John's catalogue in this passage."[8] That is, exactly the same data in Revelation 18 are explained in this case in terms of *literary antecedent,* rather than in terms of a specific authorial intention vis-à-vis commentary on *ancient, historical Rome.* For Beasley-Murray, it is not John's desire to address the contemporary situation in the Roman Empire that explains the prominence of merchants in Revelation 18, but rather the Scriptures that provide the basis for his *reflections* on that situation. John Sweet takes a similar line, albeit in a more qualified way: "If we ask why John for his dirge over Rome centers on trade, the answer may be partly that trade, with the foreign ties and wealth it brought, had in the eyes of the Old Testament prophets destroyed the primitive simplicity of Israel's national life."[9]

Then again, does the list of cargoes in our chapter signify an interest on John's part in developing an economic critique of Rome as such, or does it exist simply because it is the sort of entity that one finds in biblical laments and dirges? Bauckham himself tries to establish that the former is the case by noting the ways in which the list in Revelation 18 is not simply modeled on Ezekiel's, and by trying to demonstrate that the detail of the chapter ties John's list more to the contemporary Roman situation than to the biblical text. More recent contributions to the discussion have attempted the same. "Revelation omits items such as tin, lead, mules, honey, goats, and carpets," Craig Koester tell us, "but adds pearls, silk, citrus wood, marble, and carriages, which were fashionable in the Roman world ... It seems clear ...that the goods listed blend items from the Old Testament with those from John's context."[10] Yet, overall it remains the case that some of the cargoes mentioned in Revelation 18 (e.g., wheat, cattle, and sheep) are far from being attacked by Roman writers as extravagances, and that only half of them occur in Pliny's list of the most costly products of nature. There are indeed some surprising omissions (e.g., exotic foodstuffs) if the primary purpose of the list is to impress upon us the wicked luxuriousness of Rome as such—to lay bare what Grant Osborne describes as "the network of maritime luxury trade that supported Roman domination of the Mediterranean basin."[11]

---

8. G.R. Beasley-Murray, *The Book of Revelation* (London: Oliphants, 1974) 266-267.

9. J.P.M. Sweet, *Revelation* (London: SCM, 1979) 270-271.

10. C.R. Koester, *Revelation: A New Translation with Introduction and Commentary* (New Haven: Yale University Press, 2014) 702.

11. G.R. Osborne, *Revelation* (Grand Rapids: Baker Academic, 2002) 631, quoting A.D. Callahan, "Apocalypse as Critique of Political Economy: Some Notes on Revelation 18," *Horizons in Biblical Theology* 21 (1999) 46-65 (46). Callahan argues directly that Revelation 18 is a "critique in apocalyptic idiom of the political economy of imperial Rome" (46). For more along the same lines, see his "Babylon Boycott: The Book of Revelation," *Interpretation* 63 (2009) 48-54, where Callahan

When it comes to demonstrating that Revelation 18 concerns not only Rome's *domination* of the ancient world, but also her *oppression* of it, we find ourselves in even more difficulty, as Bauckham himself acknowledges.[12] For he is very hard pressed to establish the truth of his contention that John saw Rome's wealth as profit from the empire enjoyed *at the expense of the peoples* of the empire. The courtesan of Revelation 18 certainly enjoys an extravagant lifestyle; but where is it suggested that she does so at the *expense* of her clients? Is it not clear, in fact, that the clients have been more than happy with the economic arrangements hitherto established, and that they lament the passing of a trading system that served their own interests?

The question is this: is Revelation 18 really *intended* to have specific external reference to Rome in terms of economic critique? Or is its primary reference internal (inner-biblical), and its nature such that the sort of reading that Bauckham and others offer us is difficult to sustain? It is undeniably true that John's list of cargoes is not simply modeled on Ezekiel's. There *is* substantial overlap, however. Approximately half of the items mentioned in Rev 18 already appear in Ezekiel 27, depending on how exactly one counts.[13] Where there is no overlap, it is often possible to find another Old Testament passage that accounts for the presence of an item on the Revelation list just as well, if not better, than its significance in first-century Rome. One example is the reference to chariots in Rev 18:13. Chariots do not appear on Ezekiel's list, but they do possess a very interesting and important place alongside horses in 1 Kings 4—another biblical passage that describes at some length the goods that flow from the peripheries into the center of a world power (the Solomonic Empire). In this passage, the biblical author already alerts the reader to some of the seeds of Solomon's later apostasy as described most directly in 1 Kings 11.[14] He does so against the background of Deuteronomy 17:16, which forbids the Israelite king from acquiring "a great number of horses for himself" and from making the people "return to Egypt to get more of them." The particular significance of Solomon in relation to Ezekiel 27 is of course that, of all the kings of Israel, it is he who is most associated with trade with Tyre (1 Kings 5)—and it is Tyrian trade that is the subject of Ezek 27:12-24. Solomon is also very much associated in 1 Kings

---

argues that Revelation concerns the systemic relation between "imperialist politics, global trade, and the murderous oppression of the poor" (51).

12. R. Bauckham, "The Economic Critique of Rome in Revelation 18," in L. Alexander, ed., *Images of Empire* (Sheffield: Sheffield Academic Press, 1991) 84.

13. Koester calculates that "[f]ifteen of the twenty-nine products linked to Tyre in Ezek 27:12-24 are listed in Revelation." C.R. Koester, *Revelation: A New Translation with Introduction and Commentary* (New Haven: Yale University Press, 2014) 702.

14. I. Provan, *1 & 2 Kings* (Grand Rapids: Baker, 1995) 53-57.

with slaves, the commodity mentioned alongside horses and chariots at the end of John's list in Revelation 18. It is possible to explain the chariots, then, in terms of literary influence, and without primary reference to the situation in first-century Rome. This is not to dispute that "[h]orses were essential for chariot racing, a favorite form of entertainment in Rome and throughout the empire," and that "[l]arge sums were spent to obtain horses with the speed and stamina needed to win."[15] Still, it is impossible to deduce merely from their presence in Revelation 18 that we are dealing with a specific criticism of one aspect of Rome's economics, rather than with the sort of general criticism that world powers receive in the Old Testament as a whole. Nor is it possible, given the prominence of gold in the account of Solomon's slow slide into apostasy in 1 Kings 9:10-10:29, to deduce that gold appears at the head of the list in Revelation 18 because of its prominence in Roman thinking.[16] Nor can one persuasively argue that the presence of wheat on John's list shows how the general population of Rome survived only at the expense of the rest of the empire, since wheat already appears in Ezekiel 27; nor that John must have selected the phrase "great men of the earth" in Rev 18:23 "as corresponding to the reality of the Roman empire," since it is drawn from Isa 23:8.[17]

As to the just-mentioned "general criticism that world powers receive in the Old Testament as a whole," it is striking that it has much more to do with religion than with economics; economic sins are only ever a function of idolatry in the Old Testament, and it is on the idolatry that the emphasis falls. The stereotypical world ruler in the Old Testament is the one who considers himself to be a god, and his claim to be a material provider for his subjects is one aspect of this *hubris* (e.g., the Assyrian king Sennacherib in 2 Kings 18-19). The economics are never important in themselves, in the biblical descriptions of these kings, but only in terms of what they signify about each king's religious allegiance.

In all, then, I ask the question once again that I first asked in my original paper, convinced that intervening scholarship on Revelation 18 has done nothing to blunt its edge. Can we safely say *anything* specific, on the basis of this chapter that draws so heavily on an Old Testament background, concerning John's attitude to Rome's economics as such? Much still depends as we ponder this question on whether one agrees with Adela Yarbro Collins: "If idolatry and blasphemy were the only criticisms John

15. C.R. KOESTER, *Revelation: A New Translation with Introduction and Commentary* (New Haven: Yale University Press, 2014) 720.

16. R. BAUCKHAM, "The Economic Critique of Rome in Revelation 18," in L. ALEXANDER, ed., *Images of Empire* (Sheffield: Sheffield Academic Press, 1991) 60-61; see further I. PROVAN, *1 & 2 Kings* (Grand Rapids: Baker, 1995) 84-90.

17. R. BAUCKHAM, "The Economic Critique of Rome in Revelation 18," in L. ALEXANDER, ed., *Images of Empire* (Sheffield: Sheffield Academic Press, 1991) 72, 81.

had of Rome, his book would have been very different."[18] This is, however, precisely what I doubt—since my conviction is that what is fundamentally driving the representation of Babylon in Rev 18 is not on-the-ground reality in Rome, but rather narrative reality in the Bible. This explains, indeed, exactly why the chapter largely concerns sea-trade in the first place, when (as Jürgen Roloff notes) "Rome was neither a port city nor a shipping center." As Roloff quite rightly goes on to say: "But here John hardly intended to copy precisely the real situation; rather he wanted to round off the scene of lament by means of a third group, and for that purpose he used the material that Ezek 27:29-33 provided him."[19] Indeed—but there is more to be said! The watery chaos is the archetypal enemy of Israel's God in the Old Testament, set within its bounds at creation, but always threatening to break out and challenge the divine rule. If one is looking, then, for a reason why sea-trade in particular is given such a prominent place in Rev 18, one does not need to appeal to historical Rome's involvement in sea-trade. We can entirely account for the emphasis on the sea in this passage, first with reference to its significance in general in the Old Testament, then to the importance of Ezekiel's prophecy about Tyre as specific background, and finally to the significance of the sea within Revelation itself more broadly. It is from the sea that the beast of Rev 13:1 arises, associated with Babylon who is seated upon many waters (17:1,7). The sea is also the destination for the millstone representing Babylon in chapter 18 (vv. 22-23), as the earth returns to the silence and darkness of the primeval chaos (cf. Jer 4:23-26) that must precede the new creation in which bridegroom and bride, music and light, will be restored.

In sum, then, I see no reason to agree that "[t]he overarching theme" of Revelation 18 "is the judgment on Babylon/Rome for its economic oppression"—and I am glad to discover various authors publishing over the last twenty years who share at least some aspects of my doubt.[20]

## 3. Revelation and Rome—or Jerusalem?

All of this leads on, next, to a second question: not simply whether Revelation 18 allows us access to John's attitude toward Rome's *economics*, but

18. A. Yarbro Collins, "Revelation 18: Taunt-Song or Dirge?," in J. Lambrecht, ed., *L'Apocalypse johannique et l'Apocalyptique dans le Nouveau Testament* (Leuven: Leuven University Press, 1980) 185-204 (203).

19. J. Roloff, *The Revelation of John*, trans. J.E. Alsup (Minneapolis: Fortress Press, 1993) 206.

20. Note, e.g., D.E. Aune, *Revelation 17-22* (Nashville: Thomas Nelson Publishers, 1998) 990: "Rev 18 does not deal with the issue of economic exploitation at all."

whether it even allows us access, primarily, to his attitude to *Rome*? Is Revelation 18 really "about" Rome at all, in any substantive way?

Many modern scholars have believed that it is. John Court says of Revelation 18, for example, that "the context of the Book does seem to demand the application of this picture to Rome."[21] Adela Yarbro Collins, having discussed some of the images in both Revelation 17 and 18, asserts that "[a]ll the images examined thus far not only describe Rome but give reasons for her predicted downfall."[22] Grant Osborne states quite baldly, as if it were entirely self-evident, that "[c]hapter 17 centers on Rome as the 'great prostitute' who is drunk with the blood of the saints, while chapter 18 then looks at Rome as 'the great city' destroyed."[23] Gordon Fee writes that in Revelation 18 and 19 "John at last announces the ultimate demise of Rome,"[24] and Craig Koester is likewise of the view that chapter 18 concerns "the fall of Babylon/Rome."[25] David Aune sums up the overall situation in the modern period: "most commentators assume that 'Babylon' is a code name for Rome."[26]

This is not to say, however, that advocates of "the Rome hypothesis" have entirely prevailed in the course of recent scholarly analysis of Revelation. In my original essay, I drew attention to the work of both Josephine Massyngberde Ford and Alan Beagley, in the 1970s and 1980s, respectively—work that I considered to be important in (at the very least) raising substantive questions about any easy identification of Babylon with Rome.[27] Both scholars argued that it is in fact not Rome that is the focus of the Babylon material in Revelation, but rather Jerusalem and those associated with Jerusalem in the mind of the author. Both interpreters arrived at their conclusions, significantly, through a consideration of the Old Testament background to Revelation that was more careful and more sustained than has sometimes been the case. It is important to restate their arguments in outline at this juncture in my own argument.

Ford notes the way in which the figure of the prostitute in the Old Testament is predominantly faithless Israel, the bride who has broken her cov-

---

21. J.M. Court, *Myth and History in the Book of Revelation* (London: SPCK, 1979) 139.

22. A. Yarbro Collins, "Revelation 18: Taunt-Song or Dirge?," in J. Lambrecht, ed., *L'Apocalypse johannique et l'Apocalyptique dans le Nouveau Testament* (Leuven: Leuven University Press, 1980) 200-202.

23. G.R. Osborne, *Revelation* (Grand Rapids: Baker Academic, 2002) 605.

24. G.D. Fee, *Revelation* (Eugene, OR: Cascade Books, 2011) 242.

25. C.R. Koester, *Revelation: A New Translation with Introduction and Commentary* (New Haven: Yale University Press, 2014) 714.

26. D.E. Aune, *Revelation 17-22* (Nashville: Thomas Nelson Publishers, 1998) 985.

27. J. Massyngberde Ford, *Revelation* (Garden City: Doubleday, 1975); A.J. Beagley, *The 'Sitz im Leben' of the Apocalypse with Particular Reference to the Role of the Church's Enemies* (Berlin: De Gruyter, 1987).

enant promise to her husband. Only twice is a non-Israelite nation called a prostitute: Isa 23:15-18 (Tyre) and Nahum 3:4 (Nineveh). The metaphor is continued at Qumran in relation to Jerusalem and her priesthood, where it is evident that even texts that did not originally concern faithless Israel could be read as if they did. She also notes the way in which this priesthood is widely associated in Jewish literature with economic activity and with bloodshed. Rome, she then notes, is never mentioned in Revelation, but the New Jerusalem is—in antithesis to Babylon. There is also significant use of Jewish temple imagery in Revelation. Moreover, the phrase "great city" in Rev 11:8 appears to refer to Jerusalem, and one might therefore well expect it also to refer to Jerusalem in Rev 18:16. So for Ford, it is *Jerusalem* that is found in political alliance with the Romans in Revelation 18, "trading" (i.e., committing adultery) with the nations. Her exegesis of the chapter then works this out in detail, quite persuasively—not least in her treatment of the list of cargoes, many of which, she argues, would have been used for the Jerusalem temple and its services.[28]

Beagley argues in a similar way, noting for example that when enemies of the church are explicitly referred to in Revelation 1-3, it is the synagogues in Asia Minor and Philadelphia that are the focus, rather than the imperial authorities. The first four visions of chapters 4-8 are paralleled in Ezekiel 5-7, where Ezekiel utters threats against Jerusalem, the house of Israel and the inhabitants of the land. In Revelation 8-11 the city where the plagues of Egypt fall is clearly Jerusalem (Rev 11:8). The striking influence of Ezekiel on Revelation 17-18 generally also implies that the prostitute here is Jerusalem, and the double recompense language of Rev 18:6 clearly recalls Israel/Judah, not Babylon. The view of Jerusalem found in Revelation is in fact already foreshadowed by the Old Testament prophets, who contrast contemporary Jerusalem, mired in immorality, injustice, and apostasy, with a future, glorified city; this is exactly the pattern found in Revelation.

In the intervening decades others have added their voices to the chorus calling for reconsideration of "the Rome hypothesis," and not only some of the colleagues writing in this present volume of essays. One important contributor has been Margaret Barker, in her book *The Revelation of Jesus Christ* (2000).[29] In this volume Barker reads Revelation 17 and

28. Court himself asks a good question that is of relevance to the matter of whether Revelation 18 better fits Jerusalem than Rome: why it is, if a reference to the goddess Roma is intended in the figure of the woman in this chapter, that the author did not "make the contemporary reference more explicit ..., rather than relying so heavily in his description on the Old Testament material. At least one might expect a helmet, which seems to be a characteristic feature of the martial Roma." J.M. COURT, *Myth and History in the Book of Revelation* (London: SPCK, 1979) 151.

29. M. BARKER, *The Revelation of Jesus Christ: Which God Gave to Him to Show to His Servants What Must Soon Take Place (Revelation 1.1)* (Edinburgh: T&T

18 against the background of both the Old Testament and Jewish apocalyptic literature. The seven mountains upon which the beast that carries the woman sits (Rev 17:9), which are commonly read as the seven hills of Rome,[30] are in fact the seven mountains "of the mythic geography of Jerusalem."[31] They are also the seven kings or emperors who had dealings with Palestine (17:10). Babylon is Jerusalem, a doomed city from which Christians are told to flee (Rev 18:4), and also a prostitute-city grown rich (before its destruction by the Romans in 70 CE) by virtue of the collaboration of its elites with Rome. It was into this Jerusalem that the luxury goods described in Revelation 18 flowed—such goods as "would have been common to all the great cities of the Roman empire and cannot in themselves identify the city as, for example, Rome."[32] "Most of the merchandise," Barker notes,

> could have been destined for Jerusalem and even for the temple itself. No unclean animals are mentioned: no mules, even though they are included in the imports of Tyre, and no pigs, even though live pigs were imported into Rome for food. Cattle and sheep could be for sacrifices.[33]

Some idea of the wealth of the Jerusalem temple in the first century CE, Barker argues, can be gained from reading Josephus's account of its later looting in 70 CE.[34] "Babylon" is after this date "fallen"—the old Jerusalem has gone. All that remains in the succeeding chapters of Revelation is to describe the new version of this city: "wisdom returning to her city and the priests returning to the Garden of Eden."[35]

I find compelling much of the argument articulated in this kind of scholarship for reading Babylon as Jerusalem in Revelation 18. For this reason, I appear to have been identified sometimes in the last couple of

---

Clark, 2000) noting especially pp. 270-301.

30. So, e.g., C.R. KOESTER, *Revelation: A New Translation with Introduction and Commentary* (New Haven: Yale University Press, 2014) 690: "Since Rome was commonly known as the city on seven hills, this detail allows readers to understand that the whore personifies Rome, even though the city is not named."

31. M. BARKER, *The Revelation of Jesus Christ: Which God Gave to Him to Show to His Servants What Must Soon Take Place (Revelation 1.1)* (Edinburgh: T&T Clark, 2000) 285.

32. M. BARKER, *The Revelation of Jesus Christ: Which God Gave to Him to Show to His Servants What Must Soon Take Place (Revelation 1.1)* (Edinburgh: T&T Clark, 2000) 295.

33. M. BARKER, *The Revelation of Jesus Christ: Which God Gave to Him to Show to His Servants What Must Soon Take Place (Revelation 1.1)* (Edinburgh: T&T Clark, 2000) 295.

34. JOSEPHUS, *Jewish War* 6.388-390.

35. M. BARKER, *The Revelation of Jesus Christ: Which God Gave to Him to Show to His Servants What Must Soon Take Place (Revelation 1.1)* (Edinburgh: T&T Clark, 2000) 301.

decades as a member of the group that believes that Babylon in this chapter "is not Rome but Jerusalem."[36] This is not quite accurate. I certainly agree on the one hand that scholars like Ford, Beagley, and Barker have provided more than enough evidence to cast doubt on the claim that Babylon "is" simply Rome, if we mean by "Rome" the historical city of that name. I am far from convinced, on the other hand, that Babylon "is" simply Jerusalem, if we mean by "Jerusalem" the historical city of *that* name.

My belief is, rather, that the Scripture-saturated nature of the language of Revelation 18 concerning "Babylon," as "Jerusalemite" scholars have so carefully analyzed it, makes it very difficult to know whether any kind of reference to a particular historical reality is intended *at all* in this chapter, or—if it is—precisely what kind of reference it might be. For the language is largely borrowed from prior biblical texts in which it already possesses a supra-historical quality. It has already transcended particularity, and it has already moved into the realm of the stereotypical, the hyperbolic, and the apocalyptic. The unnamed enemies of the Psalter are not particular enemies, for example, and even a named enemy like Sennacherib, king of Assyria, is as much an archetype of the world power opposed to God as the named King Hezekiah of Judah is an archetype of the faithful ruler of God's people. In such circumstances, it is wise to exercise caution in moving from the world of the text in Revelation 18 to any world of particular social, political, and economic realities beyond the text that is allegedly "referenced" in it. John certainly wrote the Apocalypse in the midst of particular social, political, and economic realities. The question remains, however, as to whether we can ever attain reasonable certainty as to the precise manner in which analogical, symbolic, liturgical prose refers to such realities—if indeed it means to do so at all. My own view is that this is an exceedingly tricky undertaking.

## 4. Revelation and Babylon

Does this matter? Or is Edith Humphrey correct when she asserts that in any case it is "quite beside the point to enter into a debate regarding the intended historical identity of the city" of Babylon in the book of Revelation?[37] The reason why so many modern exegetes consider it *not* to be

36. D.E. Aune, *Revelation 17-22* (Nashville: Thomas Nelson Publishers, 1998) 985; G.R. Osborne, *Revelation* (Grand Rapids: Baker Academic, 2002) 635, n. 2; and possibly (but more carefully), C.S. Keener, *Revelation* (Grand Rapids: Zondervan, 2000) 405, n. 8.

37. E.M. Humphrey, *The Ladies and the Cities: Transformation and Apocalyptic Identity in Joseph and Asenath, 4 Ezra, the Apocalypse and the Shepherd of Hermas* (Sheffield: Sheffield Academic Press, 1995) 115, n. 97.

beside the point is bound up with their conviction that it is the *particular* in any given text that is the most important or authentic thing about it—its particular message, which is bound up with the particular event or situation that once gave rise to it. This being so, it is above all the concern of the biblical exegete to press into the particular. Thus it is not uncommon for commentators on the book of Revelation to be quite well aware of the difficulty of restricting this text to the particular, and to be equally well aware of the universalizing nature of the language—and yet still to insist that "[a] particular event" is, to quote Ford, "the point of departure" for John's description of the beast in Revelation 17, and therefore also for our attempts to understand that chapter.[38] As to the whole book, John's "visionary experience," Chris Rowland insists, is "conditioned by life under Roman dominion," even though it "is not determined by it."[39] Therefore, in the process of coming to understand the book of Revelation, we must begin with the particular events and circumstances in which John was writing, and *about which* (it is often assumed) he was fundamentally or at least centrally writing. But what if the opposite is the case? What if John was fundamentally and centrally concerned to write only the latest act in a great drama that spans all the ages of time, in which the main lines of the plot were already known, and the main characters embroiled in the plot had already been described? And what if John is only "plundering" Rome here and there in Revelation in order to illustrate in his contemporary situation certain aspects of this great drama, as it "touches down" in his own time and place? What if historical Rome—and for that matter historical Jerusalem—are only incidentally of interest to him as he pursues his project?

This is in fact what I believe to be true. Of course there are allusions in the book of Revelation to the social, economic, and political world in which John lived. However, I find no evidence to support the contention that a particular event is in any meaningful sense the "point of departure" for Revelation 17, nor do I think that it can be demonstrated that John's visionary experience overall was even "conditioned" in any substantial way by life under Roman dominion, much less "determined" by it. The point of departure, and the conditioning factors, of chapters like Revelation 17 and 18 lie in the Old Testament Scriptures that have shaped the worldview, the beliefs, and even the language of the author. The particular is only a function of the universal. I therefore think that Leon Morris is much more helpfully precise than many other commentators in how he writes about Babylon in the book of Revelation: Babylon is not Rome, he affirms, "though doubtless to men of the first century there was no better illustration of what Babylon means than contemporary Rome."[40] It is

38. J. Massyngberde Ford, *Revelation* (Garden City: Doubleday, 1975) 281.
39. C. Rowland, *Revelation* (London: Epworth, 1993) 24.
40. L. Morris, *The Revelation of St John* (London: Tyndale, 1969) 180.

good to see such precision also evident in more recent contributions to the discussion, even if one might still quibble with this or that aspect of their wording. Stephen Smalley, for example, encourages us

> not to restrict the identity of "Rome," or indeed "Babylon." John sees both of these in general, not civic or imperial, terms; for they are representative concepts, and images which stand for unrighteous opposition to God in any society or system at any time.[41]

Ian Boxall writes in similar tones:

> to say that Babylon equals Rome is to fail to do justice to the richness of John's vision. More satisfying is the ... interpretation ... which acknowledges the echoes of imperial Rome, but does not regard such echoes as exhausting the meaning of this woman-city. Babylon is not Rome; rather Rome represents the latest incarnation of the oppressive and idolatrous city, the "great city," which originally bore the features of Mesopotamian Babylon.[42]

Both authors are surely substantially correct, for it is typology, and not history, that is the key to understanding the picture of the great city in Revelation. Babylon, like Vanity Fair, is infinitely more than any city that might have served as its partial model.[43] If Austin Farrer can say, therefore, that John has no reason for limiting himself in his use of the Old Testament to prophecies against Babylon, "since the Rome he is denouncing is no more Babylon than she is Nineveh or Tyre,"[44] I should prefer to put it in another way: that the Babylon that John is denouncing is no more Rome than any other city of biblical times, or indeed of any time. The particular is not central to a chapter like Revelation 18, even if universals are inevitably particularized by each generation that takes its ancient scriptures seriously.

*This* is essentially why it does not matter whether we can ever attain reasonable certainty as to the precise manner in which analogical, symbolic, liturgical prose refers to social, economic, and political realities in the book of Revelation generally, or in Rev 18 in particular. This is why it is indeed "quite beside the point to enter into a debate regarding the intended historical identity of the city" of Babylon therein, or for that matter of the beast of Revelation 13,[45] or of any other "character" in the narrative.

---

41. S.S. SMALLEY, *The Revelation to John: A Commentary on the Greek Text of the Apocalypse* (Downers Grove: InterVarsity, 2005) 3.

42. I. BOXALL, *The Revelation of Saint John* (Peabody, MA: Hendrickson, 2006) 244.

43. J.P.M. SWEET, *Revelation* (London: SCM, 1979) 271.

44. A. FARRER, *The Revelation of St John the Divine* (Oxford: Clarendon, 1964) 189.

45. Note here the work of A. KING WAI SIEW, *The War between the Two Beasts and the Two Witnesses: A Chiastic Reading of Revelation 11:1-14:5* (London: T&T

## 5. Conclusion

As an Old Testament scholar, I stand much closer in the end, then, to writers on the book of Revelation like Jacques Ellul[46] than to many others. The kind of material that we find in Revelation largely resists particular and historical rather than general and universal questions about the book. Indeed, such questions distract us from what it is really about. What it is fundamentally about is the ongoing, long-fought battle, spanning the length of the Christian Bible, between God (on the one side) and those political and religious powers (on the other) that oppose even while sometimes appearing to serve God.[47] What Revelation is fundamentally about is the resolution of this conflict in the coming of the kingdom of God and of the New Jerusalem—to which old "Babylon" is simply a foil.[48] It is the generalities, rather than the particularities, of the book that are most important. This is just as well, when the very nature of the literature so evidently limits our access to anything else. Yet what we *can* access is sufficient to allow the fulfillment of John's overall purpose:

> John's visions of the end are those of an impressionist artist rather than the pictures of a photographer. For the most part they defy precision in application. But they convey sufficient to warn men of the end of state-idolatry, and enough about the kingdom of God, to encourage them to faith and adoration of God.[49]

---

Clark, 2005), whose opinion on the beast is similar to my own on the city: "When John's readers considered the beast of Revelation 13, they would no doubt *think* of Rome but ... it is unlikely that they would *identify* the beast with Rome" (266).

46. J. Ellul, *Apocalypse: The Book of Revelation* (New York: Seabury, 1977), who applies the imagery of Revelation, not to a particular city and nation, but to universal collective human realities.

47. "Throughout ch. 18, as well as in chs. 16-17, descriptions of Sodom and Gomorrah, Babylon, Tyre, Nineveh, Edom, and Jerusalem have been applied to the ungodly system that trusts only in itself." These various descriptions "are now applied to Rome"; nevertheless, "Babylon is not just one Satanic nation but a corporate, depraved worldwide system spanning the ages from the cross to the final parousia." G.K. Beale, *The Book of Revelation: A Commentary on the Greek Text* (Grand Rapids: Eerdmans, 1999) 924.

48. G. Campbell, "Antithetical Feminine-Urban Imagery and a Tale of Two Women-Cities in the Book of Revelation," *Tyndale Bulletin* 55 (2004) 81-108.

49. G.R. Beasley-Murray, *The Book of Revelation* (London: Oliphants, 1974) 23.

# *IERUSALEM (OLIM) REGINA*: JERUSALEM'S 'QUEENSHIP' IN SOME HELLENISTIC JEWISH WRITERS

**Daniele Tripaldi**

*Alma Mater Studiorum – Università di Bologna*

Résumé

Cet article examine les œuvres de trois auteurs juifs hellénistiques (Ps.-Aristée, Ps.-Salomon et Flavius Josèphe) à la recherche de références à la royauté de Jérusalem pendant la période du Second Temple. Ce faisant, d'une part, l'article vise à montrer que le langage et le discours relatifs à la royauté dans l'Apocalypse de Jean n'impliquent pas nécessairement des allusions à Rome et à la domination romaine, ni des correspondances avec des dirigeants mondiaux réels ou des villes qui dominent le monde, ni même avec une agglomération urbaine réelle selon nos normes ou celles de l'Antiquité. D'autre part, il est soutenu que, dans l'Apocalypse, la tentative de Jean de défier et de définir la royauté apparaît comme un acte délibéré de contre-propagande prophétique interne au judaïsme. Dans un premier temps, des passages de Dion de Pruse, de l'Énéide de Virgile, de la tradition synoptique et de l'apocalypse chrétienne anonyme annexée à *4 Esdras* et connue sous le titre de *5 Esdras* sont examinés afin de contrer l'erreur naïve qui consiste à assimiler automatiquement Babylone, la grande ville qui règne sur les rois de la terre dans l'Apocalypse, à la Rome impériale. Dans un deuxième temps, les œuvres des trois auteurs juifs hellénistiques susmentionnés sont passées en revue en tant que sources possibles pour reconstruire des images utopiques, idéales ou triomphalistes de Jérusalem au tournant de l'ère. Enfin, quelques conclusions générales sont tirées : le langage et le discours de la royauté étaient utilisés comme des outils rhétoriques, et ne devaient donc pas nécessairement refléter la réalité historique ; le dossier de textes d'E. Lupieri sur la domination de Jérusalem sur les nations doit et peut être élargi ; dans l'Apocalypse, Jean cible et contrecarre apparemment les espoirs de suprématie centrés sur Jérusalem et Israël et partagés par des adversaires afin de déblayer le terrain et d'affirmer sa propre vision d'Israël dans les derniers jours.

Abstract

The article investigates the works of three Hellenistic Jewish authors (Ps.-Aristeas, Ps.-Solomon, and Flavius Josephus) in search for more references to Jerusalem's queenship during the Second Temple Period. In so doing, on the one hand, it aims to show that king-/queenship language and discourse in

*"Who is Sitting on Which Beast?" Interpretative Issues in the Book of Revelation. Proceedings of the International Conference held at Loyola University, Chicago, March 30-31, 2017*, ed. by Edmondo Lupieri and Louis Painchaud, JAOC 29 (Turnhout, 2023), pp. 143–162

DOI 10.1484/M.JAOC-EB.5.131932

John's Revelation do not necessary imply allusions to Rome and Roman rule, nor correspondences with "real" world rulers or world ruling cities, not even with an actual urban agglomeration according to our or ancient standards. On the other hand, it is argued that in Revelation John's attempt to defy and define queenship emerges as a deliberate act of prophetic inner-Jewish counterpropaganda.
In a first step, passages from Dio of Prusa, Vergil's Aeneid, the Synoptic tradition, and the anonymous Christian apocalypse appended to *4 Ezra* and known as *5 Ezra* are examined in order to possibly undermine the naive fallacy of automatically equating Babylon, the great city reigning over the kings of the earth in Revelation, with imperial Rome. In a second step, the works of the three aforementioned Hellenistic Jewish authors are surveyed as possible sources for reconstructing utopian, idealizing or triumphalistic pictures of Jerusalem around the turn of the era. Finally, some general conclusions are drawn: kingship language and discourse were employed as rhetorical tools, therefore, they do not necessarily need to mirror historical *realia*; E. Lupieri's dossier of texts on Jerusalem's rule over the nations must and can be expanded; in Revelation, John seemingly targets and counters supremacy hopes centering on Jerusalem and Israel shared by "others," in order to clear the deck and assert his own vision of Israel in the last days.

## 1. Introduction

More than two decades ago, Edmondo Lupieri devoted a few lines of comment to Rev 17:3 and 17:18, arguing for the suggestion by the late Eugenio Corsini that the prostitute in Revelation 17 be identified with Jerusalem and not with Rome as usually assumed.[1] Lupieri wrote:

> On 17:18 (ἡ ἔχουσα ... γῆς): "This royalty can be a characteristic of Jerusalem (see comments on 17:3), whose ideal reign was seen as extending as far as the Euphrates (see comments on 9:14) or, in a universalistic and/or messianic context, over the whole world."[2]

In order to substantiate his hypothesis Lupieri quoted passages of pivotal relevance from the Hebrew scriptures and later Hebrew writings. In so doing he collected a small dossier of texts as evidence for his assumption, including Ezek 16:13,17; Lam 1:1; 4Q179 fr. 1 4-5; *2 Baruch* 61:7. However important and useful it actually proves to be, this dossier is in my view incomplete. By browsing through selected Hellenistic Jewish writings (in chronological order: the *Letter of Aristeas*, the *Psalms of Solomon*, and the works—and sources!—of Flavius Josephus), I will attempt to flesh it

1. E. Corsini, *Apocalisse prima e dopo* (Torino: SEI, 1980) 57, 438-470.
2. E.F. Lupieri, *A Commentary on the Apocalypse of John*, trans. M. Poggi Johnson – A. Kamesar (Grand Rapids: Eerdmans, 2006) 280.

out and fill some of its gaps. In other words, I aim to show how widespread the idea of Jerusalem's queenship over the nations was among Jewish "educated Bible readers" from the late second century BCE through the end of the first century CE by taking a selection of them as a sample.[3]

Before I delve into the *pars construens* of my argument, a good entry point into the question which I want to address is to preface it with its corresponding *pars destruens*: I intend first of all to undermine the often rash equation of Babylon with Rome and show by contrast that even though—quite obviously—in one way or another Rome openly stands or lurks behind as first in rank and universally acknowledged sovereign of the world, hyperbolical and allegedly Rome-like descriptions might and do as easily apply to other cities following after Rome, down to a Palestinian village. As a result, the identification of the queen of the nations in Revelation 17 with the actual ruling power in the world outside the text will hopefully no longer stand as self-evident as it is often uncritically assumed. This in turn will pave the way to collecting further evidence and arguments in favor of the Jerusalem hypothesis.

## 2. Testing a Fragile Premise

As I said, any interpretation of Babylon as Rome rests upon the more or less explicit, perhaps a bit too naive, assumption that John's description of the prostitute in Rev 17 as "the great city ruling as a queen (ἔχουσα βασιλείαν) over the kings of the earth" (v. 18) simply and perfectly mirrors a tangible, historical "object": 17:18 is the verse providing the explanation for the figure of the prostitute as a whole and as such it must refer to pure "facts," bridging the semantic divide between vision and reality. Given such a simplistic reading, it causes no wonder that Rome turns out to be the only possible candidate matching the requirements implied in this sort of reasoning.[4] Does this assumption however stand a more care-

3. I would expand Lucio Troiani's definition in *Letteratura giudaica di lingua greca* (vol. 5 of P. Sacchi, ed., *Apocrifi dell'Antico Testamento* [Brescia: Paideia, 1997] 20: "By Jewish-Hellenistic literature I mean writings composed by Jews in Greek during the Graeco-Roman period. The production of such writings begins with the Greek translation of the five books of the Torah [traditionally dating to the middle of the 3rd century BCE] and comes to an end in the Christian era"), as to include writings, which were originally composed in Aramaic or Hebrew, and only later were translated into and circulated in Greek. Such is the case of the *Psalms of Solomon* for example. Referring to "Hellenistic Jewish / Hebrew writings," I employ the adjectives "Hebrew" and "Jewish" as practically interchangeable ethnonyms.

4. Two examples may suffice here: in his commentary *ad locum*, D.E. Aune (*Revelation 17-22* [Nashville: Thomas Nelson Publishers, 1998] 959), first rightly observes that in Rev 11:8 the title "the great city" applies to Jerusalem and that vari-

ful reading of ancient literary evidence? In order to answer this question, I will limit myself to a small set of relevant samples.

Second biggest and greatest city under the sun, head of her inland and body, that is, Egypt, exerting control over the seas, bond and global market-place of the whole earth just as though the latter were one single, huge city, unifier of people and races: were it not for the explicit references to

ous ancient cities were designated "great city," then concludes that "it was inevitable that the title, either implicitly or explicitly, would be applied to Rome," as Rome is hidden under the name Babylon all throughout chapters 17-18 and Rome appears to be the only great city literally having worldwide dominion (960); there follows the reference to a collection of parallels from the *Neuer Wettstein*. Along these lines G. BIGUZZI (*L'Apocalisse e i suoi enigmi* [Brescia: Paideia, 2004] 259) makes the attempt to sketch the current political geography underlying Revelation 17, as no other city can be conceived of as having real worldwide dominion but the capital of a multiethnic empire. Already K. KOCH ("Vom prophetischen zum apokalyptischen Visionsbericht," in D. HELLHOLM, ed., *Apocalypticism in the Mediterranean World, and the Near East. Proceedings of the International Colloquium on Apocalypticism, Uppsala, August 12-17, 1979* [Tübingen: Mohr Siebeck, 1983] 413-446 [439]), who proved so sensitive to "apocalyptic" visionary language and style and how they work, had warned against similar modern simplifications in interpreting "apocalyptic" texts. He wondered: "Sind wir Exegeten heute auf dem richtigen Pfad, wenn wir wähnen, der makkabäische Verfasser [of the book of Daniel: D.T.] habe alle seine Aussagen so punktuell und historisch-kritisch eindeutig gemeint, wie wir es aufgrund unseres wissenschaftlichen Gewissens fordern?" (cf. also Koch's remarks on the "Übersteigerungen des real Möglichen" in Dan 8:10 ff. [434-435] preluding to his resumee in 436: "Was wir Deutung [i.e., Dan 8:20-22: D.T.] nennen und auf den zweiten Teil anwenden [i.e., Dan 8:23 ff.], bietet eigentlich keine Deutung, sondern verschiebt bloß die Darstellungsebene. Statt tierischer wie astraler Bilder wird ein menschlich-übermenschlicher Aggressor, vorgeführt, dessen Inkognito gewährt bleibt").

Such a line of reasoning fits *mutatis mutandis* Rev 17:18 as well. In the end, John was no modern exegete or historian either, as he constructed—not re-constructed!—his prostitute, no less for sure than he was or intended to be historically trustworthy, as he created his "persecution." On the construction of the latter and its highly disputable historicity, see the classical, groundbreaking work by L.L. THOMPSON, *The Book of Revelation: Apocalypse and Empire* (Oxford: Oxford University Press, 1990). More recently, R. MUCHA – S. WITETSCHEK ("Das Buch ohne Siegel. Zur zeitgeschichtlichen Referentialität der Johannesapokalypse," *Early Christianity* 4/1 [2013] 96-125) criticized old and new excesses in conventional *zeitgeschichtliche Auslegung* of the *Apocalypse*. They pointedly argued instead for interpreting *Revelation* as John's attempt both to produce an encoded, open, and polyvalent image of the world in which his addressees lived and to charge it with additional cognitive value by resorting to a strategy of visionary radicalization (on the latter see already H. ULLAND, *Die Vision als Radikalisierung der Wirklichkeit in der Apokalypse des Johannes* [Tübingen: Francke Verlag, 1997]). S.E. ROLLENS ("The Viability of Materialist Approaches to Persecution: Revelation as a Test Case," *Annali di Storia dell'Esegesi* 36/1 [2019] 75-94) exposes on a more theoretical level the risks of and the distortions generated by relying excessively on mirror readings of John's work.

Egypt and the clear statement that the author of the encomium is dealing with a city second in rank, such piling up of praises might induce to assume they apply to Rome. Instead, in his elegant prose Dio of Prusa turns out to be extolling and celebrating Alexandria *apud Aegyptum*. I quote from *Orations* 32.35-36:

> But to take just that topic which I mentioned at the beginning, see how important it is. For how you dine in private, how you sleep, how you manage your household, these are matters in which as individuals you are not at all conspicuous; on the other hand, how you behave as spectators and what you are like in the theatre are matters of common knowledge among Greeks and barbarians alike. For your city is vastly superior in point of size and situation, and it is admittedly ranked second among all cities beneath the sun. For not only does the mighty nation, Egypt, constitute the framework of your city—or more accurately—its appanage—but the peculiar nature of the river, when compared with all others, defies description with regard to both its marvellous habits and its usefulness; and furthermore, not only have you a monopoly of the shipping of the entire Mediterranean by reason of the beauty of your harbours, the magnitude of your fleet, and the abundance and the marketing of the products of every land, but also the outer waters that lie beyond are in your grasp, both the Red Sea and the Indian Ocean, whose name was rarely heard in former days. The result is that the trade, not merely of islands, ports, a few straits, and isthmuses, but of practically the whole world is yours. For Alexandria is situated, as it were, at the crossroads of the whole world, of even the most remote nations thereof, as if it were a market serving a single city, a market which brings together into one place all manner of men, displaying them to one another and as far as possible making them a kindred people (trans. Crosby, Loeb Classical Library).[5]

Alexandria is not explicitly extolled as a queen, nor any sound minded sophist and audience back then or reasonable scholar today would expect it.[6] Nonetheless, Dio's praises foreshadow motifs and *topoi* that will be

5. Unless otherwise indicated, all translations from ancient languages are mine.

6. It should not however be dismissed or underestimated that in Nero's time Lucan, *The Civil War* 10.136-171, depicts Cleopatra, *non casta* queen of Egypt, as luxuriously and extravagantly banqueting in Alexandria with sovereigns and the *maior potestas*, Caesar, her body covered with pearls and weighed down by her own ornaments, provisions, raw materials, and precious furnishings coming from all over the world. Insofar she exploited Alexandria's economical resources and commercial assets. As a result of the queen's unchaste sexual appeal and unprecedented magnificence, the poet says, "her rattle terrified the Capitol—can such things be?—/she hurled unwarlike Canopus against Roman warriors,/hoping to head an Egyptian triumph and lead a Caesar captive;/and by the waters of Leucas it was a question/whether the world should be ruled by a woman who was not even a Roman" (10.63-67; trans. Duff, Loeb Classical Library). Lucan's narrative and the discourse underlying it invite comparison with the imagery of the queen-prostitute in Revela-

fully deployed by Aelius Aristides a few years later in his *Encomium of Rome* (197-201,207,213-214,224-226 Jebb; see also Plutarch, *On the Fortune of the Romans* 317a-c and 318a-b). Dio's words thus highlight the versatility of a political discourse centered around "creating" and celebrating world *metropoleis* allegedly well integrated into the current political and economical Mediterranean order assured by Rome—although they were not Rome itself.[7]

Centuries before Alexandria *apud Aegyptum*, another city had been a valid candidate for sea and world rule. It even stood out as a prospective kingdom competing for the submission of the *gentes*: hypothetically, or better, hyperbolically, had Fate not chosen Rome in her stead, Carthage would have not been outshone in her run for supremacy over the world, sponsored as she was by the queen of the gods in person, Juno, her own patron divinity (Vergil, *Aeneid* 1.14-18):

> There was an ancient city, the home of Tyrian settlers, Carthage, over against Italy and the Tiber's mouths afar, *rich in wealth* and stern in war's pursuits. This, 'tis said, Juno loved above all other lands, holding Samos itself less dear. Here was her armour, here her chariot; that here should be the *kingdom over the nations*, should the fate perchance allow it, was the goddess's aim and cherished hope' (trans. FAIRCLOUGH, Loeb Classical Library, with revisions by the present author; emphasis mine).

So far, we still have found no mention of or allusion to Babylon though. We do find one, where we probably would not expect it. Ironically enough—and the more ironically, the more evidently do such claims and motifs prove to be rhetorical strategies not intended to simply mirror historical *realia*—even an apparently remote, unrepentant town on the shore of the Lake of Galilee, Capernaum, is in the eye of the rejected Jesus movement doomed to precipitate into hell rather than be exalted and mount up to the sky far above any human ruler's head (see Mt 11:23 // Lk 10:15): in such a manner the Galilean "city" will soon perish against its own expectations and hopes, and probably boasts of already practicing

---

tion 17. On the Lagidae as prosperous rulers over earth, sea, and rivers see already Theocritus's encomium of Ptolemy Philadelphus (*Idylls* 17.73-111); furthermore, Alexandria *apud Aegyptum* is extolled as the biggest and most prosperous city of all also in the *Letter of Aristeas* 109 and Diodorus Siculus, *Historical Library* 17.52.5-6; finally, in *Jewish War* 2.384-387 the Egyptian metropolis is still implicitly credited with far more resources and chances for successfully challenging and rivaling Rome for freedom and supremacy than the revolting Jerusalem and Judaea.

7. One might further add Aristides's cycle of orations dedicated to Smyrna (*Smyrnaikos politikos*, *Monodia*, *Palinodia* and *Epiphonetikos*): it offers another good example of the rhetoric of fashioning the world's or at least Asia's most beautiful city by remarking that it surpassed and surpasses all other cities (in beauty) and at the same time underlining the commitment of Rome and the world-ruling *basileis* in its maintenance and survival after an earthquake.

justice, not needing repentance, and rejecting Jesus and/or his followers. The fate looming large above Capernaum thus replicates in some sense the destiny of Babylon and her king as short-term would-be ruler of all the nations. As a matter of fact, Isa 14:11-15 is clearly alluded to in this Q passage.[8] It turns out then that Babylon's kingdom prophecies from Jewish sacred writings were not necessarily and monopolistically applied to Rome—or even urban agglomerations.[9]

And Babylon's replicas do not stop here—we will see one more later on. In *4 Ezra* 15:46-51 (also known as *5 Ezra*: late third century CE ?) the Roman province of Asia shows up in the row:

> And you, Asia, who share in the splendor of Babylon and the glory of her person, woe to you, miserable wretch! For you have made yourself like her; you have decked out your daughters for prostitution to please and glory in your lovers, who have always lusted after you. You have imitated that hateful one in all her deeds and devices. Therefore, God says, I will send evils upon you: widowhood, poverty, famine, sword, and pestilence, bringing ruin to your houses, bringing violation and death. And the glory of your strength shall wither like a flower, when the heat shall rise that is sent upon you. A wretched woman who is beaten and wounded, you shall be weakened, so that you cannot receive your mighty ones and your lovers (NRS; with revisions by the present author).

---

8. Cf. R. VAN DE WATER, "Reconsidering the Beast from the Sea," *New Testament Studies* 46 (2000) 246-251, 257. On the excavations in Magdala as a source of both evidences and inferences alike about the Hellenization of Galilee see most recently S. GUIJARRO OPORTO, "L'ambiente galilaico, gli scavi di Magdala e il 'documento Q,'" *Ricerche Storico-Bibliche* 29/2 (2017) 25-55. However, doubts have been raised as to whether modern Magdala actually corresponds to ancient Tarichaea/Magdala: see J.E. TAYLOR, "Missing Magdala and the Name of Mary 'Magdalene,'" *Palestine Exploration Quarterly* 146 (2014) 205-223.

9. I deliberately leave aside Qumran texts interpreting oracles against the prostitute-city of Nineveh in prophetic writings as inner-Jewish polemical references to adversaries leading "Ephraim," i.e., kings, princes, priests, commoners and strangers, astray in Jerusalem and the land of Israel (see for example 4Q169 1-2 II 7-9, interpreting Nah 3:4: "because of the countless debaucheries of the prostitute, gracefully alluring, mistress of sorcery, who enslaves nations through her debaucheries, and peoples through her sorcery"; for comments on this and similar passages, cf. E.F. LUPIERI, *A Commentary on the Apocalypse of John*, trans. M. POGGI JOHNSON – A. KAMESAR [Grand Rapids: Eerdmans, 2006] 262-263 on Rev 17:5). In Graeco-Roman times Babylon and Nineveh seem to have somehow coalesced into a single city in the mind and memory of Jewish *literati* among many others (cf. Jdt 1:1, where Nineveh, the great city, is referred to as the residence of Nebuchadnezzar, king of the Assyrians, and 4 Macc 13:9, where Hananiah, Azariah and Mishael are praised as overcoming the proof of the furnace in Assyria; see also Clement of Alexandria, *Stromata* 1.21.127.1-2). On such a confusion, its pervasiveness, and the possible historical reasons behind it, see now M. LIVERANI, *Assiria. La preistoria dell'imperialismo* (Rome - Bari: Laterza, 2017) 64-65 and 249-250.

This oracle evidently presupposes, on a first level, the Romanization of urban life in Asia, on a second, the identification of Rome with John's Babylon. It thus probably betrays some knowledge of *Revelation* and of the anti-Roman interpretation of the prostitute. Whatever we can actually make out of such a literary dependence, my point is that the new "apocalyptic" text demonstrates how influential and productive the model and brand Babylon, queen of the world, still was long after the first century CE. And so was also the rhetorical strategy of not leaving Rome alone with her Babylonian "franchised" sins and, as a practical result in our case, of aligning the province of Asia with the center of the empire.

All in all, and as a result of this brief survey, I think that the answer to the question I started with might be formulated as follows: whether by mimicking Rome (Asia) or contrasting her ambitions (Carthage), by opposing ideas and practices of an insider "Israel renewal" movement (Capernaum), or by promoting imperial Graeco-Roman culture as well as cooperating to and implementing the economic system at work (Alexandria),[10] any human aggregation form or "political" entity could potentially assert their right of gaining the "queen" and "world ruler" status. As such at least they were described—which means from time to time and case to case: praised or targeted—either explicitly or implicitly. Therefore, the assumption "under test" does not stand the proof of the literary evidence at our disposal, or at least of the texts I quoted. In the end, establishing one's kingdom over the earth should be in my view re-envisaged as a matter of discourse producing and organizing its object rather than as the bare and apparently "neutral" observation of just a fact or an existing historical reality.[11]

---

10. Let us note one possible conceptual overlapping. The idea of "making all men a kindred people," which closes Dio of Prusa, *Orations* 32.36, seems to imply, just seen from a different, positive angle, the same cultural turn which the authors of 1 and 2 Maccabees abhorred the most: all subjects of Antiochus becoming "one people" (1 Macc 1:41) and "assimilating" to foreigners (2 Macc 4:16).

11. When employing the term "discourse," I follow K.L. King (*What is Gnosticism?* [Cambridge, MA: The Belknap Press of Harvard University Press, 2005] 239-240) influenced by Foucault, for whom "the analysis of discourse focuses not on grammatical, logical, or psychological links among groups of verbal performances, but on links among statements. Statements include a principle of differentiation (for example, between orthodoxy and heresy); prescribe the position of the subjects who speak (for example, as apostolic defender of the faith or as deviant innovator); articulate an associated field (not the real context or the historical situation of a verbal performance, but, for example, the coexistence of philosophical truth or religious piety with orthodoxy); and define the status and possibilities for using and reusing elements of a strategy (such as claiming that a statement is eternal revelation from God; institutionalizing such claims in canon and creed, doctrines of apostolic succession, and ecclesiastical authority)."

## 3. From Open Metropolis to Fortress: A Tale of Two Cities

Having hopefully at least hampered the naive immediacy in the argumentation leading to equate Babylon, the great city reigning over the kings of the earth in Revelation, with imperial Rome, I turn to my *pars construens* as promised, and shift the focus on Jerusalem itself and its representations in Hellenistic Jewish writers.

From chapter 112 through 116, the *Letter of Aristeas* (second century BCE ?) delves into describing Jerusalem and Judaea respectively as the ideal city of Aristotelian flavor and its surrounding *chora*.[12] As such they build the positive counterpart to Alexandria and its inland, especially as far as the right balance between city size and countryside farming population is concerned (105-111).[13] Ps.-Aristeas writes:

> We have made this digression because Eleazar excellently showed us the aforementioned things. For the industry of those who do agriculture is great. Also, their country is plentifully wooded with olive trees and cereal crops and pulse, with grapevines and much honey as well. Other fruit trees and date palms are without number among them. And there are both many sorts of cattle and plentiful pastures for them. Therefore, they recognized well that those districts required a high population, and they laid out the construction of the city and the villages proportionally. The Arabs transport into the area a great amount of spices and precious stones and gold. The country is fully suited to agriculture and commerce. The city has many crafts, and does not want for anything imported by the sea. For it possesses convenient harbors that furnish these goods, the one at Ashkelon and Joppa and Gaza, and similarly also at Ptolemaïs, which the king

12. See L. Troiani, *Letteratura giudaica di lingua greca* (Brescia: Paideia, 1997) 25-26 and 173-175; F. Calabi, *Lettera di Aristea a Filocrate* (Milan: Rizzoli, 2006) 15-16, 92, n. 58, 96, n. 64, 98, n. 69; B.G. Wright III, *The Letter of Aristeas: Aristeas to Philocrates or On the Translation of the Law of the Jews* (Berlin: De Gruyter, 2015) 40-41 and 195-197, and Id., "Greek *Paideia* and the Jewish Community of Alexandria in the Letter of Aristeas," in J.M. Zurawski – G. Boccaccini, eds., *Second Temple Jewish* Paideia *in Context* (Berlin: De Gruyter, 2017) 93-112 (102-103 and 106-107). Following Honigmann, B.G. Wright III speaks of "utopianizing geography" (B.G. Wright III, *The Letter of Aristeas: Aristeas to Philocrates or On the Translation of the Law of the Jews* [Berlin: De Gruyter, 2015] 229-231).

13. Referring to Ps.-Aristeas's discussion of the countryside surrounding Jerusalem, B.G. Wright III clearly states ("Greek *Paideia* and the Jewish Community of Alexandria in the Letter of Aristeas," in J.M. Zurawski – G. Boccaccini, eds., *Second Temple Jewish* Paideia *in Context* [Berlin: De Gruyter, 2017] 103): "As part of that description, our author compares Alexandria and Jerusalem/Judea in which he leaves the clear impression that Jerusalem, at least in one respect, surpasses the great Egyptian metropolis," in turn defined—no need to recall—the biggest and most prosperous of all cities (*Letter of Aristeas* 109).

founded. But it is situated centrally to the aforementioned areas, not being very far away. The country has everything in abundance, being everywhere well watered and having great security. Around it flows the river that is called Jordan, which never stops flowing. The country had no less than six million aroura at the beginnings – but afterwards neighboring peoples encroached upon it – and six hundred thousand men settled one hundred aroura lots. The river, which fills up just like the Nile in the days of the harvest, irrigates much of the land.[14]

Central strategic position (cf. 84) enabling to assure safety; autarchy granted by full and ceaseless incomings from sea, earth, animal products, as well as by flourishing human activities;[15] a second Nile ceaselessly fertilizing the soil; king Ptolemy sending gifts to the High Priest as to a peer of his, i.e., a king himself:[16] this is what a functioning and land exploiting metropolis at its best is made of, at least according to Greek canons. Under the rule of a priestly kingship or of a king-like priesthood, Ps.-Aristeas's Jerusalem comfortably fits in the political and economic network of Hellenistic kingdoms, even though not explicitly named a queen on her own yet.[17]

---

14. Trans. B.G. WRIGHT III, *The Letter of Aristeas: Aristeas to Philocrates or On the Translation of the Law of the Jews* (Berlin: De Gruyter, 2015), 227-228.

15. As we saw, the text lists olive trees, cereal crops and pulse, grapevines, honey, date palms, fruit trees, cattle of all varieties, spices, precious stones, gold, commerce and crafts, harbors, mines, bronze, and iron being mentioned a little later at 119: a comparison with Rev 18:11-13,15,17-19,22-23 looks surely promising.

16. According to the *Letter of Aristeas* 98 Eleazar the High Priest wears upon the tiara on his head the βασίλειον, "the sacred diadem engraved upon gold leaf with holy letters" (B.G. WRIGHT III, *The Letter of Aristeas: Aristeas to Philocrates or On the Translation of the Law of the Jews* [Berlin: De Gruyter, 2015] 207). As a matter of fact, the term βασίλειον does not occur in any of the descriptions of the priestly *petalon* preserved in the LXX, but pertains to the king's apparel (see 2 Kings 1:10; 2 Chr 23:11; Wis 5:16; on the *petalon* as royal *diadema* see Wis 18:24 and *Testament of Levi* 8.10). Furthermore, Ptolemy's gifts to Eleazar in the *Letter of Aristeas* 320 include a crown as in 1 Macc 10:20, gold bowls and craters, purple robes (see once again 1 Macc 10:20), fine woven linen: cf. perhaps Rev 17:2; 18:4,6-7; 21:24-26?

17. "Ps.-Aristeas borrows from well-known traditions of Greek ethnography and utopian geography in order to emphasize that Eleazar, Jerusalem, and Judea are every bit the equal of Ptolemy, Alexandria, and Egypt" (B.G. WRIGHT III, *The Letter of Aristeas: Aristeas to Philocrates or On the Translation of the Law of the Jews* [Berlin: De Gruyter, 2015]). I would also add that Ps.-Aristeas borrows from the discourse of Greek encomia: cf. Theocritus's image of Egypt's prosperity under early Ptolemaic rule developed in *Idylls* 17.77-97 and 106-111. For his purpose Ps.-Aristeas might have also been working with Near Eastern city-centered mental maps: Jerusalem is imagined lying at the navel of the surrounding world, which provides it with raw materials for the maintenance of the Temple and the sacrificial service (cf. B.G. WRIGHT III, *The Letter of Aristeas: Aristeas to Philocrates or On the Translation of the Law of the Jews* [Berlin: De Gruyter, 2015] 196, who briefly

Josephus, his sources, and the *auctoritates* he quotes confirm the vitality of such a picture. Let us flip through the pages of his *Jewish Antiquities* and take a closer look at some highly significant passages:

12.6: (fragment from Agatharchides of Cnidus): fourth-third century BCE Jerusalem is "a great and strong city"; *Against Apion* 1.273 adds that it is prosperous and located in a region richer than Egypt.

12.140-141: (from a letter of Antiochus the Great): the Seleucid king grants Jerusalem tax-free provisions of cattle, wine, oil, incense, silver coins, wheat flour, wheat, salt, wood from Judea and Lebanon.[18] Four paragraphs earlier (136-137) Josephus had inserted into his own account a passage from the sixteenth book of Polybius's *Histories* marginally alluding to the ἐπιφάνεια ("renown, fame") of the Temple in Jerusalem.

13.77-78: the Temple in Jerusalem is "so ancient and the most eminent sanctuary on earth ... All the kings of Asia honored the

handles the subject; on such mental maps, see M. Liverani, *Antico Oriente. Storia, società, economia*, [Rome – Bari: Laterza, 2009] 32-33).

18. On the motif of kings, governors and merchants sending gifts and/or "tributes" to (the powerful kings of) Jerusalem, see already 1 Kings 10:14 // 2 Chr 9:13 (gold and silver brought by the kings of Arabia!); 1 Esdras LXX 2:22; 6:28-29; 8:19-20,63-64; Eupolemus in Eusebius, *Preparation for the Gospel* 9.30.1-34.3 (the Judean kingdom of Saul, David, and Solomon is here stylized as a contemporary Hellenistic state and dynasty!). Cf. also 1 Macc 15:29-36 as an echo in Maccabean propaganda. Roughly contemporary to Josephus and John, *2 Baruch* sees Jerusalem's kingship over the nations extending throughout the city's history: in Solomon's times, as reported in the aforementioned passages from 1 Kings, 2 Chronicles and Eupolemus, the land of Israel "was glorified above all the lands and the city of Sion ruled then over all the lands and regions" (*2 Baruch* 61:7); after Sion has been delivered to the Babylonians, all the idolatrous nations wonder whether "the one who used to trample on for a long time has been trampled on and the one who used to subdue has been subdued" (67:2); later on, Sion will be rebuilt and "once again the nations will come to glorify it, not fully though, as in former times" (68:5-6). Two important points for our discussion emerge from *2 Baruch*: first, given that it is undisputed that in *2 Baruch* the destruction of Solomon's temple by the Babylonians stands for the destruction of the Herodian temple by the Romans, it follows that the image of the subduing and trampling first Temple Jerusalem reflects a Jewish triumphalist and royal perception of second Temple Jerusalem; second, even if 68:5-6 only were meant to apply to Second Temple Jerusalem, nonetheless, any "tribute" paid to Sion by the nations, whether in terms of glory and honor or of raw material and artifacts, cannot be understood just as the expression of religious piety and devotion, but must be primarily taken into consideration as an act of political homage. In Jewish eyes this in turn equals to acknowledging Jerusalem's sovereignty over lands and regions (cf. especially *2 Baruch* 61:7). As a matter of fact, in the loyalist view of Justus of Tiberias the kingdom of the Jews ends with the death of Herod Agrippa, who enjoyed the favors of the Roman emperors from Nero to Domitian or Trajan (see Photius, *Library* 33.6b.26-32).

Temple with offerings and magnificent gifts" (cf. 20.49) ; moreover, in 14.186, Josephus explicitly states that he aims to highlight how much Roman emperors esteemed and supported the Jews, differing in no respect from the kings of Asia and Europe who preceded them.

14.110 : it should cause no wonder that the Temple in Jerusalem is so rich, as Jews spread throughout both Asia and Europe send offerings. The two proof-texts validating this assertion are taken from Strabo. I quote only the latter (115) : "it is not easy to find any place in the habitable world which has not received this nation and in which it has not made its power felt."[19]

15.268-276 : Herod introduces *agones* in honor of Augustus and builds a theater and an amphitheater in Jerusalem : athletes and visitors from all over the world flow into the city ; inscriptions and trophies of gold and silver, costly garments and precious stone apparels are exhibited, beasts and men fight to death (cf. 16.136-141 about Caesarea).[20]

15.412 : the Royal Portico in the Herodian Temple is so noteworthy that it has no equal under the sun.

In *Against Apion* 2.134, Josephus himself provides us with the key to understand the whole story : contrary to the Egyptians, the Jews lived free under the Greeks and ruled the surrounding cities for almost 120 years until the times of Pompey the Great.[21] Even after the Romans came, the kings of the Jews stood side by side with them as allies and friends,

19. Καὶ τόπον οὐκ ἔστι ῥᾳδίως εὑρεῖν τῆς οἰκουμένης, ὃς οὐ παραδέδεκται τοῦτο τὸ φῦλον μηδ'ἐπικρατεῖται ὑπ'αὐτοῦ (*Josephus in Nine Volumes*, with an English Translation by R. Marcus, VII: *Jewish Antiquities*, Books XII-XIV [London - Cambridge, MA: William Heinemann Ltd. - Harvard University Press, 1961] 508-509, with n. *c* discussing all the different options available for translation). Cf. Philo, *On the Embassy to Gaius* 282, who speaks of continents and main islands alike replete with Jewish colonies.

20. In *Jewish War* 1.401-428, probably relying on Herodian propaganda, Josephus had already praised Herod the Great as ideal Hellenistic king for his *euergesiai* to cities all over the Roman world. Such acts showed his innate *philotimia* and *megalonoia*. As the last sentence in 428 makes clear, by elaborating this praise Josephus—or his source—attempts to counter any persistent suspicion about Herod's aspirations for something more and higher than *basileia* over Judaea, i.e., for extending his control over further cities by conferring upon them greater benefits than those which they received from their own rulers.

21. Presenting queen Salome Alexandra's (76-67 BCE) military politics, in *Jewish War* 1.113 Josephus had earlier gone as far as to say that by doubling her army and collecting a huge body of foreign mercenaries she not only strengthened her own *ethnos*, but even scared foreign rulers (οἱ ἔξωθεν δυνάσται) as a formidable foe : in

whereas all other kings were defeated in war and subdued.[22] The apologetic move which Josephus is making in propagating this vision of deep-ranging historical events is two-folded: on the one hand, in Rome he had to counter accusations coming from the Jewish side of being anti-monarchic and anti-Roman and thus having sided with the rebels;[23] on the other hand, he had to meet the need of responding to anti-Jewish polemists as well. He therefore re-asserted along with his own his *ethnos*'s integration into Graeco-Roman world and culture and into imperial urban life and political structures alike—a re-assertion which "apocalypticists" and rebels certainly did not share or approve of.[24]

Nonetheless, the overall picture Josephus draws is not as irenic and tension free as it might seem at first sight, nor the reconstruction of such a picture can be limited to the passages I have quoted so far. In *Against Apion* 1.190-199 (citation from Hecataeus of Abdera), 209 and 2.232-233 (citation from Agatharchides), the image of Jerusalem as a stronghold and the "strongmindedness" of the Jews in their readiness to die as long as they do not transgress their ancestral laws mirror each other. Josephus shapes the former and insists upon the latter as tokens of the uncompromising willingness on the Jewish side to keep oneself pure and unassimilated and to prove not to be born to serve and easy

---

so doing—the historian concludes—she managed to rule (ἐκράτει) the others but was herself ruled by the Pharisees.

22. On Jerusalem as "royal city" cf. *Jewish War* 4.89. But already in the lengthy prologue to this work, Josephus made a big point of underlining Jewish greatness (1.7-8), defining Jerusalem as the most prosperous city on earth under Roman rule (1.59-60), and sketching the Jews as conquerors from ancient times (1.94-95). Later, in *Jewish Antiquities* 17.277 he even seems to be still implicitly dreaming of a national kingdom under Rome's patronage as a stabilizing political arrangement in Judea (cf. also *Jewish War* 2.22 and L. Troiani, *Letteratura giudaica di lingua greca* [Brescia: Paideia, 1997] 61).

23. L. Troiani, *Letteratura giudaica di lingua greca* (Brescia: Paideia, 1997) 60-62, 64-65, and Id., "Il 'tradimento' di Giuseppe," in M.B. Durante Mangoni – D. Garribba – M. Vitelli, eds., *Gesù e la storia. Percorsi sulle origini del Cristianesimo. Studi in onore di Giorgio Jossa* (Trapani: Il Pozzo di Giacobbe, 2015) 151-158 (154-158). On Josephus's silences regarding "apocalypses," cf. also P. Piovanelli, "*Odio humani generis*. Apocalypticiens messianistes et historiens intégrés à l'époque des Guerres des Judéens," in P. Piovanelli, ed., *Apocryphités. Études sur les textes et les traditions scripturaires du judaïsme et du christianisme anciens* (Turnhout: Brepols, 2016) 209-227, 211-212, 221, and notes. For the motif of the "great and famous Jerusalem" in Flavian propaganda see O. Andrei, *Rileggere 'Roma' nell'*Apocalisse. *Una riflessione sul rapporto 'testo-contesto'* (Arezzo: Università degli Studi di Siena-Facoltà di Lettere e Filosofia di Arezzo, 2007) 17-23.

24. See for example Nicolaus of Damascus's speech before Marcus Vipsanius Agrippa in *Jewish Antiquities* 16.31-57 as evidence for Josephus's consciousness of the role of Hellenistic Jewish elites in the Diaspora and as a specimen of his strategy alike (L. Troiani, *Letteratura giudaica di lingua greca* [Brescia: Paideia, 1997] 58 and 62-64).

to enslave as Egypt and the Egyptians are (1.276-277). Furthermore, in the *Antiquitates* Josephus often voices criticism of priestly elites and influential families, Herodian kings, military leaders and commoners for disobeying the Law and abandoning Jewish traditions and customs (see, e.g., 12.240-241, 286; 13.2, 4; 15.267, 281; 18.9, 340).[25] Seen from this perspective as integral part of a discourse on cultural alterity and religious zeal, Josephus's remarks do echo and probably re-cast in heavily weakened form arguments from the anti-Herodian, anti-priestly and anti-Roman repertoire of the Jewish rebels (cf. especially *Jewish War* 3.350-360 and 4.143-192).[26]

More than a century earlier an anonymous Jew was not so nuanced and politically ambiguous in his judgment about the last Hasmonean rulers. The author of the *Psalms of Solomon* (48-37 BCE ?) foresees *ex eventu* the decline of the last Hasmoneans and interprets the Roman siege of Jerusalem as general coming to terms with the harsh reality behind the appearances. He thus makes the queen literally wear new clothes: Jerusalem and her children once boasted that they had been exalted up to the stars—just like the king of Babylon in Isa 14:11-15 and Capernaum in Mt 11:23 // Lk 10:15 !—, their justice, riches and glory overflowing the inhabited earth (*Psalms of Solomon* 1:2-5); now they show up stripped off of their splendid garments, while their secret sins and iniquities committed as well as the impurities contracted are exposed as far more abominable than those perpetrated by the abhorred nations (1:6-8; 2:11-13,18-21; 4:3-6,9-13; 8:7-13; 16:7-8).[27] As a result, in his furious wrath God reached out a cup of deceit to Jerusalem, her land and its leaders.

---

25. A brief commentary of these passages is offered in D. TRIPALDI, "From Philo to Areimanios: Jewish Traditions and Intellectual Profiles in 1st – 3rd century CE Alexandria in the Light of the *Apocryphon of John*," in P. LANFRANCHI – J. VERHEYDEN, eds., *Jews and Christians in Antiquity. A Regional Perspective* (Leuven: Peeters, 2018) 101-119 (104-106).

26. Cf. L. TROIANI, *Letteratura giudaica di lingua greca* (Brescia: Paideia, 1997) 65.

27. The catalogue of sins amounts *de facto* to an almost obsessive refrain of allegations of *porneia*, *moicheia*, and profanation of the sanctuary, which was everything but unusual in second Temple Jewish literature: see Sir 9:1-9; 26:8-12; 42:9-14; *Jubilees* 22.16-21 and 23.14-18; *Testament of Levi* 14.5-8 and 17.11; *Testament of Judah* 13-16 and 23.2; *Testament of Dan* 5.5-7; *Testament of Naphtali* 4. I wonder whether all mentions of sexual sins are to be interpreted as references to women and youngsters freeing themselves from parental and male control as well as to the growing inclination towards indulging in too much of a Hellenizing or Hellenic-like symposial activity and sexual behavior (cf. Ps.-Phocylides, *Sentences* 177-183, 189-192, 198, 210-217). Seen from another, yet complementary, perspective, it might have all revolved around diverging and conflicting *halakhahs* about sex, marriage, divorce, incest and adultery, Temple incomes, and service (cf. *Damascus Document* A col. II.IV-VI).

Hence Israel's leaders welcomed the man from the West, a δράκων, actually sent to bring about their own destruction (cf. 8:15-21 with 2:25-26). Any Revelation scholar should feel quite at home with all such imagery. Were it not enough, the *Psalms of Solomon* are replete with further correspondences to John's worldview, socio-cultural imagination, and literary "creations." For instance :

- elects serving in front of God as priests (2:36) // Rev 7:9-10,13-15 ;
- tribulation, sound of trumpet announcing destruction, war and desolation overwhelming Jerusalem (8:1-2) // Rev 7:14 ; 8:2,6 ; 9:1-4,13 ; 11:1-2,7-8 ;
- trumpets blowing in Zion to gather the elect (11:1) // Rev 11:15-18 and 14:1 ;
- Jerusalem invited to stand on a high place and wear her former glory (11:2-7), as nations flow to her to see God's and his anointed One's glory (17:31-33) // Rev 21:2,22-26 ;
- elects as rejoicing God-fearers who proclaim their God as a just judge in all his ways (2:33 ; 3:12 ; 5:18 ; 8:7-8,23-26) // Rev 15:2-4 and 19:1-8 (cf. 11:15-18 ; 12:10-12 ; 18:20) ;
- the elects singing a new psalm and unscathed by famine, sword and death as they bear God's sign, whereas the evil ones have the mark of destruction upon their foreheads (15:3-9) // Rev 6:3-8,17 ; 7:2-17 ; 9:1-4 ; 13:16-17 ; 14:1-3,9-11 ;
- fleeing to the desert as prospective, temporary salvation and restoration of a faithful Israel (17:15-19) // Rev 12:14-17 and 18:4 (cf. also *Psalms of Solomon* 17:18-19 with Rev 11:1-2,6) ;
- a Davidic Messiah fulfilling the promises voiced in Psalms 2:8-9 (17:23-24) // Rev 2:27-28 and 19:15 (cf. also *Psalms of Solomon* 17:43 and Rev 3:18).

No matter what answer we give to the question of whether John knew and deliberately echoed the *Psalms of Solomon* or whether both writers shared common expectations, hopes, and biblical hypotexts, the point is that the *Psalms of Solomon* attest to the "existence" of an "other" Jerusalem under "other," not legitimate rulers and of an idolatrous Israel alike, both of them implicitly identified as the kingdom of Babylon among the nations. When targeting the unrepentant and sinful, "Gentile-like" Capernaum, the alleged "Q people" would have agreed with the rhetorical strategy underlying such critics ; at least so did in a more historically tangible way Matthew and Luke, who apparently followed and disseminated "Q" (cf. Mt 23:37-39 // Lk 13:34-35) : they employ the same *topos* to demote a smaller Galilean village, as we saw earlier. For his own part John would have consented too, and he actually turned such strategy into action within the Asian milieu where he was operating. After all, what he needed were just "other" priests, allegedly striving to acquire permanent control over Jerusalem, who were therefore liable to the accusation of leading Israel into submission to the Romans, that is, to slavery and ruin, in the name of their own conception of freedom and supremacy (cf. Flavius Josephus, *Jewish War* 4.146, 154, 166-184, 226). Alternatively, he had just to take a look around inside the Jesus movement and see "other" leaders and their followers spread successfully and "deviate" from the norms and praxis which he himself accepted and propagated. Writing after 70 CE John eventually found both ranks and typologies of adversaries and turned them into his "demons" incarnate.[28]

## 4. Concluding Remarks: Three Bullet Points

In the last paragraph I have basically searched for often overlooked literary references to Jerusalem's kingship during the Second Temple Period by surveying the writings of three Hellenistic Jewish authors. I must now admit that the search is still in progress, and perhaps, it has just begun, as my acquaintance with Jewish literature in the Hellenistic and Roman period has already been growing in the meantime and my engagement with it keeps getting deeper. Therefore, as a matter of fact, I can offer here nothing more than provisionary conclusions—and probably implicit hints at some *desiderata*:

A) Kingship language and discourse can be and were employed as rhetorical, that is laudatory or polemical, tools. As such they do not necessarily imply one-to-one references to Rome and Roman rule, or correspondences with "real" rulers or ruling cities, whose

28. On John's opponents see L. Arcari, "L'*Apocalisse di Giovanni* nel quadro di alcune dinamiche gruppali proto-cristiane: elementi per una (ri-)contestualizzazione," *Annali di Storia dell'Esegesi* 28/1 (2011) 137-183; E.F. Lupieri, "From Sodom and Balaam to the Revelation of John. Transtextual Adventures of Biblical Sins," in S. Alkier – Th. Hieke – T. Nicklas, eds., *Poetik und Intertextualität der Johannesapokalypse* (Tübingen: Mohr Siebeck, 2015) 301-318; B.E. Bruning – J.A. Hughes, "Sham Synagogues and Fake Jews: Advancing the Thesis of Pauline Pagans at Smyrna and Philadelphia (Rev. 2:9, 3:9)," *Annali di Storia dell'Esegesi* 39/1 (2022) 197-220. On the depiction of the fall of Babylon in Revelation as reenactment of the punishment of Sodom cf. Lupieri, *op. cit.* 315-316, and M. Sommer, "Pech und Schwefel. Das Motivfeld Sodom und der Tag YHWHs in der Offenbarung," in Alkier – Hieke – Nicklas, *op. cit*, 326, 328, 338-340. In my view the two scholars bring to the fore the literary "missing link" between Sodom-like Jerusalem, Babylon-queen of the world, and internal polemical issues addressed by John in Revelation 2-3.

fortunes we are able to reconstruct and survey in our history books in an allegedly objective way. Kingship language and discourse might not even apply to an actual *metropolis*, just like the case of Capernaum shows.

B) Although the word "queen" does not occur in the texts surveyed and the allusions to any queenship or to Babylon remain mostly implicit, Lupieri's literary dossier on Jerusalem's rule over the nations may be expanded to include the passages that I have focused upon. These passages revolve around the integration of Jerusalem and Judaea first into the Hellenistic and then the Roman political, economic, and cultural systems, explained as a form of social intercourse with the kings of Asia and the Romans as more or less equal partners. Such integration could be considered as a token of "Babylonian" royalty (*Psalms of Solomon*). On the opposite side, it could and was indeed perceived and depicted as an aftermath of Jerusalem's independence from foreigners, the contaminating "nations," as the new freedom led to the establishment of a "national" Jewish rule over Judaea and the surrounding cities (*Jewish War* and *Against Apion*).[29]

C) What if, then, leaving aside the artificial distinction between Palestinian and Diaspora Judaism, we study Revelation as one "chapter" among many belonging to the Jewish Hellenistic literature and therefore as one expression among many "of specific *milieus* and ferments in Hellenistic Judaism" ?[30] I offer here only

29. On Hasmonean and Herodian royal ideologies as political efforts to accommodate Jewish tradition to Hellenistic *Königsdogma* and *vice versa* cf. E. Regev, *The Hasmoneans: Ideology, Archaeology, Identity* (Göttingen: Vandenhoeck & Ruprecht, 2013) and A.K. Marshak, *The Many Faces of Herod the Great* (Grand Rapids: Eerdmans, 2015) 58-72 and 230-311.

30. So L. Troiani, *Letteratura giudaica di lingua greca* (Brescia: Paideia, 1997) 70, referring more generally to the New Testament corpus. On the historical and exegetical task of reading Revelation as a Jewish work belonging to Graeco-Roman literature see respectively E. Pagels, "How John of Patmos' Readers Made Him into a Christian," in T.G. Petrey, ed., *Re-Making the World: Christianity and Categories. Essays in Honor of Karen L. King* (Tübingen: Mohr Siebeck, 2019) 35-47 and M. Karrer, *Johannesoffenbarung (Offb. 1,1-5,14)* (Göttingen/Ostfilden: Vandenhoeck & Ruprecht/Patmos Verlag, 2017) 45-48, 91-102. Cf. programmatically D. Tripaldi, *Apocalisse di Giovanni. Introduzione, traduzione e commento* (Rome: Carocci, 2012) 34. Already K. Berger, *Theologiegeschichte des Urchristentums* (Tübingen: Francke Verlag, 1995) 615-626, emphasized John's ideological proximity to Judaism, although he actually seemed to work with a too sharp contrastive distinction between Judaism and Hellenism.

a partial and specific answer: reading Revelation against Jewish Hellenistic images of *Ierusalem regina*, I would profile John's attempt to defy and define queenship in Revelation as a deliberate act of counterpropaganda. John reverses *de facto* supremacy hopes centering on Jerusalem and Israel other than his own. It probably made no difference to him how similar such hopes actually were to his. He did not wonder either whether they embodied the political dreams of the Jewish ruling class or those of the rebels (i.e., the Herodian dynasty; priests like Ananos and Josephus himself after surrendering; the very same Josephus before his surrender; the priestly leadership of the "zealots"). Nor did it really matter to him to discern instead if they reflected diverging Jewish – or non Jewish – Asian identities or even the growing authority and successful preaching of other prophets and would-be leaders among the *ekklesiai* of groups of Jesus followers, which he regarded as the remnant of Israel.[31] He just lumped everything together: any other "queen" had to be unmasked and promptly debased once and for all as one single incarnation of the sitting *Iudaea capta* waiting for restoration and an actual kingdom. One incarnation, but surely not the only, since the roughly contemporary picture of the mourning woman in *4 Ezra* has been convincingly interpreted as a reverberation of the *Iudaea capta* motif on Roman coins.[32] The only restoration and kingdom that John envisages and could promise, or ever conceive of, centers exclusively on *his own* vision of Israel, Jerusalem and the *ekklesiai*. This vision builds upon the ideal of a holy "Temple-city," which is currently under the siege of the nations but will turn ἐν τάχει into a new earth

31. See R. Van de Water, "Reconsidering the Beast from the Sea," *New Testament Studies* 46 (2000) 251-261 (even though not convincing in every detail); U. Sals, *Die Biographie der „Hure Babylon". Studien zur Intertextualität der Babylon-Texte in der Bibel* (Tübingen: Mohr Siebeck, 2004) 76, 103-106, 143; J. Dochhorn, *Schriftgelehrte Prophetie. Der eschatologische Teufelsfall in Apc Joh 12 und seine Bedeutung für das Verständnis der Johannesoffenbarung* (Tübingen: Mohr Siebeck, 2010) 123-130; L. Painchaud, "Assemblées de Smyrne et de Philadelphie et congrégation de Satan: vrais et faux Judéens dans l'Apocalypse de Jean (2,9; 3,9)," *Laval Théologique et Philosophique* 70/3 (2014) 475-492.

32. See P. Piovanelli, "*Odio humani generis.* Apocalypticiens messianistes et historiens intégrés à l'époque des Guerres des Judéens," in P. Piovanelli, ed., *Apocryphités. Études sur les textes et les traditions scripturaires du judaïsme et du christianisme anciens* (Turnhout: Brepols, 2016) 216-219. More generally, on the depiction of the woman in *4 Ezra* and its socio-historical context and meaning see L. Arcari, *"Una donna avvolta nel sole ..." (Apoc 12,1) Le raffigurazioni femminili nell'*Apocalisse *di Giovanni alla luce della letteratura apocalittica giudaica* (Padua: Edizioni del Messaggero, 2008) 199-225.

and a new heaven under the rule of God, of the risen Jesus as God's legitimate Davidic anointed one, and of their true priestly "delegates."[33]

33. D. TRIPALDI, *Apocalisse di Giovanni. Introduzione, traduzione e commento* (Rome: Carocci, 2012) 27-29. J. Dochhorn pointedly writes: "die Ekklesiologie der Apc Joh ist eine Israelologie oder Zionslehre" (J. DOCHHORN, *Schriftgelehrte Prophetie. Der eschatologische Teufelsfall in Apc Joh 12 und seine Bedeutung für das Verständnis der Johannesoffenbarung* [Tübingen: Mohr Siebeck, 2010] 159); see also Pagel's brief conclusions in "How John of Patmos' Readers Made Him into a Christian," in T.G. PETREY, ed., *Re-Making the World: Christianity and Categories. Essays in Honor of Karen L. King* (Tübingen: Mohr Siebeck, 2019) 46-47. For the evidence cf. Rev 2:27-28; 11:1-2,15-17; 19:15-16; 20:4-5,9; 21:1-4,24-26; 22:3-5, and Dochhorn's discussion (86-96, 140-159, 308-310). On the governmental function entrusted to scribal and priestly figures in Q and Qumran as integral part of the discourse on (God's) kingship and kingdom see G.B. BAZZANA, *Kingdom of Bureaucracy: The Political Theology of Village Scribes in the Sayings Gospel Q* (Leuven: Peeters, 2015) 272-313.

# Third Part

# The Dragon and the Beasts

# DRAGON'S ATONEMENT: ESCHATOLOGICAL YOM KIPPUR IN THE BOOK OF REVELATION

**Andrei A. Orlov**
*Marquette University, Milwaukee*

Résumé

Cet article suggère que la représentation du dragon dans l'Apocalypse reprend les principales caractéristiques des derniers moments du rituel du bouc émissaire telles qu'elles ressortent des témoignages apocalyptiques, mishnaïques et patristiques. Ces caractéristiques comprennent les motifs suivants: l'enlèvement du bouc émissaire; le manipulateur qui le lie et le pousse du haut de la falaise; sa ligature; le scellement de l'abîme; la guérison temporaire de la terre; la déliaison temporaire du bouc émissaire avant sa disparition finale; et, enfin, la bande écarlate. Comme dans d'autres réinterprétations apocalyptiques de l'image du bouc émissaire que l'on trouve dans le *Livre des Veilleurs* et l'*Apocalypse d'Abraham*, le bannissement du bouc émissaire apocalyptique, représenté par le dragon dans l'Apocalypse, se déroule en deux temps. Il est d'abord banni sur la terre au chapitre 12, puis dans le royaume souterrain, qui est représenté par l'abîme au chapitre 20. Cette progression en deux temps de l'exil de l'antagoniste ressemble aux deux étapes des déplacements du bouc émissaire terrestre que l'on retrouve dans des sources rabbiniques et patristiques plus tardives: d'abord, le bannissement du bouc émissaire dans le désert, puis sa précipitation dans l'abîme lorsque l'animal est poussé de la falaise.

Abstract

This paper suggests that the portrayal of the dragon in the Book of Revelation reiterates the main features of the final moments of the scapegoat ritual, as reflected in apocalyptic, Mishnaic, and patristic testimonies. These features include the following elements: the motif of the scapegoat's removal; the motif of the handler who binds and pushes the scapegoat off the cliff; the motif of the scapegoat's binding; the motif of sealing the abyss of the scapegoat; the motif of the temporary healing of the earth; the motif of the scapegoat's temporary unbinding before its final demise; and, finally, the motif of the scarlet band of the scapegoat. As in other apocalyptic re-interpretations of the scapegoat imagery found in the *Book of the Watchers* and the *Apocalypse of Abraham*, the banishment of the apocalyptic scapegoat, represented by the dragon in the Book of Revelation, encompasses a two-stage development. He

*"Who is Sitting on Which Beast?" Interpretative Issues in the Book of Revelation. Proceedings of the International Conference held at Loyola University, Chicago, March 30-31, 2017*, ed. by Edmondo Lupieri and Louis Painchaud, JAOC 29 (Turnhout, 2023), pp. 165–184

DOI 10.1484/M.JAOC-EB.5.131933

is first banished to the earth in chapter 12, and then to the underground realm, which is represented by the abyss in chapter 20. Such a two-stage progression of the antagonist's exile resembles the two stages of the earthly scapegoat's movements, found in later rabbinic and patristic sources: first, the scapegoat's banishment to the wilderness, and then its descent into the abyss when the animal was pushed off the cliff.

## 1. Introduction

There are striking differences between the classic description of the scapegoat ritual found in Leviticus 16 and later renderings of this rite in rabbinic and early Christian authors. For instance, several enigmatic additions to the Levitical blueprint of the scapegoat ritual appear in later interpretations of this rite found in Mishnaic, targumic, and talmudic accounts, especially in the description of the conclusion of the scapegoat ceremony. Some of these accounts insist that in the final moments of the ritual in the wilderness the crimson band of the scapegoat was removed and then placed back onto the animal. The scapegoat was then pushed off the cliff by its handler. These traditions are not attested to in the biblical description of Leviticus, yet they figure into many rabbinic and early Christian interpretations. *Mishnah Yoma* 6:6, for example, contains the following tradition:

> What did he do? He divided the thread of crimson wool and tied one half to the rock and the other half between its horns, and he pushed it from behind; and it went rolling down, and before it had reached half the way down the hill it was broken in pieces.[1]

This account depicts the climax of the scapegoat ceremony, in which the scapegoat's handler strips away the infamous crimson band from the cultic animal, and then, according to the Mishnah, the band was divided into two pieces, one of which was tied to a rock, and the other bound again around the animal's horns. Scholars have previously suggested that the scarlet band[2] here is envisioned as an impure garment, or more specifically, as the attire of sins,[3] which the cultic animal was predestined to carry into

1. H. Danby, *The Mishnah* (Oxford: Oxford University Press, 1992) 170.

2. The tradition of the scarlet band is also reflected in *m. Sheqalim* 4:2: "The [Red] Heifer and the scapegoat and the crimson thread were bought with the *Terumah* from the Shekel-chamber." (H. Danby, *The Mishnah* [Oxford: Oxford University Press, 1992] 155); *m. Shabbat* 9:3: "Whence do we learn that they tie a strip of crimson on the head of the scapegoat? Because it is written, though your sins be as scarlet they shall be as white as snow." (H. Danby, *The Mishnah* [Oxford: Oxford University Press, 1992] 108).

3. *m. Yoma* 4:2 attests to the initial "clothing" of two goats of the Yom Kippur ritual in which one crimson band is tied around the horns of the scapegoat, while

an uninhabitable realm, in this case, the wilderness.[4] Loosing the cultic band at the end of the rite possibly signifies the forgiveness of the sins of the Israelites,[5] since, in some Jewish accounts, the imagery of loosing is closely connected to the forgiveness of transgressions.[6]

The aforementioned Mishnaic passage also hints at the fact that the final destination of the scapegoat's exile was not merely the desert, like it was described in Leviticus 16, but rather the underworld or abyss, the descent to which is symbolically expressed through the action of pushing the animal off a cliff. This tradition of the unusual demise of the atoning agent is attested in a panoply of rabbinic sources.[7] Early Christian testi-

---

the other is tied around the neck of the immolated goat; it reads: "He bound a thread of crimson wool on the head of the scapegoat and he turned it towards the way by which it was to be sent out; and on the he-goat that was to be slaughtered [he bound a thread] about its throat" (H. DANBY, *The Mishnah* [Oxford: Oxford University Press, 1992] 166).

4. A. DORMAN, "'Commit Injustice and Shed Innocent Blood.' Motives behind the Institution of the Day of Atonement in the Book of Jubilees," in TH. HIEKE – T. NICKLAS, eds., *The Day of Atonement: Its Interpretation in Early Jewish and Christian Traditions* (Leiden: Brill, 2012) 57; A. ORLOV, *Divine Scapegoats: Demonic Mimesis in Early Jewish Mysticism* (Albany: SUNY, 2015) 24-28.

5. Cf. R. HIERS, "'Binding and Loosing': The Matthean Authorizations," *Journal of Biblical Literature* 104 (1985) 233-250 (233). It also can be understood as release from the oath placed on the cultic animal by the high priest. Some studies suggest that the meaning can be understood in terms of later rabbinic usage, namely, the authority to absolve or release a person from some sort of vow. (R. HIERS, "'Binding and Loosing': The Matthean Authorizations," *Journal of Biblical Literature* 104 [1985] 233-250 [233]).

6. C. FLETCHER-LOUIS, "The Revelation of the Sacral Son of Man," in F. AVEMARIE – H. LICHTENBERGER, eds., *Auferstehung-Resurrection* (Tübingen: Mohr Siebeck, 2001) 284; J.A. EMERTON, "Binding and Loosing—Forgiving and Retaining," *Journal of Theological Studies* 13 (1962) 325-331 (329-330).

7. See *b. Yoma* 67a: "What did he do? He divided the thread of crimson wool, and tied one half to the rock, the other half between its horns, and pushed it from behind. And it went rolling down and before it had reached half its way down hill it was dashed to pieces. He came back and sat down under the last booth until it grew dark. And from when on does it render his garments unclean? From the moment he has gone outside the wall of Jerusalem. R. Simeon says: from the moment he pushes it into the Zok." (I. EPSTEIN, *The Babylonian Talmud. Yoma* [London: Soncino, 1935-1952] 67a); *y. Yoma* 6:3: "All during Simeon the Just's lifetime he [the scapegoat] did not fall down half the mountain before he dissolved into limbs; after Simeon the Just's death he fled to the desert and was eaten by the Saracens." (H.W. GUGGENHEIMER, ed., *The Jerusalem Talmud. Tractates Pesahim and Yoma. Edition, Translation and Commentary* [Berlin: De Gruyter, 2013] 559); *Targum Pseudo-Jonathan* on Lev 16:21-22: "Aaron shall lay both his hands on the head of the live goat, in this fashion: his right hand upon his left. He shall confess over it all the iniquities of the children of Israel and all their rebellions, whatever their sins; he shall put them on the head of the goat with a declared and explicit oath by the great and glorious Name. And he shall let (it) go, in charge of a man who has been designated previously, to go to the desert of Soq, that is Beth Haduri.

monies reflected in the *Epistle of Barnabas*,[8] Justin Martyr,[9] and Tertullian[10] are also cognizant of the peculiar details of the final demise of the scapegoat in the wilderness.

---

The goat shall carry on himself all their sins to a desolate place; and the man shall let the goat go into the desert of Soq, and the goat shall go up on the mountains of Beth Haduri, and the blast of wind from before the Lord will thrust him down and he will die" (M. McNamara – M. Maher – R. Hayward, eds., *Targum Neofiti 1, Leviticus; Targum Pseudo-Jonathan, Leviticus* [Collegeville: Liturgical Press, 1994] 169).

8. *Barnabas* 7:6-11 reads: "Pay attention to what he commands: 'Take two fine goats who are alike and offer them as a sacrifice; and let the priest take one of them as a whole burnt offering for sins.' But what will they do with the other? 'The other,' he says, 'is cursed.' Pay attention to how the type of Jesus is revealed. 'And all of you shall spit on it and pierce it and wrap a piece of scarlet wool around its head, and so let it be cast into the wilderness.' When this happens, the one who takes the goat leads it into the wilderness and removes the wool, and places it on a blackberry bush, whose buds we are accustomed to eat when we find it in the countryside. (Thus the fruit of the blackberry bush alone is sweet.) And so, what does this mean? Pay attention: 'The one they take to the altar, but the other is cursed,' and the one that is cursed is crowned. For then they will see him in that day wearing a long scarlet robe around his flesh, and they will say, 'Is this not the one we once crucified, despising, piercing, and spitting on him? Truly this is the one who was saying at the time that he was himself the Son of God.' For how is he like that one? This is why 'the goats are alike, fine, and equal,' that when they see him coming at that time, they may be amazed at how much he is like the goat. See then the type of Jesus who was about to suffer. But why do they place the wool in the midst of the thorns? This is a type of Jesus established for the church, because whoever wishes to remove the scarlet wool must suffer greatly, since the thorn is a fearful thing, and a person can retrieve the wool only by experiencing pain. And so he says: those who wish to see me and touch my kingdom must take hold of me through pain and suffering" (B.D. Ehrman, ed., *The Apostolic Fathers* [2 vols; Cambridge, MA: Harvard University Press, 2003] 2.37-41).

9. Justin Martyr's *Dialogue with Trypho* 40:4-5 reads: "Likewise, the two identical goats which had to be offered during the fast (one of which was to be the scapegoat, and the other the sacrificial goat) were an announcement of the two comings of Christ: Of the first coming, in which your priests and elders send him away as a scapegoat, seizing him and putting him to death; of the second coming, because in that same place of Jerusalem you shall recognize him whom you had subjected to shame, and who was a sacrificial offering for all sinners who are willing to repent and to comply with that fast which Isaiah prescribed when he said, loosing the strangle of violent contracts, and to observe likewise all the other precepts laid down by him (precepts which I have already mentioned and which all believers in Christ fulfill). You also know very well that the offering of the two goats, which had to take place during the fast, could not take place anywhere else except in Jerusalem" (T.F. Falls – T.P. Halton, eds., *St. Justin Martyr. Dialogue with Trypho* [Washington, DC: Catholic University of America Press, 2003] 62).

10. In *Against Marcion* 3:7, Tertullian writes: "If also I am to submit an interpretation of the two goats which were offered at the Fast, are not these also figures of Christ's two activities? They are indeed of the same age and appearance because the Lord's is one and the same aspect: because he will return in no other

## 2. Demise of the Eschatological Scapegoat in Jewish Apocalypticism

I have previously argued that these additions to the scapegoat ritual found in rabbinic and early Christian sources, including the motifs of the scapegoat's binding, the hurling of the scapegoat off a cliff, and the alteration of its garment of sins represented by the crimson band immediately before its death, all stem from the eschatological reinterpretations of the scapegoat rite found in some early Jewish apocalyptic writings including the *Book of the Watchers*, the *Animal Apocalypse*, and the *Apocalypse of Abraham*.[11] In these accounts, which were written earlier than the aforementioned rabbinic and patristic testimonies, one finds a striking refashioning of the traditional atoning rite, where the scapegoat's features are transferred to an otherworldly antagonist bearing the name "Asael" or "Azazel."

One of the earliest apocalyptic reinterpretations of the scapegoat ritual in Jewish tradition may be found in the *Book of the Watchers*, in which the story of the cultic gatherer of impurities receives a novel conceptual makeup. This early Enochic booklet refashions the scapegoat rite in a paradoxical angelological way, incorporating details from the sacrificial

---

form, seeing he has to be recognized by those of whom he has suffered injury. One of them however, surrounded with scarlet, cursed and spit upon and pulled about and pierced, was by the people driven out of the city into perdition, marked with manifest tokens of our Lord's passion: while the other, made an offering for sins, and given as food to the priests of the temple, marked the tokens of his second manifestation, at which, when all sins have been done away, the priests of the spiritual temple, which is the Church, were to enjoy, as it were, a feast of our Lord's grace, while the rest remain without a taste of salvation" (E. Evans, ed., *Tertullian. Adversus Marcionem* [2 vols; Oxford: Clarendon Press, 1972] 1.191). Similar testimony appears in *Against the Jews* 14:9: "In fact, thus also let me make an interpretation of the two goats that were offered at the fast. Do these not also show the two conditions of the Christ who is already come? They are indeed of the same age and appearance on account of the one and the same aspect of the Lord, because he will return in no other form, seeing that he has to be recognized by those from whom he has suffered injury. One of them, however, which was surrounded with scarlet, cursed and spat upon and perforated and punctured, was driven outside the city by the people to ruin, marked with obvious emblems of the suffering of Christ, who, having been surrounded with a scarlet garment, spat upon and knocked about with every physical violence, was crucified outside the city. The other, however, made an offering for offences, and given as food only to the priests of the temple, is marked with the proof of his second manifestation, because when all offences have been done away, the priests of the spiritual temple—that is, the church—were to enjoy as it were a feast of our Lord's grace, while the rest remain without a taste of salvation" (G.D. Dunn, ed., *Tertullian* [London: Routledge, 2004] 103).

11. A. Orlov, *Divine Scapegoats: Demonic Mimesis in Early Jewish Mysticism* (Albany: SUNY, 2015) 9-36.

ritual into the story of its main antagonist, the fallen angel Asael. *1 Enoch* 10:4-7 presents a striking depiction laden with familiar sacerdotal details:

> And further the Lord said to Raphael: "Bind Asael by his hands and his feet, and throw him into the darkness. And split open the desert which is in Dudael, and throw him there. And throw on him jagged and sharp stones, and cover him with darkness; and let him stay there forever, and cover his face, that he may not see light, and that on the great day of judgment he may be hurled into the fire. And restore the earth which the angels have ruined, and announce the restoration of the earth, for I shall restore the earth ..."[12]

Several scholars have noticed numerous details of Asael's punishment that are reminiscent of the scapegoat ritual as it is reflected in *Mishnah Yoma*. Daniel Olson, for instance, argues that "a comparison of *1 Enoch* 10 with the Day of Atonement ritual... leaves little doubt that Asael is indeed Azazel."[13] Additionally, Daniel Stökl Ben Ezra observes that "the punishment of the demon resembles the treatment of the goat in aspects of geography, action, time and purpose."[14] He further notes that "both in the description of the prison of the demon in *1 Enoch* and in traditions about the precipice of the scapegoat ritual an element of ruggedness appears. This ruggedness could reflect an early Midrash on the meaning of *gzr* (cut, split up) in *ʿrṣ gzrh* (Lev 16:22) and/or historical memory of the actual cliffs in the mountains of Jerusalem."[15] Furthermore, the place of Asael's punishment designated in *1 Enoch* as Dudael is reminiscent of the terminology used for the designation of the ravine of the scapegoat in later rabbinic interpretations of the Yom Kippur ritual, down which the scapegoat was hurled.[16] This tradition is explicitly attested in *m. Yoma* and *Targum Pseudo-Jonathan*.[17]

---

12. M. Knibb, ed., *The Ethiopic Book of Enoch: A New Edition in the Light of the Aramaic Dead Sea Fragments* (2 vols; Oxford: Clarendon Press, 1978) 2.87-88.

13. D. Olson, *Enoch. A New Translation: The Ethiopic Book of Enoch, or 1 Enoch* (North Richland Hills, TX: Bibal Press, 2004) 34.

14. D. Stökl Ben Ezra, *The Impact of Yom Kippur on Early Christianity: The Day of Atonement from Second Temple Judaism to the Fifth Century* (Tübingen: Mohr Siebeck, 2003) 87; D. Olson, *Enoch. A New Translation: The Ethiopic Book of Enoch, or 1 Enoch* (North Richland Hills, TX: Bibal Press, 2004) 38.

15. D. Stökl Ben Ezra, *The Impact of Yom Kippur on Early Christianity: The Day of Atonement from Second Temple Judaism to the Fifth Century* (Tübingen: Mohr Siebeck, 2003) 88.

16. A. Geiger, "Einige Worte über das Buch Henoch," *Jüdische Zeitschrift für Wissenschaft und Leben* 3 (1864) 196-204 (200).

17. See *Targum Pseudo-Jonathan* to Lev 16:10: "The goat on which the lot of Azazel fell shall be set alive before the Lord to make atonement for the sinfulness of the people of the house of Soq, that is Beth Haduri." (M. McNamara – M. Maher – R. Hayward, eds., *Targum Neofiti 1, Leviticus; Targum Pseudo-Jonathan, Leviticus* [Collegeville: Liturgical Press, 1994] 167); *Targum Pseudo-Jonathan*

The tradition of apocalyptic reinterpretations of the scapegoat ritual reaches its symbolic pinnacle in the *Apocalypse of Abraham*. This Jewish text, which was most likely written during the period in which the Mishnaic descriptions of the atoning rite received their conclusive textual codification, provides us with a unique glimpse into the final stages of the ever-changing scapegoat imagery that began many centuries earlier in the Enochic books. Although the early traits of the Enochic apocalyptic blueprint and the Watchers tradition still play a formative role in the *Apocalypse of Abraham*, this conceptual core is now greatly enhanced by some novel developments that are essential in Mishnaic and early Christian versions of the atoning ritual. Thus, the imagery of the celestial scapegoat's clothing, only vaguely alluded to in the early Enochic books, in the symbolism of covering the antagonist with darkness, now receives its distinctive conceptual expression as the impure vestment of human sins.[18]

The details of the angelic scapegoat's exile into the lower realms found in the Slavonic apocalypse are similarly indebted to the early Enochic blueprint. As with Asael in the Enochic tradition, the antagonist's exile in the *Apocalypse of Abraham* encompasses two movements: first, to the earth,[19] and second, to the fiery abyss of the subterranean realm.[20] Although early

---

to Lev 16:22: "The goat shall carry on himself all their sins to a desolate place; and the man shall let the goat go into the desert of Soq, and the goat shall go up on the mountains of Beth Haduri, and the blast of wind from before the Lord will thrust him down and he will die" (M. McNamara – M. Maher – R. Hayward, eds., *Targum Neofiti 1, Leviticus; Targum Pseudo-Jonathan, Leviticus* [Collegeville: Liturgical Press, 1994] 169).

18. In *Apocalypse of Abraham* 13:7-14, the following mysterious encounter between the heavenly high priest Yahoel and the celestial scapegoat Azazel takes place: "... Reproach is on you, Azazel! Since Abraham's portion is in heaven, and yours is on earth, since you have chosen it and desired it to be the dwelling place of your impurity. Therefore the Eternal Lord, the Mighty One, has made you a dweller on earth. And because of you [there is] the wholly evil spirit of the lie, and because of you [there are] wrath and trials on the generations of impious men. Since the Eternal Mighty God did not send the righteous, in their bodies, to be in your hand, in order to affirm through them the righteous life and the destruction of impiety. ... Hear, adviser! Be shamed by me, since you have been appointed to tempt not all the righteous! Depart from this man! You cannot deceive him, because he is the enemy of you and of those who follow you and who love what you desire. For behold, the garment which in heaven was formerly yours has been set aside for him, and the corruption which was on him has gone over to you" (A. Kulik, *Retroverting Slavonic Pseudepigrapha: Toward the Original of the Apocalypse of Abraham* [Atlanta: Scholars Press, 2004] 20).

19. *Apocalypse of Abraham* 13:8: "Since Abraham's portion is in heaven, and yours is *on earth*, since you have chosen it and desired it to be the dwelling place of your impurity" (A. Kulik, *Retroverting Slavonic Pseudepigrapha: Toward the Original of the Apocalypse of Abraham* [Atlanta: Scholars Press, 2004] 20).

20. *Apocalypse of Abraham* 14:5: "May you be the fire brand of the *furnace of the earth*!" (A. Kulik, *Retroverting Slavonic Pseudepigrapha: Toward the Original of*

versions of the scapegoat ritual found in the Book of Leviticus attest only to a one-step removal of the goat to the wilderness, the tradition of the two-step removal plays a prominent role in later Mishnaic versions of the rite, in which the cultic animal is first taken to the wilderness and then pushed from a cliff into the abyss.

The *Apocalypse of Abraham* clearly contains the tradition of sending the scapegoat into the lower realm, since in chapters 13 and 14 the heavenly priest-angel Yahoel banishes Azazel first to the earthly realm and then into the abyss of the subterranean sphere. It is noteworthy that, much like the scapegoat in Mishnaic testimonies, the antagonist's exile in the Slavonic apocalypse coincides with his disrobing and re-robing. The text reports that the fallen angel was first disrobed of his celestial garment and then re-clothed in the ominous attire of human sins; it reads: "For behold, the garment which in heaven was formerly yours has been set aside for him, and the corruption which was on him has gone over to you."[21]

## 3. Book of Revelation

It is possible that the Book of Revelation also belongs to the aforementioned group of the apocalyptic writings that offers an eschatological reinterpretation of the scapegoat ritual. Unfortunately, the limited scope of my paper does not allow me to explore all of the allusions to Yom Kippur found in the Book of Revelation.[22] So, my study will focus only on the

---

*the Apocalypse of Abraham* [Atlanta: Scholars Press, 2004] 21).

21. A. Kulik, *Retroverting Slavonic Pseudepigrapha: Toward the Original of the Apocalypse of Abraham* (Atlanta: Scholars Press, 2004) 20.

22. On Yom Kippur traditions in the Book of Revelation, see P. Carrington, *The Meaning of Revelation* (London: SPCK, 1931) 348, 392; D.T. Niles, *As Seeing the Invisible* (New York: Harper and Brothers, 1961) 110-113; A.M. Farrer, *A Rebirth of Images* (Gloucester: Peter Smith, 1970) 177-178; J. Massyngberde Ford, *Revelation* (Garden City: Doubleday, 1975) 277, 287; G.L. Carey, "The Lamb of God and Atonement Theories," *Tyndale Bulletin* 32 (1981) 97-122; K.A. Strand, "An Overlooked Old Testament Background to Rev 11:1," *Andrews University Seminar Studies* 22 (1984) 317-325; B. Snyder, *Combat Myth in the Apocalypse: The Liturgy of the Day of the Lord and the Dedication of the Heavenly Temple* (Ph.D. Diss.; Graduate Theological Union, 1991); R.D. Davis, *The Heavenly Court Judgment of Revelation 4-5* (Lanham: University Press of America, 1992) 220-226; A.R. Treiver, *The Day of Atonement and the Heavenly Judgment* (Siloam Springs, AR: Creation Enterprises International, 1992); J. Paulien, "The Role of the Hebrew Cultus, Sanctuary, and Temple in the Plot and Structure of the Book of Revelation," *Andrews University Seminar Studies* 33 (1995) 245-264 (255-256); E.F. Lupieri, "Apocalisse, sacerdozio e Yom Kippur," *Annali di Storia dell'Esegesi* 19/1 (2002) 11-21; R. Stefanović, *Revelation of Jesus Christ: Commentary on the Book of Revelation* (Berrien Springs, MI: Andrews University Press, 2002) 31-32; J. Ben-Daniel – G. Ben-Daniel, *The Apocalypse in the Light of the Temple: A New*

tradition of the dragon's demise in the Book of Revelation and its possible connection with the scapegoat ritual.

Before we proceed to a close analysis of the conceptual developments found in the Book of Revelation, let us again reiterate the main features of the final moments of the scapegoat ritual, as reflected in apocalyptic, Mishnaic, and patristic testimonies; they include the following elements:

1. The motif of the scapegoat's removal, represented as a two-stage movement, which includes, first, the antagonist's banishment into the wilderness, and second, placing him into the abyss or underworld, which is symbolized in the atoning ritual by pushing the goat off the cliff;
2. The motif of the (angelic) handler who binds and pushes the scapegoat off the cliff;
3. The motif of the scapegoat's binding;
4. The motif of sealing the abyss of the scapegoat;
5. The motif of the temporary healing of the earth;
6. The motif of the scapegoat's temporary unbinding before its final demise;
7. The motif of the scarlet band of the scapegoat.

### 3.1 The Motif of the Antagonist's Banishment

Let us start with exploration of the eschatological scapegoat's processions. As mentioned, in *1 Enoch* 10, the Deity orders Raphael to open the pit in the desert and throw Asael into the darkness. The text further describes the celestial scapegoat's fall into the depths of the abyss. Yet, the exile of the apocalyptic scapegoat may begin even earlier when the infamous watcher descends from heaven to earth with other members of the rebellious angelic group.

My previous analysis of the otherworldly scapegoat traditions demonstrates that, both in the *Book of the Watchers* and the *Apocalypse of Abraham*, the exile of the apocalyptic scapegoat encompasses a two-stage development. First, the antagonist descends to the earth, and then into the underground realm, represented by the abyss.[23] I have previously argued that such a two-stage progression of the antagonist's exile corresponds to the two stages of the earthly scapegoat's movements, reflected in later rabbinic and patristic sources, represented respectively by the scapegoat's ban-

---

*Approach to the Book of Revelation* (Jerusalem: Beit Yochanan, 2003); R. Boustan, *From Martyr to Mystic: Rabbinic Martyrology and the Making of Merkavah Mysticism* (Tübingen: Mohr Siebeck, 2005) 197.

23. A. Orlov, *Divine Scapegoats: Demonic Mimesis in Early Jewish Mysticism* (Albany: SUNY, 2015) 66.

ishment to the wilderness and its descent into the abyss when the animal was pushed off the cliff.[24]

In the Book of Revelation, we may see a similar two-stage progressive movement when the main antagonist, the dragon, is first banished to the earth in chapter 12, and then to the underground realm, represented by the abyss in chapter 20. We should explore these traditions more closely.

Rev 12:9 relates the following tradition: "the great dragon was thrown down ... he was thrown down to the earth, and his angels were thrown down with him."[25] It is intriguing that in the Book of Revelation, as in the *Book of the Watchers*, and the *Apocalypse of Abraham*, the eschatological scapegoat is demoted along with his "portion."

One important detail of the aforementioned story of the angelic descent in Rev 12:9 is that the antagonist and his angels did not descend to earth voluntarily, like in the early Enochic booklets, but they "were thrown down," which correlates the tradition found in the Book of Revelation even more closely to the scapegoat ritual, in which the animal was involuntary led out into the wilderness by its handler. It also places the Book of Revelation's rendering of the celestial antagonist's demotion in very close connection to the interpretation found in the *Apocalypse of Abraham*. There, the main antagonist of the story—the fallen angel Azazel—is also forcefully demoted by his angelic handler, Yahoel.

Furthermore, it is noteworthy that the dragon's exile to the earth coincides in Revelation 12 with the wilderness motif, since upon his exile to earth the dragon pursues the woman clothed with the sun in the desert (εἰς τὴν ἔρημον). This motif might be relevant for our study of the imagery of the scapegoat, whose exile to the wilderness represents an important topological marker in many apocalyptic Yom Kippur accounts. Thus, in the *Apocalypse of Abraham* Yahoel banishes Azazel not simply to the earth, but to "the untrodden parts of the earth." The word "untrodden" (Slav. беспроходна, lit. "impassable")[26] is significant since it designates a place uninhabitable to human beings, reminiscent of the language of Leviticus 16, where the scapegoat is dispatched to the solitary place in the wilderness.[27]

Second, the "underground" stage of the scapegoat's exile is then attested in Revelation 20, where the antagonist is now thrown into the

24. A. Orlov, *Divine Scapegoats: Demonic Mimesis in Early Jewish Mysticism* (Albany: SUNY, 2015) 73-74.

25. All biblical quotations are taken from the New Revised Standard Version (NRSV) unless otherwise indicated.

26. B. Philonenko-Sayar – M. Philonenko, *L'Apocalypse d'Abraham. Introduction, texte slave, traduction et notes* (Paris: Librairie Adrien-Maisonneuve, 1981) 68.

27. Lev 16:22: "The goat shall bear on itself all their iniquities to a barren region; and the goat shall be set free in the wilderness."

subterranean chamber.[28] Rev 20:2-3 relates the following tradition: "He seized the dragon ... and threw him into the pit, and locked and sealed it over him ..."

Furthermore, it is noteworthy that in Revelation, like in the *Book of the Watchers*[29] and the *Apocalypse of Abraham*, this underground imprisonment is temporary, since on the Day of Judgment the antagonist will be thrown for a second time—but this time—into the abyss of fire,[30] an event labeled in Revelation as "the second death."[31]

*1 Enoch* 10:6 describes Asael's second punishment in the following terms: "on the great day of judgment he may be hurled into the fire ..."[32] In Rev 20:10 this second ordeal is rendered in the following way: "And the devil who had deceived them was thrown into the lake of fire and sulfur, where the beast and the false prophet were, and they will be tormented day and night forever and ever." It is noteworthy that both apocalyptic descriptions betray a similar symbolism, namely, the distinctive imagery of fire.

---

28. The biblical roots of the motif of the incarceration of heavenly beings in the subterranean realm can be found in Isa 24:21-22: "On that day the Lord will punish the host of heaven in heaven, and on earth the kings of the earth. They will be gathered together like prisoners in a pit; they will be shut up in a prison, and after many days they will be punished." Regarding this tradition, see D.E. AUNE, *Revelation 17-22* (Nashville: Thomas Nelson Publishers, 1998) 1078.

29. In relation to this tradition, Patrick Tiller suggests that "the temporary rocky prison of Asael may be somehow related to the offering of a live goat, which bears the sins of Israel, to Azazel on the Day of Atonement (Leviticus 16)." P.A. TILLER, *A Commentary on the Animal Apocalypse of 1 Enoch* (Atlanta: Scholars Press, 1993) 371.

30. Scholars note that the complex nature of the angelic imprisonment's imagery in early Enochic materials operates with various types of subterranean/desert prisons, temporary as well as permanent. Sometimes these separate entities are combined into a single prison. With respect to this, Patrick Tiller observes that "in both the *Book of the Watchers* and the *Animal Apocalypse*, there are two prisons into which the Watchers will be cast. The first, a temporary prison, is described as two separate places in 10.4-5 (= 88.1) and 10.12 (= 88.3). In 18.12-16 and 21.1-6 these two places are combined into a single prison for both the wandering and the fallen angels. In the later part of the *Book of the Watchers* (18.12-16; 21.1-6), this prison is not an abyss at all but a dark, desert wasteland. In chapters 6-12, it is not clear whether the temporary prisons are abysses or not. The permanent prison, the abyss of fire, is described in 10.6,13; 18.9-11; and 21.7-10 in the *Book of the Watchers* and in 90.24-25 in the *Animal Apocalypse*. The abyss described by Jude seems to be a composite of all of these prisons: it is dark (10.4-5; 88.1); it is reserved for the wandering stars (18.12-16; 21.1-6); and it is eternal (10.6, 13; 21.7-10)" (P.A. TILLER, *A Commentary on the Animal Apocalypse of 1 Enoch* [Atlanta: Scholars Press, 1993] 252-254).

31. Rev 20:14: "Then Death and Hades were thrown into the lake of fire. This is the second death, the lake of fire."

32. M. KNIBB, ed., *The Ethiopic Book of Enoch: A New Edition in the Light of the Aramaic Dead Sea Fragments* (2 vols; Oxford: Clarendon Press, 1978) 2.88.

In the *Apocalypse of Abraham*, the pit of the eschatological scapegoat is also portrayed with fiery imagery. There, the underground domain of the antagonist is depicted as the very place of fire. In Yahoel's speech, for instance, found in chapter 14, which reveals the true location of the chief antagonist, the arch-demon's abode is designated as the furnace of the earth. Azazel himself, moreover, is depicted as the "burning coal" or the "firebrand" of this infernal kiln.

Unlike the Book of Revelation, the *Book of the Watchers* does not describe a temporary release of its antagonist. Yet such activity might be hinted at in the *Apocalypse of Abraham*, where Azazel, despite his exile into the underground prison, still retains his ability to corrupt humankind.

### 3.2 The Motif of the Angelic Handler

A prominent feature of the Mishnaic depiction of the scapegoat ritual is the motif of the scapegoat's handler, who performs ritual actions with regards to the animal by leading it into the wilderness, binding and unbinding its crimson band, and finally throwing the animal into the pit. In the apocalyptic versions of the atoning rite, these sacerdotal actions are performed by angelic figures, namely, Raphael in the *Book of the Watchers* and Yahoel in the *Apocalypse of Abraham*. Like in the *Book of the Watchers* and the *Apocalypse of Abraham*, in the Book of Revelation there is an angelic figure that binds and handles the eschatological scapegoat.

As it is known, in rabbinic renderings of the scapegoat ritual the animal is thrown into the abyss by its handler. The same order of events can be seen in the *Book of the Watchers*, where Raphael throws Asael into the dark underground pit, and in Rev 20:3, where the angelic figure throws the dragon into the abyss. In the *Apocalypse of Abraham*, the angel Yahoel orders Azazel to be banished into exile to the lower realm, namely, the abyss.

### 3.3 The Motif of the Scapegoat's Binding

Although the biblical account of the scapegoat ritual found in Leviticus does not mention the binding of the scapegoat, this motif became very prominent in the Mishnaic accounts, including a passage found in *Mishnah Yoma* 4:2, where the scapegoat is bound with scarlet thread upon its selection by lottery. Even more important for our study is a tradition found in *Mishnah Yoma* 6:6, which relates that, in the final moments of the scapegoat ceremony, immediately before its demise off the cliff, the go-away goat was unbound and then re-tied with the crimson band.[33] The

---

33. It is possible that the loosing of the band at the end of the ritual signified the forgiveness of the Israelite sins. Some studies point to the connection of the formulae of loosing with the theme of forgiveness. On this see R. Hiers, "'Binding and Loosing': The Matthean Authorizations," *Journal of Biblical Literature* 104 (1985) 233-250 (234).

features that Mishnaic authors weave into the fabric of the ancient rite are intriguing, and seemingly novel. Yet it should not be forgotten that, several centuries before the composition of the Mishnah, some apocalyptic accounts already link the scapegoat ritual with the symbolism of binding.[34] Already in *1 Enoch* 10, the handler of the celestial scapegoat, the archangel Raphael, is instructed to bind the demon by his hands and feet immediately before throwing him into the subterranean pit. This tradition represents a remarkable parallel to *Mishnah Yoma* 6:6, in which the cultic animal is bound with a crimson band *immediately* before its demise.

The motif of the antagonist's binding receives its distinctive expression also in the Book of Revelation. In Rev 20:1-2 the seer reports that he saw an angel coming down from heaven, holding in his hand the key to the bottomless pit and a great chain.[35] The angel then seized the dragon and bound him for a thousand years. Already Robert Henry Charles had noted a parallel between this passage and the tradition of Asael's binding in the *Book of the Watchers*.[36]

---

34. Scholars have noted that the binding motif was very prominent in the tradition of the fall of the Watchers. On this see R. BAUCKHAM, *Jude, 2 Peter* (Waco: Word Books, 1983) 53. On the binding motif, see also *1 Enoch* 13:1; 14:5; 18:16; 21:3-6; 54:3-5; 56:1-4; 88:1; *Jubilees* 5:6; 10:7-11; *2 Enoch* 7:2; *2 Baruch* 56:13; *Sibylline Oracles* 2.289; Origen, *Contra Celsum* 5:52.

35. A curious parallel to the motif of a great chain can be found in *1 Enoch* 54, where Enoch sees iron chains of "immeasurable weight" which are prepared for "the hosts of Asael/Azazel." *1 Enoch* 54:3-5 reads: "And there my eyes saw how they made instruments for them—iron chains of immeasurable weight. And I asked the angel of peace who went with me, saying: 'These chain-instruments—for whom are they being prepared?' And he said to me: 'These are being prepared for the hosts of Azazel, that they may take them and throw them into the lowest part of Hell; and they will cover their jaws with rough stones, as the Lord of Spirits commanded'" (M. KNIBB, ed., *The Ethiopic Book of Enoch: A New Edition in the Light of the Aramaic Dead Sea Fragments* [2 vols; Oxford: Clarendon Press, 1978] 2.138). The peculiar details of the punishment, which includes the motif of the "rough stones," brings to mind Asael's demise in *1 Enoch* 10.

36. Charles argued that "this idea of binding the powers of evil in prison for an undefined period is already found in Isa xxiv. 22, and of their final judgment in xxiv. These powers consist of the host of heaven and the kings of the earth. This idea of the angels and the kings of the earth being judged together reappears in *1 Enoch* liii. 4 – liv. 5, and the idea of the binding of the fallen angels in a place of temporary punishment till the day of the final judgment is found in *1 Enoch* xviii. 12-16, xix. 1-2, xxi. 1-6, from which the final place of their punishment an abyss of fire is carefully distinguished, x. 13-15, xviii. 11, xxi. 7-10, liv. 6, xc. 24-25. Their leader Azazel is bound in a place by himself (x. 4-5) as a preliminary punishment, but at the final judgment is to be cast into a place of everlasting punishment (x. 6). In nearly all cases the evil spirits are spoken of in *1 Enoch* as being 'bound' in a preliminary place of punishment, just as in Isa. xxiv. 22 and in our text" (R.H. CHARLES, *A Critical and Exegetical Commentary on the Revelation of St. John* [2 vols; Edinburgh: T&T Clark, 1920] 2.141-142).

David Aune,[37] and recently Kelley Coblentz Bautch,[38] also both reaffirm the connection between Revelation 20 and *1 Enoch* 10 by noting numerous parallels. Coblentz Bautch concludes that "the binding and imprisonment of Satan in an abyss and a second punishment by fire strongly evoke the fate of the rebellious angels as presented in numerous accounts."[39] Although Aune and Coblentz Bautch do not discuss the relationships between the dragon's binding and the scapegoat motif, Lester Grabbe entertains this implicit connection. He argues that the punishment of the dragon in Revelation has been assimilated to the apocalyptic scapegoat tradition found in *1 Enoch* 10.[40]

37. David Aune notes that in "Rev 20:1-3, 7-10: (1) An angel descends from heaven with a key and a chain (v. 1). (2) The angel seizes and binds Satan (v. 2a). (3) Satan will be imprisoned one thousand years (v. 2b). (4) Satan is cast into a pit that is locked and sealed (v. 3). (5) Satan is released for an unspecified period (vv. 3b,7-9). (6) Satan and his associates are cast into the lake of fire for eternal torment (v. 10). *1 Enoch* 10:4-6 contains the following motifs: (1) God sends an angel (Raphael). (2) Azazel (an alias for Satan) is bound by the angel. (3) Azazel is thrown into darkness and imprisoned 'forever.' (4) The time of imprisonment, however, will actually end at the great day of judgment. (5) On the great day of judgment Azazel is thrown into the fire. A similar sequence is evident in *1 Enoch* 10:11-13: (1) God sends an angel (Michael). (2) The angel binds Semyaza (another alias for Satan) and his associates. (3) They are imprisoned under the earth. (4) The period of imprisonment is limited to seventy generations. (5) On the day of judgment they are thrown into the abyss of fire." D.E. AUNE, *Revelation 17-22* (Nashville: Thomas Nelson Publishers, 1998) 1078. Aune concludes his comparative analysis with the following: "Since the narrative pattern found twice in Rev 20:1-10 (i.e., in vv. 1-3 and 7-10) also occurs twice in *1 Enoch*, it seems likely that both authors are dependent on a traditional eschatological scenario. The enumeration of motifs found in these three passages exhibits a striking similarity, though John has introduced the innovation of the temporary release of Satan" (D.E. AUNE, *Revelation 17-22* [Nashville: Thomas Nelson Publishers, 1998] 1078-1079).

38. K. COBLENTZ BAUTCH, "The Fall and Fate of Renegade Angels: The Intersection of Watchers Traditions and the Book of Revelation," in A. KIM HARKINS – K. COBLENTZ BAUTCH – J.C. ENDRES, eds., *The Fallen Angels Traditions* (Washington, DC: The Catholic Biblical Association of America, 2014) 69-93.

39. K. COBLENTZ BAUTCH, "The Fall and Fate of Renegade Angels: The Intersection of Watchers Traditions and the Book of Revelation," in A. KIM HARKINS – K. COBLENTZ BAUTCH – J.C. ENDRES, eds., *The Fallen Angels Traditions* (Washington, DC: The Catholic Biblical Association of America, 2014) 83.

40. Grabbe notes that "although there is no explicit reference to the scapegoat ceremony, Rev 20,1-3.10 has clear connections with *1 Enoch* 10, 4-5. Note the common features: Asael is bound prior to the judgment just as is Satan. This binding seems to include chains, according to *1 Enoch* 54, 3-5, though the exact date of the Parables is disputed. Just as Satan is cast into the abyss, so are Asael and others according to Syncellus's version of *1 Enoch* 9, 4: 'Then the Most High commanded the holy archangels, and they bound their leaders [sc. of the fallen angels] and threw them into the abyss until the judgment.' In the final judgment, just as Satan is cast into a 'lake of fire' ... so Asael and his companions are cast into an 'abyss of fire' ... Thus, the punishment of Satan has been assimilated to the Asael

### 3.4 The Motif of Sealing the Scapegoat's Abyss

Another important connection that ties Revelation 20 to *1 Enoch* 10 is the motif of sealing the abyss of the antagonist's first imprisonment. From Rev 20:3 one learns that, after the dragon was thrown into the abyss, the executing angel then locked and sealed the pit over him.

Similarly, in the *Book of the Watchers*, Raphael seals the abyss of the eschatological scapegoat with sharp rocks and darkness. In *1 Enoch* 10 God commands Raphael to throw onto Asael jagged and sharp stones and cover him with darkness. The motif of sealing the tomb of the eschatological scapegoat might also be present in the story of another—this time Christian—eschatological scapegoat, namely Jesus, whose temporarily placement in the underground chamber was also accompanied by the sealing of his tomb with a stone.

### 3.5 The Motif of the Temporary Healing of the Earth

In his analysis of the similarities between the punishment of Asael in *1 Enoch* 10 and Yom Kippur traditions, Daniel Stökl ben Ezra notes that the restoration of the earth by the removal of the sin in *1 Enoch* 10:7-8 alludes to the cathartic rationale behind Yom Kippur.[41] It is noteworthy that in the *Book of the Watchers* "the healing of the earth" occurs immediately after Asael's banishment into the abyss but before his fiery demise. This final ordeal will happen much later, on the Day of Judgment, which will occur as in the case of the other Watchers after seventy generations of entombment.[42] Such sandwiching of "the healing of the

---

tradition of *1 Enoch*" (L.L. GRABBE, "The Scapegoat Tradition: A Study in Early Jewish Interpretation," *Journal for the Study of Judaism in the Persian, Hellenistic, and Roman Periods* 18 [1987] 165-179 [160-161]).

41. D. STÖKL BEN EZRA, *The Impact of Yom Kippur on Early Christianity: The Day of Atonement from Second Temple Judaism to the Fifth Century* (Tübingen: Mohr Siebeck, 2003) 88.

42. Reflecting on the punishment of Asael and other fallen angels in the *Book of the Watchers*, Archie Wright notes that "*1 Enoch* 10:4-15 describes the punishment of the Watchers for their crimes against God and His creation. Asa'el is first to face his punishment for his role in the Instruction motif of *Book of the Watchers* (10:4-6, 8). He will be bound and cast into the darkness where he will be entombed until the Day of Judgment at which time he will be destroyed in the fire. The angels from the Shemihazah tradition face a similar punishment in 10:11-14. They will first view the death of their offspring (10:12) and secondly, they shall be bound under the earth until their judgment (10:12). The judgment occurs after seventy generations of entombment at which time they shall be cast into the fire where they will be destroyed (10.13-14)" (A.T. WRIGHT, *The Origins of Evil Spirits: The Reception of Genesis 6.1-4 in Early Jewish Literature* [Tübingen: Mohr Siebeck, 2005] 145-146). Other Enochic booklets reaffirm the same pattern. Thus, Coblentz Bautch notes that "the pattern recurs in the *Animal Apocalypse* as the Watchers are first consigned to

earth" between the antagonist's first and second punishments is noteworthy since it brings to mind several developments found in the Book of Revelation, where the dragon's first banishment precedes the peace of the millennium, which will later be interrupted by the dragon's brief release. The removal of the antagonist into the bottomless pit appears to accomplish, as in Asael's episode, cathartic and purifying functions which allow the earth to flourish. This context underlines the principal "elimination" aspect of the scapegoat ritual whereby impurity must be removed from the human *oikoumene* and sent into the uninhabitable realm.[43] This period of prosperity, however, ends with the unchaining of the dragon. Scholars have previously noted that "the millennium is deliberately framed by the chaining of the dragon and his unchaining which follows in Rev 20:7-10."[44] The apocalyptic portrayal of earth's healing as a temporary event might be rooted in Yom Kippur traditions, according to which the purification of the land and the community must be repeated on a regular basis.

### 3.6 The Motif of the Scapegoat's Temporary Unbinding before His Final Demise

From *Mishnah Yoma* 6:6 we learned that immediately before the scapegoat's final demise its handler briefly removed its crimson band. Such a procedure might signify a short-term release of the antagonist from bondage. It is possible that this theme of the temporary unbinding of

---

an abyss (*1 Enoch* 88:1,3) described as deep, dark and of the earth. At the time of the eschaton, the angels are brought forward for judgment (*1 Enoch* 90:21) and then thrown into a fiery abyss along with other sinners (*1 Enoch* 90:24-26). The *Book of Parables* describes a similar fate: chains are prepared for the host of Azazel (a later rendering of Asael and a reference to one of the Watchers) so that they might be thrown into an abyss of complete judgment and covered with jagged stones (cf. *1 Enoch* 10:5). On the day of judgment, we are told, the archangels will throw the rebels into a burning furnace because they became servants of Satan and led astray humankind (54:3-6)" (K. Coblentz Bautch, "The Fall and Fate of Renegade Angels: The Intersection of Watchers Traditions and the Book of Revelation," in A. Kim Harkins – K. Coblentz Bautch – J.C. Endres, eds., *The Fallen Angels Traditions* [Washington, DC: The Catholic Biblical Association of America, 2014] 84).

43. Reflecting on the dynamics of the scapegoat ritual Jacob Milgrom notes that "purgation and elimination rites go together in the ancient world. Exorcism of impurity is not enough; its power must be eliminated. An attested method is to banish it to its place of origin (the wilderness or the netherworld) or to some place where its malefic powers could work in the interest of the sender" (J. Milgrom, *Leviticus. A Book of Ritual and Ethics. A Continental Commentary* [Minneapolis: Fortress Press, 2004] 172).

44. P. de Villiers, "Prime Evil and its Many Faces in the Book of Revelation," *Neotestamentica* 34 (2000) 57-85 (62).

the cultic ribbon is also attested in some apocalyptic scapegoat traditions. As it is known, in addition to the motif of the Dragon's binding, the Book of Revelation reports a theme of his release from captivity. Thus, after the description of the millennium in Rev 20:4-6, during which the dragon remains chained in the bottomless pit, the text discloses the mystery of his release from imprisonment. Scholars have previously noticed that the narrative about the dragon's release is closely tied to the previous section pertaining to his imprisonment through several terminological connections, namely the subtle and often unnoticed link between the chaining and the unchaining, which is formulated by λυθῆναι in Rev 20:3 and λυθήσεται in Rev 20:7.[45]

### 3.7 The Motif of the Red Band

An important motif, which is absent in Leviticus 16 but present in Mishnaic and early Christian testimonies, is the theme of the scapegoat's crimson band that was put on the animal's head during the ritual of the goats' selection.[46] This scarlet band is often reinterpreted in the apocalyptic Yom Kippur traditions as the red garment. Thus, for example, the *Apocalypse of Abraham* speaks about Azazel's garment and the *Epistle of Barnabas* reinterprets the crimson band as a long scarlet robe around Christ's flesh. As one can see in apocalyptic scapegoat traditions, the crimson color was often projected onto the entire extent of the eschatological characters.

In light of these developments, special attention should be drawn to Rev 12:3 where the dragon is associated with a fiery red color (πυρρός). Many scholarly interpretations of this color symbolism have been offered through a panoply of references to various Egyptian,[47] Mesopotamian,[48] and Greek traditions.[49] What was often forgotten in these scholarly debates is that in ancient Jewish lore the color red was

---

45. P. DE VILLIERS, "Prime Evil and its Many Faces in the Book of Revelation," *Neotestamentica* 34 (2000) 57-85 (63-64).

46. Thus, *m. Yoma* 4:2 contains the following tradition: "He bound a thread of crimson wool on the head of the scapegoat and he turned it towards the way by which it was to be sent out; and on the he-goat that was to be slaughtered [he bound a thread] about its throat" (H. DANBY, *The Mishnah* [Oxford: Oxford University Press, 1992] 166).

47. E. LOHMEYER – H. LIETZMANN – G. BORNKAMM, *Die Offenbarung des Johannes* (Tübingen: Mohr, 1970) 99; A. YARBRO COLLINS, *The Combat Myth in the Book of Revelation* (Missoula: Scholars Press, 1976) 79.

48. R.H. CHARLES, *A Critical and Exegetical Commentary on the Revelation of St. John* (2 vols; Edinburgh: T&T Clark, 1920) 1.318-319; A. YARBRO COLLINS, *The Combat Myth in the Book of Revelation* (Missoula: Scholars Press, 1976) 77.

49. D.E. AUNE, *Revelation 6-16* (Nashville: Thomas Nelson Publishers, 1998) 683; C.R. KOESTER, *Revelation: A New Translation with Introduction and Commentary* (New Haven: Yale University Press, 2015) 545.

often associated with impurity and defilement. Already Isa 1:18 hints at such an understanding, delivering a promise from the deity that although Israel's "sins are like scarlet, they shall be like snow; though they are red like crimson, they shall become like wool." This passage, which associates sin with the color red, was predestined to play a special role in the Mishnaic testimonies concerning the crimson band of the scapegoat. Thus, both *m. Yoma* 6:8[50] and *m. Shabbat* 9:3[51] connect the tradition of the crimson band to the aforementioned passage from Isaiah that speaks about the forgiveness of sins. Elsewhere, a connection was made between the scarlet thread and human sins, since Jewish lore often associated the color red with sin, and white with forgiveness. The *Book of Zohar* II.20a-b neatly summarizes this understanding of the color symbolism:

> Sin is red, as it says, "Though your sins be as scarlet"; man puts the sacrificial animal on fire, which is also red; the priest sprinkles the red blood round the altar, but the smoke ascending to heaven is white. Thus, the red is turned to white: the attribute of Justice is turned into the attribute of Mercy.[52]

A very similar appropriation of the color imagery appears to be reflected in the scapegoat ritual. The band's transformation from red to white, signaling the forgiveness of Israel's sins, strengthens the association of the red coloration with sin.[53] Numerous Mishnaic and talmudic passages

50. *m. Yoma* 6:8: "R. Ishmael says: Had they not another sign also?—a thread of crimson wool was tied to the door of the Sanctuary and when the he-goat reached the wilderness the thread turned white; for it is written, Though your sins be as scarlet they shall be as white as snow" (H. DANBY, *The Mishnah* [Oxford: Oxford University Press, 1992] 170).

51. *m. Shabbat* 9:3: "Whence do we learn that they tie a strip of crimson on the head of the scapegoat? Because it is written, Though your sins be as scarlet, they shall be as white as snow" (H. DANBY, *The Mishnah* [Oxford: Oxford University Press, 1992] 108).

52. H. SPERLING – M. SIMON, *The Zohar* (5 vols; London - New York: Soncino, 1933) 3.6.

53. *b. Yoma* 39a: "Our Rabbis taught: Throughout the forty years that Simeon the Righteous ministered, the lot ['For the Lord'] would always come up in the right hand; from that time on, it would come up now in the right hand, now in the left. And [during the same time] the crimson-colored strap would become white. From that time on it would at times become white, at others not." (I. EPSTEIN, *The Babylonian Talmud. Yoma* [London: Soncino, 1935-1952] 39a); *b. Yoma* 39b: "Our Rabbis taught: During the last forty years before the destruction of the Temple the lot ['For the Lord'] did not come up in the right hand; nor did the crimson-coloured strap become white" (I. EPSTEIN, *The Babylonian Talmud. Yoma* [London: Soncino, 1935-1952] 39b).

attest to the whitening of the band[54] during the scapegoat ritual, which signifies the removal of sins.[55]

The Book of Revelation might also be cognizant of this symbolic conception, in which the color red is paradoxically able to turn white, thus signifying the removal of human transgressions.[56] So, for example, in Rev 7:14 one finds a paradoxical statement which reports that the righteous had "washed their robes and made them white in the blood of the Lamb."

In light of the aforementioned traditions, it does not appear to be coincidental that in the Book of Revelation many antagonists, onto some of which human sins were literally heaped in the course of the story, are associated with the color red. These agents of impurity and transgression, which now include the Scarlet Beast and the Harlot,[57] are portrayed with similar color attributes, being fashioned in crimson (κόκκινον) garments.[58]

54. *b. Yoma* 67a: "But let him tie the whole [thread] to the rock? — Since it is his duty [to complete his work with] the he-goat, perhaps the thread might become fast white, and he would be satisfied. But let him tie the whole thread between its horns? — At times its head [in falling] is bent and he would not pay attention. Our Rabbis taught: In the beginning they would tie the thread of crimson wool on the entrance of the Ulam without: if it became white they rejoiced; if it did not become white, they were sad and ashamed. Thereupon they arranged to tie it to the entrance of the Ulam within. But they were still peeping through and if it became white, they rejoiced, whereas, if it did not become white, they grew sad and ashamed. Thereupon they arranged to tie one half to the rock and the other half between its horns. R. Nahum b. Papa said in the name of R. Eleazar ha-Kappar: Originally they used to tie the thread of crimson wool to the entrance of the Ulam within, and as soon as the he-goat reached the wilderness, it turned white. Then they knew that the commandment concerning it had been fulfilled, as it is said: If your sins be as scarlet, they shall be as white wool" (I. EPSTEIN, *The Babylonian Talmud. Yoma* [London: Soncino, 1935-1952] 67a).

55. Cf. also *m. Shabbat* 9:3: "Whence do we learn that they tie a strip of crimson on the head of the scapegoat? Because it is written, Though your sins be as scarlet they shall be as white as snow" (H. DANBY, *The Mishnah* [Oxford: Oxford University Press, 1992] 108).

56. E.F. LUPIERI, "Apocalisse, sacerdozio e Yom Kippur," *Annali di Storia dell'Esegesi* 19/1 (2002) 11-21 (19).

57. Rev 17:3-4: "So he carried me away in the spirit into a wilderness, and I saw a woman sitting on a scarlet beast (ἐπὶ θηρίον κόκκινον) that was full of blasphemous names, and it had seven heads and ten horns. The woman was clothed in purple and scarlet (κόκκινον), and adorned with gold and jewels and pearls, holding in her hand a golden cup full of abominations and the impurities of her fornication." The *Epistle of Barnabas* uses the same terminology in its descriptions of scarlet band: *Barnabas* 7:8: "and wrap a piece of scarlet wool (τὸ ἔριον τὸ κόκκινον) around its head."

58. The red colored attributes of the antagonists present a striking contrast with the white attributes of the sinless and the righteous (Rev 2:17; 3:4-5; 6:11; 7:9-14) and their eschatological leaders (Rev 1:14; 4:4). Scholars previously noted that "in Revelation the color 'white' consistently denotes purity" (L.T. STUCKEN-

Some scholars have previously suggested that these color associations evoke the memory of the scarlet band of the scapegoat.[59] Future investigations of these intriguing developments might help to bring clarity to the true extent and nature of the Yom Kippur traditions found in the Book of Revelation.

---

BRUCK – M.D. MATHEWS, "The Apocalypse of John, *1 Enoch*, and the Question of Influence," in J. FREY – J.A. KELHOFFER – F. TÓTH, eds., *Die Johannesapokalypse. Kontexte – Konzepte – Rezeption* (Tübingen: Mohr Siebeck, 2012) 191-234 (198). See also D.E. AUNE, *Revelation 1-5* (Dallas: Word Books, 1997) 222-223.

59. P. CARRINGTON, *The Meaning of Revelation* (London: SPCK, 1931) 348, 392; J. MASSYNGBERDE FORD, *Revelation* (Garden City: Doubleday, 1975) 277, 287.

# THE DRAGON, THE BEASTS, AND THE GOLD: THE NUMBER OF THE BEAST IN THE APOCALYPSE OF JOHN*

À LA MÉMOIRE DE BERNARD BARC (1940-2021),

« … SON SOUVENIR NE DISPARAÎTRA PAS … »

## PART ONE: "AND IT STOOD ON THE SAND OF THE SEA" (REV 12:18): THE DRAGON, THE SEED OF THE WOMAN, AND THE BEAST FROM THE SEA

**Louis PAINCHAUD**

*Université Laval, Québec*

Yet you said, "I will do you great good
and make your offspring as the sand of the sea,
which shall not be counted for multitude."

(Gen 32:13 LXX).[1]

Résumé

Comme beaucoup d'autres passages obscurs dans l'Apocalypse de Jean, le chiffre de la bête, le nombre 666, doit être interprété à partir de son parallèle scripturaire, un *hapax* en 1 R 10,13. Cette hypothèse n'est pas nouvelle puisqu'elle a été formulée pour la première fois par Bède le Vénérable au début du VIIIe siècle. Dans cette première partie de ma contribution au présent volume, je propose un état sommaire de la recherche concernant l'identité du

* I would like to thank, for their helpful comments and criticisms, all colleagues who read drafts of these chapters, in particular the late Bernard Barc and Wolf-Peter Funk, as well as Edmondo Lupieri and Paul-Hubert Poirier, and also all those who contributed to the development of its English version or revision, Michael Kaler, Shane Gormley, Jared Teschner.

1. Σὺ δὲ εἶπας καλῶς εὖ σε ποιήσω καὶ θήσω τὸ σπέρμα σου ὡς τὴν ἄμμον τῆς θαλάσσης, ἣ οὐκ ἀριθμηθήσεται ἀπὸ τοῦ πλήθους (Gen 32:13 LXX). The Greek texts of the Septuagint are taken from A. RAHLFS, ed., *Septuaginta. Id est Vetus Testamentum graece iuxta lxx interpretes* (Stuttgart: Deutsche Bibelgesellschaft, 1982). English translations are taken from A. PIETERSMA – B.G. WRIGHT, eds., *A New English Translation of the Septuagint* (Oxford: Oxford University Press, 2007).

*"Who is Sitting on Which Beast?" Interpretative Issues in the Book of Revelation. Proceedings of the International Conference held at Loyola University, Chicago, March 30-31, 2017,* ed. by Edmondo Lupieri and Louis Painchaud, JAOC 29 (Turnhout, 2023), pp. 185–226

DOI 10.1484/M.JAOC-EB.5.131934

dragon et des deux bêtes issues de la mer et de la terre et j'aborde l'utilisation des Écritures par Jean comme clé de l'interprétation de son texte, qu'il compose comme un tissu dont la trame narrative est supportée par une chaîne d'allusions scripturaires. Je propose ensuite des critères de repérage des allusions scripturaires et j'examine leur utilisation dans le prologue (Ap 1,4-8) et dans la vision de la femme et du dragon (Ap 12) et son énigmatique conclusion, « Il se tint sur le sable de la mer » (Ap 12,18 ; cf. Gn 32,13). Enfin, je propose d'interpréter la bête issue de la mer (Ap 13,1-10) non seulement comme une représentation de l'empire romain, mais comme une récapitulation de tous les empires étrangers qui ont successivement exercé leur domination sur Israël jusqu'au dernier, celui de Rome.

Abstract

Like many other obscure passages in the Apocalypse of John, the number of the beast, 666, must be interpreted from its scriptural parallel, a *hapax* in 1 Kings 10:13. This hypothesis is not new, since it was first formulated by the Venerable Bede at the beginning of the eighth century. In this first part of my contribution to this volume, I offer a summary of the research concerning the identity of the dragon and the two beasts from the sea and from the land, and I discuss John's use of Scripture as a key to the interpretation of his text, which he composes as a fabric whose narrative weave is supported by a chain of scriptural allusions. I then propose criteria for identifying scriptural allusions and examine their use in the prologue (Rev 1:4-8), and in the vision of the woman and the dragon (Rev 12), and its enigmatic conclusion, "He stood on the sand of the sea" (Rev 12:18; cf. Gen 32:13). Finally, I propose to interpret the beast from the sea (Rev 13:10) not only as a representation of the Roman Empire, but as a recapitulation of all the foreign empires that successively exercised their domination over Israel until the last one, that of Rome.

## 1. Introduction

In the Apocalypse of John, the visions of the woman in heaven and the dragon, and of the two beasts from the sea and the land, form a whole (Rev 12-13) that offers the reader enigmas to decipher. The dragon standing on the sand of the sea (Rev 12:18) is one, as is the famous number of the beast (Rev 13:18). Furthermore, the beast from the land (Rev 13:11-17), who is the false prophet (Rev 16:13; 19:20; 20:10), also remains a riddle. The hypothesis proposed here is that the solution to these riddles can be reached by identifying the scriptural allusions in these passages and understanding the links between them.

This is the first part of a diptych devoted to these visions; it addresses the essential theoretical and methodological questions and deals specifically with the vision of the woman confronted by the dragon and its enigmatic conclusion (Rev 12:1-18), and that of the beast from the sea

(Rev 13:1-10). The second part will deal with the vision of the beast from the land (Rev 13:11-17) and the number of the beast (Rev 13:18).

This first part is divided into five unequal sections: 1) a brief state of research that questions the reading of the Apocalypse according to a "theory of persecution" or an "anti-imperial theory"; 2) the important question of the actual dating of the text and its chronotope[2] (Rev 1:9-10); 3) a theoretical and methodological framework proposing the reading of the Apocalypse as a scriptural prophecy whose proper interpretation depends on recognizing the scriptural allusions it contains and understanding the links between them; 4) the application of this reading to the allusions contained in the inaugural address (Rev 1:4-8); and 5) its application to the three following passages: the vision of the fight in heaven between the woman and the dragon (Rev 12:1-17); the riddle of the dragon standing on the sand of the sea (Rev 12:18); and the vision of the beast coming out of the sea (Rev 13:1-10).

## 2. The State of Research

Traditional iconography has fixed the image of a single beast with seven heads;[3] yet there are a dragon and two beasts in the text. The dragon has seven heads and ten horns, and on its heads are seven diadems (Rev 12:3); it appears in heaven where it stands in front of a pregnant woman clothed with the sun (Rev 12:3-4); Michael and his angels fight it (Rev 12:7); it is thrown down to earth (Rev 12:9) where it pursues the woman who had given birth to a male child (Rev 12:13), who escapes from it in the desert; then the dragon continues the fight against the remnants of her seed (Rev 12:17) and stands on the sand of the sea (Rev 12:18).

Then a first beast rises from the sea (Rev 13:1a); it has seven heads and ten horns like the dragon (Rev 13:1b), and ten diadems on the ten horns, three more than the dragon; it has the appearance of a leopard, a bear, and a lion; the dragon gives the beast its own power, its throne, and a great authority (Rev 13:2); one of its heads, wounded to death, is healed (Rev 13:3); its number is six hundred and sixty-six, or six hundred and sixteen according to certain manuscripts (Rev 13:18).[4]

---

2. That is the time and space of the Apocalypse as they are configured in the first chapter of Revelation; on the concept of chronotope, see M. Bakhtine, *Esthétique et théorie du roman* (Paris: Gallimard, 1978) 237-238.

3. On the influence of the traditional iconography of the Apocalypse on its scholarly reception, see R. Burnet, "D'où proviennent nos clefs de lecture de l'Apocalypse? *Auslegungsgeschichte* de l'épisode de la Femme et du Dragon," in A. Yarbro Collins, ed., *New Perspectives on the Book of Revelation* (Leuven: Peeters, 2017) 315-332.

4. On the variant six hundred and sixty, see below, pp. 241 ff.

A second beast rises from the earth/land, it does not have the seven heads, nor the ten horns, nor the crowns of the dragon ; it has two horns like those of a lamb, but it speaks like a dragon (Rev 13:11). It exercises all the authority of the first beast under its supervision (Rev 13:12) ; it causes fire to come down from heaven (Rev 13:13) and incites people to make an image of the first beast (Rev 13:14) ; it imposes a mark upon everyone, which is the name and the number of the first beast, in order to buy or sell (Rev 13:16-17) ; elsewhere in the text, it is identified with the false prophet (Rev 16:13 ; 19:20 ; 20:10).

### 2.1 The Identity of the Dragon

The identity of the dragon is made clear through scriptural allusion : it is explicitly identified with the "ancient serpent" (Gen 3:1-4), with the devil and Satan (Rev 12:9) ; it personifies the mythical Adversary par excellence.

As for the two beasts, the issue is more complex. On the eschatological level, commentators identify the beast with the Antichrist who is to come at the end of time.[5] However, opinions differ as to which of the two beasts should be identified with him.[6] There has been a broad consensus that the two beasts represent historical realities contemporary to the composition of the text.[7]

---

5. The secondary literature devoted to this subject is immense; see W. BOUSSET, *The Antichrist Legend. A Chapter in Christian and Jewish Folklore* (Atlanta: Scholars Press, 1999) repr. of the English translation by A.H. KEANE (London: Hutchison, 1896) of *Der Antichrist in der Überlieferung des Judentums, des Neuen Testaments und der alten Kirche. Ein Beitrag zur Auslegung der Apokalypse* (Göttingen: Vandenhoeck & Ruprecht, 1895), esp. the introduction and bibliography by David Frankfurter, pp. iii-xx; D.E. AUNE, *Revelation 6-16* (Nashville: Thomas Nelson Publishers, 1998) 751-754; C. BADILITA, *Métamorphoses de l'Antichrist chez les pères de l'Église* (Paris: Beauchesne, 2005) ; C. BADILITA – L. CICCOLINI, *L'Antichrist* (Paris: J.-P. Migne, 2011).

6. For Irenaeus of Lyon (*Against Heresies* V, 28, 2), it is the beast coming from the sea that is the Antichrist, whereas the beast coming from the earth, which is also the false prophet, is its servant (*armigero ejus*) ; A. ROUSSEAU – L. DOUTRELEAU – Ch. MERCIER, *Irénée de Lyon. Contre les Hérésies, Livre V. Édition critique d'après les versions arménienne et latine, tome II. Texte et traduction* (Paris: Cerf, 1969) 352-357 ; he is followed by Victorinus of Poetovio (*Commentary on the Apocalypse* XIII,1) which initiates speculation about the heads of the beast and the Roman emperors, and echoes the legend of the *Nero redivivus* (M. DULAEY, *Victorin de Poetovio. Sur l'Apocalypse suivi du Fragment chronologique et de La construction du monde* [Paris: Cerf, 1997] 104-111); for Hippolytus of Rome (*On Christ and Antichrist* XLIX, 1), it is the second beast that represents the coming reign of the Antichrist, its two horns representing the Antichrist himself and the false prophet (E. NORELLI, *L'Anticristo. De Antichristo* [Firenze: Nardini Editore, 1987] 122-125 ; 233-235).

7. For a different perspective, see in this book the contribution by Iain Provan.

## 2.2 The Identity of the First Beast

The identification of the first beast with the Roman Empire is traditional and makes sense given the historical background of the text. It is consistent not only with a certain prophetic tradition that sets Israel, the chosen people, against other nations, but also, and more precisely, with the identification of God's eschatological adversary with Rome in certain texts contemporary with the Apocalypse,[8] but this is perhaps too reductive. We shall propose that this first beast should be seen not only as the empire of Rome, but also as a recapitulation of all the empires that dominated Israel.

## 2.3 The Identity of the Second Beast

As for the second beast, the situation is less clear. It is most often associated with the Roman imperial cult or with an institution attached to it,[9] for example the *koinon* of Asia ; however, this identification is hardly compatible with the ambiguous character of the second beast, the imperial cult being in no way ambiguous, nor with its designation as "the false prophet" (ψευδοπροφήτης Rev 16:13 ; 19:20 ; 20:10). The identification of the second beast with the Roman imperial cult thus remains problematic ; this conclusion reached by David Aune twenty years ago is still valid today.[10] In my view, this particular identification rests less on internal elements of the text than on postulates according to which : 1) the Apocalypse was directed against the Roman empire, either in reaction to real or perceived persecution (persecution theory), or for ideological reasons (anti-imperial theory) ; and 2) the imperial cult constituted an important threat to the followers of Jesus. As it will be discussed below, these assumptions have been challenged and we must now abandon them.

### 2.3.1 The Theory of Persecution

Historical-critical exegetes have sought to explain the Apocalypse as a reaction to a crisis caused by the persecution of Christians by the Roman Empire. Thus, the influential George Arthur Buttrick wrote in 1951, "In one way, Revelation is a brilliant and deadly attack upon the Roman

---

8. For example, in the Syriac *Apocalypse of Baruch*, where it is represented by the forest opposite to the vine (*2 Baruch* 39), in the *Sibylline Oracles* (5:137-183), where the reference to Nero is clear, as well as in the *Ascension of Isaiah* 4:1-4.

9. See P. Prigent, *L'Apocalypse de Saint Jean. Édition revue et augmentée* (Geneva : Labor et Fides, 2000) 321 ; D.E. Aune, *Revelation 6-16* (Nashville : Thomas Nelson Publishers, 1998) 773-779.

10. D.E. Aune, *Revelation 6-16* (Nashville : Thomas Nelson Publishers, 1998) 756.

Empire as it sets to destroy the Christian faith."[11] Research since then has found no proof of any systematic persecution of "Christians" in the province of Asia Minor in the first century, neither under Domitian, whose reign lasted from 81 to 96, nor before him.[12] Indeed, it seems that Judeans[13] who lived in these cities, and followers of the Messiah Jesus, later to be called Christians, who likely lived among them,[14] could lead a serene, even prosperous existence,[15] relatively well integrated into the social fabric of the cities.[16] In order to preserve this interpretation of the Apocalypse as the one intended by its author and earliest readers, Adela Yarbro Collins postulated the existence of a perception or apprehension of a crisis among the "Christians" of Asia Minor, at least by John himself.[17] Neither verifiable nor falsifiable, this postulate has been generally accepted, so much

---

11. G.A. Buttrick, *The Interpreter's Bible: The Holy Scriptures in the King James and Revised Standard Versions with General Articles and Introduction, Exegesis, Exposition for Each Book of the Bible.* vol. 12 (New York: Abingdon-Cokesbury Press, 1951) 588.

12. Concerning the absence of systematic or widespread persecution of Christians in Asia Minor in the first two centuries, see L.L. Thompson, *The Book of Revelation: Apocalypse and Empire* (Oxford: Oxford University Press, 1990); also J.C. Wilson, "The Problem of the Domitianic Date of Revelation," *New Testament Studies* 39/4 (1993) 587-616 (589-595); P.A. Harland, *Associations, Synagogues, and Congregations. Claiming a Place in Ancient Mediterranean Society* (Minneapolis: Fortress Press, 2003) 185-189; also D.E. Aune, *Revelation 1-5* (Dallas: Word Books, 1997) lxvi-lxx.

13. Preferably to "Jew," the ethnonym "Judean" will be used in this text to designate persons originating from Judea and living according to the laws and customs of this territory in Palestine or in the diaspora; see S.C. Mimouni, *Le judaïsme ancien du VIe siècle avant notre ère au IIIe siècle de notre ère. Des prêtres aux rabbins* (Paris: PUF, 2012) 22-24; also S. Mason, "Jews, Judeans, Judaizing, Judaism: Problems of Categorization in Ancient History," *Journal for the Study of Judaism* 38 (2007) 457-512.

14. Considering the Apocalypse of John as a sectarian messianic Judean text and not as a Christian text, the term "Messiah" will be used, as in the translations of Septuagint and of Judeo-Hellenistic literature, to render the Greek χριστός, and not the term "Christ" which belongs to the Christian idiom.

15. In the Apocalypse itself, John's rebukes to the ἐκκλησία of Laodicea "which thinks itself rich" (Rev 3:15-19) testify to this.

16. L.L. Thompson, *The Book of Revelation: Apocalypse and Empire* (Oxford: Oxford University Press, 1990) 95-167 (esp. 146-167); P.R. Trebilco, *Jewish Communities in Asia Minor* (Cambridge, U.K.: Cambridge University Press, 1991); also, *The Early Christians in Ephesus from Paul to Ignatius* (Tübingen: Mohr Siebeck, 2004) esp. for Ephesus 344-347; P.A. Harland, *Associations, Synagogues, and Congregations. Claiming a Place in Ancient Mediterranean Society* (Minneapolis: Fortress Press, 2003); also, *Dynamics of Identity in the World of Early Christians: Associations, Judeans, and Cultural Minorities* (New York: T&T Clark, 2009).

17. A. Yarbro Collins, *Crisis and Catharsis: The Power of the Apocalypse* (Philadelphia: Westminster Press, 1984) esp. 84-110. Whatever one's conception of the relationship that may exist between a given social situation and the apocalyptic dis-

so that the idea that this book is a writing of resistance, not only against Rome, but also against any form of empire, remains influential, even if the belief in a persecution of "Christians" by Rome has meanwhile vanished.

### 2.3.2 Anti-Imperial Theory

More recently, a new "anti-imperial" theory has emerged, which is not unrelated to the disappearance of the "theory of persecution."[18] It has been well received and amplified by liberation theology and post-colonial studies, for obvious reasons.[19] Thus, Stephen Friesen could write the following in 2001:

> John's vision of the world has implications beyond his first century setting, for John was not simply anti-Roman; he was anti-empire. His understanding of his world produced a religious critique of hegemony that transcended his particular historical location. The visionary argument built a broader case, one that questions *every* imperialist project. John's apocalyptic imagery depicted Rome in ruins and would lay waste to the structures of modern hegemony as well. John's religious criticism elevates Revelation as a crucial voice in the contrapuntal Christian canon. His criticism also makes the Apocalypse an important witness to humanity's struggles for the establishment of a just community in the context of humanity's record of ubiquitous oppression.[20]

Even today, the reception of the Apocalypse as a Christian work of anti-imperial or even anti-imperialist resistance still dominates much of the research, at least in the Anglo-Saxon world. Steven Friesen summed up this viewpoint in 2017, writing that

> [The Apocalypse] is the most strident anti-imperial text in the surviving Christian literature, and perhaps the most striking piece of an extant resistance literature from the first-century Mediterranean world."[21]

---

course, this idea has become quite widely accepted; see L.L. THOMPSON, *The Book of Revelation: Apocalypse and Empire* (Oxford: Oxford University Press, 1990) 27-28.

18. S.J. FRIESEN, "Apocalypse and Empire," in J.J. COLLINS, ed., *The Oxford Handbook of Apocalyptic Literature* (Oxford: Oxford University Press, 2014) 172.

19. See D.L. SMITH-CHRISTOPHER, "A Post-Colonial Reading of the Apocalyptic Literature," in J.J. COLLINS, ed., *The Oxford Handbook of Apocalyptic Literature* (Oxford: Oxford University Press, 2014) 180-200.

20. S.J. FRIESEN, *Imperial Cults and the Apocalypse of John: Reading Revelation in the Ruins* (Oxford: Oxford University Press, 2001) 4. In this excellent book on the imperial cult in Asia Minor, Friesen takes for granted, but without demonstrating it, that this cult constitutes a fundamental problem for the Jewish diaspora in Asia Minor and in particular for the Apocalypse of John.

21. S.J. FRIESEN, "Apocalypse and Empire," in J.J. COLLINS, ed., *The Oxford Handbook of Apocalyptic Literature* (Oxford: Oxford University Press, 2014) 172; see also A. PORTER-YOUNG, "Jewish Apocalyptic Literature as Resistance Literature," in COLLINS, *op. cit.*, 145-162.

In fact, this reading of the Apocalypse as a text of resistance to the empire of Rome dates back to the beginning of the third century, to Hippolytus, who wrote from a Roman point of view and fully endorsed the identification of the first beast with "the empire of the Romans" (ἡ βασιλεία Ῥωμαίων, *Antichrist* XLIX, 2, see also XXVIII).[22] A little later, Victorinus, bishop of Poetovio in Upper Pannonia (today's Ptuj, Slovenia), wrote his commentary on the Apocalypse probably around 258-260,[23] in the wake of persecutions under Decius and Valerian. Victorinus is the first to speculate on the identification of the seven kings (Rev 17:9-11) with seven emperors and to introduce the figure of Nero, risen by God to be king and messiah of the persecutors and of the Judeans (13:2-3).[24]

The Pannonian bishop is thus the first known figure to assimilate the first beast to both the Antichrist and the Roman Empire and to introduce the legend of *Nero redivivus* as a false messiah. Thanks to its revision and editing by Jerome, his commentary would later be widely disseminated in western Christianity. As David Potter points out, the anti-imperial reception of the Apocalypse of John may well owe something to the hostility towards Decius, Valerian and Diocletian that developed in the fourth century, at the time of the early circulation of Victorinus's commentary.[25] Consequently, it seems that we can retain neither the theory of persecution, nor the popular but anachronistic anti-imperial theory that has taken its place.[26]

### 2.3.3 Imperial Worship

Furthermore, the similarly popular idea that the imperial cult played a crucial role in the production of John's text[27] should also be put into perspec-

22. E. Norelli, *Ippolito. L'Anticristo. De Antichristo* (Firenze: Nardini Editore, 1987) 124-125, also 96-97; for the identification of Hippolytus and the dating of *De Christo et Antichristo*, see 9-40 and C. Badilita – L. Ciccolini, *L'Antichrist.* (Paris: J.-P. Migne, 2011) 57-62.

23. M. Dulaey, *Victorin de Poetovio. Sur l'Apocalypse suivi du Fragment chronologique et de La construction du monde* (Paris: Cerf, 1997) 15-17.

24. M. Dulaey, *Victorin de Poetovio. Sur l'Apocalypse suivi du Fragment chronologique et de La construction du monde* (Paris: Cerf, 1997) 106-109.

25. See D. Potter, "Decius and Valerian," in D.P.W. Burgersdijk – J. Ross, eds., *Imagining Emperors in the Late Roman Empire* (Leiden: Brill, 2018) 18-38; also, J.K. Zangenberg, "*Scelerum inventor et malorum machinator.* Diocletian and the Tetrarchy in Lactantius *De mortibus persecutorum*," in Burgersdijk – Ross, *op. cit.*, 39-62.

26. For a possible ideological matrix of this anti-imperial reading of the Apocalypse, see P.F. Esler, "Social-Scientific Approaches to Apocalyptic Literature," in J.J. Collins, ed., *The Oxford Handbook of Apocalyptic Literature* (Oxford: Oxford University Press, 2014) 133.

27. S.J. Friesen, *Imperial Cults and the Apocalypse of John: Reading Revelation in the Ruins* (Oxford: Oxford University Press, 2001) 3; see also J.N. Kraybill, *Imperial Cult and Commerce in John's Apocalypse* (Sheffield: Sheffield Academic

tive, as there is no evidence of an imperial policy to promote and impose the cult of the emperor under Domitian or before his reign.[28] Moreover, the imperial authorities, recognizing the ethnic laws, those of the Judeans as well as those of other ethnic groups within the empire, could not impose on the Judeans to participate in a cult that went against the laws of their *ethnos*.[29] This necessarily applied also to the Judean followers of Jesus of Nazareth, since they could hardly be distinguished from the other Judeans whose ethnic identity they shared.[30] This is all the more true since it is to be assumed, given John's constant allusive use of Scriptures, that the followers of Jesus for whom he intended his prophecy must have been mainly Judeans who were familiar with these Scriptures.[31] Moreover, Philip Harland's research, which seeks to contextualize the imperial cult

---

Press, 1996) in particular about merchant wealth 102-141 ; but see a different perspective in I. PROVAN, "Foul Spirits, Fornication and Finance : Revelation 18 from an Old Testament Perspective," *Journal for the Study of New Testament* 64 (1996) 81-100, as well as in the present book.

28. J.W. VAN HENTEN, "The Intertextual Nexus of Revelation," in S. ALKIER – TH. HIEKE – T. NICKLAS, eds., *Poetik und Intertextualität der Johannesapokalypse* (Tübingen : Mohr Siebeck, 2015) 410-412. The Greco-Roman social and cultural context of the composition and reception of the Apocalypse fully justifies an "intertextual" approach that seeks to contextualize the symbolic content of Revelation in relation to Greco-Roman culture, as van Henten does, but this does not mean that John borrows his symbolic material from it.

29. This does not imply that the Judeans enjoyed a privileged status in the empire, nor does it totally exclude occasional sporadic trouble in the cities, see M. SARTRE, *L'Orient romain : provinces et sociétés provinciales en Méditerranée orientale d'Auguste aux Sévères. 31 avant J.-C. – 235 après J.-C.* (Paris : Seuil, 1991) esp. 393-395 ; P.R. TREBILCO, *Jewish Communities in Asia Minor* (Cambridge, UK : Cambridge University Press, 1991) 12-19 ; also S. SAULNIER, "Lois romaines sur les Juifs selon Flavius Josèphe," *Revue Biblique* 88 (1981) 161-198 ; T. RAJAK, "Was there a Roman Charter for the Jews ?," *Journal of Roman Studies* 64 (1984) 107-123 ; on contacts and interaction between Judeans and non-Judeans see also L.V. RUTGERS, *The Jews in Late Ancient Rome : Evidence of Cultural Interaction in the Roman Diaspora* (Leiden : Brill, 1995) esp. 262-268 about isolation and assimilation. The recently proposed attempt to see in the dragon, the beast rising from the sea, and the beast rising from the land the three Dumezilian functions does not solve any of these problems (J. POON, *The Identities of the Beast from the Sea and the Beast from the Land in Revelation 13* [Eugene, OR : Wipf & Stock, 2017]).

30. Presumably, only the non-Judean followers of Jesus could have been harassed. Moreover, studies devoted to the construction of Christian identity in the first century come to the conclusion that it was impossible, at the time of the writing of the Apocalypse of John, to distinguish a "proto-Christian," that is to say a messianic Judean disciple of Jesus of Nazareth, from another Judean ; see J. GALAMBUSH, *The Reluctant Parting : How the New Testament's Jewish Writers Created a Christian Book* (San Francisco : Harper, 2005).

31. P. HIRSCHBERG, "Jewish Believers in Asia Minor according to the Book of Revelation and the Gospel of John," in O. SKARSAUNE – R. HVALVIK, eds., *Jewish Believers in Jesus : The Early Centuries* (Peabody : Hendrickson, 2007) esp. 218-230.

within the framework of associative life in the cities of Asia Minor, leads him to conclude

> Scholars have often overplayed the significance of imperial cults for early Christianity (as well as Judaism) without recognizing the broader framework within which these cults were embedded."[32]

That being said, the fact remains that the imperial cult practiced in the cities of Asia Minor, and more broadly the cult surrounding the statues, could not but abhor a Judean prophet who obviously considered the making of images to be an abomination.

On the other hand, one verifiable fact to which the prophet John could have been reacting is the risk of accommodation to the surrounding culture; Judeans, and among them followers of Jesus, might have been tempted to jeopardize their identities by adapting to the standards of the Greco-Roman city. In fact, the provinces in general, and Asia Minor in particular, experienced a period of prosperity in the last decades of the first century,[33] and the members of the messianic ἐκκλησίαι to which John addresses himself likely saw their condition improve during this period, as did the rest of the population.[34] Epigraphy and archaeology provide evidence of the integration of the Jewish communities of Asia Minor, and even of their prosperity in the following centuries, and there is every reason to believe that this situation also prevailed in the first century. Yet these messages to the ἐκκλησίαι seem to be more concerned with internal dissensions caused by tensions between rich and poor,[35] whereas for John, poverty, as well as dietary laws, would have been a boundary marker for the identity of Jesus's Judean followers.[36]

---

32. P.A. HARLAND, *Associations, Synagogues, and Congregations. Claiming a Place in Ancient Mediterranean Society* (Minneapolis: Fortress Press, 2003) 239-240.

33. On the economic situation and relative prosperity of the cities of Asia Minor in the first and second centuries, see M. SARTRE, *L'Orient romain. Provinces et société provinciales en Méditerranée orientale d'Auguste aux Sévères. 31 avant J.-C. – 235 après J.-C.* (Paris: Seuil, 1991) 295-308.

34. P.B. DUFF, *Who Rides the Beast? Prophetic Rivalry and Rhetoric of Crisis in the Churches of the Apocalypse* (Oxford: Oxford University Press, 2001) 17-30.

35. P.B. DUFF, *Who Rides the Beast? Prophetic Rivalry and Rhetoric of Crisis in the Churches of the Apocalypse* (Oxford: Oxford University Press, 2001) 47 and 61-70; "Not only was there a mixture of social levels in each congregation; but also, in each individual or category that we are able to identify there is evidence of divergent rankings in the different dimensions of status" (W.M. MEEKS, *The First Urban Christians: The Social World of the Apostle Paul* [New Haven: Yale University Press, 1983] 73); these observations made by Wayne Meeks about the Pauline communities likely also apply to the *ekklesiai* which John was addressing; see also M. ROSTOVTZEFF, *The Social and Economic History of the Roman Empire* (Oxford: Clarendon, 1926) 111.

36. P.R. TREBILCO, *The Early Christians in Ephesus from Paul to Ignatius* (Tübingen: Mohr Siebeck, 2004) 434-445. See also M.D. MATHEWS, *Riches, Poverty, and*

## 2.4 A Real Crisis, the First Judean War and the Ruin of the Temple

The now common understanding of John as a messianic Judean prophet and follower of Jesus,[37] rather than as a "Christian," was prompted by studies which have made considerable progress over the past half century in refining our understanding of early Jewish and Christian identities. This new understanding requires the abandonment of the dichotomy between Jews and Christians on the one hand and, on the other hand, the correction of the anachronistic reading of John's prophecy through the lens of Rome's oppression of the Christians, which has dominated the reception of the Apocalypse up to the present day. John W. Marshall has summed it up perfectly:

> There can be no mistake that John's apocalypse knows of no such identity as "Christianity," describes no break with Judaism, undertakes no polemic against it, does not conceive of the world in a three-part taxonomy of Christians/Jews/Pagans, and does not consider itself to be a hybrid of Judaism and Christianity. On the other hand, John's language, name, literary universe, social habitus, political loyalties, cosmological vision, and even his messianism all stand squarely within Second Temple Judaism.[38]

This being the case, there is no need to imagine any crisis caused by real or perceived anti-Christian persecution in the background of the Apocalypse, nor any anti-imperialist ideology, for at the time that John was writing, a major crisis was affecting all Judeans in Palestine and in the Diaspora, whatever the particular form of Judaism to which they adhered. This crisis, to which *4 Ezra* and *2 Baruch*, among other texts, witness, is the crisis that was provoked by the fall of Jerusalem and the ruin of the Temple in 70 CE. This tragic event was a human, political and religious disaster for

---

*the Faithful: Perspectives on Wealth in the Second Temple Period in the Apocalypse of John* (Cambridge, UK: Cambridge University Press, 2013) esp. 141-224.

37. J.W. MARSHALL, *Parables of War: Reading John's Jewish Apocalypse* (Waterloo, ONT: Wilfrid Laurier University Press, 2001) 1-9; P.A. HARLAND, *Associations, Synagogues, and Congregations. Claiming a Place in Ancient Mediterranean Society* (Minneapolis: Fortress Press, 2003) 1; E.F. LUPIERI, *A Commentary on the Apocalypse of John*, trans. M. POGGI JOHNSON – A. KAMESAR (Grand Rapids: Eerdmans, 2006) 35-44; E. PAGELS, *Revelations: Visions, Prophecy & Politics in the Book of Revelation* (New York: Viking, 2012).

38. J.W. MARSHALL, "John's Jewish (Christian?) Apocalypse," in M. JACKSON-MCCABE, ed., *Jewish Christianity Reconsidered: Rethinking Ancient Groups and Texts* (Minneapolis: Fortress Press, 2007) 235. This reception of John is at the antipodes of the one expressed in 1984 by Adela Yarbro Collins of a John "alienated from the Judaism of his time to a significant degree" ("Numerical Symbolism in Jewish and Early Christian Apocalyptic Literature," in W. HAASE, *Aufstieg und Niedergang der römischer Welt* 2.21.2. *Hellenistisches Judentum in römischer Zeit: Philon und Josephus* [Berlin: De Gruyter, 1984] 1278).

Judeans,[39] all of whom, including the followers of the Messiah Jesus of Nazareth, interpreted it in different ways in the light of their Scriptures, read according to their particular convictions.[40]

The voices of the prophets inspire John; like Jeremiah, Ezekiel, and Zechariah, John announces the just punishment of the holy city. For him, the fall of Jerusalem is due to the accommodations of its leaders with the nations; it is, therefore, the earthly Jerusalem defiled by its prostitution, and not Rome, that he represents under the guise of the whore Babylon.[41]

---

39. S.C. MIMOUNI, *Le judaïsme ancien du VIe siècle avant notre ère au IIIe siècle de notre ère. Des prêtres aux rabbins* (Paris: PUF, 2012) 453-478 and 611-612.

40. For an overview, see H.M. DÖPP, *Die Deutung der Zerstörung Jerusalems und des zweiten Tempels im Jahre 70 in den ersten drei Jahrhunderten n. Chr.* (Tübingen: Francke, 1998). On the importance of the Jerusalem temple among the followers of Jesus, see E. REGEV, *The Temple in Early Christianity: Experiencing the Sacred* (New Haven: Yale University Press, 2019) esp. chapter 7, "The Book of Revelation: The Alternative Temple," 222-251.

41. J.C. Wilson is wrong to assert that no scholar doubts that this woman, Babylon, should be identified with Rome (J.C. WILSON, "The Problem of the Domitianic Date of Revelation," *New Testament Studies* 39/4 [1993] 599). Although still marginal to the mainstream research, this thesis has been convincingly presented by Josephine Massyngberde Ford and by the roughly contemporary Eugenio Corsini: see J. MASSYNGBERDE FORD, *Revelation* (Garden City: Doubleday, 1975); also "The Heavenly Jerusalem and Orthodox Judaism," in C.K. BARRETT – E. BAMMEL – W.D. DAVIES, eds., *Donum Gentilicium. New Testament Studies in Honour of David Daube* (Oxford: Clarendon Press, 1978) 215-226; and E. CORSINI, *Apocalisse prima e dopo* (Torino: Società Editrice Internazionale, 1980) = *The Apocalypse: The Perennial Revelation of Jesus Christ*, trans. F.J. MOLONEY (Wilmington, DE: Glazier, 1983) = *L'Apocalypse maintenant*, trans. R. ARRIGHI (Paris: Éditions du Seuil, 1984). Massyngberde Ford is said to have subsequently abandoned this idea, under the influence of Ugo Vanni, apparently for fear of being accused of anti-Semitism (see E.F. LUPIERI, "L'Apocalisse dopo Corsini: un'eredità in evoluzione," in C. LOMBARDI – L. SILVANO, eds., *Apocalisse ieri oggi e domani. Atti della giornata di studio im memoria di Eugenio Corsini. Torino, 2 ottobre 2018* [Alessandria, Edizioni dell'Orso, 2019] 21). Massyngberde Ford and Corsini had been preceded by Philip Carrington, Anglican bishop of Quebec (1935-1960) and Metropolitan of Canada (1944-1960), see P. CARRINGTON, *The Meaning of Revelation* (London/New York: SPCK/Macmillan, 1931); see also more recently, A.J. BEAGLEY, *The 'Sitz im Leben' of the Apocalypse with Particular Reference to the Role of the Church's Enemies* (Berlin: De Gruyter, 1987) 1: "The way [John] uses this material leaves little doubt that he has in mind above all judgments which are to come (or which have come) upon the nation of Israel, and especially upon the city of Jerusalem"; also, I. PROVAN, "Foul Spirits, Fornication and Finance: Revelation 18 from an Old Testament Perspective," *Journal for the Study of New Testament* 64 (1996) 91-92; E.F. LUPIERI, *L'Apocalisse di Giovanni* (Milan: Arnoldo Mondadori Editore, 1999) (= *A Commentary on the Apocalypse of John*, trans. M. POGGI JOHNSON – A. KAMESAR [Grand Rapids: Eerdmans, 2006]); ID., "From Sodom and Balaam to the Revelation of John. Transtextual Adventures of Biblical Sins," in S. ALKIER – TH. HIEKE – T. NICKLAS, eds., *Poetik und Intertextualität der Johannesapokalypse* (Tübingen: Mohr Siebeck, 2015) 301-318; R. VAN DE WATER, "Reconsidering the Beast from

His faith in the Messiah Jesus assures him that the punishment of the earthly Jerusalem, the prostitute, was necessary for the advent of the new Jerusalem, the bride of the Lamb.[42]

In the absence of a real or perceived crisis caused by persecution at the hands of local or imperial authorities, John's Apocalypse (like other Judean apocalypses of the same time) can be read as a reaction to the events of 66-70 CE in Judaea. It is in this general context that we must seek to understand the meaning of the beasts and of the famous number.

As John Marshall and Martha Himmelfarb have clearly demonstrated, the Apocalypse of John is primarily a sectarian Judean text.[43]

## 3. Dating and Chronotope

John is reacting to the ruin of the earthly Jerusalem, which he announces after the fact (*vaticinium ex eventu*), just like *2 Baruch* and *4 Ezra*, two contemporary texts. This reading rests on a clear textual basis, namely the proclamation that the "holy city," that is, Jerusalem, will be trampled underfoot by the nations (Rev 11:2).[44] In Rev 11:7-8, Jerusalem is referred

the Sea (Rev 13.1)," *New Testament Studies* 46 (2000) 245-261) ; F.J. Moloney, *The Apocalypse of John : A Commentary* (Grand Rapids : Baker, 2020).

42. According to Stanilas Giet, John's writing of the Apocalypse might reflect the perception of the fall of Jerusalem in the prophetic tradition by Judean followers of Jesus, "who were quick to see in this catastrophe ... a providential disposition" (S. Giet, *L'Apocalypse et l'histoire, étude historique sur l'Apocalypse johannique* [Paris : PUF, 1957] 1).

43. J.W. Marshall, *Parables of War : Reading John's Jewish Apocalypse* (Waterloo, ONT : Wilfrid Laurier University Press, 2001) ; M. Himmelfarb, *A Kingdom of Priests : Ancestry and Merit in Ancient Judaism* (Philadelphia : University of Pennsylvania Press, 2006) 135-136.

44. In the same chapter, the beast rising from the abyss, which will make war on the two witnesses, will defeat them and cause them to perish, after which their bodies will remain in the place of the "great city," still evokes in a barely veiled way the taking of Jerusalem in 70 CE ; cf. L. Painchaud, "Temple et sacerdoce dans l'Apocalypse de Jean ou Zorobabel et Josué, témoins de Jésus Christ (Ap 11,3-14)," in L. Painchaud – S.C. Mimouni – D. Hamidović, eds., *La sacerdotalisation dans le judaïsme synagogal, dans le christianisme et dans le rabbinisme. Actes du colloque de Québec, 18-20 septembre 2014* (Turnhout : Brepols, 2018) 229-246. The "great city" appears also in Rev 17:18 ; 18:10. It is wrong to believe that the "great city that reigns over the kings of the earth" (Rev 17:18) is necessarily Rome. See Daniele Tripaldi's contribution in the present book. One may add to his compilation the striking expression "from the great Jerusalem to the little Alexandria" (*TJ Hagigah*, II, 2 [77d, col. 787] quoted by E. Friedheim, "Quelques notes sur la signification historique du silence philonien à propos de la bibliothèque d'Alexandrie," in C. Rico – A. Dan, eds., *The Library of Alexandria : A Cultural Crossroads of the Ancient World. Proceedings of the Second Polis Institute Interdisciplinary Conference* [Jerusalem : Polis Institute Press, 2017] n. 27).

to as the "great city" where the Lord was crucified, the same "great city" whose destruction is described in chapter 18.[45] This postulate requires some discussion regarding the dating of John's Apocalypse, both actual dating and literary or narrative (fictitious) dating.

### 3.1 Dating

The dating generally accepted today places the composition of the Apocalypse, at least in its final form, under the reign of Domitian. This dating is based on the testimony of Irenaeus and on the thesis developed by Joseph B. Lightfoot concerning a persecution that would have been carried out against the Christians under this emperor; however, this thesis is only supported by circumstantial evidence.[46] As we have seen, this alleged persecution may not have taken place, thus weakening Lightfoot's argument. As for the testimony of Irenaeus, who situates the writing of the Apocalypse "*ad finem Domitiani imperii*" (*Against Heresies* V, 30, 3), it is hardly more reliable than the identification he makes of the author of the Apocalypse with the "disciple of the Lord" (*Against Heresies* IV, 20, 11) following Justin (*Dialogue with Trypho* 81, 4).

The announcement of the siege of Jerusalem (Rev 11:2) requires that the composition of the text be placed after 70 CE, or at least at a time when the capture of Jerusalem had become foreseeable, if not inevitable. This seems unlikely before the beginning of the siege in the spring of 70, and so Rev 11:2 must therefore be a prophecy *ex eventu*. The year 70 marks a *terminus post quem*, and Justin's writing of the *Dialogue with Trypho*, which seems to refer to the Apocalypse (1:3; 9:3), shortly after the revolt of Bar Kochba (132-135), marks a *terminus ante quem*.[47] Since there is no necessity to go very late within this range, and since the violence of the text could easily be due to its proximity to the tragic events announced,

---

45. In the septets, Stanislas Giet suggested that the sixth phase should refer each time to the first Jewish war (S. GIET, *L'Apocalypse et l'histoire : étude historique sur l'Apocalypse johannique* [Paris : PUF, 1957] v-vi) ; he observed that the four angels (Rev 7:1-3) chained on the Euphrates (Rev 9:13-15) or the kings of the East crossing the dry Euphrates (Rev 16:12) have their correspondent in *2 Baruch* (6:4-5 ; 7:1) where four angels are associated with the destruction of Jerusalem ; see also S. GIET, "La guerre des Juifs de Flavius Josèphe et quelques énigmes de l'Apocalypse," *Revue des sciences religieuses* 26 (1952) 1-19 and 325-362 ; ID., "Retour sur l'Apocalypse," *Revue des sciences religieuses* 38 (1964) 225-264.

46. J.B. LIGHTFOOT, *The Apostolic Fathers : Clement, Ignatius, and Polycarp : Revised Texts with Introduction, Notes, Dissertations and Translations* (London : Macmillan, 1889 ; repr. Peabody : Hendrickson, 1989) passim, esp. vol. 1, 104-115.

47. D.E. AUNE, *Revelation 1-5* (Dallas : Word Books, 1997) 56-70. For the dating of the *Dialogue* in the years following the Second Jewish War, see P. BOBICHON, *Justin Martyr, Dialogue avec Tryphon*, vol. 1 (Fribourg : Academic Press Fribourg, 2003) 92-98.

we can plausibly situate the composition of the Apocalypse between the 70s and the end of the first century CE.

### 3.2 The "Lord's Day in Patmos," the Chronotope of the *Reception* of the Revelation

The hypothesis of an *ex eventu* prophecy also requires that the author uses a fictitious backdating, if the prophecy is to be credible.[48] John Wilson rejects this hypothesis, noting first that the Apocalypse is not a pseudepigraph, and second that it contains no injunction to keep its contents secret.[49] In this respect, there has been much speculation about the reasons for John's stay in Patmos,[50] but little consideration has been given to how Patmos itself functions in the text. This spatio-temporal reception of the revelation, "the day of the Lord at Patmos" (Rev 1:10), inserted just after an introduction establishing the foundation of the discursive universe of the revelation outside of time and space,[51] has the effect of establishing the concrete chronotope[52] of the revelation, of its dating and of its place of reception. The mention of the "day of the Lord" establishes the day of the week,[53] and perhaps also the occasion (an assembly of the faithful) for the reception of the revelation.[54] The mention of Patmos might establish not only the geographical location of the revelation, but likely also its time, month or year for the intended readers who would have been informed of this sojourn, which would have taken place shortly before the taking of Jerusalem announced in Rev 11:2, since the prophecy announces "that which must soon come to pass" (ἃ δεῖ γενέσθαι ἐν τάχει Rev 1:1).

In a different form, this chronotope could have the same backdating function as those found at the beginning of *4 Ezra* and *2 Baruch*, each

48. See, for example, P.M. Bogaert, "La ruine de Jérusalem et les apocalypses juives après 70," in L. Monloubou, ed., *Apocalypses et théologie de l'espérance* (Paris: Cerf, 1977) 137.

49. J.C. Wilson, "The Problem of the Domitianic Date of Revelation," *New Testament Studies* 39/4 (1993) 603.

50. D.E. Aune, *Revelation 1-5* (Dallas: Word Books, 1997) 75-85. Concerning the unlikelihood of John's exile to Patmos because of persecution, and the theory of persecution as applied to the Apocalypse generally, see R.A. Briggs, *Jewish Temple Imagery in the Book of Revelation* (New York: Peter Lang, 1999), 35-36 n. 96. See also in the present book, the contribution by Luca Arcari, p. 23.

51. S. Alkier – T. Nicklas, "Wenn sich Welten Berühren. Beobachtungen zu zeitlichen und räumlichen Strukturen in der Apokalypse des Johannes," in S. Alkier – Th. Hieke – T. Nicklas, eds., *Poetik und Intertextualität der Johannesapokalypse* (Tübingen: Mohr Siebeck, 2015) 205-226.

52. On the concept of chronotope, see footnote 2.

53. On the possible symbolic meaning of this mention, see P. Prigent, *L'Apocalypse de Saint Jean. Édition revue et augmentée* (Geneva: Labor et Fides, 2000) 98-99.

54. On ecstatic phenomena in assemblies, see Paul's instructions to the Corinthians (1 Cor 12:1-11; 14:26-39).

of which was composed around the same time as the Apocalypse. This short backdating, dealing with the reception of the revelation and not its writing in a book (Rev 1:11,19),[55] leaves a gap in which "what was to come soon" could occur. From a rhetorical point of view, the foundation of the revelation in an abstract chronotope in time and space and the insertion of a concrete fictitious antedating of an autobiographical nature[56] have the same function: namely, to assure the readers of the authority of the prophet John and the credibility of his message, his *ethos*.[57] This is, needless to say, precisely the work that any introduction must do.[58]

## 4. The Use of Scriptures in the Apocalypse of John

As Elizabeth Schüssler Fiorenza has noted, while John's use of Scripture is evident in almost every line, there is no overall study of the question, and this observation formulated in 1985 is still valid.[59] There have been to

55. This injunction to write down the revelation received, is contrasting with the Pharisee Paul's silence (2 Cor 12:5). Contradictory to the prohibition of writing of the Oral law among the sages, the insistence on writing will characterize the literature of the Palaces and could well be an indication of the priestly background of the prophet John; see R. Elior, "The Priestly Struggle on the Sacred Written Authority as Reflected in the Merkaba Tradition," in D. Hamidović – S.C. Mimouni – L. Painchaud, eds., *La 'sacerdotalisation' dans les premiers écrits mystiques juifs et chrétiens. Actes du colloque international tenu à l'Université de Lausanne du 26 au 28 octobre 2015* (Turnhout: Brepols, 2021) 13-40.

56. On the legitimizing function of this data both chronologically and geographically, see D. Tripaldi, *Gesù di Nazareth nell'Apocalisse di Giovanni. Spirito, profezia e memoria* (Brescia: Morecelliana, 2010) 53-57.

57. On recent research concerning rhetorical criticism of the Apocalypse of John, and in particular the rhetorical function of Rev 1:1-20, see D.A. DeSilva, "What has Athens to Do with Patmos? Rhetorical Criticism of the *Revelation of John* (1980-2005)," *Currents in Biblical Research* 6 (2008) 256-289.

58. As for the title "the Apocalypse of Jesus the Messiah" (ἀποκάλυψις Ἰησοῦ Χριστοῦ, Rev 1:1), there has been much discussion about its interpretation, but mainly about how to interpret the term "apocalypse" and what precise content of prophecy it refers to; see for example M. Jauhiainen, "Ἀποκάλυψις Ἰησοῦ Χριστοῦ (Rev. 1:1): The Climax of John's Prophecy?" *Tyndale Bulletin* 54 (2003) 99-117. One must also consider the rhetorical function of the formula as legitimizing John's prophecy, comparable to its use by Paul a few decades earlier to legitimize the heavenly origin of his gospel (Gal 1:12; 2:2; Eph 3:3), which is certainly more than a mere coincidence; see. L. Painchaud, "'*Apokalupsis Iesou Christou*' (Ap 1,1). L'étonnant *incipit* du livre de la prophétie de Jean," in C.G. Pardee – J.M. Tripp, eds., *Sacred Texts & Sacred Figures. The Reception and Use of Inherited Traditions in Early Christian Literature. A Festschrift in Honor of Edmondo F. Lupieri* (Turnhout: Brepols, 2022) 175-200.

59. E. Schüssler Fiorenza, *The Book of Revelation. Justice and Judgment* (Philadelphia: Fortress Press, 1985) 28, n. 39.

date no studies that deal with this issue as a whole, rather, research deals with John's use of this or that particular book,[60] and tends to privilege the later prophets, valued by the Christian tradition, to the detriment of the earlier prophets.[61] As for the general commentaries, they point out the "scriptural parallels," often according to an arbitrary selection,[62] and without always analyzing their function in the text.[63]

## 4.1 The Apocalypse of John, a Scriptural Prophecy

Yet these often-allusive scriptural references are as essential to understanding the Apocalypse as are the explicit scriptural references that a modern author would make by referring to the divisions of the biblical text into numbered chapters and verses. Ancient authors had recourse to an entirely different system of reference, inserting into their texts characteristic words or formulas supposedly understood by the addressees and establishing an analogical link between the text that was read or heard and the text that was used as a source. John J. Collins has summarized this allusive mode of reference very well:

> In many cases, however, the use of older texts consists only in the use of a phrase that brings a biblical passage to mind without claiming to interpret

60. This "book approach" is not without introducing a certain bias insofar as the book, as we understand it, does not constitute a significant unit from the point of view of the traditional reading of the Scriptures; see B.D. SOMMER, "The Scroll of Isaiah as Jewish Scripture, or, Why Jews Don't Read Books," *Society of Biblical Literature 1996 Seminar Papers* (Atlanta: SBL Scholars Press, 1996) 225-242 (esp. 230); J. BARTON, "What is a Book? Modern Exegesis and the Literary Conventions of Ancient Israel," in J.C. DE MOOR, *Intertextuality in Ugarit and Israel* (Leiden: Brill, 1998) 1-14.

61. See, for example, B.J. KOWALSKI, *Die Rezeption des Propheten Ezechiel in der Offenbarung des Johannes* (Stuttgart: Katolisches Bibelwerk, 2004); A. VANHOYE, "L'utilisation du Livre d'Ézéchiel dans l'Apocalypse," *Biblica* 43 (1962) 463-476; M. JAUHIAINEN, *The Use of Zechariah in Revelation* (Tübingen: Mohr Siebeck, 2005). For more references, see Stéphanie Audet, "Intertextuality in the Apocalypse: The Desert and the Woman" in the present book, esp. n. 2.

62. For example, for the fire coming down from heaven, the prodigy of Carmel will be cited, but not the other occurrences of the same prodigy in Exodus and 2 Chronicles.

63. The recent survey by Adela Yarbro Collins shows that there is still no comprehensive study of the function of the Scriptures in this text (A. YARBRO COLLINS, "The Use of Scripture in the Book of Revelation," in A. YARBRO COLLINS, ed., *New Perspectives on the Book of Revelation* [Leuven: Peeters, 2017] 11-32). Older works most often use the anachronistic Old Testament designation for Scriptures, which is not without introducing an interpretative bias; see G.K. BEALE, *John's Use of the Old Testament in Revelation* (Sheffield: Sheffield Academic Press, 1998); S. MOYISE, *The Old Testament in the Book of Revelation* (Sheffield: Sheffield Academic Press, 1995); J. CAMBIER, "Les images de l'Ancien Testament dans l'Apocalypse de Saint Jean," *Nouvelle revue théologique* 77 (1955) 113-122.

> it in a definitive way ... allusiveness encircles the language by building associations and analogies between the biblical contexts and the new context in which the phrase is used.[64]

The competent reader, which in this case would be one who knew the Scriptures, would not need a marginal note to know that a word or phrase referred to a particular passage of Scripture by this verbal analogy. He or she would not be dependent on any outside "authority" to decide arbitrarily whether a verbal analogy was meaningful or merely coincidental. Such readers would know that it was referring to another text, and that this text was necessary to understand the text they were reading (or hearing). In other words, the source text was intended to be an integral part of the text read (or heard). As Bernard Barc notes in connection with the writing of the Hebrew Bible: "... these implicit quotations can in many cases provide the key to the interpretation of a text."[65]

This system of implicit quotation, or allusion, through verbal analogy is clearly at work in John's compositional process. Richard Bauckham has best summarized this aspect of the Apocalypse:

> Secondly, Revelation's use of the Old Testament scriptures is an essential key to its understanding. The pattern of almost continuous allusion to the Old Testament throughout the book is not a haphazard use of Old Testament language by a writer so soaked in the Old Testament that he naturally uses its language, as some scholars have mistakenly thought. It is a pattern of disciplined and deliberate *allusion* to specific Old Testament texts. Reference to and interpretation of these texts is an extremely important part of the meaning of the text of the Apocalypse. It is a book designed to be read in constant intertextual relationship with the Old Testament. John was writing what he understood to be a work of prophetic inspiration, the climax of prophetic revelation, which gathered up the prophetic meaning of the Old Testament scriptures and disclosed the way in which it was being fulfilled in the last days. It presupposes and conveys an extensive interpretation of large parts of Old Testament prophecy. Allusions are meant to recall the Old Testament context, which thereby becomes part of the meaning the Apocalypse conveys, and to build up, sometimes by a network of allusions to the same Old Testament passage in various parts of the Apocalypse, an interpretation of whole passages of Old Testament prophecy. The interpretation is highly disciplined, employing contempo-

---

64. J.J. COLLINS, *The Apocalyptic Imagination: An Introduction to Jewish Apocalyptic Literature* (Grand Rapids: Eerdmans, 1998) 18. On the problems raised by the identification of allusions, see, among others, J. PAULIEN, "Elusive Allusions: The Problematic Use of the Old Testament in Revelation," *Biblical Research* 33 (1988) 37-53.

65. See on this subject B. BARC, *Siméon le Juste: l'auteur oublié de la Bible hébraïque* (Turnhout: Brepols, 2015) 79-83.

> rary methods of Jewish exegesis, especially the technique of *gezērâ šāwâ*, by which passages sharing common words or phrases are interpreted in relation with each other. Frequently in these essays, we shall find that obscure passages in Revelation regularly misunderstood by the commentators can be correctly understood when the Old Testament allusions are identified and John's interpretation of the Old Testament reconstructed in terms of Jewish exegetical practice.[66]

Bauckham helpfully describes both the method of allusive writing used by John, and the way in which his text should be approached. Our approach, therefore, will be guided by the following three methodological guidelines: 1) passages sharing common words or expressions with Scriptures and/or within the text itself must be related to each other according to the exegetical technique of the *gezarah shawah* or verbal analogy;[67] 2) a network of allusions to the same scriptural text appearing in various passages of the Apocalypse must be understood as a whole; 3) the function of the allusions is to recall not only a scriptural word or expression, *but the entire context from which they are drawn and any associated texts, so that this context and these associated texts are to be understood as integral to the meaning of the Apocalypse.*[68]

More recently, Jan Dochhorn has taken this approach in his application of the concept of "scriptural prophecy" (*Schriftgelehrte Prophetie*) to the Apocalypse:

> The identification of the apocalypse as a scriptural prophecy is decisive for its interpretation. In accordance with this genre, the author of the Apocalypse expects his readers to decode the signals and signal constellations (*Zeichenkonstellationen*) that he deliberately designed as confusing. This is made possible by the identification of contextual references (a), scriptural

66. R. BAUCKHAM, *The Climax of Prophecy: Studies on the Book of Revelation* (Edinburgh: T&T Clark, 1993) x-xi; it can only be regretted that the Scottish scholar did not always apply the method of reading which he described so acutely.

67. This analogy can also go beyond the simple verbal level and be multidimensional, encompassing theological and social aspects; see D.H. WENKEL, "*Gezarah Shawah* as Analogy in the Epistle to the Hebrews," *Biblical Theology Bulletin: Journal of Bible and Culture* 37/2 (2007) 62-68. In a number of cases, it is possible to apply the *binyan'av* rule (the paternal edifice or paradigm), whereby the meaning of a word or expression must be inferred from its first occurrence in Scripture. This principle of *midrash halakhah* may well be at work in the apocalypse as elsewhere in canonized and uncanonized literature, see for example B. BARC, "La descente aux enfers du grand prêtre Ananias dans les Actes de Philippe," in R. GOUNELLE – B. MOUNIER, eds., *La littérature apocryphe chrétienne et les Écritures juives* (Lausanne: Éditions du Zèbre, 2015) 313-324.

68. For an interesting illustration of this "contextual" approach to a scriptural allusion, see G.K. BEALE, "The Old Testament Background of Rev 3.14," *New Testament Studies* 42 (1996) 133-152.

passages (b), and a knowledge of the tradition common to the author and readers (c).[69]

When adopting such an approach, one must postulate the consistency of the set of scriptural references at work in the text. It follows from this postulate that any verbal analogy that is recognized or recognizable in the Apocalypse must be examined, not through the distorting prism of a tradition external to the text and conditioned by the text's reception in various milieus and at various times, but in the light of the coherent network that it forms with other scriptural analogies in the text itself.

## 4.2 Allusions

It will suffice here to define allusion as a literary process within a text that simultaneously activates in the mind of the reader or listener two texts whose meaning is illuminated by one another.[70] Our treatment of these allusions will be drawn from Zvi Ben-Porat's fundamental article distinguishing four phases in the process of understanding an allusion on the part of the readers:[71] 1) they must recognize that an element of the text read also belongs to another text; 2) they must then identify the evoked text that contains this element; 3) they will modify their interpretation of this element in the text read according to its presence in the evoked text; and finally 4) they will establish connections between the two texts that are not based only on the common element, but that will involve other elements of these texts. *This implementation of additional elements is, in Ben-Porat's opinion, the specific purpose of the literary allusion.*[72] The recognition of literary allusions, when they are present in a text, is essential

---

69. "Hermeneutisch entscheidend ist vor allem die Identifikation der Apocalypse als schriftgelehrte Prophetie. Dieser Gattungsbestimmung entsprechend erwartet der Verfasser der Apokalypse von seinen Lesern eine Dekodierung der von ihm absichtlich rätselhaft gestalten Zeichen und Zeichenkonstellationen. Diese soll [...] erfolgen durch die Identifikation von Kontextbezügen (a), alludierten Schriftstellen (b) und eines Verfasser wie Lesern gemeinsamen Traditionswissens (c)." J. DOCHHORN, *Schriftgelehrte Prophetie: Der eschatologische Teufelsfall in Apc Joh 12 und seine Bedeutung für das Verständnis der Johannesoffenbarung* (Tübingen: Mohr Siebeck, 2010) 19.

70. On allusion as an argumentative figure, see C. OLBRECHTS-TYTECA – L. PERELMAN, *Traité de l'argumentation. La nouvelle rhétorique* (Bruxelles: Éditions de l'Université de Bruxelles, 1988) esp. 229 and 239. This implies that this play of allusion also reveals the reception of the source text and its interpretation by its user, so it is not a unidirectional movement as the use of the term "source" might lead one to believe, but a bidirectional movement from the source text to the new text and vice versa.

71. Z. BEN-PORAT, "The Poetics of Literary Allusions," *PTL: A Journal of Poetics and Theory of Literature* 1 (1976) 105-128.

72. Z. BEN-PORAT, "The Poetics of Literary Allusions," *PTL: A Journal of Poetics and Theory of Literature* 1 (1976) 111.

to the full understanding of the text, otherwise the allusion is lost, and the text is misunderstood.[73]

As has often been noted, the major challenge in studying allusions is the risk of assuming that the ancient author shares the modern author's subjective interpretations of the source text or the text studied, and one of the main methodological issues has been the determination of objective criteria for identifying an allusion. To address this question, Jeffery M. Leonard proposes a series of eight methodological principles, which will be used as a guide here:

> (1) Shared language is the single most important factor in establishing a textual connection. (2) Shared language is more important than no shared language. (3) Shared language that is rare or distinctive suggests a stronger connection than does language that is widely used. (4) Shared phrases suggest a stronger connection than do individual shared terms. (5) The accumulation of shared language suggests a stronger connection than does a shared single term. (6) Shared language in similar contexts suggests a stronger connection than does shared language alone. (7) Shared language need not to be accompanied by shared form to establish a connection. (8) Shared language need not to be accompanied by shared ideology to establish a connection.[74]

These principles are useful guides for *identifying* with some objectivity the allusion as a literary device used by an author. They are, however, of no use for its *interpretation*, which is always subjective.[75] In fact, *interpretation* depends on several subjective factors on the part of both the reader and the author, among which the interpretation of the text evoked (e.g., the Book of Zechariah) by the given text (the Apocalypse) must be placed at the forefront. In the conclusion to his study of the use of Zechariah in the Apocalypse, Marko Jauhiainen rightly insists on the influence that the presuppositions of the reader will have on his or her reception and interpretation of the allusions found in a text.[76] For example, an allusion to the text of Zechariah 12 announcing the siege and the taking of Jerusalem along with the salvation of the tents of Judah and of the house of David will take on different meaning depending who is reading it. The interaction of the texts of Zechariah and the Apocalypse could well be understood quite differently by a Christian of the third century CE perse-

73. See L. Pernot, *L'art du sous-entendu : histoire – théorie – mode d'emploi* (Paris : Fayard, 2018) esp. 85-111.

74. J.M. Leonard, "Identifying Inner-Biblical Allusions : Psalm 78 as a Test Case," *Journal of Biblical Literature* 127 (2008) 246.

75. See remarks on this subject by M. Jauhiainen, *The Use of Zechariah in Revelation* (Tübingen : Mohr Siebeck, 2005) 33-35.

76. M. Jauhiainen, *The Use of Zechariah in Revelation* (Tübingen : Mohr Siebeck, 2005) 163-164.

cuted by civic or imperial Roman authorities than it would by a messianic Judean of the first century who was a follower of Jesus of Nazareth upset by the fall of Jerusalem.

Before discussing the visions of the dragon and the first beast, it will be useful to apply the approach described by Richard Bauckham to the inaugural address (Rev 1:4-8), for it contains the essence of John's prophecy *in nuce*. This address must be read in the light of the allusions it contains; they mark the beginning of a chain of scriptural allusions that underlies the narrative frame of the text until its conclusion. One can indeed compare John's compositional process to a woven pattern whose warp threads, made of scriptural allusions, serve as a support for the threads of the narrative weft that intertwine them, giving it unity, coherence and meaning.[77] To take up the weaver analogy, John, in the opening address, sets up his loom, that is to say, he attaches the warp threads on which he will weave the weft of his narrative.

## 5. The Inaugural Address (Rev 1:4-8) : Davidic Messianic Promise and the Disobedience of the Sons of David

The inaugural address contains several elements deriving from scriptural texts. These elements are recognized by commentators: they belong to Exodus (3:14; 19:6), Psalm 89:28, 38 (88:28, 38 LXX), the books of Daniel (7:13) and Zechariah (12:10). However, they are most often seen as "pastiches" or echoes rather than allusions, and comments rarely go beyond the first two steps described by Ben-Porat. Yet, the contexts from which these allusions are borrowed must be "activated" to grasp their full meaning and function in the text, and then linked together to understand this inaugural address.

"On the part of him who is, who was and who will be" (ἀπὸ ὁ ὢν καὶ ὁ ἦν καὶ ὁ ἐρχόμενος, Rev 1:4c, 8b)[78] is generally considered as an expansion of Exod 3:14 LXX (ἐγώ εἰμι ὁ ὤν).[79] There has been discussion of its precise theological meaning and the syntactical problems it poses, but

77. On this analogy, see J. Cazeaux, *La trame et la chaîne. Ou les structures littéraires et l'exégèse des traités de Philon d'Alexandrie* (Leiden: Brill, 1983) esp. 6-22. The same analogy is used by I. Boxall, *The Revelation of Saint John* (Peabody, MA: Hendrickson, 2006).

78. Greek quotations are taken from B. Aland – K. Aland – J. Karavidopoulos – C.M. Martini – B. Metzger, *Nestle – Aland Novum Testamentum Graece*, 27th ed. (Stuttgart: Deutsche Bibelgesellschaft, 1993).

79. The question of the language of the scriptural text to which John refers will not be considered here since John may be referring to a Greek written text or a Hebrew text, or to a rough oral transmission. Since the Apocalypse was composed in Greek, we will use the Septuagint as a reference text for convenience.

there has been to date no discussion of its allusive function.[80] Now in Exodus, the phrase in question appears in the context of the authentication of Moses's prophetic vocation; its introduction at the beginning of the Apocalypse would thus be likely to lead the reader to see in it, as in Exodus, an authentication of John's prophetic mission.

Continuing the reading, in the formula "from the seven spirits before the throne" (Rev 1:4d), there might be an allusion to Isa 11:2, but due to its ambiguity, we will leave it out.[81] On the other hand, the two titles attributed to Jesus (Rev 1:5) "the faithful witness" (ὁ μάρτυς ὁ πιστός) and "the firstborn from the dead and prince of the kings of the earth" (ὁ πρωτότοκος τῶν νεκρῶν καὶ ὁ ἄρχων τῶν βασιλέων τῆς γῆς), are two indisputable allusions to Ps 89 (88 LXX): ὁ μάρτυς ἐν οὐρανῷ πιστός (Ps 88:38 LXX) and πρωτότοκον θήσομαι αὐτόν, ὑψηλὸν παρὰ τοῖς βασιλεῦσιν τῆς γῆς (Ps 88:28 LXX). This reference to Ps 88 LXX is very strong, since it is based not only on one, but on two phrases borrowed from the same text.

These two formulas are rare. The expression "faithful witness" used in the messianic and Davidic context of Psalm 89:38 is unique in the Scriptures.[82] Similarly, the formula "firstborn, the most high among the kings of the earth" (κἀγὼ πρωτότοκον θήσομαι αὐτόν, ὑψηλὸν παρὰ τοῖς βασιλεῦσιν τῆς γῆς Ps 88:28 LXX) is a *hapax*.[83] They send a strong signal to the reader or listener: If you want to understand the prophecy, remember the psalm.[84] The formula "a firstborn, high among the kings

80. D.E. Aune, *Revelation 1-5* (Dallas: Word Books, 1997) 30-32; P. Prigent, *L'Apocalypse de Saint Jean. Édition revue et augmentée* (Geneva: Labor et Fides, 2000) 87.

81. See D.E. Aune, *Revelation 1-5* (Dallas: Word Books, 1997) 33-35.

82. The other two occurrences of the expression "faithful witness" in Proverbs occur in a legal context (Prov 14:5,25).

83. This expression also recalls 2 Kings 25:28, where Ewil-Merodach, king of Babylon, gave to Yoyakin, the last king of Judah of the lineage of David, a higher seat than that of the other kings who shared his lot in Babylon. I owe this observation to the late Bernard Barc. This passage means that the end of the temple and the kingdom in no way marks the end of the Davidic lineage that survives the taking of Jerusalem and the ruin of the temple. However, Yoyakin does not owe his elevation to the Lord, but to a foreign king, Nebuchadnezzar's successor; see B. Barc, *Siméon le Juste: l'auteur oublié de la Bible hébraïque* (Turnhout: Brepols, 2015) 295.

84. The formula is borrowed from I. Provan, "Foul Spirits, Fornication and Finance: Revelation 18 from an Old Testament Perspective," *Journal for the Study of New Testament* 64 (1996) 87: "read Ezechiel if you want to understand what I am saying here." In the Psalm, this "faithful witness" is generally considered to be the moon; for a different interpretation, see S. Kuk Kim, *Psalms in the Book of Revelation. Ph.D. Diss. in Biblical Studies (New Testament)* (University of Edinburgh, 2013) 64; in the Apocalypse, it refers to the Messiah. The fact that the expression is used by John without regard to its original meaning in the psalm further rein-

of the earth," which applies to David in the psalm, indicates the Davidic character of the risen Messiah Jesus, hence the addition of τῶν νεκρῶν, according to a tradition which also finds an echo in the Epistle to the Colossians (1:18).

These signals, therefore, lead the reader back to Ps 89 (88 LXX), a lament over the Lord's silence and apparent abandonment of his covenant with David and his descendants. Psalm 89 (88 LXX) is a messianic psalm that nourishes the hope of a return for the dynasty of David temporarily destroyed by its enemies;[85] it is a psalm that reaffirms the Lord's faithfulness to his covenant in favor of his Anointed One:

> Nor will I violate my covenant and set aside what proceeds from my lips. Once and for all, I swore by my holiness, "If I will lie to David." His seed shall remain forever, and his throne is like the sun before me, and like the moon established forever. And the witness in heaven is faithful. (Ps 88:35-38 LXX)

The Lord also reminds us that if the sons of David abandon his law and do not "keep his commandments," they will be punished with a rod (Ps 88:31-34 LXX). This whole psalm is an interpretation of the oracle of Nathan in 2 Sam 7.[86]

Through these allusions, Rev 1:5 evokes the whole of Psalm 88 LXX, a psalm whose grave tone is in perfect resonance with the dark years following the fall of Jerusalem. It expresses the distress of the vanquished (Ps 88:39-52 LXX) and the fidelity of the Lord—who masters the power of the sea (σὺ δεσπόζεις τοῦ κράτους τῆς θαλάσσης, Ps 88:10 LXX); who crushes the sea monster Rahav in the Hebrew text (Ps 89:11),[87] the very monster which will be found at the heart of the Apocalypse in the

---

forces its function as a signal to refer the reader or listener back to that psalm and its message.

85. W.C. POHL IV, "A Messianic Reading of Psalm 89: A Canonical and Intertextual Reading," *Journal of the Evangelical Theological Society* 58 (2015) 507-525.

86. See on this subject the excellent study by N.N. SARNA, "Psalm 89: A Study in Inner Biblical Exegesis," in A. ALTMANN, ed., *Biblical and Other Studies* (Cambridge, MA: Harvard University Press, 2013) 29-46, and D. VOLGGER, *Notizen zur Textanalyse von Ps 89* (Emming: Eos Verlag, 1994); also S. RAMOND, "La voix discordante du troisième livre du Psautier (Psaumes 74, 80, 89)," *Biblica* 96 (2015) 39-66.

87. It should also be noted that the victory of the horseman who calls himself "Faithful and True" (πιστὸς καὶ ἀληθινός) over the beast (Rev 19:11), despite the difference in vocabulary, could well be an allusion to Ps 88 LXX, where "faithfulness and truth" (ἔλεος καὶ ἀλήθεια) precede the face of the Lord (Ps 88:15 LXX) given the similarity of the two contexts, which describe the victory of the Lord over the power of the sea (or monster Rahav, Ps 89:11) and that of the Messiah over the beast from the sea, and the similarity of the two pairs πιστὸς καὶ ἀληθινός and ἔλεος καὶ ἀλήθεια.

image of the beast rising from the sea (Rev 13:1-10)—to his covenant with David and his lineage in spite of the disobedience of David's sons (Ps 88:31-37 LXX).

This royal and Davidic theme underlying the inaugural address will return in the epilogue where Jesus says: "I am the offspring and lineage of David" (ἐγώ εἰμι ἡ ῥίζα καὶ τὸ γένος Δαυίδ, Rev 22:16).[88] Reading the inaugural address in the light of the psalm, one cannot but agree with Knut Heim's observation that:

> In Rev 1, each allusion (to Ps 89) makes a statement about Jesus the Christ which identifies him as the answer to the question posed by Psalm 89:50 [88:50 LXX] ... 'Lord, where is your steadfast love of old, which by your faithfulness you swore to David?'"[89]

It is therefore in Jesus the Messiah that the promises of the Lord in Psalm 88 LXX are fulfilled (see also Rev 3:7; 5:5).[90]

The phrase "a kingdom and priests for God" (βασιλείαν, ἱερεῖς τῷ θεῷ Rev 1:6) refers to Exod 19:6 LXX: "And you shall be for me a royal

---

88. In the formula "ἡ ῥίζα ... Δαυίδ," the word ῥίζα is to be understood both in the sense of original root and germ or sucker. The designation of the Living One as "the one who holds the key of David" (ὁ ἔχων τὴν κλεῖν Δαυιδ Rev 3:7) "is a clear allusion to Isa 22:22" (D.E. AUNE, *Revelation 1-5* [Dallas: Word Books, 1997] 235), and more broadly to the text of Isa 22-23 which tells of the siege and devastation of Jerusalem, followed by the dismissal of an unworthy high official, possessing—like Solomon—many chariots (Isa 22:18), and the Lord's calling back to his servant Eliakim son of Hilkiah, who will be "a father to the inhabitants of Jerusalem and to the house of Judah." Here again, this allusion brings to the mind of the reader a context which tells about the siege of Jerusalem.

89. K.M. HEIM, "The (God-)Forsaken King of Psalm 89: A Historical and Intertextual Enquiry," in J. DAY, ed., *King and Messiah in Israel and the Ancient Near East: Proceedings of the Oxford Old Testament Seminar* (Sheffield: Sheffield Academic Press, 1998) 319-321.

90. And not in the Hasmonaean dynasty or even less in the Herodian one, without Davidic ancestry, who "set up a monarchy because of their arrogance; they despoiled the throne of David with arrogant shouting." (*Psalms of Solomon* XVII, 6; trans. by R.B. WRIGHT, in J.H. CHARLESWORTH, ed., *The Old Testament Pseudepigrapha*, vol. II [Peabody: Hendrickson, 1983] 666); see D.K. ROOKE, "Kingship as Priesthood: The Relationship between the High Priesthood and the Monarchy," in J. DAY, ed., *King and Messiah, in Israel and the Ancient Near East: Proceedings of the Oxford Old Testament Seminar* (Sheffield: Sheffield Academic Press, 1998) 206-208. From the moment we understand the punishment of the whore in the Apocalypse as being that of the earthly unholy Jerusalem, the ideological links of the Apocalypse of John with the Psalms of Solomon become obvious. On the dating and context of the composition of the Psalms of Solomon, see R.B. WRIGHT, "Psalms of Solomon," in J.H. CHARLESWORTH, ed., *The Old Testament Pseudepigrapha*, vol. II (Peabody: Hendrickson, 1983) 640-643; also A.-M. DENIS, *Introduction à la littérature judéo-hellénistique vol. 1. Pseudépigraphes de l'Ancien Testament* (Turnhout: Brepols, 2000) 520-523.

priesthood and a holy nation" (ὑμεῖς δὲ ἔσεσθέ μοι βασίλειον ἱεράτευμα καὶ ἔθνος ἅγιον). It evokes the covenant of Sinai and announces the fulfilment of the promise made in the psalm while referring the reader to the great Exodus narrative; it associates the royal and priestly themes underlying the whole of the Apocalypse; it contains John's project for his audience in a nutshell.[91] The reunification of the royal and priestly functions in messianic times is accomplished.[92] Henceforth, kingship and priesthood belong to those whom Jesus delivered from their sins by his blood, those whom he made kings and priests (Rev 1:4). It is in them that the promise made to the lineage of David in the psalm is fulfilled; they will reign with the Messiah in the millennium (Rev 20:1-6).

"He comes in the midst of the clouds" (ἰδοὺ ἔρχεται μετὰ τῶν νεφελῶν Rev 1:7) evokes the mysterious "son of man ... coming upon the clouds of heaven" of Daniel (καὶ ἰδου ἐπὶ τῶν νεφελῶν τοῦ οὐρανοῦ ὡς υἱὸς ἀνθρώπου ἤρχετο Dan 7:13 LXX), whose appearance marks the end of the sovereignty of empires over Israel.

Likewise, "him whom they have pierced, for whom they will mourn" (καὶ οἵτινες αὐτὸν ἐξεκέντησαν, καὶ κόψονται ἐπ' αὐτόν, Rev 1:7) takes up the words of Zechariah (12:10 LXX, καὶ ἐπιβλέψονται πρός με ἀνθ' ὧν κατωρχήσαντο καὶ κόψονται ἐπ' αὐτὸν κοπετόν). The context in Zechariah evokes the siege of Jerusalem, the coming of the Messiah and the defeat of the nations, following a time of trial, and the purification of the land from which the idols will be removed.[93] Marko Jauhiainen, who has studied John's use of Zechariah, points out the importance of this particular reference to Zechariah given its place at the beginning of the document.[94] Zechariah's text explicitly refers to the siege of Jerusalem: "Behold, I set Ierousalem as shaking doorways for all the peoples round about, and in Judea there will be a siege against Ierousalem" (Zech 12:2 LXX). The rest of the text describes the coming tragedy (Zech 12:3-6 LXX), then announces the salvation that the Lord will bring and the expulsion of the false prophets and the unclean spirit from the land (καὶ τοὺς ψευδοπροφήτας καὶ τὸ πνεῦμα τὸ ἀκάθαρτον ἐξαρῶ ἀπὸ τῆς γῆς, Zech 13:2 LXX). This allusion would open the revelation

91. See M. Himmelfarb, *A Kingdom of Priests: Ancestry and Merit in Ancient Judaism* (Philadelphia: University of Pennsylvania Press, 2006) 135-142.

92. See B. Barc, *Siméon le Juste: l'auteur oublié de la Bible hébraïque* (Turnhout: Brepols, 2015) 293-298.

93. About the use of Zechariah in the Apocalypse, see M. Jauhiainen, *The Use of Zechariah in Revelation* (Tübingen: Mohr Siebeck, 2005); also, "The Minor Prophets in Revelation," in J.J. Maartens – J.J. Menken – S. Moyise, eds., *The Minor Prophets in the New Testament* (London: T&T Clark, 2009) 159-172.

94. M. Jauhiainen, "The Minor Prophets in Revelation," in J.J. Maartens – J.J. Menken – S. Moyise, eds., *The Minor Prophets in the New Testament* (London: T&T Clark, 2009) 158.

of Jesus the Messiah (Rev 1:1) by presenting it as a response to the fall of Jerusalem.[95]

There is, therefore, a noteworthy convergence between the contexts to which these allusions refer. Through his allusions to Ps 88 LXX, Zechariah, and Daniel, the prophet John invites the reader to interpret "what is to come soon" (Rev 1:1), that is, the fall of Jerusalem. Seen in the light of Scripture, the fall of Jerusalem is the punishment for the rebellion of the sons of David, while the death and resurrection of the Messiah Jesus is the manifestation of the Lord's unfailing fidelity to his covenant with David and his lineage.

The function of these scriptural allusions is not limited to the understanding of the inaugural address; rather they attach the threads of the warp on which the weft of the revelation is woven, threads whose extension can be seen throughout the text, and especially through chapters 12 and 13.

## 6. The Dragon, the Woman, and the Beast from the Sea

Chapters 12 and 13 of the Apocalypse form a whole made up of three visions closely connected to one another by the links established between the dragon (Rev 12) and the two beasts (Rev 13).[96] Considered at the level of the narrative, the descriptions of the dragon and these two beasts position them from the outset as opponents of the pregnant woman (Rev 12:1), the remnants of her seed (Rev 12:13-14), and the saints (Rev 13:7), dragging into idolatry the whole earth/land (Rev 13:3) and its inhabitants (Rev 13:8,12,14). In order to understand the deeper meaning of these visions, however, it is necessary to recognize the signals referring to the Scriptures, which form the chain of allusions on which the narrative is

95. For example, Marko Jauhiainen does not attach any importance to the announcement of the siege of Jerusalem in Zech 12:1-2 in his analysis of the allusion to this text in Rev 1:7, no doubt because for him the Apocalypse of John is not concerned with the fall of Jerusalem but only with the coming of Jesus; M. Jauhiainen, *The Use of Zechariah in Revelation* (Tübingen: Mohr Siebeck, 2005) 143.

96. The intertwining of the images of the dragon and the two beasts has been widely studied by all commentators of Revelation, both in their scriptural roots and in their possible parallels in ancient culture; see recently V. Dorneles, "A besta de sete cabeças e seus antecedentes em textos da cultura antiga," *Horizonte* 48 (2017) 1423-1445 (1441). He concludes that the similarity between the monstrous figures of the ancient stories and the biblical text demonstrates the contact of the authors of the biblical texts with the ancient culture. Although this conclusion is quite relevant, it does not do much to illuminate the particular use of these images in Revelation.

woven, and to read these visions in the light of the scriptural contexts to which they refer.

In the vision of Rev 12, the dragon, as we have seen, is identified with the ancient serpent, which necessarily evokes the serpent of the Garden of Eden. But this identification of the serpent and the dragon might also recall the promise of the Lord's victory announced by the prophet Isaiah over a dragon which is a serpent, "On that day God will bring his holy and great and strong dagger against the dragon, a fleeing snake—against the dragon, a crooked snake—and he will kill the dragon" (Isa 27:1 LXX).[97]

## 6.1 The Dragon and the Remnants of the Seed of the Woman (Rev 12)

There is much to be said about chapter 12 and the debates over its interpretation.[98] Whatever one might imagine with regard to hypotheses of a "pagan" or astrological influence for the *reception* of this chapter,[99] the fact remains that in terms of *composition*, scriptural references are constant. Thus, the great sign appearing in the sky, the moon and the sun, cannot fail to evoke for the readers the account of the creation of the lights, moon, and sun as "signs in the sky" (Gen 1:16), and the twelve stars, the dream of Joseph and the twelve tribes of Israel (Gen 37:9-11). As for the woman and the pains of childbirth, they evoke, of course, Gen 3:16 and

97. Τῇ ἡμέρᾳ ἐκείνῃ, ἐπάξει ὁ θεὸς τὴν μάχαιραν τὴν ἁγίαν καὶ τὴν μεγάλην καὶ τὴν ἰσχυρὰν ἐπὶ τὸν δράκοντα ὄφιν φεύγοντα, ἐπὶ τὸν δράκοντα ὄφιν σχολιὸν καὶ ἀνελεῖ τὸν δράκοντα (Isa 27:1 LXX).

98. L. ARCARI, *"Una donna avvolta nel sole ..." (Apoc 12,1): le raffigurazioni femminili nell'Apocalisse di Giovanni alla luce della letteratura apocalittica giudaica* (Padova: Edizioni Messaggero Padova, 2008). On the history of the reception of this vision and the influence of iconography on it, see R. BURNET, "D'où proviennent nos clefs de lecture de l'Apocalypse? *Auslegunsgeschichte* de l'épisode de la Femme et du Dragon," in A. YARBRO COLLINS, eds., *New Perspectives on the Book of Revelation* (Leuven: Peeters, 2017) 315-332.

99. It is not impossible that all this passage reflects Greco-Roman or Eastern traditions and myths, especially Leto's story, and even more possible that it could have been received in the light of these traditions. The literature on this subject is abundant; see A. YARBRO COLLINS, *The Combat Myth in the Book of Revelation* (Missoula: Scholars Press, 1976); P. BUSCH, *Der gefallene Drache: Mythenexegese am Beispiel von Apokalypse 12* (Tübingen: Francke, 1996), and in the present book, the contribution by Luca Arcari, p. 24, and note 27. This does not, however, diminish the importance of the scriptural references that are integrated into the narrative, especially to Exodus and the Book of Daniel. It is noteworthy that in his attempts at "remythologising" the analysis of this chapter, Steven J. Friesen could identify clear and precise use of mythical traditions about Behemoth and Leviathan and to the beast from the Book of Daniel, but only loose implicit association with what he calls "the mythology of imperial cults," while leaving aside all allusions to Exodus; see S.J. FRIESEN, "Myth and Symbolic Resistance in Revelation 13," *Journal of Biblical Literature* 123 (2004) 281-313.

the whole story of paradise to which the ancient serpent (Rev 12:9) is referred a little further down in the text. All these scriptural references invite the reader to read in the text a summary of the history of Israel, and to see in this woman in labor, the mother of the Messiah who is to lead all the nations with a rod of iron (Ps 2:9 ; Rev 2:27 ; 19:15), a figure of messianic expectation.

The eagle's wings given to the woman chased by the dragon in the desert and the food she receives there are all signals referring to the Exodus narrative (Exod 16:1-36 ; 19:4), inviting the reader to read the vision in the light of this background.[100] In this context, the earth that "opens and swallows up" (ἤνοιξεν ἡ γῆ τὸ στόμα αὐτῆς καὶ κατέπιεν, Rev 12:16) the river vomited up by the dragon could not fail to evoke by verbal analogy the rebellion of Korah and the earth that "opens its mouth and swallows" the rebels (καὶ ἀνοίξασα ἡ γῆ στόμα αὐτῆς καταπίεται αὐτούς … καὶ ἠνοίχθη ἡ γῆ καὶ κατέπιεν αὐτούς, Num 16:30, 32 LXX ; cf. also 26:10 ; Deut 11:16) ; John has borrowed the exact phrasing of the scriptural texts. Just as in the inaugural address, the reference to Psalm 88 LXX recalls the Lord's fidelity to his covenant and the rebellion of the lineage of David, here the evocation of the wings of the eagle and of manna recalls the Lord's benevolence towards his people to which the rebellion of Korah and part of the people respond, and their punishment (Num 17:6-15). We have here the same sequence as in Psalm 106 (Ps 106:17 [105 LXX]), which takes up exactly the same formula, and juxtaposes the episode of the sons of Korah (the band of Abiram) and that of the golden calf, as a double expression of the rebellion of the fathers. This evocation of the rebellion of Korah reminds the readers that the plagues do not affect only the nations, but sometimes also the rebellious sons of Israel, and prepares them to understand the true identity of the beast from the earth/land and the meaning of the plagues to come.

---

100. See J. DOCHHORN, *Schriftgelehrte Prophetie : Der eschatologische Teufelsfall in Apc Joh 12 und seine Bedeutung für das Verständnis der Johannesoffenbarung* (Tübingen : Mohr Siebeck, 2010). Notwithstanding Adela Yarbro Collin's criticism ("The Use of Scripture in the Book of Revelation," in A. YARBRO COLLINS, ed., *New Perspectives on the Book of Revelation* [Leuven : Peeters, 2017] 29-30), which does not seem justified to me, because John's constant use of scriptural references, as Dochhorn sees it, in no way implies that John considers his addressees as completely detached from their socio-cultural environment. It is perfectly normal that John uses the Scriptures, here the Exodus account, which have a traditional and normative value to convince his addressees. One must evaluate Dochhorn's reading by its capacity to reveal the coherence of John's text. Concerning the reference to the Exodus in this passage, see E.F. LUPIERI, "A Beast and a Woman in the Desert, or the Sin of Israel : A Typological Reflection," in E.F. MASON – E.F. LUPIERI, eds., *Golden Calf Traditions in Early Judaism, Christianity, and Islam* (Leiden : Brill, 2018) 157-175.

As for the dragon (δράκων) identified with Satan and the ancient serpent, it is no mere coincidence that its occurrences in Scripture are also found in Exodus, in a passage where the dragon and the serpent seem interchangeable (Exod 7:8-12). It appears also in the Song of Moses (Deut 32:33), which sings of the Lord's goodness to his people, whose ingratitude deserves a punishment. Here, the dragon is great (δράκων μέγας, Rev 12:3), a formula that echoes Ezek 29:3, where the "great dragon" refers to Pharaoh (Φαραω τὸν δράκοντα τὸν μέγαν), another evocation of Exodus. As for the seven heads and ten horns that John attributes to this dragon, he borrows them from the four beasts from the sea in the Book of Daniel (Dan 7:3-8). Thus, the few features attributed to the dragon swarm with allusions to Exodus and the Book of Daniel, and extend the scriptural chain set up by the inaugural address.

Finally, the dragon bears its wrath against the woman and goes to war "against the remnants of her seed" (τῶν λοιπῶν τοῦ σπέρματος αὐτῆς, Rev 12:17). The phrase "the remnants of her [i.e., the woman's] seed" would be doubly unexpected since the woman gave birth to one son who was caught up "to God and to his throne" (Rev 12:5) and because, from the point of view of the embryological theories of antiquity, in the process of generation, the semen comes from the man and not from the woman.[101] This reference to the remnants of the woman's seed is incongruous. Once again, we have to look for the explanation of this enigma in the Scriptures.

David Aune is rightly of the opinion that the simultaneous presence of the motifs of the woman, the seed, and the serpent evokes a reference to Gen 3:15,[102] that is, to the hostility between the seed of Eve and the serpent. However, the incongruous expression "the remnants of her seed" also evokes the notion of the "remnant" which has been so important in prophetic eschatology since the prophet Amos;[103] here again, the text

---

101. The passage in the Epistle to the Hebrews about Sarah, which is sometimes quoted against this opinion: "By faith, Sarah, barren, received power for the foundation of a seed" (Πίστει καὶ αὐτὴ Σαρρα στεῖρα δύναμιν εἰς καταβολὴν σπέρματος ἔλαβεν, Heb 11:11) does not attribute this seed to Sarah herself and therefore does not contradict this belief, since the whole context (Heb 11:11-12) clearly refers to the promise made by the Lord to Abraham: "I will indeed bless you with blessings, and I will make your offspring as numerously numerous as the stars of heaven and as the sand that is by the seashore" (ἦ μὴν εὐλογῶν εὐλογήσω σε καὶ πληθύνων πληθυνῶ τὸ σπέρμα σου ὡς τοὺς ἀστέρας τοῦ οὐρανοῦ καὶ ὡς τὴν ἄμμον τὴν παρὰ τὸ χεῖλος τῆς θαλάσσης, Gen 22:17 LXX).

102. D.E. Aune, *Revelation 6-16* (Nashville: Thomas Nelson Publishers, 1998) 708.

103. See for example Amos 5:15 LXX: Μεμισήκαμεν τὰ πονηρὰ καὶ ἠγαπήκαμεν τὰ καλά. καὶ ἀποκαταστήσατε ἐν πύλαις κρίμα, ὅπως ἐλεήσῃ κύριος ὁ θεὸς ὁ παντοκράτωρ τοὺς περιλοίπους τοῦ Ιωσηφ ("'We have hated evil

refers to a constellation of prophetic passages.[104] Read in this perspective, the remnants of the woman's seed cannot but represent the holy Israel, formed, in John's perspective, of those who keep the commandments and the testimony of Jesus.

This reference illustrates once again, if more proof is needed, that the inconsistencies in the narrative framework resolve themselves if we look for an explanation in the Scriptures without diminishing the richness and polysemy proper to any symbol. This applies as well to the figure of the woman in heaven. Luca Arcari reminds us that one of the immediate referents of the woman in heaven is the Judaism of which John becomes the herald, the holy Israel from which the messiah comes.[105]

## 6.2 The Seed of the Woman and the Sand of the Sea

"And he stood upon the sand of the sea" (Καὶ ἐστάθη ἐπὶ τὴν ἄμμον τῆς θαλάσσης, Rev 12:18):[106] this passage is a real aporia, so much so that already the ancient manuscript tradition corrects it.[107] As for modern translations, they sometimes transform it by trivializing it.[108] While it is just as intriguing as the more famous number of the beast, this passage has not exerted the same fascination, probably because of its apparent banality. However, we know from Philo, amongst others, that the apparent absurdities of a text are the driving force behind allegorization.[109] It is under the double light of the immediate context and of the Scriptures that one must seek the veiled meaning of this passage.

---

things and loved the good things.' Restore judgment in the gates, that the Lord God the Almighty might have mercy on the remnant of Ioseph").

104. e.g., Mic 4:7, etc.; see V. Herntrich, "The Remnant in the Old Testament," *s.v.* λεῖμμα κτλ., in G. Kittel, ed., *Theological Dictionary of the New Testament*, vol. 4 (Grand Rapids: Eerdmans 1967) 196-209.

105. L. Arcari, *"Una donna avvolta nel sole ..." (Apoc 12,1): le raffigurazioni femminili nell'Apocalisse di Giovanni alla luce della letteratura apocalittica giudaica* (Padova: Edizioni Messaggero Padova, 2008) 357-358. These remnants of the Woman seed would form the true Israel, distinct from the "congregation of Satan" (Rev 2:9; 3:9).

106. D.E. Aune underlines the problematic nature of this verse (*Revelation 6-16* [Nashville: Thomas Nelson Publishers, 1998] 732-733).

107. Manuscript tradition attests to the variant ἐστάθην (I stood, I stood up) instead of ἐστάθη (he/it stood, he/it stood up). This is clearly a correction seeking to make sense with a passage that was problematic; see the details in D.E. Aune, *Revelation 6-16* (Nashville: Thomas Nelson Publishers, 1998) 716.

108. For example, the current French translation: "Le dragon se tint sur le bord de la mer"; as for the Jerusalem Bible, which adopts the reading ἐστάθην, it translates: "Et je me tenais sur la grève de la mer."

109. J. Pépin, *La tradition de l'allégorie, de Philon d'Alexandrie à Dante* (Paris: Études augustiniennes, 1987) 22; about the functions of allegorical writing, see 91-136.

Now the verb ἵστημι is already used in connection with the dragon that rises, threatening, in front of the woman, ready to devour the unborn child (Rev 12:4), and it is the same Greek verb ἵστημι that is used in the vision of the Lamb on the throne (Rev 4:5). In these contexts, the verb ἵστημι (to stand, to rise) is given a strong meaning. The present occurrence should be related to the one that opens the account of the vision of the Lamb at the beginning of chapter 14, which echoes it: "And I saw, behold, the Lamb standing on Mount Zion" (Καὶ εἶδον, καὶ ἰδοὺ τὸ ἀρνίον ἑστὸς ἐπὶ τὸ ὄρος Σιών, Rev 14:1):

| the dragon | the Lamb |
|---|---|
| standing | standing |
| on the sand of the sea | on the mountain of Sion |

Now, the dragon represents Satan (Rev 12:9), while the Lamb represents the Messiah Jesus,[110] and Mount Zion is obviously not simply a geographical location but rather the mountain of the temple, a metaphor for the Holy Jerusalem. So, what does the sand of the sea represent? Certainly not an ordinary beach, the shore or the bottom of the sea. Here again, the solution to this enigma is to be sought in the Scriptures where the sand of the sea is associated with the seed of Abraham and Jacob, which is "as the sand of the sea": "I will make your offspring as numerously numerous as the stars of heaven and as the sand that is by the seashore" (τὸ σπέρμα σου ὡς τοὺς ἀστέρας τοῦ οὐρανοῦ καὶ ὡς τὴν ἄμμον τὴν παρὰ τὸ χεῖλος τῆς θαλάσσης, Gen 22:17), or to Jacob (τὸ σπέρμα σου ὡς τὴν ἄμμον τῆς θαλάσσης, Gen 32:13).[111] This association of the sand and the seed is suggested by the mention of the woman's seed (τὸ σπέρμα αὐτῆς, Rev 12:17) in the immediate context.

110. The Lamb, the principal messianic figure in the Apocalypse of John (29 occurrences), is often considered a non-violent symbol, in accordance with certain contemporary sensibilities, but not very compatible with his anger (Rev 6:16), which is related with God's wrath (Rev 15-16) and his victory in battle (Rev 17:14). It is by no means obvious that the use of this image in the Apocalypse emphasizes the vulnerability of the Lamb. In Scripture, the Lamb is essentially a sacrificial figure, which should not necessarily be associated with the Passover as many commentators do, but rather with temple worship; see the discussion in L.L. JOHNS, *The Lamb Christology of the Apocalypse of John: An Investigation into its Origins and Rhetorical Force* (Tübingen: Mohr Siebeck, 2003) esp. 128-132. In the context of the Apocalypse, the Lamb is essentially a symbol expressing the sacrificial character of the Messiah Jesus, inseparable from his priestly function, high priest of heavenly worship associated with the divine throne (Rev 7:9), both sacrificial victim and priest as in the Epistle to the Hebrews (8-10).

111. See also Isa 10:20-22; 48:17-19; Hos 1:8-10; and the parallel formula, the sand or dust of the earth (Gen 13:16; 28:14 [or of the sea A]).

Thus, read according to the rule of verbal analogy, this sentence is no longer trivial: it signifies the domination of the dragon over Israel as it has already been rightly understood by Edmondo Lupieri.[112] It thus continues the chain of allusions to the sin of Israel or of the sons of David evoked by Ps 88 LXX and the rebellion of Korah. However, this allusion leads the reader back to contexts that announce the triumph of the seed of Abraham over their external enemies (Gen 22:17) and over their internal divisions (Gen 32:13), evoked by the conflict between Esau and Jacob. Read in this light, the antithetical parallelism of verses 12:18 and 14:1 takes on its full meaning: framing the vision of the two beasts, it certainly announces the provisional domination of Satan over Israel. Moreover, it anticipates the final triumph of the Lamb, which will be explained later (Rev 19:11-21).

### 6.3 The Two Beasts

At one level, these two beasts refer to the two legendary monsters Leviathan (or Rahav of Ps 89:11) and Behemoth, dominating the sea and the land, created on the fifth and sixth day (Gen 1:9-10), and set aside to serve as food for the chosen ones at the end of time: these beasts are the dual protological and eschatological figures of the Adversary.[113] This tradition is very much alive at the time of the writing of the Apocalypse, as evidenced by *1 Enoch* 60:7-11; 24; *4 Ezra* 6:49-52 and *2 Baruch* 29:4. These monsters provide John with the traditional background from which he borrows his two beasts. John attributes to them a historical significance, following the Book of Daniel, which used the image of the sea monster to represent four empires. For John, these two symbolic beasts become the double manifestation of the dragon, that is, Satan, in the history of Israel.

### 6.4 The Beast from the Sea (Rev 13:1-10)

The description of the first beast is in perfect continuity with the vision of the woman and the dragon, both from the point of view of the narrative weave, since it is the dragon that gives the beast its power, and from the point of view of the scriptural chain, since its description, like that

---

112. See E.F. Lupieri, *A Commentary on the Apocalypse of John*, trans. M. Poggi Johnson – A. Kamesar (Grand Rapids: Eerdmans, 2006) 200. For an overview of misinterpretations arising from the misunderstanding of the scriptural allusion in this passage, see D.E. Aune, *Revelation 6-16* (Nashville: Thomas Nelson Publishers, 1998) 731-732.

113. L. Ginzberg, *The Legends of the Jews* vol. 1, *Bible Times and Character from the Creation to Jacob* (Philadelphia: The Jewish Publication Society of America, 1968) 26-31; P. Prigent, *L'Apocalypse de Saint Jean. Édition revue et augmentée* (Geneva: Labor et Fides, 2000) 311, n. 1; D.E. Aune, *Revelation 6-16* (Nashville: Thomas Nelson Publishers, 1998) 728-729.

of the dragon, largely borrows from the Book of Daniel. A strange aspect of this description is that the number of the first beast will be given only after the account of the vision of the second beast.

### 6.4.1 The Beast from the Sea Recapitulates All the Empires in the History of Israel

The beast has ten horns and seven heads (Rev 13:1-2a). These features, which are parallel to those of the dragon, indicate that this beast is the dragon's *alter ego*. It has also the features of the leopard, the bear, and the lion, which are the first three beasts of the Book of Daniel (Dan 7:3-6), while the ten horns are borrowed from the fourth beast, the most terrible of all (Dan 7:7-8).[114] David Aune sees nothing more in this description than a simple pastiche and does not see a direct correspondence between the seven heads of the beast imagined by John and the beasts of Daniel; he believes that John is describing only one beast because he is aiming at only one kingdom, the empire of Rome.[115] In fact, David Aune's reasoning must be reversed. Instead of interpreting the text on the basis of an *a priori* assumption that John would describe only one empire, we must start from the text to form the hypothesis that John turns the four beasts of Daniel into one beast in order to recapitulate in a single figure all the empires that dominated Israel.

Beyond the legend of Leviathan and the four beasts of Daniel 7, this beast from the sea could not but awaken in the mind of the reader or listener the passages of Ezekiel and Isaiah concerning Tyre (Sor), "which lives at the entrance to the sea" (τῇ Σορ τῇ κατοικούσῃ ἐπὶ τῆς εἰσόδου τῆς θαλάσσης, Ezek 27:3 LXX) and its prince who proclaims himself god and boasts of his riches (Ezek 28); the prince against whom the Lord has stretched out his hand (Isa 23:11). This is all the more likely since Rev 18 will make ample reference to these passages, as Iain Provan has well demonstrated.[116]

---

114. It must be remembered that the number of the ten horns (Rev 13:1) and their identification with ten kings (Rev 17:12) are not a creation of John who borrows them from Daniel (Dan 7:8,24); any attempt to make them coincide with a precise list of rulers at the time of John, especially Roman emperors, would be only secondary.

115. D.E. AUNE, *Revelation 6-16* (Nashville: Thomas Nelson Publishers, 1998) 734. The beast from the sea as an allusion to the Roman empire is generally taken for granted. Given the lack of evidence of persecution of Christians under Domitian however, Rick van de Water sees in the two beasts an allusion to Jewish messianism as opposed to Christian messianism (R. VAN DE WATER, "Reconsidering the Beast from the Sea (Rev 13.1)," *New Testament Studies* 46 [2000] 245-261).

116. I. PROVAN, "Foul Spirits, Fornication and Finance: Revelation 18 from an Old Testament Perspective," *Journal for the Study of New Testament* 64 (1996) 81-100.

There is no doubt that for the prophet John and for his readers and listeners, as well as for the author and audience of *4 Ezra* (12:11), the Roman Empire was the ultimate avatar of this beast from the sea, who had received its power from the dragon (Rev 13:4), that is, from Satan (Rev 12:9). The identification of the seven heads with seven mountains in Rev 17:9 might well have been received as a reference to the seven hills of Rome; however, the number seven is not a creation of John; rather, he takes it from Daniel's vision, where they cannot have this meaning (i.e., the hills of Rome). Werner Foerster observes on the one hand that the mountains, in the ancient East and in the Scriptures, are a common expression for power, including political power, and that, on the other hand, the beast, which displays all the characteristics of Daniel's beasts, cannot correspond to a single empire, so that the seven mountains here might well have been intended to represent the totality of political foreign powers in the history of Israel.[117]

On the other hand, the seven mountains that are the seat of the woman (Rev 17:9) can also be read in the light of the prophetic tradition where the mountains are the place of idolatry, of prostitution, the object of the Lord's wrath (Ezek 6:1-7; Jer 3:6).[118] In any case, the primary function of these seven heads, which are seven mountains, is to stress the continuity between the dragon that is Satan and the beast from the sea.

Further on, the angel will show John the great harlot sitting on "great waters" (ἐπὶ ὑδάτων πολλῶν, Rev 17:1) which could again allude to Tyre, whose merchants cross the sea on "much water" (ἐν ὕδατι πολλῷ Isa 23:3 LXX). John will see "a woman sitting on a scarlet beast" (Rev 17:3), and the angel will explain that the waters that he saw, on which the harlot is sitting, are "peoples and multitudes and tongues and nations" (Rev 17:15b). Beyond any particular past or contemporary empire, the nations (τὰ ἔθνη)

117. As W. FOERSTER, puts it "a power which spans the centuries" (art. "ὄρος," in G. KITTEL, ed., *Theological Dictionary of the New Testament*, vol. 5 [Grand Rapids, Mich.: Eerdmans, 1967] 487); against the identification of these seven heads with seven mountains which would be the hills of Rome, see also critiques by L. ARCARI, "L'Apocalisse di Giovanni nel quadro di alcune dinamiche gruppali proto-cristiane: elementi per una (ri-)contestualizzazione," *Annali di Storia dell'Esegesi* 28 (2011) 146.

118. *1 Enoch* also knows seven mountains, which obviously have nothing to do with the seven hills of Rome (18:7-9; 24-25): made of precious stones, they are the place of paradise, and one of them is compared to the throne of the Lord. With these seven mountains, *1 Enoch* also knows seven rivers and seven islands (*1 Enoch* 77:1-4). On the other hand, in *1 Enoch* 21, the seven stars which have transgressed the commandments of the Lord and are cast down and bound together in a chaotic place where they are burning are compared to great mountains. There is no reason to believe that the seven mountains of Revelation allude to those of Enoch; however, these parallels may well illustrate a traditional use of the number seven in a symbolic geography without any reference to reality.

are all that is *not* the holy nation, the chosen people. More than foreign nations, they are unbelievers, infidels, pagans.[119] This beast should not, therefore, be assumed to represent the Roman Empire alone, as it is generally understood.

On these heads is a blasphemous name (or names) (καὶ ἐπὶ τὰς κεφαλὰς αὐτοῦ ὀνόμα βλασφημίας, Rev 13:1c).[120] This could well evoke the titles attributed to the Roman emperors, "lord" (κύριος, *dominus*), "savior" (σωτήρ), "son of god" (*divi filius*) as is often thought,[121] but it might also bring to the mind of the reader the Prince of Tyre, who proclaims himself god (Ezek 28:11). Since there is every reason to believe that this beast from the sea recapitulates all the empires that dominated Israel, we can think of the Hellenistic, Lagid, or Seleucid rulers, for example Ptolemy *Soter* or Antiochus IV *Epiphanes*.

### 6.4.2 *Imperium redivivum*

Like the Lamb standing on the throne who "seemed to be put to death" (ὡς ἐσφαγμένον, Rev 5:6; see also 5:9,12; 13:8), one of the heads of the beast "seemed to be put to death" (ὡς ἐσφαγμένον εἰς θάνατον, Rev 13:3),[122] which marks a kind of parallelism between this head and the Lamb, whose mortal wound was healed. If this beast rising from the sea recapitulates the empires that dominated Israel, this wound inflicted on one of its heads could evoke, more than the legend of *Nero redivivus*, the violent death of a sovereign or the end of one empire, which would have been replaced by another and therefore would not have put an end to the reign of the beast. One example could be the violent death of Darius III,[123]

119. J.P. Louw – E.A. Nida, *Greek-English Lexicon of the New Testament Based on Semantic Domains*, vol. I (New York: United Bible Society, 1988) § 11.37.

120. The manuscript tradition is divided, although the oldest seems to favor the singular. D.L. Mathewson, *Revelation: A Handbook on the Greek Text* (Waco: Baylor University Press, 2016) 169. The difference may not be significant, see G.K. Beale, *The Book of Revelation: A Commentary on the Greek Text* (Grand Rapids: Eerdmans, 1999) 685.

121. D.E. Aune, *Revelation 6-16* (Nashville: Thomas Nelson Publishers, 1998) 734.

122. At the opening of the first six seals, the same verb is applied to those who perished "because of the word of God and the testimony they bore" (Rev 6:9); also to saints and prophets (Rev 18:24). In the New Testament, the verb σφάζω connotes the idea of violence but not that of sacrificial immolation; see J.P. Louw – E.A. Nida, *Greek-English Lexicon of the New Testament Based on Semantic Domains*, vol. I (New York: United Bible Society, 1988) § 20.72.

123. The last Achaemenid ruler, he reigned from 336 to 330; defeated by Alexander in 331, he was assassinated by a party of conspirators in 330 and is probably the Darius mentioned in Neh 12:22. Notwithstanding the relative oblivion into which Darius III fell under the shadow of Alexander, his memory was alive in

which put an end to the hegemony of the Persian Empire but did not lead to the death of the beast, since Alexander's empire succeeded him.[124]

The association of this image with the legend of *Nero redivivus* is less obvious than is usually claimed.[125] Indeed, one does not see how the continuation of the text "The whole earth/land marveled (and walked) behind the beast" (Καὶ ἐθαυμάσθη ὅλη ἡ γῆ ὀπίσω τοῦ θηρίου, Rev 13:3b) could evoke Nero; on the other hand, it would be perfectly suitable for Alexander the Great and his successors, all of whom "put on crowns," the description of which opens the First Book of Maccabees (1 Macc 1:1-7). Flavius Josephus, recounting Alexander's legendary visit to Jerusalem, tells how its inhabitants and its priests welcomed him.[126]

### 6.4.3 Submission to Empires

In the visions of the two beasts, one is struck by the recurrence of the verb προσκυνεῖν, always in connection with the dragon, the beast, or its image (Rev 13:4[*bis*],8,12,15; cf. also 14:9,11; 16:2; 19:4; 20:4).[127] Should it be

John's time, and the tragic end of the last Achaemenid emperor as soon as he was replaced by Alexander and a new empire might well have inspired John, reflecting on the succession of empires, with this image of a head put to death to be immediately reborn. See, about the death of Darius III, the excerpts gathered in A. KUHRT, *The Persian Empire: A Corpus of Sources from the Achaemenid Period* (London: Routledge, 2010) 451-455.

124. On the contradictory traditions that developed around the death of Darius and the succession of Alexander, see P. BRIANT, *Darius dans l'ombre d'Alexandre* (Paris: Fayard, 2003) esp. 443-521.

125. This so-called obviousness stems more from an *a priori* "Neronian" reading than from the text itself; see E.F. LUPIERI, *A Commentary on the Apocalypse of John*, trans. M. POGGI JOHNSON – A. KAMESAR (Grand Rapids: Eerdmans, 2006) 203-204.

126. F. JOSEPHUS, *Judean Antiquities* 11.329-339 (W. WHISTON, *The Works of Josephus* [Peabody: Hendrickson, 1987] 307). On the legendary nature of this story, see M. SARTRE, *D'Alexandre à Zénobie. Histoire du Levant antique, IVe siècle avant J.-C. – IIIe siècle après J.-C.* (Paris: Fayard, 2001) 79-82 and S.C. MIMOUNI, *Le Judaïsme ancien du VIe siècle avant notre ère au IIIe siècle de notre ère. Des prêtres aux rabbins* (Paris: PUF, 2012) 309-312.

127. Elsewhere, the verb is used in the description of the heavenly liturgy, always in connection with the verb πίπτειν, in the sense of "falling down and bowing down before," obviously in an attitude of adoration (Rev 4:10; 5:14; 7:11; 11:16; 19:4); in various situations, in relation to human beings or to God in 11:1, it expresses in a general way the activity of the faithful in the earthly temple. In the same way, on two occasions John falls down at the feet of the *angelus interpres* to prostrate himself before him, and each time the angel answers that one should only prostrate oneself before God (Rev 19:10; 22:8-10). It does not always have a cultic meaning and can also express submission or homage in a political context; see Luca Arcari's observations in this book (p. 28-29 with notes 39 and 40) and the references he gives on this subject. In a more general sense in the Apocalypse, those who

given a cultic meaning as is usually done? It is true that the beast is guilty of blasphemy against God (Rev 13:5-6), but as David Aune rightly points out, it does not explicitly claim to be divine,[128] which makes a cultic reference less likely. So, John does not seem to be aiming at worship as such, but rather at a more general attitude of submission to the empires represented by the beast from the sea. It seems preferable, in the absence of any other explicit cultic reference, to understand this verb in the more general sense of bowing to a power or a reality to which one submits.

In addition to its recurrence, the use of the verb προσκυνεῖν is striking for what appears to be a certain temporal inconsistency. First, the verb is in the aorist: "the whole earth marveled (and walked) after the beast, and *they bowed down*[129] before the dragon, and they bowed down before the beast" (Καὶ ἐθαυμάσθη ὅλη ἡ γῆ ὀπίσω τοῦ θηρίου καὶ προσεκύνησαν τῷ δράκοντι ... καὶ προσεκύνησαν τῷ θηρίῳ ... Rev 13:3-4). Then the verb is used again, but this time in the future tense: "all who dwell on the earth *shall bow down* before the beast" (καὶ προσκυνήσουσιν αὐτὸν πάντες οἱ κατοικοῦντες ἐπὶ τῆς γῆς, Rev 13:8). This tension between the "already" and the "not yet" will find a partial explanation in the following vision with the entry of the beast that will rise from the earth/land and make "those who dwell on the earth/land" (τοὺς κατοικοῦντες ἐπὶ τῆς γῆς, Rev 13:14) bow down before the first beast. This explanation, however, does not resolve the apparent contradiction between the statement in verse 4 ("the whole earth/land marveled and walked behind the beast") and verse 8 ("all that dwell on the earth/land shall bow down before him"),[130] unless "the whole earth/land" and "those who dwell on

---

call themselves Judeans but are not, will come and *bow down* before the assembly of Philadelphia (Rev 3:9b), a formula which could well evoke Isa 60:14 (also 49:23), passages where it is Gentiles who bow down before Israel. David Aune (*Revelation 1-5* [Dallas: Word Books, 1997] 237-239) sees this as a reversal of Isaiah's meaning since, according to him, the Jews of Philadelphia would come to worship before "this (largely Gentile) Christian community." This postulate of a largely Gentile congregation is hardly compatible with the character of Revelation, especially John's constant allusive use of the Scriptures, which would probably have been rather obscure for a pagan disciple.

128. "One of the striking features of the eschatological antagonist presented as the beast from the sea in 13:1-10 is that it is never explicitly made to claim that he is God and demand worship on that basis; nor does it take residence in the temple and broadcast its claim from there. The absence of these features which figure prominently in many Jewish versions of the eschatological-antagonist myth, probably results from the author's reshaping of the myth in light of the historical realities that he wishes the myth to reflect" (D.E. AUNE, *Revelation 6-16* [Nashville: Thomas Nelson Publishers, 1998] 740).

129. The plural must be interpreted here as an agreement *ad sensum*, the earth being considered as a collective.

130. Relying on the fact that v. 8 is the only occurrence of *all* the inhabitants of the earth, David Aune (*Revelation 6-16* [Nashville: Thomas Nelson Publishers,

the earth/land" point toward two different realities: this is made possible by the polysemy of the Greek word γῆ, which can mean either the earth or the land.[131]

"He was given a mouth speaking great things" (στόμα λαλοῦν μεγάλα Rev 13:5): this sentence takes up an aspect of the description of the little horn which grows on the head of the fourth beast of Daniel and which has a "mouth speaking great things" (στόμα λαλοῦν μεγάλα, Dan 7:8). Daniel then attributes to it an action that clearly recalls Antiochus IV Epiphanes, who, Daniel declares, "shall speak words against the Most High and wear down the holy ones of the Most High" (καὶ ῥήματα εἰς τὸν ὕψιστον λαλήσει καὶ τοὺς ἁγίους, Dan 7:25 LXX) and desires to change the calendar and the Law (Dan 7:25), which may well be echoed in the rest of John's text (Rev 13:6-7a).[132] More than the emperor Nero, or even Caligula, John could well, by this allusion to Daniel, be intending to evoke the reign of Antiochus IV, who attributed to himself the epithet Epiphanes, usually reserved for the gods, a "blasphemy against his Name and his tabernacle" (βλασφημίας πρὸς τὸν θεὸν βλασφημῆσαι τὸ ὄνομα αὐτοῦ καὶ τὴν σκηνὴν αὐτοῦ, Rev 13:6) referring to the profanation of the temple in 168 BCE (1 Macc 1:21-24; 2 Macc 5:15-23).

### 6.4.4 Dominion Over the Earth and the Land

The rest of the text asserts in the past tense the universal domination of the beast "over every tribe, language, people, and nation" (καὶ ἐδόθη αὐτῷ

1998] 746) thinks that this statement can only concern the eschatological future. However, this does not hold since "all the earth" (ὅλη ἡ γῆ) is already marveling at the beast and bowing down before the dragon (Rev 13:3-4).

131. The Greek word γῆ refers to the space inhabited by humans, either the earth as opposed to the heaven, the dry land as opposed to the sea, or the land as a region or a country (H. SASSE, "art. γῆ," in G. KITTEL, ed., *Theological Dictionary of the New Testament*, vol. 1 [Grand Rapids: Eerdmans, 1964] 677-681; also J.P. LOUW – E.A. NIDA, *Greek-English Lexicon of the New Testament Based on Semantic Domains*, vol. 2 [New York: United Bible Society, 1988] § 1.39-79).

132. It is generally taken for granted that the "saints" (ἅγιοι) refer to "Christians"; yet the concept of holiness plays a major role in the religion of Israel, not only in connection with worship, but also in prophetic literature; see K.G. KUHN, art. "ἅγιος," in G. KITTEL, ed., *Theological Dictionary of the New Testament*, vol. 1 (Grand Rapids: Eerdmans, 1964) 88-110. Of course, in the Apocalypse of John, the saints refer to those who "keep the commandments of God and faith in Jesus" (Rev 14:12), but its use should be understood not as a break but as a continuation of Jewish usage, for example, in the formula "the prophets, the saints, and those who fear the name" (Rev 11:18). As is stated by M. JAUHIAINEN (*The Use of Zechariah in Revelation* [Tübingen: Mohr Siebeck, 2005] 160-161), "Indeed, the cry and its overall context suddenly gain new depth once we see it as an allusion to the OT expectation of the restoration of God's people, rather than as a reference to sporadic and rather limited persecution of Christians during the preceding 35-60 years."

ἐξουσία ἐπὶ πᾶσαν φυλὴν καὶ λαὸν καὶ γλῶσσαν καὶ ἔθνος, Rev 13:7b; a formula which likely designates all the pagan nations over which the beast exercises its authority),[133] whereas in the following passage, in the future and no longer in the preterit, the reference to "all those who dwell on the earth/ land whose names are not written in the book of life of the Lamb slain since the foundation of the world" (Rev 13:8),[134] which is not likely including pagans, who *will* bow down before the beast (αὐτόν προσκυνήσουσιν, Rev 13:8) could designate the Judean inhabitants of the land of Israel or dispersed on earth, that is to say, the Judeans who do not keep the commandments.[135] We would then have a thinly veiled reference to the Hellenization of Judeans both in Judaea and in the diaspora, in Asia Minor and elsewhere, those whose "name is not written in the holy book." This could correspond, in Judean history, to the party of the "Hellenists," close to the temple and the great priestly families, and, in the messianic ἐκκλησίαι that John addresses, to the followers of Jesus who were inclined to make accommodations to the pagan lifestyle in the Greek cities of Asia Minor.[136]

The beginning of v. 9, "He who has ears to hear, let him hear," takes up a formula already used at the end of the message to the angel of the assembly in Smyrna to underline the importance of messages to the ἐκκλησίαι (Rev 2:11). Commentators generally consider it to introduce the reference to Jeremiah that immediately follows,[137] but it can also refer to what precedes, as the addresses to the reader or listener that close each of the messages do (Rev 2:7,11,17,29 ; 3:6,13,22).

### 6.4.5 Jeremiah, the Perversion of the Fathers, and the Destruction of Jerusalem

The proverbial statement that follows, "If anyone is destined for captivity, he will go into captivity; if anyone is destined to die by the

133. As suggested by E.F. LUPIERI, *A Commentary on the Apocalypse of John*, trans. M. POGGI JOHNSON – A. KAMESAR (Grand Rapids: Eerdmans, 2006) 207.

134. Καὶ προσκυνήσουσιν αὐτὸν πάντες οἱ κατοικοῦντες ἐπὶ τῆς γῆς, οὗ οὐ γέγραπται τὸ ὄνομα αὐτοῦ ἐν τῷ βιβλίῳ τῆς ζωῆς τοῦ ἀρνίου τοῦ ἐσφαγμένου ἀπὸ καταβολῆς κόσμου (Rev 13:8; cf. 17:8).

135. As is rightly pointed out by Edmondo Lupieri, "Here *gê* could refer to the whole world or the Holy Land of Israel" (E.F. LUPIERI, *A Commentary on the Apocalypse of John*, trans. M. POGGI JOHNSON – A. KAMESAR [Grand Rapids: Eerdmans, 2006] 207).

136. On the binomial "Judaism" and "Hellenism," see M. HIMMELFARB, *Between Temple and Torah: Esssays on Priests, Scribes, and Visionaries in the Second Temple Period and Beyond* (Tübingen: Mohr Siebeck, 2013) esp. 191-256; also S.C. MIMOUNI, *Le Judaïsme ancien du VIe siècle avant notre ère au IIIe siècle de notre ère. Des prêtres aux rabbins* (Paris, PUF, 2012) 313-376.

137. D.E. AUNE, *Revelation 6-16* (Nashville: Thomas Nelson Publishers, 1998) 749.

sword, he will die by the sword" (Rev 13:10a),[138] does not seem to connect naturally with the plot of the story, but it clearly evokes Jer 15:2 LXX (cf. also 50:11 LXX; 43:11 MT). In order to understand the meaning of this reference to Jeremiah's text, one should not limit oneself to seeing in it a description of how the "Christian" must resist the threat of the beast.[139] Rather, it should be read in the light of the context from which it is taken. This context describes the guilt of the people of Israel, announces their punishment by the Lord, and denounces the false prophets who deny this punishment. To the people who ask for forgiveness ("Where shall we go?"), the Lord answers: "Those destined for death, to death, and those destined for a dagger, to a dagger; and those destined for famine, to famine, and those destined for captivity, to captivity" (Jer 15:2).[140] The Lord then evokes the sin of Manasseh, son of Ezekias king of Judah, given all that he did in Jerusalem (Jer 15:3-4), whose destruction he announces with his hand (Jer 15:6). As Ps 88 LXX, which was alluded to in the inaugural address, announces the punishment of Israel for the disobedience of the sons of David, and as the allusion to the rebellion of Korah also alludes to punishment (Rev 12:16), so too does the text of Jeremiah announce the punishment of the people for Manasseh's deeds. This allusion to Jeremiah's text therefore invites the readers to understand the visionary account of the beast coming from the sea in the light of this scriptural chain that extends from the inaugural address. This chain evokes the sin of the sons of David, the disobedience of the people, and the just punishment that follows. It prepares the reader to understand the description of the second beast rising from the earth/land and the terrible punishment that will soon strike the great city. If this proverbial statement seems at first glance disconnected from the weft of the narrative, it is on the other hand in line with the scriptural warp that underlies it.

John closes the account of this vision with an exhortation to perseverance implicitly addressed to its recipients: "This is the hour of the perseverance and faith of the saints" (Rev 13:10; cf. 14:12, "those who keep the commandments of God and faith in Jesus the Messiah"), marking a pause between the descriptions of the two beasts.

---

138. Εἴ τις εἰς αἰχμαλωσίαν, εἰς αἰχμαλωσίαν ὑπάγει. εἴ τις ἐν μαχαίρῃ ἀποκτανθῆναι αὐτὸν ἐν μαχαίρῃ ἀποκτανθῆναι (Rev 13:10a).

139. "... how Christians should face the threat of the beast from the sea" (D.E. AUNE, *Revelation 6-16* [Nashville: Thomas Nelson Publishers, 1998] 749).

140. Ὅσοι εἰς θάνατον, εἰς θάνατον. καὶ ὅσοι εἰς μάχαιραν, εἰς μάχαιραν. καὶ ὅσοι εἰς λιμόν, εἰς λιμόν. καὶ ὅσοι εἰς αἰχμαλωσίαν, εἰς αἰχμαλωσίαν (Jer 15:2 LXX).

## 7. Provisional Conclusion

The dragon and the Lamb, the two eschatological adversaries, are face to face in the final confrontation. One stands on the sand of the sea (i.e., on the seed of Jacob); the other stands on Mount Zion. In this confrontation, the dragon takes the form of two beasts, the first coming from the sea, fighting against the saints and exercising its power over all nations, the second coming from the earth/land.

We have seen that the beast rising from the sea, which evokes the legend of Leviathan, the vision of Daniel, and likely also Hiram, the prince of Tyre, recapitulates the empires that have dominated Israel throughout its history, right down to the last of these: the empire of Rome.

The dragon takes yet another form, at the same time more ambiguous and more dreadful: that of a beast from the earth/land, which is also the false prophet. This remains to be deciphered.

# THE DRAGON, THE BEASTS, AND THE GOLD: THE NUMBER OF THE BEAST IN THE APOCALYPSE OF JOHN

## Part Two: "Its Number is Six Hundred and Sixty-Six" (Rev 13:18): The Rulers of Jerusalem, the Gold of the Nations, and the Beast from the Land

**Louis Painchaud**

*Université Laval, Québec*

And the weight of gold that had come
to Salomon in one year was
six hundred sixty-six talents of gold ...

(3 Kgdms 10:14 LXX)[1]

Résumé

Cette deuxième partie porte sur la vision de la bête issue de la terre/du pays (Ap 13,11-17) et sur l'énigmatique chiffre de la bête, 666 (Ap 13,18). J'y analyse la description de l'action de la bête issue de la terre ou du pays, qui fait descendre le feu du ciel et qui fabrique des images, à partir de parallèles scripturaires mettant en scènes les figures sacerdotale et royale d'Aaron et de Salomon, pour proposer que cette bête récapitule l'apostasie de la royauté et du sacerdoce anciens souillés par l'or des nations. Ils sont désormais remplacés par ceux dont Jésus a fait un royaume et des prêtres pour Dieu son père en les purifiant par sa mort (Ap 1,5-6). Le chiffre de la bête, en renvoyant à l'or de Salomon, un roi qui a multiplié l'or, les chevaux et les femmes étrangères, révèle la source de cette souillure de la royauté et du sacerdoce anciens, soit leur compromission avec les empires, dont l'or des nations fut de tout temps l'instrument.

1. Καὶ ἦν ὁ σαθμὸς τοῦ χρυσίου τοῦ ἐληλυθότος τῷ Σαλωμων ἐν ἐνιαυτῷ ἑνὶ ἑξακόσια καὶ ἑξήκοντα ἓξ τάλαντα χρυσίου (3 Kgdms 10:14 LXX). The Greek texts of the Septuagint are taken from A. Rahlfs, ed., *Septuaginta. Id est Vetus Testamentum graece iuxta lxx interpretes* (Stuttgart: Deutsche Bibelgesellschaft, 1982). English translations are taken from A. Pietersma – B.G. Wright, eds., *A New English Translation of the Septuagint* (Oxford: Oxford University Press, 2007).

*"Who is Sitting on Which Beast?" Interpretative Issues in the Book of Revelation. Proceedings of the International Conference held at Loyola University, Chicago, March 30-31, 2017,* ed. by Edmondo Lupieri and Louis Painchaud, JAOC 29 (Turnhout, 2023), pp. 227–262

DOI 10.1484/M.JAOC-EB.5.131935

Abstract

This second part focuses on the vision of the beast from the earth/land (Rev 13:11-17) and on the enigmatic number of the beast, 666 (Rev 13:18). I analyze the description of the action of the beast from the earth/land, which brings down fire from heaven and makes images, from scriptural parallels involving the priestly and royal figures of Aaron and Solomon, to propose that this beast recapitulates the apostasy of the ancient kingship and priesthood defiled by the gold of the nations. They are now replaced by those whom Jesus has made a kingdom and priests for God his father by purifying them through his death (Rev 1:5-6). The number of the beast, referring to the gold of Solomon, a king who multiplied gold, horses and foreign women, reveals the source of this defilement of the ancient kingship and priesthood, that is, their compromise with the empires, of which the gold of the nations was always the instrument.

## 1. Introduction

This second part is divided into three sections that deal successively with the beast from the earth/land (Rev 13:11-17), the number of the beast (Rev 13:18), and its origin in Scriptures (1 Kgs 10:14 MT; 3 Kgdms 10:14 LXX).

## 2. The Beast from the Earth/Land (Rev 13:11-17)

The identity of the first beast is clear from the first lines of its description, which points towards the Book of Daniel and the empires to which Daniel explicitly refers. By contrast, the description of the second beast is obscure and is gradually revealed through allusions to a constellation of scriptural passages revolving around the fire coming down from heaven and the making of images, down to the last of them, the number of the beast. This scriptural constellation could be called "the rebellious rulers of Zion" (Isa 1:23).[2]

The second beast rises from the earth/land (Rev 13:11a); it exercises the authority of the first beast and makes the earth/land and those who live in it bow down before it (Rev 13:12). It has two horns like those of a lamb, but speaks like a dragon (Rev 13:11b) and causes fire to come down from heaven (Rev 13:13). It causes the inhabitants of the earth/land to make an image for the first beast (Rev 13:14) and has power to kill those

2. Πῶς ἐγένετο πόρνη πόλις πιστὴ Σιων, πλήρης κρίσεως ... οἱ ἄρχοντές σου ἀπειθοῦσιν, κοινωνοὶ κλεπτῶν, ἀγαπῶντες δῶρα ... (Isa 1:21-23 LXX).

who do not bow down before it (Rev 13:15) ; and, finally, it controls commercial activity (Rev 13:16-17).

## 2.1 The Imperial Cult Deadlock

There are two conflicting (but not mutually exclusive) interpretative trends regarding the second beast. One trend sees in the beast's appearance and the wonders it performs a parody of the Messiah, or a prophet who must come at the end of time to announce the Antichrist.[3] The second detects an allusion to a contemporary reality linked to the imperial cult or to an institution of the Roman province of Asia, priests and priestesses of the imperial cult, *koinon* of Asia Minor, Roman governor of the province of Asia, or wealthy elites whose members provided the priests and priestesses of the imperial cult.[4]

Since these interpretations are generally taken for granted, no scriptural reference is sought in this passage, even though all agree that the fire coming down from heaven must refer to the prodigy Elijah performed on mount Carmel (1 Kgs 18:38 ; 2 Kgs 1:10). Pierre Prigent points out that "the first beast alone exhausts the symbolism of the vision of Daniel 7" and adds, "The second beast can hardly claim a traditional model borrowed from the OT."[5] Yet it is in the Scriptures, not in the traditional Greek or Roman cults, that fire comes down from heaven ; and the making of images, "this ancient sin of Aaron,"[6] is central in the Scriptures.

This identification of the second beast with an institution or group linked to the Roman imperial cult raises many problems : 1) it does not account for the fact that the second beast has neither the seven heads nor the ten horns of the first beast and the dragon, which distinguishes it from the first beast even more than the first beast was distinguished from the dragon ; 2) it ignores the antonymic aspect of the two beasts, the

3. D.E. Aune, *Revelation 6-16* (Nashville : Thomas Nelson Publishers, 1998) 756.

4. S.J. Friesen, "The Beast from the Land. Revelation 13:11-18 and Social Setting," in D.L. Barr, ed., *Reading the Book of Revelation. A Resource for Students* (Atlanta : Society of Biblical Literature, 2003) 49-64. If, as Friesen suggests, the inscriptions confirm that these elites did indeed provide the cadres for the imperial cult, they do not in any way confirm the identification of the second beast with these elites ; an identification suggested by A. Yarbro Collins, "'What the Spirit Says to the Churches' : Preaching the Apocalypse," *Quarterly Review* 4 (1984) 82.

5. P. Prigent, *L'Apocalypse de Saint Jean. Édition revue et augmentée* (Geneva : Labor et Fides, 2000) 320.

6. E.F. Lupieri, *A Commentary on the Apocalypse of John*, trans. M. Poggi Johnson – A. Kamesar (Grand Rapids : Eerdmans, 2006) 209 ; L. Arcari, "L'Apocalisse di Giovanni nel quadro di alcune dinamiche gruppali proto-cristiane : elementi per una (ri-)contestualizzazione," *Annali di Storia dell'Esegesi* 28 (2011) 155.

first coming from the sea, the second from the earth/land, to the point of amalgamating them into one;[7] 3) the identification of this beast with the Roman imperial cult cannot account for its dragon/lamb ambiguity; 4) the identification of the beast from the land as the false prophet (ψευδοπροφήτης Rev 16:13; 19:20; 20:10), would more likely point toward an internal conflict,[8] as it is the case about the prophetess in Thyatira (Rev 2:20); and 5) if the first beast recapitulates all the empires that have ruled Israel and not only the last one (Rome), as I suggested in the previous chapter, a second beast recapitulating the whole history of Israel, and not only the Roman imperial cult, would be expected. It may well be that in constructing his description of the false prophet, John has in mind Jeremiah's denunciation of the ungodly prophets and priests of Jerusalem (Jer 23:9-15).[9]

In a recent article, Craig Koester examines the seemingly incongruous nature of this description in literary, historical, and ethical terms, as well as in the history of its reception. He sees this incongruity as a literary device designed to make the reader perceive the insidious connections between political power and commerce on the one hand, and loyalty to God on the other, while leaving the reader free to respond to this connection in his or her own social context.[10] Koester's analysis is partly correct insofar as there is indeed a discrepancy between the social context in which John's recipients live in the cities of Asia Minor and the description of this beast. He is also right when reading in it the

7. David G. Dunbar provides an excellent example of this amalgamation: "In the book of Revelation the basically religious motif of the Antichrist theme – the beast out of the earth (Rev 13:11-18) – is merged with a political interpretation which views the Antichrist – the beast out of the sea (Rev 13:1-10) – as the head of the Roman empire" (D.G. DUNBAR, "Hippolytus of Rome and the Eschatological Exegesis of the Early Church," *Westminster Theological Journal* 45 [1983] 327).

8. The polemic between prophets and the accusation of false prophecy, in the Scriptures and in the early canonized Christian writings, are most often, if not always, the witnesses of internal conflicts or dissensions; see G. FRIEDRICH, art. "προφήτης κτλ.," in G. KITTEL, ed., *Theological Dictionary of the New Testament*, vol. 6 (Grand Rapids: Eerdmans, 1967) 855-856. In the case of the Apocalypse of John, in the messages to the assemblies, the activity of the false prophet is intrinsically related to the description of John's opponents (L. ARCARI, "L'Apocalisse di Giovanni nel quadro di alcune dinamiche gruppali proto-cristiane: elementi per una [ri-]contestualizzazione," *Annali di Storia dell'Esegesi* 28 [2011] 178).

9. See J.T. HIBBARD, "True and False Prophecy: Jeremiah's Revision of Deuteronomy," *Journal for the Study of the Old Testament* 35 (2011) 339-358; S. BAKON, "True and False Prophets," *Jewish Bible Quarterly* 39 (2011) 152-158.

10. C.R. KOESTER, "The Image of the Beast from the Land (Rev 13:11-18). A Study in Incongruity," in A. YARBRO COLLINS, ed., *New Perspectives on the Book of Revelation* (Leuven: Peeters, 2017) 333-352, esp. 352.

insidious connections between political power and commercial activity, and even religious power. However, he fails in identifying the target of John's prophetic criticism.

As David Aune pointed out twenty years ago, and as Luca Arcari has underlined recently, the identity of the beast from the earth/land remains problematic and controversial.[11]

This impasse stems from the fact that the scriptural references contained in the description of the second beast have been ignored or neglected until now because of the consensus that it was aimed at imperial worship in the cities of Asia Minor. To get past this impasse, one must recognize the scriptural references and read this description of the beast from the earth/land in the light of the passages to which it refers. Like that of the first beast, the narrative weave of the vision of the second beast is woven on a warp of scriptural allusions. However, whereas this warp was perfectly clear in the vision of the first beast and unequivocally referred the reader first and foremost to the Book of Daniel and to Jeremiah, that of the second beast is more complex. It is composed of ambiguous signals referring to different scriptural passages, but still forming a constellation, linked together by a golden thread that the number of the beast will make manifest. In other words, the description of the second beast is somewhat comparable to a guessing game that could be formulated in the following way. "I come from the earth/land, but I receive my power from the nations (i.e., the beast from the sea); I bring down fire from heaven like a prophet, but I make an image of the beast. Who am I?"

## 2.2 The Description of the Beast from the Earth/Land Under the Light of Scriptures

"Then I saw another beast from the earth/land" (Καὶ εἶδον ἄλλο θηρίον ἐκ τῆς γῆς, Rev 13:11).[12] This sentence parallels the one that introduces the vision of the first beast: "And I saw a beast rising out of the sea" (13:1). David Aune rightly observes that we have here the only occurrence of the word "beast" to designate this second figure, to which John

11. D.E. Aune, *Revelation 6-16* (Nashville: Thomas Nelson Publishers, 1998) 756; L. Arcari, "L'Apocalisse di Giovanni nel quadro di alcune dinamiche gruppali proto-cristiane: elementi per una (ri-)contestualizzazione," *Annali di Storia dell'Esegesi* 28 (2011) 149.

12. The English language offers the choice of translating the Greek word γῆ as "earth" or "land." While almost all English translations opt for the first, "earth," to my knowledge, only Young's Literal Translation (1888) and, recently, the Jubilee Bible (2000) opt instead for the second, "land," which seems to me more appropriate, because it better renders the opposition land/sea. The choice of the formula earth/land is a compromise intended to fully maintain the ambiguity of the Greek word γῆ.

will refer later, until the end of chapter 13, only by a series of eight verbs in the third person singular and by a pronoun.[13] This observation confirms what has already been pointed out: the second beast is *not* an *alter ego* of the first beast. In this pericope (Rev 13:11-18), the word "beast" (θηρίον) appears nine more times, but in v. 12, the text specifies that it is the "first beast" (τὸ θηρίον τὸ πρῶτον). Later, when the word *beast* (θηρίον) is used, it always refers to the first beast (Rev 13:14a): its image (Rev 13:14b,15a.b), its mark, its name (Rev 13:17), and its number (Rev 13:18). Thereafter, the second beast is referred to as the false prophet (Rev 16:13; 19:20; 20:10). Everything happens as if the designation of this second figure as a beast had no other function than to evoke, through the legend of Leviathan and Behemoth, the inseparable pair that this figure forms with the foreign, pagan empires, without, however, assimilating them to each other.

### 2.2.1 It Rises from the Earth/Land (ἀναβαῖνον ἐκ τῆς γῆς Rev 13:11)

On one level, the opposition between sea and land obviously refers to the opposition between water (ὕδωρ) and dry ground (ξηρά) separated on the fifth day of creation, which God called "sea" (θάλασσα) and "land" (γῆ) respectively (Gen 1:9-10). In the context of Revelation 13, and of the pair of two beasts (the first one coming from the "sea"), "land," as opposed to "sea," is a better English translation of the Greek word γῆ than "earth," which would form an antonymic pair with "heaven." On another level, we have also seen (given the features borrowed from the Book of Daniel attributed to the beast) that the beast rising from the sea represents the empires that dominated Israel through history, and more broadly, "peoples, multitudes, nations and languages" (Rev 17:15b). Since the Greek word γῆ can also designate a particular country, it might well point toward the country that is Israel, as opposed to the empires, as Edmondo Lupieri has observed.[14] Recognizing the chain of scriptural allusions on which this description is woven will make it possible to establish that the more likely concern of the text is the land of Israel, together with its rebellious leaders, priests, and kings.

---

13. D.E. Aune, *Revelation 6-16* (Nashville: Thomas Nelson Publishers, 1998) 755.

14. "A remarkable number of references to Jewish religious practices are used in the description of the false prophet-beast, which suggests that it may not represent only, or primarily, pagan religions, but also the corrupt form of Judaism that has compromised with the pagan world. The γῆ which is mentioned four times in four verses, may actually be Israel ... If so, John would echo the traditional prophetic accusation that Israel has become corrupt and has devoted herself to idolatry" (E.F. Lupieri, *A Commentary on the Apocalypse of John*, trans. M. Poggi Johnson – A. Kamesar [Grand Rapids: Eerdmans, 2006] 209-210).

### 2.2.2 It Has Two Horns Like (those of) a Lamb and Speaks Like a Dragon (Rev 13:11b)

The number of its horns distinguishes this second beast both from the dragon and from the first beast which have ten horns (Rev 12:3; 13:1), and from the Messianic Lamb, which has seven horns (Rev 5:6). This beast would therefore be at least by these two horns similar to the Lamb, a kind of deceptive counterfeit of the Messiah, the Lord's anointed one.[15] On the other hand, these horns could refer to those of the false prophet (1 Kgs 22:11; 2 Chr 18:10), as Enrico Norelli suggests.[16] Worse, this second beast speaks like the dragon, that is, Satan. This enigmatic image thus indicates a reality that is not only ambiguous, but also deceptive: the second beast is by some aspects at the same time similar to a lamb and a dragon, which makes it the image par excellence of the Antichrist.

### 2.2.3 It Exercises the Authority of the First Beast Under Its Gaze (Rev 13:12)

After describing the symbolic features that distinguish the second beast from the first one, the prophet describes the link that unites them: it exercises the authority of the first beast under its gaze, i.e., its supervision, to make the earth/land and those who dwell in it bow down before it. This statement would be entirely appropriate in order to describe the political and religious power of the kings and high priests in Jerusalem in the Hasmonean and Herodian periods under the Roman rule. Herod the Great and his successors were clients of Rome, on which their power depended, and they were devoted to the interests of the empire. The same is true of the high priesthood. Simon Mimouni summed it up perfectly:

15. It could be that these two horns represent the double priestly and royal power of the Messiah. Like the two witnesses of Jesus in chapter 11, who are not said to be "faithful" (Rev 11:3) and who will prophesy "clothed in sackcloth," a sign of penance and mourning, at the time when the holy city will be trampled on by the nations, represent ancient kingship and priesthood destroyed when Jerusalem was taken, but already purified and resurrected with Jesus; for the reference to Zorobabel, the Prince, and Josuah, the Priest (Zech 3-4), see L. Painchaud, "Temple et sacerdoce dans l'Apocalypse de Jean ou Zorobabel et Josué, témoins de Jésus Christ (Ap 11, 3-14)," in L. Painchaud – S.C. Mimouni – D. Hamidović, eds., *La sacerdotalisation dans le judaïsme synagogal, dans le christianisme et dans le rabbinisme. Actes du colloque de Québec, 18-20 septembre 2014* (Turnhout: Brepols, 2018), 229-246; see also M. Goodman, *The Ruling Class of Judaea. The Origins of the Jewish Revolt against Rome A.D. 66-70* (Cambridge, UK: Cambridge University Press, 1987) esp. 129-133.

16. E. Norelli, *L'Ascensione di Isaia* (Bologna: EDB) 93-113; L. Arcari, "L'Apocalisse di Giovanni nel quadro di alcune dinamiche gruppali proto-cristiane: elementi per una (ri-)contestualizzazione," *Annali di Storia dell'Esegesi* 28 (2011) 151.

> Aux yeux des Judéens, les Hérodiens apparaissent essentiellement comme les suppôts des Grecs dont la langue et la culture, tant intellectuelle que matérielle, triomphent partout en Palestine, au mépris des préceptes religieux Judéens fondamentaux dont la tendance est le maintien des traditions ancestrales. Quant au grand sacerdoce, il est totalement instrumentalisé, choisi par le roi ou le gouverneur romain, le grand-prêtre représente certes une certaine autorité religieuse dont l'assise est le temple, mais cette autorité est affligée d'une souillure dont la garde des vêtements du grand-prêtre par le gouverneur romain pourrait bien être le signe le plus manifeste.[17]

Mimouni's description of the Herodian dynasty may well have its counterpart in Revelation's description of those ten kings "who have not yet received kingship, but receive authority as kings for one hour with the beast" (Καὶ τὰ δέκα κέρατα ἃ εἶδες δέκα βασιλεῖς εἰσιν, οἵτινες βασιλείαν οὔπω ἔλαβον, ἀλλὰ ἐξουσίαν ὡς βασιλεῖς μίαν ὥραν λαμβάνουσιν μετὰ τοῦ θηρίου, Rev 17:12).[18] It is therefore possible, and even quite likely, that the beast rising from the earth/land represents the kings to whom God has given a temporary kingship at the service of the beast from the sea until his words are fulfilled (Rev 17:17).[19]

### 2.2.4 The Earth/Land and Those Who Dwell in It (Rev 13:12b)

"And it makes the land and those who dwell *in* it bow down before the first beast" (καὶ ποιεῖ τὴν γῆν καὶ τοὺς *ἐν* αὐτῇ κατοικοῦντας ἵνα προσκυνήσουσιν τὸ θηρίον τὸ πρῶτον, Rev 13:12b). In Rev 13:8, the expression "those who dwell on the earth" is usually constructed with the preposition ἐπί ("on"; οἱ κατοικοῦντες ἐπὶ τῆς γῆς: cf. Rev 3:10; 6:10; 8:13; 11:10 [bis]; 17:8). Here the formula is constructed with the preposition ἐν ("in"). Explanations offered in order to understand this difference in the preposition include secondary intervention or a concern for parallelism with Rev 12:12; however, neither of these explanations is convincing.[20] This variation could be better explained if γῆ here does not refer

17. S.C. MIMOUNI, *Le judaïsme ancien du VIe siècle avant notre ère au IIIe siècle de notre ère. Des prêtres aux rabbins* (Paris: PUF, 2012) 412, 430-434; on the relationship between Rome and Jerusalem, see also M. GOODMAN, *Rome and Jerusalem. The Clash of Ancient Civilizations* (London: Penguin, 2007).

18. About the number of kings, we must take into account that it is determined by Daniel's vision, not by any historical accuracy.

19. Adela Yarbro Collins saw the importance of this passage as a hermeneutic key to understanding the description of the city in chapter 18 (A. YARBRO COLLINS, "Rewritten Prophets. The Use of Older Scriptures in Revelation," in S. ALKIER – TH. HIEKE – T. NICKLAS, eds., *Poetik und Intertextualität der Johannesapokalypse* [Tübingen: Mohr Siebeck, 2015] 299).

20. D.E. AUNE, *Revelation 6-16* (Nashville: Thomas Nelson Publishers, 1998) 758.

to the whole earth, but to a particular land, a country. In the Septuagint, the expression κατοικεῖν ἐν ("to live in") is applied overwhelmingly to the inhabitants of a city or a country.[21] This variation in the formulation may therefore provide a clue that we are dealing here with the country, i.e., Israel, and its inhabitants.

### 2.2.5 It Performs Great Signs (σημεῖα μεγάλα) Until Fire Comes Down from Heaven to Earth (Rev 13:13)

The word "sign" (σημεῖον) refers in Revelation to a reality of heavenly origin, such as the appearance of the woman and the dragon in heaven (Rev 12:1.3) or seven angels holding plagues (Rev 15:1). Here, the signs (σημεῖα) are fulfilled by an agent who is not of heavenly origin; however the fact that this ability is *given* to him (τὰ σημεῖα ἃ ἐδόθη αὐτῷ ποιῆσαι Rev 13:14), as well as to the false prophet (Rev 16:14; 19:20), indicates the heavenly origin of this gift. This is another indication of the radical difference between the two beasts; neither the dragon nor the first beast is given the ability to perform signs.

This ability is granted to it so that it may bring down fire from heaven in the sight of men (ἵνα καὶ πῦρ ποιῇ ἐκ τοῦ οὐρανοῦ καταβαίνειν εἰς τὴν γὴν ἐνώπιον τῶν ἀνθρώπων, Rev 13:13). Most commentaries rightly see here the beast's or false prophet's *imitation* or *counterfeit version* of the true prophet par excellence, Elijah, whose prayer made fire come down from heaven on mount Carmel (1 Kgs 18:24-38; 2 Kgs 1-10), confirming his status as a prophet of the true God. It is difficult, however, to connect this trait convincingly with imperial worship or another Roman institution.[22] Moreover, this interpretation does not account for the fact that this ability is *given* to the beast.

To this second beast, which is the false prophet, is therefore given the ability to *imitate* Elijah, the true prophet; this ability has a positive connotation. To understand the significance of this passage, however, we must go back to the Scriptures and to all passages where fire comes down from heaven, and not only to the episode of Mount Carmel. This prodigy knows several occurrences. The first is twofold; it is

---

21. H. SASSE, art. "γῆ," in G. KITTEL, ed., *Theological Dictionary of the New Testament*, vol. 1 (Grand Rapids: Eerdmans, 1967) 677-681.

22. Luca Arcari lists a number of attestations of the use of fire in a religious or magical context in antiquity, sometimes thanks to the tricks of illusionists ("L'Apocalisse di Giovanni nel quadro di alcune dinamiche gruppali proto-cristiane: elementi per una [ri-]contestualizzazione," *Annali di Storia dell'Esegesi* 28 [2011] 177-178 and note 99). However, the fact that this ability to perform signs *is given* to the second beast (Rev 13:14, cf. D.E. AUNE, *Revelation 6-16* [Nashville: Thomas Nelson Publishers, 1998] 760-761) does not call into question the reality of these signs.

found in Leviticus, where the formulation is somewhat different: the fire "came down from the Lord" and not from heaven (καὶ ἐξῆλθεν πῦρ παρὰ κυρίου), at the dedication of the tent of meeting (Lev 9:24; 10:2 LXX), after Aaron had offered the sacrifice first (Lev 9:8-22), and then to punish the sons of Aaron who had brought a strange fire (Lev 10:2). The second is found in the First Book of Chronicles, where the Lord answered David's prayer "with fire from the sky" (ἐν πυρὶ ἐκ τοῦ οὐρανοῦ, 1 Chr 21:26), confirming the choice of Mount Zion as the site for his house (1 Chr 22:1). The prodigy occurs again at the prayer of Solomon at the dedication of the Temple: "fire also descended from the sky ... And all the sons of Israel saw the fire descend" (καὶ τὸ πῦρ κατέβη ἐκ τοῦ οὐρανοῦ ... καὶ πάντες οἱ υἱοὶ Ισραηλ ἑώρων καταβαῖνον τὸ πῦρ, 2 Chr 7:1-3 LXX), meaning that the glory of the Lord "filled the house."[23]

The whole of these scriptural passages describing the descent of fire from heaven forms a constellation. If the attribution of this sign to the beast from the earth/land, which is also the false prophet, is rightly understood as a counterfeit of the true prophet par excellence (Elijah), and of the true king (David), we must nevertheless ask how the whole of these scriptural episodes and the attribution of this sign to the beast from the earth/land in the Apocalypse of John can illuminate one another. These episodes present prophetic, priestly, and royal figures of an ancient kingship and priesthood (Elijah, Aaron, David and Solomon), now replaced by those whom Jesus the Messiah delivered from their sins by his blood (Rev 1:5-6). Among these figures, Aaron, high priest of the Lord (Exod 28:1-2; 29:1-9) and craftsman of the golden calf (Exod 32:1-6), and Solomon, son of David and apostate, who is rich in gold, horses and women (1 Kgs 10-11), both anointed and apostates,[24] are two highly ambiguous figures, just like the second beast.

### 2.2.6 It Deceives Those Who Dwell on the Earth/Land (Rev 13:14a)

Deception characterizes the action of Satan (Rev 12:9; 20:10), but also that of Babylon/Jerusalem, the great city (Rev 18:21-23), which deceives the nations with its spells, and of the prophetess of Thyatira

---

23. For a first overview of the Levitical *ethos* of the Books of Chronicles and their exaltation of the figures of David and Solomon, see R. NOTH, "The Chronicler: 1-2 Chronicles, Ezra, Nehemiah," in R.E. BROWN – J.A. FITZMYER – R.E. MURPHY, eds., *The New Jerome Biblical Commentary* (London: Geoffrey Chapman, 1990) 362-365.

24. TH. RÖMER, "Salomon d'après les deutéronomistes: un roi ambigü," in CL. LICHTERT – D. NOCQUET, eds., *Le roi Salomon, un héritage en question: hommage à Jacques Vermeylen* (Bruxelles: Lessius, 2008) 98-130.

whom John calls by the ignominious name of Jezebel, who deceives the servants of the Living One (Rev 2:20). This action of the second beast comes from its capacity as a false prophet (see Jer 23:9-15) : it exercises deception thanks to the signs that it is given to accomplish. Here, "those who dwell on earth/land" (τοὺς κατοικοῦντας ἐπὶ τῆς γῆς) could encompass the Judean diaspora as well as all humankind (cf. Dan 3:1).

### 2.2.7 It Prompts Those Who Dwell on the Earth/Land to Make an Image in Honor of the Beast (Rev 13:14b)

In line with the chain of allusions to the Book of Daniel contained in the vision of the dragon, and especially in the vision of the beast from the sea, "making an image" (εἰκόνα ποιεῖν) inevitably refers the reader to the golden image made by King Nebuchadnezzar (ἐποίησεν εἰκόνα χρυσῆν Dan 3:1 LXX) before which all were commanded to bow (προσκυνεῖν Dan 3:5 LXX). The making of images obviously refers to the ban on making idols and prostrating oneself before them on Sinai (Exod 20:4-5), but also to its first transgression by the priest Aaron, and the people with him, who made the golden calf and worshipped it (Exod 32:1-10).[25]

According to Flavius Josephus, a contemporary of John, Solomon himself also transgressed this interdict, both in the temple and in the royal house, even before his marriage to foreign princesses, by making images of bulls (1 Kgs 7:25-28 ; 2 Chr 4:3-4,15) to support the bronze sea, and images of lions surrounding his throne (1 Kgs 10:19-20 ; 2 Chr 9:18-19).[26] Likewise, Jeroboam, the first king of the northern kingdom, made two golden calves and established shrines in Dan and Bethel (1 Kgs 12:28-33) ;

---

25. Often recalled in the Scriptures (e.g. Amos 5:25-27 LXX), this episode is evoked in the discourse of Stephen (Acts 7:39-43) in the same way as John uses it to describe the activity of the second beast; see L. ARCARI, "L'Apocalisse di Giovanni nel quadro di alcune dinamiche gruppali proto-cristiane : elementi per una [ri-]contestualizzazione," *Annali di Storia dell'Esegesi* 28 (2011) 157-161. In Judean history, this passage could also refer to the desecration of the Temple under the Hellenized High Priests Jason and Menelaus in the time of Antiochus IV Epiphanius as well as to the golden eagle placed by Herod above the great entrance of the Temple, see F. JOSEPHUS, *Wars of the Judeans* 1.650 (W. WHISTON, ed., *The Works of Josephus* [Peabody : Hendrickson, 1987] 595) ; see also P. PRIGENT, *Le judaïsme et l'image* (Tübingen : J.C.B. Mohr, 1990) 15 ; S.C. MIMOUNI, *Le judaïsme ancien du VI^e siècle avant notre ère au III^e siècle de notre ère. Des prêtres aux rabbins* (Paris : PUF, 2012) 396.

26. F. JOSEPHUS, *Judean Antiquities* 8.195 (W. WHISTON, *The Works of Josephus* [Peabody : Hendrickson, 1987] 226) ; on the ambivalent reception of Solomon by Flavius Josephus, see J. VERHEYDEN, "Josephus on Solomon," in J. VERHEYDEN, ed., *The Figure of Solomon in Jewish, Christian and Islamic Tradition. King, Sage and Architect* (Leiden : Brill, 2013) 85-106, esp. 99-102.

Manasseh, who reigned in Jerusalem for 55 years, made an image, and brought it into the temple. He placed there a statue of Ashera that he had made (2 Kgs 21:7; 2 Chr 33:7).

Thus, two ambiguous figures were given the capacity to bring down fire from heaven in the Scriptures. The first, the high priest Aaron, is guilty of having fashioned the golden calf. The second, the apostate king Solomon, is guilty, according to Flavius Josephus, of having violated this same interdict by introducing images into the temple. In a way, this places them halfway between the type of the true prophet Elijah and the true king, David, and the type of the enemies of Israel, Babylon and its king Nebuchadnezzar.

These passages form a *constellation*, a scriptural network, which we can visualize in the following table, forming a perfectly coherent scheme:

| **Fire from heaven** | | **Image making** |
|---|---|---|
| Figures pleasing to the Lord | Ambiguous characters | Figures abominable to the Lord |
| Elijah the true prophet | Aaron, high priest, craftsman of the golden calf | Nebuchadnezzar, King of Babylon |
| David, the true King | King Solomon, son of David and apostate | Jeroboam, King of Israel |
| | | Manasseh, King in Jerusalem |

In the light of this scriptural network, we can understand the nature of this ambiguous beast that rises from the earth/land and that is similar to both the Lamb and the dragon. It represents the ancient unclean kingship and priesthood, guilty of idolatry,[27] of which Solomon and Aaron are the types.

In order to understand the meaning of this double reference to Aaron and Solomon, it is necessary to set aside the prism of the "Christian" tradition which sees in the Apocalypse a reaction to the persecution of Christians by Rome and to read it in its Judean messianic context. It is also necessary to imagine an environment in which King Solomon is received and understood as an ambiguous figure, in the Deuteronomist manner[28] and

27. For a critique of ancient royalty and priesthood found in palace literature, see C. Heszer, "'He Who Sits Crowned on the Throne of His Glory': Body Posture in Hekhalot Rabbati and in Rabbinic Literature," in D. Hamidović – S.C. Mimouni – L. Painchaud, eds., *La 'sacerdotalisation' dans les premiers écrits mystiques juifs et chrétiens. Actes du colloque international tenu à l'Université de Lausanne du 26 au 28 octobre 2015* (Turnhout: Brepols, 2021) 41-56.

28. On the irony and subversiveness of the Deuteronomistic narrative of 1 Kgs 1-11, see J. Koulagna, *Salomon de l'histoire deutéronomiste à Flavius*

in the tradition behind Matt 6:29; 12:42; Luke 11:31; 12:27 (also Acts 4:46-53), and Flavius Josephus.[29]

### 2.2.8 Putting to Death Anyone Who Does Not Bow Down Before the Beast (Rev 13:15b)

This verse could recall the scriptural theme of the murder of the prophets (Jer 2:30; 26:23; 2 Chr 24:21-22) taken up by Matthew in relation to Jerusalem (Matt 23:37-38 [Luke 13:34]; see also Matt 5:12; 21:31; 23:30) and evoked by Stephen's speech (Acts 7:54-8:1).[30] The killing of the saints is already mentioned many times by the prophet John (Rev 2:10,13; 6:9; 11:7-8). It would have brought to the readers' mind the martyrdom of Eleazar, and the seven brothers and their mother under Antiochus IV (2 Macc 6:18-7:42). There is no need to look outside of Scripture for events in history to which this passage might have referred a Judean reader or listener. Nevertheless, this could have reminded them of the massacre of six thousands men perpetrated by Alexander Jannaeus, king and high priest, in 96 BCE on the Feast of Tabernacles,[31] or the episode of the golden eagle placed by Herod's orders above the temple door, which resulted in the massacre of the men who dared to destroy it.[32] Finally, among the followers of Jesus, it might have evoked the stoning of Stephen by the Judeans (Acts 7:54-8:1) or that of James, the brother of the Lord, in 61-62 CE.[33]

---

*Josèphe. Problèmes textuels et enjeux historiographiques* (Paris: Publibook, 2009) 19-53.

29. The staging of episodes in Solomon's portico (John 10:22-23; Acts 3:1-10; 5:12) may well bear witness to a veiled polemic against the Jerusalem temple establishment in the canonized writings of the New Testament, to say nothing of Stephen's discourse (Acts 7:47-50); see A.L.A. HOGETREP, "King Solomon in the New Testament," in J. VERHEYDEN, ed., *The Figure of Solomon in Jewish, Christian and Islamic Tradition: King, Sage and Architect* (Leiden: Brill, 2013) 142-163.

30. L. ARCARI, "L'Apocalisse di Giovanni nel quadro di alcune dinamiche gruppali proto-cristiane: elementi per una (ri-)contestualizzazione," *Annali di Storia dell'Esegesi* 28 (2011) 157-160.

31. F. JOSEPHUS, *Judean Antiquities* 13.372-373 (W. WHISTON, *The Works of Josephus* [Peabody: Hendrickson, 1987] 360).

32. F. JOSEPHUS, *Wars of the Judeans* 1.650-656 (W. WHISTON, *The Works of Josephus* [Peabody: Hendrickson, 1987] 595-596); see P. RICHARDSON, *Herod: King of Jews and Friend of the Romans* (Columbia S.C.: University of South Carolina Press, 1996) 15-18.

33. S.C. MIMOUNI – P. MARAVAL, *Le christianisme des origines à Constantin* (Paris: PUF, 2006) 155. For the link established by the tradition between the stoning of James and the siege of Jerusalem, see J. BOURGEL, "Jacques le Juste, un Oblias parmi d'autres," *New Testament Studies* 59 (2013) 222-246.

### 2.2.9 The Economic Activity and the Mark of the Beast (Rev 13:16)

The beast that comes from the earth/land makes everyone bear a "mark" (χάραγμα) on the hand or forehead, in order that they be able to buy or sell. There has been much speculation about the referent of the word "character" or "mark" (χάραγμα); it has been seen as a traditional eschatological motif, or as a reference to some concrete reality, *tephillim*, tattoos or something else.[34] It is a mark that comes up repeatedly in connection with the announcement of the punishment of all those who bear it (Rev 14:9-11; 16:2; 19:20; 20:4), an indication that having this mark confers a moral stigma in the eyes of the prophet. However, it is obviously not a real, concrete mark that should be worn on the hand or forehead and displayed in the marketplace or in shops.

Here, as elsewhere, in order to clarify the meaning of an enigmatic passage, it might be illuminating to turn to the Scriptures. The "mark on the forehead" (τὸ χάραγμα ... ἐπὶ τὸ μέτωπον) imposed by the beast cannot but recall the "sign upon the foreheads" (τὸ σημεῖον ἐπὶ τὰ μέτωπα Ezek 9:4) imposed by the man clothed in linen on the inhabitants of Jerusalem resisting the abominations that are committed there in order to preserve them from extermination,[35] of which it would be the antithesis. This mark would prolong the chain of scriptural allusions to the announcement of the punishment of the holy city that has been going on since the beginning of the text, and in the immediate context, the reference to its announcement by Jeremiah inserted at the end of the description of the beast from the sea.

In a context that evokes economic activity, we can think that the replacement of the word σημεῖον (sign), used by Jeremiah, by the word χάραγμα (brand) would have the function of evoking the notion of currency, money, which is at the same time an instrument of economic activity, and a symbol of wealth.[36] Indeed, without money, no one can buy or sell; for John, having money or being wealthy would reveal the true identity of any follower of the beast. In this hypothesis, referring to money as

---

34. D.E. Aune, *Revelation 6-16* (Nashville: Thomas Nelson Publishers, 1998) 766-767.

35. This passage recalls also the blood on the lintel of the doors of the Israelites as a sign to protect them from the destructive scourge directed against Egypt (Exod 12:7). This man dressed in linen is found also in Dan 10:5 with a belt of gold (cf. Rev 1:13); see B. Barc, *Les arpenteurs du temps. Essai sur l'histoire religieuse de la Judée à la période hellénistique* (Lausanne: Éditions du Zèbre, 2000) 171-173 = *Du sens visible au sens caché de l'Écriture. Arpenteurs du temps. Essai sur l'histoire religieuse de la Judée à la période hellénistique*. Nouvelle édition (Turnhout: Brepols, 2021) 171-173.

36. And this notwithstanding the fact that the mark is here on the hand and on the forehead; see D.E. Aune, *Revelation 6-16* (Nashville: Thomas Nelson Publishers, 1998) 766-767.

the instrument of commercial activity, the mark of the beast, i.e., money, or its form par excellence, gold, would be the means by which the beast from the earth/land would subjugate anyone to the beast from the sea. The rest of the text contains insignificant variants,[37] and seems to indicate that brand, name, and number are each interchangeable and designate the same reality.

## 3. The Number of the Beast (Rev 13:17-18)

The number of the beast raises a twofold problem, first textual, since the text is not sure; secondly, of interpretation, because of the isopsephic impasse that has persisted since the second century. Here is the text:

> Here is wisdom, let him that has understanding calculate the number of the beast, it is a man's number. Its number is six hundred and sixty-six.
>
> Ὧδε ἡ σοφία ἐστίν. ὁ ἔχων νοῦν ψηφισάτω τὸν ἀριθμὸν τοῦ θηρίου, ἀριθμὸς γὰρ ἀνθρώπου ἐστίν, καὶ ὁ ἀριθμὸς αὐτοῦ ἑξακόσιοι ἑξήκοντα ἕξ. (Rev 13:18)

### 3.1 The Textual Problem

The number six hundred and sixty-six (ἑξακόσιοι ἑξήκοντα ἕξ), is written in full in the great codices of the fourth century, Sinaiticus (א), Alexandrinus (A), or in the form ΧΞϚ, in a papyrus of the third century P[47] Nestle – Aland).[38] As for the number six hundred and sixteen (ἑξακόσιοι δέκα ἕξ),[39] it is found in a papyrus of Oxyrhynchus (P[115] Nestle – Aland) also dated in the late third or early fourth century, in the form ΧΙϚ and in full, in a palimpsest of the fifth century, the Codex Ephraimi Rescriptus (C. 04).[40] In the Latin tradition, the reading "six hundred and sixteen" is attested neither in the *Vetus Latina* nor in the Vulgate, but it is found in the commentary of Tyco-

37. All textual witnesses have the same sequence "mark – name – number"; the variations concern the place of the word "beast" in the series and the use of possessives.

38. F.G. Kenyon, *The Chester Beatty Biblical Papyri. Descriptions and Texts of Twelve Manuscripts on Papyrus of the Greek Bible. Fasciculus III Pauline Epistles and Revelation* (London: Emery Walker, 1934) xii and 28.

39. For textual witnesses of the six hundred and sixteen variant, see J.N. Birdsall, "Irenaeus and the Number of the Beast: Revelation 13,18," in A. Denaux ed., *New Testament Textual Criticism and Exegesis: Festschrift J. Delobel* (Leuven: Peeters, 2002) 349-352; also K. Bodner – B.A. Strawn, "Solomon and 666 (Revelation 13.18)," *New Testament Studies* 66 (2020) 299 note 2.

40. C. Tischendorf, *Codex Ephraemi Rescriptus* (Leipzig, 1845) 301, l. 40.

nius Afer;[41] among later Latin commentators, only Caesarius of Arles adopts this reading.[42] It is also found in Armenian versions of the fifth or sixth centuries.[43] In the indirect tradition, the two readings are attested around 180 by Irenaeus of Lyon, a proponent of the reading six hundred and sixty-six (*Against the Heresies* V, 30, 1-4). The two numbers, therefore, have both a textual and a traditional basis.

## 3.2 The Interpretative Problem: the Isopsephic Deadlock

While the generally accepted harmful symbolic meaning of the number made of six units, six tens and six hundreds is supported by a plausible argument,[44] any attempt to see it as an isopsephic reference to a name that would have the same numerical value remains highly speculative given the large number of possibilities it would open.[45] In the first

41. This commentary is lost, but Roger Gryson was able to reconstruct it with the help of the later authors who used it, Caesarius of Arles, Primasius, the Venerable Bede, Beatus of Liébana (R. GRYSON, *Tyconii Afri Expositio Apocalypseos: accedunt eiusdem Expositionis a quodam retractatae fragmenta Taurinensia* [Turnhout: Brepols, 2011] and the French translation, *Tyconius. Commentaire de l'Apocalypse* [Turnhout: Brepols, 2011]); see also K.B. STEINHAUSER, *The Apocalypse Commentary of Tyconius: A History of its Reception and Influence* (Berlin: Peter Lang, 1987).

42. A.G. HAMMAN, *L'Apocalypse expliquée par Césaire d'Arles. Scholies attribuées à Origène; commentaire de l'Apocalypse, traduit par dom Joël Courreau, moine de Ligugé; scholies attribuées à Origène, traduites par Solange Bouquet; introduction par I. de la Potterie et A.-G. Hamman* (Paris: Desclée de Brouwer, 1989).

43. For later Armenian witnesses, see J.N. BIRDSALL, "Irenaeus and the Number of the Beast: Revelation 13,18," in A. DENAUX, ed., *New Testament Textual Criticism and Exegesis: Festschrift J. Delobel* (Leuven: Peeters, 2002) 351.

44. On the symbolism of numbers, see F. DORNSEIFF, *Das Alphabet in Mystik und Magie* (Leipzig: B.G. Teubner, 2nd ed., 1925); G. IFRAH, *Histoire universelle des nombres. L'intelligence des hommes racontée par les chiffres et le calcul* (Paris: Laffont, 1994); studies on the use of numbers in ancient Christianity are numerous, we can refer to the still relevant article by F. BOVON, "Des noms et des nombres dans le christianisme primitif," *Études théologiques et religieuses* 82 (2007) 337-360. For apocalyptic literature in general, see A. YARBRO COLLINS, "Numerical Symbolism in Jewish and Early Christian Apocalyptic Literature," in *Aufstieg und Niedergang der römischer Welt* 21.2 *Hellenistisches Judentum in römischer Zeit* (Berlin: De Gruyter,1984) 1221-1287. About the number seven, see G.G. REINHOLD – V. GOLINETS, *Die Zahl Sieben im Alten Orient: Studien zur Zahlensymbolik in der Bibel und ihrer altorientalischen Umwelt = The Number Seven in the Ancient Near East: Studies on the Numerical Symbolism in the Bible and its Ancient Near Eastern Environment* (Frankfurt am Main: Peter Lang, 2008).

45. The isopsephic approach is based on the fact that Greek letters are also used as numerical signs, so that words, expressions or stichs whose sum of the numerical values of the letters that form them is equal will be called isopsephs; see P. PERDIZET, "Isopséphie," *Revue des études grecques* 17 (1904) 350-360. These calculations can lead to the development of mysterious links between words or names with the same numerical value. Reference is also often made to *gematria*, a rabbinic exegetical rule using the numerical value of letters (see D.E. AUNE, *Revelation 6-16*

half of the nineteenth century, four German scholars saw in it, independently from each other and in various forms, but always using a Hebrew transliteration, a reference to Emperor Nero,[46] the archetypal "persecutor of Christians."

An interesting discussion on this subject marked the first publications of the *Zeitschrift für die neutestamentliche Wissenschaft* at the beginning of the last century. Considering it unlikely that the editor of Revelation or an earlier editor would have required Hebrew knowledge from his readers, and rejecting possible references to Hadrian or Trajan, C. Clemen proposed in 1901 ἡ ἰταλὴ βασιλεία, whose value is 666, and ἡ λατίνη βασιλεία, whose value is 616.[47] The following year, Peter Corssen objected that the "name of the beast" should be the name of a person.[48] In 1903, Eberhard Vischer stressed the hazardous nature of any attempt to arrive at a name determined from a number and cited the symbolic and scriptural

---

[Nashville: Thomas Nelson Publishers, 1998] 771), which does not strictly speaking apply here.

46. There is some confusion about the origin of this idea; an excellent summary can be found in F. Bleek, *Vorlesungen über die Apokalypse* (Berlin: Georg Reimer, 1862) 292-293. Ferdinand Benary published this idea in the first issue of the *Zeitschrift für spekulative Theologie* launched by Bruno Bauer in 1836 (F. Benary, "Erklärung der Zahl 666 in der Apocalypse [13,18] und ihrer Variante 616," *Zeitschrift für spekulative Theologie I. Miscellen* [1836] 205-206). The following year, Ferdinand Hitzig claimed authorship of this interpretation, which he would have proposed for the first time during a series of lectures devoted to the Apocalypse of John in the summer of 1836 (F. Hitzig, *Ostern und Pfingsten. Zur Zeitbestimmung im Alten und Neuen Testament* [Heidelberg: C.F. Winter, 1837] 3; also F. Benary, "Offene Erklärung gegen Dr Ferd. Hitzig," *Haller Allgemeine Literaturzeitung Intelligenzblatt August 1837* [1837] 428); Édouard Reuss, in Strasbourg, also claimed to be behind this idea (E. Reuss, *Haller Allgemeine Literaturzeitung Intelligenzblatt September 1837* [1837]). And yet, fatherhood does not belong to any of them, but to Karl Friedrich August Fritzsche, in 1831 (K.Fr.A. Fritzsche, "Ueber die Zahl 666 in der Apokalypse, eine Abhandlung über Apocal. 13,16-18," *Annalen der gesammten theologischen Literatur und der christlichen Kirche Überhaupt* 1/3. [Coburg und Leipzig, 1831] 42-64, spec. pp. 58-60). Fritzsche first considers the transliteration of the expression *Caesar Romae*, in Hebrew קיסר רום, which would be worth 616 (100 + 10 + 60 + 200 / + 200 + 6 + 40 = 616), which he rejects, because, according to him, it requires a proper name, and then proposes *Caesar Neron*, in Hebrew קסר נרון, worth 666 (100 + 60 + 200 / + 50 + 200 + 6 + 50 = 666). Note the graphic variants used to obtain the desired figure. It was later observed that the number 616 corresponded to the Hebrew transliteration of the Latin form *Nero Caesar* without the final N.

47. C. Clemen, "Die Zahl des Tieres Apc 13,18," *Zeitschrift für die neutestamentliche Wissenschaft und die Kunde der älteren Kirche* 2 (1901) 109-114.

48. P. Corssen, "Noch einmal die Zahl des Tieres in der Apokalypse," *Zeitschrift für die neutestamentliche Wissenschaft und die Kunde der älteren Kirche* 3 (1902) 238-246.

approach of Irenaeus as an example.[49] In 1920, Wilhelm Hadorn returned to the isopsephic interpretation, and saw in it a reference to the Emperor Trajan.[50] Here we have, in summary, the difficulties that are still raised a century later.

Today, the common opinion holds the number six hundred and sixty-six for the original reading, and the Neronian hypothesis, despite its fragility, is taken up and accepted as possible by most commentators, most often with a prudent reserve,[51] sometimes with excessive enthusiasm.[52] However, J. Neville Birdsall, an eminent professor of New Testament and textual criticism, who devoted an article to this problem a few years before his death in 2005, retained six hundred and sixteen as the original reading according to the criterion of *lectio difficilior*.[53] According to him, in fact, the number six hundred and sixteen is less susceptible to symbolic interpretations than six hundred and sixty-six, and refers to the Emperor Caligula (Caius Caesar), the numerical value of ΓΑΙΟΣ ΚΑΙΣΑΡ being six hundred and sixteen. The origin of this application of the number six hundred and sixteen to Caligula would be linked to his threat to have his statue erected in the temple of Jerusalem and would, according to Birdsall, have been prior and external to the writing of Revelation. A symbol of threat, this number would have been integrated into the final form of Revelation. Later, early in the second century, this number would have been transformed into six hundred and sixty-six "easier to interpret."[54] This totally speculative hypothesis is unverifiable; moreover, it is not based on any analysis of the function of this possible reference to Caligula within

---

49. E. VISCHER, "Die Zahl 666 Apc 13,18," *Zeitschrift für die neutestamentliche Wissenschaft und die Kunde der älteren Kirche* 4 (1903) 167-174.

50. W. HADORN, "Die Zahl 666, ein Hinweis auf Trajan," *Zeitschrift für die neutestamentliche Wissenschaft* 19 (1920) 25; and *Die Offenbarung des Johannes* (Leipzig: A. Deicherische Verlagsbuchhandlung, 1928) 147.

51. See discussion in D.E. AUNE, *Revelation 6-16* (Nashville: Thomas Nelson Publishers, 1998) 770-771.

52. According to Richard Bauckham, "Although the emperor Nero is not named in Revelation, his name plays a key role in it" (R. BAUCKHAM, *The Climax of Prophecy: Studies on the Book of Revelation* [Edinburgh: T&T Clark, 1993] 384).

53. J.N. BIRDSALL, "Irenaeus and the Number of the Beast: Revelation 13,18," in A. DENAUX, ed., *New Testament Textual Criticism and Exegesis: Festschrift J. Delobel* (Leuven: Peeters, 2002) 349-359; see also L. VAN HARTINGSVELD, "Die Zahl des Tieres, die Zahl eines Menschen, Apokalypse XIII,18," in T. BAARDA, ed., *Miscellanea Neotestamentica*, vol. 2 *Studia ad Novum Testamentum praesertim pertinentia a Sociis Sodalicii Batavi c.n. studiosorum Novi Testamenti conventus anno MCMLXXVI quintum lustrum feliciter complentis suscepta* (Leiden: Brill, 1978) 191-201.

54. J.N. BIRDSALL, "Irenaeus and the Number of the Beast: Revelation 13,18," in A. DENAUX, ed., *New Testament Textual Criticism and Exegesis: Festschrift J. Delobel* (Leuven: Peeters, 2002) 358.

the context of the Apocalypse of John. Little progress has been made on this issue since Irenaeus.

Any hypothesis identifying the beast with any person or institution based on the search for a name whose numerical value would be six hundred and sixty-six is not only fragile, as Pierre Prigent points out,[55] but is also highly unlikely, for three reasons. The first is the text itself, which in no way requires finding a word or a name with a numerical value of six hundred and sixty-six, but only the calculation of the number of the beast, the result of which is immediately given. The second is the infinite number of possibilities that such an interpretation opens up. The third, which stems from the second, is textual pragmatics: for the communication of an information as important as the identity of the beast to be effective, the name would have had to be already known to the addressees of the text, which is postulated but not demonstrated. From a methodological point of view, as Luca Arcari rightly points out,[56] one cannot base the interpretation of the text on such a fragile hypothesis. Let us add to this that the examples generally put forward in support of this hypothesis, Pompeii's graffito, the *Sibylline Oracles*, Barnabas's *Epistle*, when considered closely, are rather unfavorable to it. The graffito is not meant to be understood except by one person, and in the other texts the numbers are always accompanied by unequivocal clues allowing the reader to identify the reference.[57]

---

55. "Il faut simplement avoir la sagesse de reconnaître que c'est une hypothèse possible, mais seulement une hypothèse" (P. PRIGENT, *L'Apocalypse de Saint Jean. Édition revue et augmentée* [Geneva: Labor et Fides, 2000] 329).

56. L. ARCARI, *"Una donna avvolta nel sole ..." (Apoc 12,1): le raffigurazioni femminili nell'Apocalisse di Giovanni alla luce della letteratura apocalittica giudaica* (Padova: Edizioni Messaggero Padova, 2008) 298, n. 112.

57. However, these examples, when examined closely, tend rather to exclude this possibility as far as the Apocalypse of John is concerned. Thus, the graffito of Pompeii published by Antonio Sogliano in 1901, φιλῶ ἧς ἀριθμός φμε "I love the one whose number is 545" presumably assumes that the beloved only will recognize herself, and is probably not intended to be deciphered by those it does not concern (A. SOGLIANO, "Isopsepha Pompeiana," *Rendiconti della Reale Accademia dei Lincei* 10 [1901] 256-259, in A. DEISSMANN, *Light from the Ancient East: The New Testament Illustrated by Recently Discovered Texts of the Graeco-Roman World. New and Completely Revised Edition with Eighty-five Illustrations from the Latest German Ed.* [Grand Rapids: Baker Book House, 1965] 277). Richard Bauckham rightly points out: "Presumably the beloved herself is expected to recognize the numerical value of her name, but few others would take the trouble to work out which name has this numerical value (as most probably several Greek feminine names have)" (R. BAUCKHAM, *The Climax of Prophecy: Studies on the Book of Revelation* [Edinburgh: T&T Clark, 1993] 385). With regard to the numerous examples taken from the *Sibylline Oracles*, where numbers are used to suggest names of sovereigns, each of the passages concerned gives details such that these names can be easily found without risk of error: the numerical value of only the initial of the name is

### 3.3 A Hypothetical Well Known Number?

This is why an ancient apocalyptic tradition of using the number six hundred and sixty-six has been imagined,[58] and commentators, proposing to associate the number of the beast with a particular Roman emperor, will sometimes stress, as Birdsall did, that for this identification to be effective, it had to be widely used and already known by John's addressees. Thus, George R. Beasley-Murray suggests that the identification of Nero with the number 666 was the work of a Palestinian zealot during Nero's lifetime or of a Judeo-Christian prophet in the apocalyptic tradition.[59] Some authors have proposed other equivalents, sometimes foreign to the world of this text.[60] All this remains purely speculative since no such attestation

---

first given, an unequivocal clue, which is not based on any calculation, to which is added a second clue, historical (Sib. Or. 11-14 passim) or other, which removes any ambiguity. For example, for Cleopatra (Κλεοπάτρα) the text gives the number 20, which is the numerical value of the initial of her name, K, and clearly identifies her: "A queen of the land by the streams of the Nile" (*Sibylline Oracles* 11, 254-256 [J.H. CHARLESWORTH, ed., *The Old Testament Pseudepigrapha*, vol. 1 *Apocalyptic Literature and Testaments* (Peabody: Endrickson, 2009) 40]); likewise, Alexander Severus (Marcus Aurelius) is said to bear the name of the "mighty Macedonian prince" (Sib. Or. 12, 270 [CHARLESWORTH 452]); for Solomon, the text gives the numerical value of his initial S, 200, but also its rank in the alphabet, 18 (*Sibylline Oracles* 11, 80-103) and specifies, among other things, that he built the temple. Similarly, the passage which gives the numerical value 888 for the name of Jesus introduces him as the incarnate Son of God and gives the number of vowels and consonants which make up his name (*Sibylline Oracles* 1, 324-330). The only real enigma is therefore the divine name in 1, 137-146, and here again the text gives not only the numerical value of this name, but also the number of letters and syllables that make it up. If the simple enumeration of these uses of numbers by the Sibylline Oracles—it is not strictly speaking isopsephy—to indicate the name of an emperor of Rome or of another character may at first sight seem to militate in favor of the use by John of the number six hundred and sixty-six to refer to a Roman emperor, a serious examination of these passages falsifies this hypothesis. In fact, this procedure is never used without other clues that remove any ambiguity. The *Epistle of Barnabas* offers a typological interpretation of the number of the 318 servants circumcised by Abraham (Gen 17:23-27) according to which this number would refer to Jesus, whose cross imitates the shape of the letter τ, whose numerical value is 300, and whose name includes the two letters ι, and η, whose sum is eighteen. This explanation is taken up by Clement of Alexandria (*Stromateis* VI, 11 § 84). But in the epistle and in Clement, the interpretation of numbers is very explicitly exposed and leaves nothing to the uncertain perspicacity of the reader, however intelligent he or she may be.

58. See D.E. AUNE, *Revelation 6-16* (Nashville: Thomas Nelson Publishers, 1998) 389, n. 18C.

59. G.R. BEASLEY-MURRAY, *The Book of Revelation: Based on the Revised Standard Version* (Grand Rapids: Eerdmans, 1981) 219-220; he is followed by B. WITHERINGTON III, *Revelation* (Cambridge, UK: Cambridge University Press, 2003) 185.

60. For example the Phoenician name for the constellation of the triangle (*delto-ton*); see B.J. MALINA – J.J. PILCH, *Social-science Commentary on the Book of Revela-*

has reached us in Jewish or Christian sources, either before or after the writing of the Apocalypse of John.

### 3.4 The Number of Its Name

In order to find the solution to this problem, we must first get rid of the assumption that the phrase "the number of its name" (τὸν ἀριθμὸν τοῦ ὀνόματος αὐτοῦ Rev 13:17; cf. also 15:2) is pointing to a proper name. Grammatically speaking, the Greek word ὄνομα, like the English word "noun" designates the part of speech used to designate "a body or an action," to use the terminology of Dionysius of Thrace. It can be common or proper:

> A 'noun' (ὄνομα) is a declinable part of the sentence indicating a physical entity, such as 'stone,' or a non-physical entity, such as 'education,' it can be general, such as 'man,' 'horse,' or particular, such as 'Socrates.' It has five properties: gender, type, form, number, declension.[61]

In this sentence, therefore, the expression "its name" (τοῦ ὀνόματος αὐτοῦ) may simply mean the word that designates the beast, i.e., the Greek word θηρίον.

### 3.5 Calculate the Number of the Beast

The reader is engaged to *calculate* the number of the beast, not to interpret it,[62] much less to look for a reality to which this number would correspond. Since the number of a reality is the sum of the numerical values of the letters of the noun that designates it, the simplest interpretation of the text is to calculate the number of the word θηρίον. This hypothesis, qualified as new by Pierre Prigent,[63] was first proposed, it seems with astonishment, by Hadorn a hundred years ago,

---

*tion* (Minneapolis: Fortress Press, 2000) 177-178.

61. Ὄνομά ἐστι μέρος λόγου πτωτικόν, σῶμα ἢ πρᾶγμα σημαῖον, σῶμα μὲν οἷον λίθος, πρᾶγμα δὲ οἷον παιδεία, κοινῶς τε καὶ ἰδίως λεγόμενον, κοινῶς μὲν οἷον ἄνθρωπος, ἵππος, ἰδίως δὲ οἷον Σωκράτης. Παρέπεται δὲ τῶι ὀνόματι πέντε. γένη, εἴδη, σχήματα, ἀριθμοί, πτώσεις. G. Uhlig, *Grammatici Graeci I/I, Dionysii Thracis Ars grammatica* (Leipzig: B.G. Teubner, 1883) § 14 (translation. A. Alcock, *The Grammar of Dionysus Thrax Translated into English* Published on Academia.Edu) 7; see also, for example, Plato's dialogue *Cratylus*, devoted to the correctness of names (τῶν ὀνομάτων), whether proper or common.

62. As the French translation of TOB understands it the wrong way "... celui qui a de l'intelligence, qu'il *interprète* le chiffre de la bête" and the translation in everyday French (traduction en français courant "*trouver le sens* ..."), influenced by the many speculations that this number inspires.

63. P. Prigent, *L'Apocalypse de Saint Jean. Édition revue et augmentée* (Geneva: Labor et Fides, 2000) 330, n. 55.

in 1920.[64] It is an apparently easy operation. However, according to the numerical value of the Greek letters, this sum is not six hundred and sixty-six, but two hundred and forty-seven, or, if we calculate the numerical value of the genitive form, θηρίου, as it appears in the text, five hundred and ninety-seven.[65]

To obtain the result given in the text, that is the number six hundred and sixty-six, it is necessary to transliterate with Hadorn the word θηρίον using the Hebrew characters תריון (*triyn*). Thus transliterated, the Greek word θηρίον has the value six hundred and sixty-six (= נ + ו + י + ר + ת 666 = 400 + 200 + 10 + 6 + 50).[66]

Calculating the number of the beast is therefore more difficult than it seems, especially since the text is most often accessed orally: it is necessary to transliterate the nominative form of a Greek word that appears in the genitive in the text. This is why the text immediately gives the solution of the calculation: "its number is six hundred and sixty-six" (ὁ ἀριθμὸς αὐτοῦ ἑξακόσιοι ἑξήκοντα ἕξ, Rev 13:18). As for the ancient variant six hundred and sixteen, it corresponds to the numerical value of the genitive form θηρίου transliterated into Hebrew (616 = 400 + 200 + 10 + 6 = ו + י + ר + ת).[67]

---

64. "Auffallenderweise ist nun die Summe der Zahlenwerte des griechischen Wortes θηρίον ins Hebräische umgeschrieben genau 666" (W. HADORN, "Die Zahl 666, ein Hinweis auf Trajan," *Zeitschrift für die neutestamentliche Wissenschaft* 19 [1920] 23; and *Die Offenbarung des Johannes* [Leipzig: A. Deicherische Verlagsbuchhandlung, 1928] 148). After mentioning the hypothesis that the number six hundred and sixty-six would be the sum of the numerical value of the expression Nero Caesar in Hebrew characters, Eduard Lohse adds, but without reference to Hadorn: "Gleichzeitig ergibt das griechische Wort *therion* = Tier die Zahl 666" (E. LOHSE, *Die Offenbarung des Johannes*, 9. Aufl. 2., neubearb. [Göttingen: Vandenhoeck & Ruprecht, 1966] 82); see also U. WILCKENS, art. "χάραγμα," in G. KITTEL, ed., *Theological Dictionary of the New Testament*, vol. 9 (Grand Rapids: Eerdmans, 1974) 417 n. 7; O. RÜHLE, art. "ἀριθμέω," in G. KITTEL, ed., *op. cit.*, vol. 1, 463. David Aune mentions Hadorn's article in his bibliography for the chapter 13 (D.E. AUNE, *Revelation 6-16* [Nashville: Thomas Nelson Publishers, 1998] 714), but he makes no mention of it in his commentary. This observation is rarely noticed by commentators, let alone considered seriously.

65. Θηρίον (9 + 8 + 100 + 10 + 70 + 50 = 247); θηρίου (9 + 8 + 100 + 10 + 70 + 400 = 597).

66. To obtain this result, not only must θηρίον be written in Hebrew characters, but also the *theta* must be rendered as a *tav* rather than a *thet*. Concerning the possibility of this spelling, see H.B. ROSÉN, "Palestinian κοινή in Rabbinic Illustration," *Journal of Semitic Studies* 8 (1963) 65.

67. One can imagine that a scribe will have corrected the number in order to take into account the genitive form of the word in the text. This would have happened before 180 CE, since the testimony of Irenaeus provides us with a *terminus ante quem*, no doubt in an environment where the necessity of the passage through Hebrew had been remembered, but had lost sight of the function of the number six hundred and sixty-six as an allusion to Scriptures (see further section 4).

### 3.6 The Number of a Human Being or a Human Number?

As David Aune notes, the expression "it is a man's number" (ἀριθμὸς γὰρ ἀνθρώπου ἐστίν) is problematic.[68] The genitive ἀνθρώπου can have two meanings. It is a possessive genitive, and in this case ἀνθρώπου can be either generic and refer to the human race, or specific and refer to a particular human being. It is an attributive genitive which indicates that it is a human number, i.e., of the order of human realities.[69] The parallel formula in Rev 21:17, μέτρον ἀνθρώπου, is not without similar problems of interpretation, so that it is difficult to argue one way or the other.[70] That being said, nothing obliges us to conclude that these refer to a contemporary of the Apocalypse.[71] However, there is no indication that it is the number of the name of a human being as is generally taken for granted. It should therefore be remembered that, on the one hand, as we have just seen, this number 666 is that of the noun *beast* (θηρίον), and that, on the other hand, this number belongs to a human being or points in the direction of a human being, but not necessarily to the *name* of this human being.

### 3.7 Not an Enigma, but the Solution of an Enigma

Given at the very end of the accounts of the three visions it crowns, this number cannot be a riddle to solve; it must be the key to understanding these chapters. Now, since the prophet John does not leave it to the "intelligent reader" to calculate this number and provides it at once, it is all the more unlikely that he would expect the reader or listener to find its meaning by some even more hazardous recalculation consisting in looking for another name or expression whose numerical value would be six hundred and sixty-six.

Again, in order to discover the meaning of the number of the beast, as well as to elucidate any other apparently obscure passage in Revelation, we must turn to Scriptures.

---

68. D.E. Aune, *Revelation 6-16* (Nashville: Thomas Nelson Publishers, 1998) 769.

69. D.L. Mathewson, *Revelation: A Handbook on the Greek Text* (Waco: Baylor University Press, 2016) 184.

70. See D.E. Aune, *Revelation 17-22* (Nashville: Thomas Nelson Publishers, 1998) 1163; D.L. Mathewson, *Revelation: A Handbook on the Greek Text* (Waco: Baylor University Press, 2016) 293-294. On the possible meaning of this *man* as *angel*, see E.F. Lupieri, *A Commentary on the Apocalypse of John*, trans. M. Poggi Johnson – A. Kamesar (Grand Rapids: Eerdmans, 2006) 343.

71. J. Behm, *Die Offenbarung des Johannes* (Göttingen: Vandenhoeck & Ruprecht, 1953) *ad. loc.*, in H. Bietenhard, art. "Ὄνομα, ὀνομάζω, ἐπονομάζω, ψευδώνυμος," in G. Kittel, ed., *Theological Dictionary of the New Testament*, vol. 5 (Grand Rapids: Eerdmans, 1974) 280.

## 4. A Number Well Known in Scriptures: The Gold of Solomon

The number six hundred and sixty-six has three occurrences in the Scriptures. Two of them indicate the amount of gold that Solomon received in one year, that is, six hundred and sixty-six talents of gold (1 Kgs 10:14 [3 Kgdms 10:14 LXX]; 2 Chr 9:13); the other corresponds to the number of the sons of Adoniqam returning from Babylon, six hundred and sixty-six in Ezra 2:13 MT (2 Ezra 2:13 LXX), but six hundred and sixty-seven, or six hundred and forty-seven, in Neh 7:18 MT (1 Ezra 5:14 LXX). This latter, independent occurrence, which is drowned in an enumeration that includes many numbers, will be left aside.[72] The text of 1 Kgs 10:14 and its parallel 2 Chr 9:13 exhibit no variant for this number, neither in Hebrew nor in Greek, so that the number is assured, and practically constitutes a *hapax* in Scripture:[73]

> And the weight of gold that had come to Salomon in one year was six hundred sixty-six talents of gold ...

### 4.1 An Old Idea

This rapprochement is not a new idea. In his commentary on the Apocalypse (*Expositio Apocalypseos* XXII, 79-101) written between 703 and 710,[74] the Venerable Bede[75] notes that the number six hundred and sixty-six corresponds to the weight of gold received each year by Solomon. Here is the text:

> Aliter. Senarium numerum, quo mundus factus est, perfectionem operis significare quis nesciat, qui siue simplex siue per decem centumue multi-

72. This does not mean that the analogical link between these two occurrences of the number is meaningless; in fact, they both appear in texts recounting the construction of the first and second temple with the gold of the nations.

73. Καὶ ἦν ὁ σταθμὸς τοῦ χρυσίου τοῦ ἐληλυθότος τῷ Σαλωμων ἐν ἐνιαυτῷ ἑνὶ ἑξακόσια καὶ ἑξήκοντα ἓξ τάλαντα χρυσίου (3 Kgdms 10:14); Καὶ ἦν ὁ σταθμὸς τοῦ χρυσίου τοῦ ἐνεχθέντος τῷ Σαλωμων ἐν ἐνιαυτῷ ἑνὶ ἑξακόσια ἑξήκοντα ἓξ τάλαντα χρυσίου (2 Chr 9:13).

74. R. Gryson, *Baede Presbyteri. Expositio Apocalypseos. Baede Opera II, 5* (Turnhout: Brepols, 2001) 153.

75. Bede was one of the most brilliant spirits of his time; see J.J. Contreni, "Bede's Scientific Works in the Carolingian Age," in J.J. Contreni, ed., *Learning and Culture in Carolingian Europe: Letters, Numbers, Exegesis, and Manuscripts* (Farnham: Ashgate, 2011) 247-259. His scientific originality has been well summarized by Wesley M. Stevens, who writes: "He not only could see more than others, but also could explain well what no one had explained before him" (W.M. Stevens, "Bede's Scientific Achievements: The Jarrow Lecture 1985 [Revised 1995]," in W.M. Stevens, ed., *Cycles of Time and Scientific Learning in Medieval Europe* [London: Routledge, 1995] 53-59).

> plicatus eiusdem perfectionis tricesimum sexagesimum centesimumque fructum demonstrat ? Erat autem pondus auri quod adferebatur Salomoni per singulos annos sexcenta sexaginta sex talentorum. Quod ergo uero regi iure munus et debetur et soluitur, hoc etiam sibi seductor tyrannus exigere praesumet.[76]

This connection seems to be an original idea of the Northumbrian monk because we find no evidence of it either in Tyconius or in Primasius, from whom he borrows a lot,[77] or elsewhere in the patristic tradition. It is not found in the later tradition, in the medieval period, nor in Ambrosius Autpertus, nor in Haimo of Auxerre, nor later.

Again, in the middle of the twentieth century, the Anglican philosopher and theologian Austin Mardsen Farrer, who does not seem to have been familiar with Bede's commentary, proposed the same idea as self-evident in his essay, *A Rebirth of Images : The Making of St John's Apocalypse*,[78] without demonstrating it, except by a few pertinent but insufficient observations.[79] For Farrer, the story of Solomon, son of David and apostate, the very type of the Antichrist, was the source of the enigmatic number of the

76. The text is found in R. Gryson, *Baede Presbyteri. Expositio Apocalypseos, Baede Opera II, 5* (Turnhout: Brepols, 2001) 417. F. Wallis (*Bede: Commentary on Revelation* [Liverpool: Liverpool University Press, 2013] 206) translates, "Another [explanation]: who does not know that the number six, in which the world was made, signifies the completion of an action? Either by itself or multiplied by ten or one hundred, it demonstrates the *thirty*-fold or *sixty-fold* or *hundred-fold* fruit of this same perfection. For *every year, a weight of gold was brought to Solomon of six hundred and sixty-six talents*. What in fact is a gift rightfully owed to the true king, this tyrant and seducer will presume to exact for himself" (italics original).

77. J.-M. Vercruysse, "Bède lecteur de Tyconius dans l'*Expositio Apocalypseos*," in S. Lebecq – M. Perrin – O. Szerwiniak, eds., *Bède le Vénérable. Entre tradition et postérité / The Venerable Bede. Tradition and Posterity* (Villeneuve d'Ascq: Publications de l'Institut de recherches historiques du Septentrion, 2002) 19.

78. A.M. Farrer, *A Rebirth of Images: The Making of St John's Apocalypse* (Westminster: Dacre Press, 1949) 256-257. Farrer was chaplain at Trinity College, Oxford, when he published his essay; his claim to "get into John's head" was obviously received coldly by the exegetes and only a few reviews were made. One of them is due to John J. Collins (a Jesuit professor at the Weston School of Theology, not to be confused with John J. Collins, professor at Yale) "Review of A Rebirth of Images. By Austin Farrrer. Westminster: Dacre Press, 1949," *Theological Studies* 11 (1950) 417-418; see also T.W. Manson, "A Rebirth of Images, by Austin Farrer. Pp 348. London: Dacre Press, 1949," *The Journal of Theological Studies* 1 (1950) 206-208. Although reprinted several times, *A Rebirth of Images* is only rarely mentioned in subsequent commentaries.

79. Without knowing its previous formulation by Bede and Farrer, I myself proposed this idea more recently, in a series of lectures given at the École pratique des Hautes études, Paris in May 2014 at the invitation of Simon Claude Mimouni; see L. Painchaud, "L'Apocalypse de Jean de Patmos," in *Annuaire EPHE, sciences religieuses* 122 (Paris: École pratique des Hautes études, 2014) 237.

beast. He later abandoned this idea, which he did not even mention in his commentary on Revelation published fifteen years later.[80]

This idea has never been seriously discussed until recently. Two likely reasons for this are as follows: 1) in the eighth century, as in the middle of the last century, this idea went against all preconceived ideas; 2) each time it has been presented as self-evident and without any supporting arguments. On the web, among the innumerable publications devoted to the number six hundred and sixty-six, there are several, which it would be useless to list here, which make this comparison without appearing to know Bede or Farrer.[81] One can distinguish two categories: on the one hand, there are those who reject the connection to Solomon without further argument, seeing in it a mere coincidence; on the other hand, there are those who, like Farrer, perceive Solomon as an apostate king who, multiplying gold, horses and women, sank into idolatry and who, as a result, prefigures the Antichrist. However, these publications fail to integrate this possible relationship between Solomon and the beast into a coherent reading of Revelation and, failing to demonstrate its relevance on a rigorous theoretical and methodological basis, drift into often-fanciful speculations. As a result, this idea is generally considered far-fetched. The connection made by Bede and Farrer has therefore been relegated to the margins of research, at best judged worthy of a footnote by some scholars, but never considered a serious hypothesis.[82]

---

80. A.M. FARRER, *The Revelation of St John The Divine: Commentary on the English Text* (Oxford: Clarendon Press, 1964).

81. See, for example, "Gold, Money and the Mark of the Beast," *Riding the Beast.com* (https://www.ridingthebeast.com/articles/gold-money-666/) consulted January 12, 2020.

82. Charles Brütsch mentions it, without more, with the six days of the week, the six cubits of Goliath or the weight of his spear, the dimensions of the statue of Nebuchadnezzar that we find in the Old Testament; see Ch. BRÜTSCH, *La clarté de l'Apocalypse, 5ᵉ éd. enrichie et complétée par 10 années de recherche* (Geneva: Labor et Fides, 1966) 232. G.K. Beale is more explicit: "The mention in 1 Kgs 10:14 of 666 talents of gold accumulated by Solomon may also be in John's field of reference. The 666 talents are mentioned immediately after Solomon has reached the peak of his kingship. After telling such a greatness, 1 Kings immediately tells how Solomon broke a series of God's laws for kings (Deut 17:14-17) by multiplying gold, horses, chariots, and foreign wives and by becoming involved in idolatry (1 Kgs 10:14-11:13). Consequently, the 666 from 1 Kings would have served as an excellent candidate for a number to symbolize the perversion of kingship through idolatry and economic evil" (G.K. BEALE, *The Book of Revelation: A Commentary on the Greek Text* [Grand Rapids: Eerdmans, 1999] 727). Giancarlo Biguzzi also mentions this rapprochement and quotes the passage from Bede, but without commenting on it (G. BIGUZZI, *L'Apocalisse e i suoi enigmi* [Brescia: Paideia, 2004] 143). Iain Provan also saw a link of the second beast with the figure of Solomon, but without reference to the number six hundred sixty-six, in the excellent contribution he devoted to sea trade in Revelation 18, which he relates to the book of Ezekiel and the ora-

As I was doing the final editing of this chapter before it went to press, I came across the excellent 2020 article by Keith Bodner and Brent Strawn, two Old Testament scholars such as Iain Provan, who argue convincingly that the origin of the number in Revelation should be related to Solomon receiving 666 talents of gold.[83]

From an arithmetic point of view, the probability that two identical numbers will come out simultaneously and independently depends on the number of possibilities. In a series with only two digits, for example, one and two, the probability is one out of two. If we imagine that Solomon's annual income and the number of the beast could be any number between 1 and 999, there would be only a 1 in 999 chance that this coincidence would occur. Given John's use of Scripture throughout his text, the hypothesis of a deliberate reference must be considered primarily. Indeed, providing a scriptural basis for the postulate of the circulation of the number six hundred and sixty-six prior to the writing of the Apocalypse, this hypothesis has the merit of simplicity since it leads to a *hapax*. If confirmed, it would provide both a definitive solution to the problem of textual criticism and an unequivocal basis for understanding the number six hundred and sixty-six and its function in the text. Moreover, inserted in a context that, as is generally understood, evokes commercial activity and money (Rev 13:17), an allusion that would refer the reader to the commercial activity of Solomon, son of David and apostate and to the gold of the nations, is far from incongruous.

## 4.2 Solomon, Son of David and Apostate

Christian commentaries on the Book of Kings give little or no importance to the number six hundred and sixty-six and its possible symbolic significance, and rarely consider its twin in Rev 13:18.[84] Yet this num-

---

cles against the prince of Tyre. He points out that Solomon was of all the kings who reigned in Jerusalem, the most involved in maritime trade, with Hiram king of Tyre in particular. He also points out that the mention of chariots and horses (Rev 18:13) echoes their mention in the Book of Kings (1 Kgs 5:6; 10:26-29), a mention, as we shall see, linked to the apostasy of this king; see I.W. Provan, "Foul Spirits, Fornication and Finance: Revelation 18 from an Old Testament Perspective," *Journal for the Study of New Testament* 64 (1996) 87-88.

83. K. Bodner – B.A. Strawn, "Solomon and 666 (Revelation 13.18)," *New Testament Studies* 66 (2020) 299-312.

84. Commentators generally wonder how the number six hundred and sixty-six is reached in the Book of Kings to describe Solomon's income in a single year and what its historical plausibility is, but never address its possible symbolic value. According to Martin Noth, the number six hundred and sixty-six talents would be exaggerated and would seem to exceed the historically acceptable amount. The question would be whether "in one year" means "every year" or in a particular year with a higher income; even in the latter case, such an amount would be exaggerated! Rather, it would be, according to him, the artificial result of adding

ber appears after the account of the building of the temple, with the help of Hiram king of Tyre, at the heart of the account of Solomon's apostasy—Solomon, who turns away from the Lord and turns to foreign gods (1 Kgs 11:4-13).

In this account, by multiplying horses and chariots from Egypt (1 Kgs 10:26-29), gold (1 Kgs 10:14-25), and foreign women (1 Kgs 11:1-3), King Solomon goes against the description of the ideal king in Deut 17:16-17:

> For he shall not multiply cavalry for himself or return the people to Egypt in order to multiply cavalry for himself, but the Lord has said to you, "you shall never add to return that way." And he shall not multiply wives for himself, neither shall his heart turn away; also, silver and gold he shall not multiply exceedingly for himself. (Deut 17:16-17 LXX)

The Deuteronomist account in 1 Kings indeed describes King Solomon as the wise king amongst all, but who turned away from the Law. Kim Ian Parker has demonstrated the consistency of this account, which earlier research had seen as an arrangement of disparate material from mul-

---

up the amounts of gold talents received by Solomon from Hiram king of Tyre (120 talents, 1 Kings 9:14), from Ophir (420 talents, 1 Kings 9:28), given by the queen of Sheba (120 talents, 1 Kings 10:10). Again, according to Noth, the author will have added these amounts and added a little more, "to reach the beautiful number" 666 ("um die schöne zahl 666 zu gewinnen," M. NOTH, *Könige, 3. Aufl.* [Neukirchen-Vluyn: Neukirchener Verlag, 2003] 228). Ernst Wurthwein asks the same question: every year or exceptional year? He opts for the second hypothesis since it is a question of highlighting Solomon's dependence on gold, but this number has, according to him, no historical reliability (E. WÜRTHWEIN, *Das erste Buch der Könige, 2. durchgesehene und überarbeitete Aufl.* [Göttingen: Vandenhoeck & Ruprecht, 1985] 122-123). As for Noth and Wurthein, this number is usually considered to be clearly exaggerated and cannot correspond to historical reality. Donald J. Wiseman, on the other hand, considers that this amount is not implausible (D.J. WISEMAN, *1 and 2 Kings: An Introduction and Commentary* [Leicester: InterVarsity Press, 1993] 131-132). In all this discussion, it seems that only Martin J. Mulder reports the occurrences of the number 666 not only in the parallel passage of 2 Chr 9:13, but also Ezra 2:13 and Rev 13:18. And he adds that this number could be the result of an exaggeration (M.J. MULDER, *1 Kings, vol. 1: Kings 1-11*, trans. J. VRIEND [Leuven: Peeters, 1999] 523-524). As for recent studies on the figure of Solomon, neither Jacques Cazeaux, who nevertheless attaches great importance to the presence of gold, the "fateful symbol," in these chapters, who sees it as the sign par excellence of the fall of Solomon, and with him, of the monarchy in general (*Saül, David, Salomon: la royauté et le destin d'Israël* [Paris: Cerf, 2003] 325-336), nor Jean-Pierre Sonnet ("Côté cour, côté jardin. Salomon, l'Adam royal," in Cl. LICHTERT – D. NOCQUET, eds., *Le roi Salomon, un héritage en question: hommage à Jacques Vermeylen* [Bruxelles: Lessius, 2008] 247-260), nor Thomas Römer ("Salomon d'après les deutéronomistes: un roi ambigü," in LICHTERT – NOCQUET, eds., *Le roi Salomon, un héritage en question: hommage à Jacques Vermeylen*, 98-130) attach importance to this number.

tiple sources.[85] The apostasy of the son of David[86] prefigures, announces, and recapitulates the apostasy of most of the Davidic lineage after him (to which there is a hint in the opening address of Revelation through the allusion to Psalm 89).[87] It is the etiological account of the defilement of Davidic royalty, just as the episode of the golden calf erected by the high priest Aaron is the etiological account of the defilement of the Aaronic priesthood. If the number six, one hundred times, ten times, and one time, placed at the heart of the account of Solomon's apostasy is indeed a symbol of deficiency,[88] it may well have the function in the Book of Kings

---

85. K.I. PARKER, "Repetition as Structuring Device in 1 Kings 1-11," *Journal for the Study of the Old Testament* 42 (1988) 19-27.

86. No matter where in the book you start that decline. For M. NOTH (*Könige, 3. Aufl.* [Neukirchen-Vluyn: Neukirchener Verlag, 2003] 60-61) followed by K.I. PARKER ("Repetition as Structuring Device in 1 Kings 1-11," *Journal for the Study of the Old Testament* 42 [1988] 19-27) and A. FRISCH ("Structure and Significance: The Narrative of Solomon's Reign," *Journal for the Study of the Old Testament* 51 [1991] 3-14), the description of the temple (1 Kgs 9:1-9) is the turning point of the story, that Marc Brettler instead places in 1 Kings 9:26 (M. BRETTLER, "The Structure of Kings 1-11," *Journal for the Study of the Old Testament* 49 [1991] 87-97).

87. Contemporary to Book of Revelation, the *Syriac Apocalypse of Baruch* uses the theme of the defilement or perversion of kings in connection with the punishment of Jerusalem in the visions of the black waters (*2 Baruch* 62 and 64); however, Solomon is not incriminated, but only Jeroboam, Jezebel and Manasseh; see A.F.J. KLIJN, "*2 (Syriac Apocalypse of) Baruch*," in J.H. CHARLESWORTH, ed., *The Old Testament Pseudepigrapha*, vol. 1, *Apocalyptic Literature and Testaments* (Peabody: Hendrickson, 2009) 642-643. In the epilogue of *4QHalakhic Letter* (4QMMT frags. 11-13) Solomon, the son of David, appears in a context of blessings and curses that occurred in his days and in those of Jeroboam and his successors until the exile. Because of the fragmentary nature of this text, it is not clear whether the figure of Solomon is associated with blessings or curses. The restitution of "blessings" [*habera*]*ko*[*th*] at the beginning of the fragment in relation with "the days of Solomon" by the first editors (E. QIMRON – J. STRUGNELL, "An Unpublished Halakhic Letter from Qumran," *Israel Museum Journal* 4 [1985] 9-12; reproduced in F. GARCÍA MARTÍNEZ – E.J.C. TIGCHELAAR, *The Dead Sea Scrolls, Study Edition. Vol. 2 [4Q272-11Q31]* [Leiden: Brill, 1998] 802-803) is considered plausible but uncertain by R.G. KRATZ, "Moses und die Propheten: Zur Interpretation von 4QMMT," in F. GARCÍA MARTÍNEZ – A. STEUDEL – E.J.C. TIGCHELAAR, eds., *From 4QMMT to Resurrection. Mélanges qumraniens en hommage à Émile Puech* (Leiden: Brill, 2006) 165; it is considered "paleographically problematic" by H. von Weissenberg, *4QMMT: Reevaluating the Text, the Function, and the Meaning of the Epilogue* (Leiden: Brill, 2009) 56. In any case, the curse of Solomon's successors is clear. In the same fragment it is written that it is the end of time and the return to Israel and the law, and that the wicked will continue to act wickedly (Dan 12:10; cf. Rev 22:11).

88. We can note with Irenaeus the 600 years of Noah at the time of the flood (Gen 7:6), the measurements of the statue Nebuchadnezzar (Gen 3:1) or the number of the pharaoh's chariots (Exod 14:7). The approach by the symbolism of numbers consists in seeing in this number composed of six units, six tens and six hundreds,

of recapitulating all idolatry, iniquity, deceit, and apostasy, as Irenaeus understands it in the Apocalypse of John (*Against Heresies* V 29:2).[89]

Irenaeus, who knew the Scriptures and sought the key to understanding the number of the beast, did not take into account the only passage where it is attested, probably because for him, King Solomon no longer had this ambiguous character. Later, in the context of Christian interpretation, Tyconius had well understood this ambiguity of King Solomon, who represented for him the "bipartite Church" (*Book of Rules* 9:3-4),[90] but he read in Revelation the number six hundred and sixteen, which he could not relate to Solomon, and in which he saw the Christic monogram (*Exposition of the Apocalypse* 4:46).[91] As for Bede the Venerable (*Exposition of the Apocalypse* 22,100), who sought to read the number six hundred and sixty-six in the light of its occurrence in the Scriptures, he saw in Solomon the figure of the "true king" (*uero regi*),[92] which prevented him from grasping the full significance of this connection.

Understood in the light of John's use of Scriptures, this reference to the Book of Kings could remind the reader not only of the apostasy of Solomon, but also and more broadly of the construction of the earthly temple, thanks to his alliance with Hiram, king of Tyre (1 Kgs 5:15-32) "who dwells in the avenues of the sea" (Ezek 27:1).[93] The prophet John rejects all compromise with the nations, whether it be for the followers of Jesus and the other Judeans in the cities of Asia Minor or in the history of Israel and Judah. For him, the covenant of King Solomon with Hiram, the prince of the sea, for the construction of the royal house and the temple, is

---

a number generally considered to signify deficiency, imperfection, as opposed to the number seven symbolizing totality, perfection. This is how Irenaeus understands it, for whom the number six hundred and sixty-six recapitulates all evil, all iniquity, all apostasy. A variant of this symbolic approach is based on the fact that six hundred and sixty-six is a triangular number, the sum of all the numbers between 1 and 36, itself being the triangular number of the number 8. On the symbolism of numbers, see supra note 51.

89. A. Rousseau – L. Doutreleau – Ch. Mercier, *Irénée de Lyon, Contre les Hérésies, Livre V. Édition critique d'après les versions arménienne et latine, tome II, Texte et traduction* (Paris: Cerf, 1969) 366-367.

90. J.-M. Vercruysse, *Tyconius. Le livre des règles* (Paris: Cerf, 2004) 236-239.

91. R. Gryson, *Tyconii Afri Expositio Apocalypseos: accedunt eiusdem Expositionis a quodam retractatae fragmenta Taurinensia* (Turnhout: Brepols, 2011) 186-187; on this see H.-I. Marrou, "Autour du monogramme constantinien," in *Mélanges offerts à Étienne Gilson* (Paris/Toronto: Librairie philosophique J. Vrin/Pontifical Institute of Medieval Studies, 1959) 409-414.

92. R. Gryson, *Baede Presbyteri. Expositio Apocalypseos. Baede Opera II, 5* (Turnhout: Brepols, 2001) 417.

93. On the ambiguity of the account of the construction of the temple in the First Book of Kings, see J.-P. Sonnet, "Salomon construit le Temple (1 Rois 5-10)," in C. Focant, ed., *Quelle maison pour Dieu?* (Paris: Cerf, 2003) 111-142.

the very expression of the covenant between the beast from the land and the beast from the sea.[94]

### 4.3 The Gold of the Nations, Source of All Defilement

By referring his reader to Solomon's gold with the number six hundred and sixty-six, John reveals the thread that runs from the idol fashioned by the high priest Aaron to Solomon's apostasy. This guiding thread is the gold of the nations; the gold of the Egyptians, put on the sons and daughters of Israel (Exod 3:21-22; 12:35) and torn off to make the golden calf (Exod 32:2-3); the gold of the Queen of Sheba (1 Kings 10:10), the gold of Ofir (1 Kgs 9:27-28) brought by the ships of Hiram (1 Kgs 10:11), the prince of Tyre. For John, it is the gold of the nations that links together the two aspects, priestly and royal, of the beast from the earth/land and enslaves it to the beast from the sea; it is this gold obtained from trade with the nations that has defiled the ancient kingship and priesthood.[95] This golden thread runs to the woman sitting on the scarlet beast, "who sparkles with gold" (κεχρυσωμένη χρυσίῳ) and holds in her hand a "golden cup" (ποτήριον χρυσοῦν) full of abomination, the filth of her corruption (Rev 17:4) and is opposed to the "pure gold" (χρυσίον καθαρόν) from which the New Jerusalem will be made (Rev 21:18). Certainly, this unclean gold may well evoke the wealth of Rome, but we must not forget that Jerusalem, especially its temple, was the "economic lung of Judaea,"[96] and its wealth was inseparable from its compromise with Rome.

As an unequivocal reference to a *hapax* in Scriptures in 1 Kgs 10:14 (2 Chr 9:10), the number six hundred and sixty-six is not an enigma. It reveals that the second beast is the ancient royalty and priesthood soiled by the gold of the nations, brought by the first beast, a soiled gold inseparable from the construction of the material temple, whether it be the first

---

94. For the prophet John, the building of the temple by Solomon through his covenant with Hiram and the oracles against Tyre and its prince (Ezek 26-29; Isa 23:1-17) were undoubtedly points forming another scriptural "constellation" which is in the background of chapter 18 (see I. PROVAN, "Foul Spirits, Fornication and Finance: Revelation 18 from an Old Testament Perspective," *Journal for the Study of New Testament* 64 [1996] 81-100).

95. It is possible that the astonishing oracle against the prince of Tyre of Ezekiel (28:11-18) was originally directed against the high priest of Jerusalem as suggested P.-M. BOGAERT, "Montagne sainte, jardin d'Éden et sanctuaire (hiérosolomytain) dans un oracle d'Ézéchiel contre le prince de Tyr (Ez 28,11-19)," in H. LIMET – J. RIES, eds., *Le mythe, son langage et son message* (Louvain-la-Neuve: Centre d'Histoire des Religions, 1983) 131-153; also "Le Chérub de Tyr (Ez 28,14.16) et l'hippocampe de ses monnaies," in R. LIWAK – S. WAGNER, eds., *Prophetie und Wirklichkeit im alten Israel. Festschrift für Siegfried Herrmann zum 65. Geburtstag* (Stuttgart: Kolhammer, 1991) 29-38.

96. E. FRIEDHEIM, "Richesse et pauvreté dans le judaïsme intertestamentaire et talmudique," *Pardès* 54 (2013) 157.

temple built by Solomon with the help of Hiram, king of Tyre, the second temple built by Zerubbabel and Joshua with the gold of the nations (Ezra 1:4-6 ; 6:8),[97] or the magnificent temple rebuilt by Herod the Great under the Roman rule.

## 5. Conclusion

For half a century now, many scholars have emphasized John's sectarian Jewish or Judean character rather than Christian seen as an anachronism. This point of view is part of the broader context of discussions about the construction of Christian identity in the face of a Jewish/Judean identity, and of considerations internal to the text itself on which the distinction between Jewish and Christian editorial layers was once based. It is time to restore the Apocalypse of John to its rightful place not only in Christian origins but also in ancient Judaism, to use the wording of the present collection.

If John is to be labeled at last, he must surely be considered as a faithful messianic Judean prophet of the resurrected Messiah Jesus, who may well have belonged to those "priestly-prophetic-visionary-mystical-liturgical circles that maintained direct communication with the heavenly realm through dreams, visions, prophecy, divine inspiration, angelic revelation or mystical ascents" described by Rachel Elior.[98]

The capture of Jerusalem by Titus in 70 CE was undoubtedly as disturbing for John as it was for the authors of *2 Baruch and 4 Ezra*, his contemporaries, and as that of 63 BCE by Pompey was for the author of the *Psalms of Solomon*. John read this event prophetically, both in the light of his faith in the risen Jesus, the Messiah of the lineage of David, and in the light of the Scriptures, especially the prophets, notably Ezekiel, Zechariah and Daniel, whose books also react to the taking of Jerusalem by Nebuchadnezzar in 587/586 and the events that followed.

---

97. About the two witnesses of Jesus, Zerubbabel and Joshua, whom the beast defeated and destroyed (Rev 11:3-7) and who were resurrected with the Messiah Jesus (Rev 11:11), see L. Painchaud, "Temple et sacerdoce dans l'Apocalypse de Jean ou Zorobabel et Josué, témoins de Jésus Christ (Ap 11, 3-14)," in L. Painchaud – S.C. Mimouni – D. Hamidović, eds., *La sacerdotalisation dans le judaïsme synagogal, dans le christianisme et dans le rabbinisme. Actes du colloque de Québec, 18-20 septembre 2014* (Turnhout: Brepols, 2018) 229-246.

98. R. Elior, "The Priestly Struggle on the Sacred Written Authority as Reflected in the Merkaba Tradition," in D. Hamidović – S.C. Mimouni – L. Painchaud, eds., *La 'sacerdotalisation' dans les premiers écrits mystiques juifs et chrétiens. Actes du colloque international tenu à l'Université de Lausanne du 26 au 28 octobre 2015* (Turnhout: Brepols, 2020) 13-40; also R. Elior, *The Three Temples: On the Emergence of Jewish Mysticism* (Oxford: Littman Library of Jewish Civilization, 2004).

The accumulation of the gold of the nations by Rome was not John's concern at all. The abomination in his eyes was the accumulation of unholy gold by kings and priests in Jerusalem with all that this entailed in compromising with the nations, especially from high priesthood. This is what had brought about the fall of the holy city.

John makes Solomon and Aaron the paired symbols of the ancient royalty and priesthood, soiled by the gold of the nations, which dragged Zion, the city full of justice, into prostitution (Isa 1:26).[99] Jesus, the royal and priestly Messiah, together with his disciples, would replace them and will be priests of God, reigning for a thousand years (Rev 20:6). They would worship and reign for ever and ever in the New Jerusalem (Rev 22:3-5). For John, the prostitute had to disappear so that the New Jerusalem, the bride of the Lamb, might come into being.

As Adela Yarbro Collins has clearly shown, the function of apocalypses is always to convince their recipients to adopt a particular course of action.[100] The real issue for John in daily life is not about Jerusalem itself, but about the Judean communities in Asia Minor. For him, all Judeans, especially but not only, the disciples of the Messiah Jesus, should maintain the state of ritual purity required by the priesthood and the royalty to which they are called, so as not to know the fate reserved for the earthly Jerusalem prostituted by its kings and high priests. They must turn away from the prostitution to which the Jezebels and Balaams who are rampant in the cities of Asia Minor are leading them. In a certain way, his addressees live in cities where the defilement of accommodation with the pagan world threatens them at every moment, just like Jerusalem which has been given over to prostitution by its leaders.[101] They must come out of it. They must renounce the defiled gold, that of the beast, the one from whom the scarlet woman sparks (Rev 17:4), and exchange it for a purified gold, that of the Lamb (Rev 3:18), the one of which the heavenly Jerusalem will be made (Rev 21:18).

John calls the servants of the Lamb to leave the unclean city (Rev 18:4) and to live in the holiness required by the new kingship and priesthood,[102]

---

99. Πῶς ἐγένετο πόρνη πόλις πιστὴ Σιων, πλήρης κρίσεως ... οἱ ἄρχοντές σου ἀπειθοῦσιν, κοινωνοὶ κλεπτῶν, ἀγαπῶντες δῶρα ... (Isa 1:21-23 LXX Ralphs).

100. A. YARBRO COLLINS, "Introduction to Apocalyptic Literature," *Semeia* 36 (1986) 1-11.

101. In this sense, these cities, where the religious cohabitation requires accommodations, are the theater where the ancient drama of the prostitution of Jerusalem, as portrayed by the prophets, is played out again and again in the daily life of the followers of the Lamb and of all the Judeans; see the whole contribution of Luca Arcari in this volume.

102. In this respect, the Apocalypse of John is in line with an ideology that Charles Perrot describes as Leviticus or priestly, according to which the ideal of holiness for all the righteous consists in living in a continual state of ritual purity,

in order to reign in the New Jerusalem (Rev 22:5), where nothing unclean will enter (Rev 21:27).[103]

That is why John holds in contempt the prophetess of Thyatira, whom he calls Jezebel, and her "companions in adultery" (Rev 2:2-22), as well as in Pergamos, those who hold to the doctrine of Balaam (Rev 2:14), and in Smyrna and Philadelphia, his fellow Judeans, who form in his eyes a "congregation of Satan,"[104] no doubt because they are too well-integrated into the city.[105] For the same reason, he vilified the wealth of the messianic assembly of Laodicea (Rev 3:17-18), or of some members of it. It is against this background, which is not far from the ideology of the sectarian writings of the Dead Sea Scrolls, that we must understand the praise and blame distributed through the messages to the *ekklesiai* of followers of Jesus.

What the Prophet saw first when he was in the Spirit (Rev 1:10) were seven golden lampstands (ἑπτὰ λυχνίας χρυσᾶς, Rev 1:12) that could not fail to evoke for the reader or listener the lampstand of pure gold with seven lamps that the Lord commanded Moses to make for the tent (Καὶ ποιήσεις λυχνίαν ἐκ χρυσίου [...] καὶ ποιήσεις τοὺς λύχνους αὐτῆς ἑπτά Exod 25:31-37; also Zech 4:1-14).[106] It is a clear indication, right from the beginning of the book that the vision and the words of the prophecy (Rev 1:30) are about the temple. Of course, the voice will later identify the seven lamps with the seven *ekklesiai* (Rev 1:20), signifying to the recipients of the prophecy that they themselves were part of what was soon to come to the temple and to Jerusalem.

When he was in the Spirit, the prophet's eyes were not on Rome, but on Jerusalem and its temple where "the blood of the prophets and saints and of all who were slain on the earth/land was found" (καὶ ἐν αὐτῇ αἷμα προφητῶν καὶ ἁγίων εὑρέθη καὶ πάντων τῶν ἐσφαγμένων ἐπὶ τῆς γῆς,

---

following the example of the priests in service, without exalting the earthly temple; see Ch. Perrot, "La 'Maison de Dieu' à l'époque intertestamentaire," in C. Focant, ed., *Quelle maison pour Dieu?* (Paris: Cerf, 2003) 228-254; also, M. Himmelfarb, *A Kingdom of Priests: Ancestry and Merit in Ancient Judaism* (Philadelphia: University of Philadelphia Press, 2003) particularly Chapter 4 "Priesthood and Sectarianism: The Rule of the Community, the Damascus Document, and the Book of Revelation," 115-142.

103. L. Painchaud, "Identité chrétienne et pureté rituelle dans l'Apocalypse de Jean de Patmos. L'emploi du terme *koinon* en Ap 21,25," *Laval théologique et philosophique* 62 (2006) 345-357.

104. To be compared with the "Belial congregation" of the *Hodayot* (1QH), see F. García Martínez – E.J.C. Tigchelaar, *The Dead Sea Scrolls, Study Edition*, vol. 1 *(1Q1-4Q273)* (Leiden: Brill, 1997) 163.

105. L. Painchaud, "Assemblées de Smyrne et de Philadelphie et congrégation de Satan. Vrais et faux Judéens dans l'Apocalypse de Jean (2,9; 3,9)," *Laval théologique et philosophique* 70 (2014) 275-292.

106. See D.E. Aune, *Revelation 1-5* (Dallas, Word Books, 1997) 88-90.

Rev 18:24). What he saw was the holy city trampled underfoot by the nations, in ruin and desolate, and all the saints who had perished there. He heard the voice of the Scriptures that denounced the disobedience of the people and their rulers, and also announced the just punishment of the defiled city and the Lord's faithfulness to his promise to David.

The Scriptures and his faith in Jesus the Messiah made John understand that the prostitute had to disappear for the bride of the Lamb to come, that the old kingship and priesthood had to perish for the new kingship and priesthood of the Lamb's followers to come.[107] The advent of Jesus, the offspring of David, and the fall of Jerusalem sealed the double fulfillment of a prayer, as witnessed in the *Psalms of Solomon* (17:21-22):

> Look, O Lord, and raise up their king, the son of David, at the time you know, O God, that he may reign over Israel your servant! And gird him with strength, that he may break the unjust princes, that he may cleanse Jerusalem from the nations that tread it down and ruin it.[108]

To understand the Apocalypse of John, we must turn our eyes away from Rome and its emperors and, like John in the dark years following the fall of the holy city, turn them to Jerusalem prostituted by her rebellious leaders, and listen to the voice of the prophets that had foretold its ruin and its salvation.

107. Thus, John bears witness to a messianic royal ideology reinterpreted in the perspective of a "democratization"; see R. MASON, "The Messiah in Postexilic Old Testament Literature," in J. DAY, ed., *King and Messiah in Israel and the Ancient Near East* (London: Bloomsbury 2013) 339-364.

108. R.B. WRIGHT, "Psalms of Solomon," in J.H. CHARLESWORTH, ed., *The Old Testament Pseudepigrapha*, vol. 2 (Peabody: Hendrickson, 2009 [1983]) 667.

# Fourth Part

# The Reception, from Irenaeus of Lyon to William Blake

# THE RECEPTION OF BABYLON THE GREAT PROSTITUTE IN LATE ANTIQUITY

**Scott K. Brevard**
*Loyola University Chicago*

Résumé

L'une des énigmes les plus tenaces de l'Apocalypse est la figure de Babylone la Grande (Ap 17-18). Alors que le texte offre une explication allégorique interne du symbole, « la grande cité, celle qui règne sur les rois de la terre » (Ap 17,18), sa désignation est loin d'être claire et a conduit à diverses interprétations modernes qui l'examinent à travers des lentilles historico-critiques, littéraires et théologiques pour tenter d'identifier le référent de ce symbole énigmatique. Cependant, plutôt que de se demander qui elle est, ce chapitre s'intéresse à ce qu'elle signifie en posant une question différente : comment ce symbole a-t-il été transmis, reçu et interprété ? Il propose une histoire représentative de la réception en examinant les réceptions implicites et explicites du texte de l'Apocalypse à travers les œuvres de plusieurs auteurs chrétiens anciens, notamment Irénée, Tertullien, Victorinus, Tyconius, Oecuménius et André de Césarée. Plutôt que d'argumenter en faveur d'une compréhension particulière du texte basée sur un contexte déterminé, cette histoire représentative de la réception cherche à comprendre les dynamiques changeantes, et pourtant imbriquées, du texte, du contexte et des premiers récepteurs chrétiens, qui ont présenté ce symbole comme formateur et pertinent dans l'Antiquité tardive et au-delà.

Abstract

One of Revelation's most enduring enigmas is the figure of Babylon the Great (Rev 17-18). While the text offers an internal allegorical explanation of the symbol—"the great city, the one reigning over the kings of the earth" (Rev 17:18)—her designation is far from clear and has led to a variety of modern interpretations examining her through historical-critical, literary, and theological lenses in attempts to identify the referent of this enigmatic symbol. However, rather than questioning who she *is*, this chapter instead looks at what she *means* by asking a different question: *how has this symbol been transmitted, received, and interpreted?* This chapter offers a representative reception history examining implicit and explicit receptions of the text of Revelation through the works of several early Christian authors, particularly Irenaeus, Tertullian, Victorinus, Tyconius, Oecumenius, and Andrew

*"Who is Sitting on Which Beast?" Interpretative Issues in the Book of Revelation. Proceedings of the International Conference held at Loyola University, Chicago, March 30-31, 2017,* ed. by Edmondo Lupieri and Louis Painchaud, JAOC 29 (Turnhout, 2023), pp. 265–286
 DOI 10.1484/M.JAOC-EB.5.131936

of Caesarea. Rather than arguing for a particular understanding of the text based on a determinative context, this representative reception history seeks to understand the changing, yet interlocking, dynamics of text, context, and early Christian receptors as they presented this symbol as formative and relevant in late antiquity and beyond.

## 1. Introduction

For nearly two millennia, interpreters have wrestled with how to handle the symbolic language of Revelation. Its vivid imagery has captured countless audiences, and "Christians in every century down to the present have turned to the book for symbols to express their fundamental hopes and fears."[1] Allegorical attempts at rendering Revelation's complex symbols intelligible have led to many different interpretations of the text, but this is not a new phenomenon, nor is Revelation the first text to engender such reactions. Jewish-Christian communities in the first century CE seem to have made use of allegory as they scrutinized their scriptures to make sense of historical realities "for signs that the true prophecies are being fulfilled" in the contemporary world of those engaged in the "process of rereading, interpretation, and adjustment of earlier prophecies," a process that early Christians participated in frequently as they produced their own writings.[2] From a literary standpoint, however, there are instances in the text of Revelation that beg for allegorical interpretation by offering a "first level of allegory" in which an angelic interpreter provides an explanation of symbols or provides an analogy for the visionary.[3] Inasmuch as this method of approaching the text can produce multifaceted, intricate, or even "disastrous" interpretations,[4] an allegorical approach to the text is

1. J.J. Collins, *The Apocalyptic Imagination: An Introduction to Jewish Apocalyptic Literature* (Grand Rapids: Eerdmans, 1998) 279. Within the last several decades, pop culture works like the *Left Behind* series or *Good Omens* have offered both Christian and secular audiences a contemporary narrative drawing from—or claiming to draw from—many of the same apocalyptic and eschatological themes in Revelation.

2. E.F. Lupieri, *A Commentary on the Apocalypse of John*, trans. M. Poggi Johnson – A. Kamesar (Grand Rapids: Eerdmans, 2006) 34-35. Not all Christians engaged in this process produced "apocalyptic" works in the generic sense. The "fulfillment motif" in Matthew sees scripture and prophecy frequently referenced in light of Jesus's fulfillment (cf. Matt 2:15,17-18,23; 3:3; 4:14-16; 8:17). Lupieri also points to Luke 4:21 as an example of early Christians portraying Jesus's ministry as self-reflective of "updating" earlier prophecies, and the author of Revelation, John of Patmos, participates in this prophetic process by drawing on Daniel, particularly Daniel 7.

3. E.F. Lupieri, *A Commentary on the Apocalypse of John*, trans. M. Poggi Johnson – A. Kamesar (Grand Rapids: Eerdmans, 2006) 33. Cf. Rev 7:13-14; 17:7-18.

4. "Few writings in all of literature have been so obsessively read with such generally disastrous results as the Book of Revelation (= the Apocalypse). Its history of

not particularly unwarranted; indeed, "when handling the Apocalypse, it is both legitimate and necessary to proceed allegorically."[5]

Of the few passages interpreted allegorically for the visionary by an angelic companion, perhaps there is no better example of allegorical possibility than that of Babylon, the Great Prostitute (τῆς πόρνης τῆς μεγάλης) in Revelation 17. The chapter opens when the visionary is called out to witness the judgment (κρίμα, 17:1) of "Babylon the Great, the Mother of Prostitutes and of the Abominations of the Earth" (Βαβυλὼν ἡ μεγάλη, ἡ μήτηρ τῶν πορνῶν καὶ τῶν βδελυγμάτων τῆς γῆς, 17:5). She is adorned in fine clothing and jewelry (περιβεβλημένη πορφυροῦν καὶ κόκκινον, καὶ κεχρυσωμένη χρυσίῳ καὶ λίθῳ τιμίῳ καὶ μαργαρίταις, 17:4), drunk with the blood of the martyrs (17:6) and sitting on the many waters and on a seven-headed scarlet beast (θηρίον κόκκινον, 17:3). Part of the confusion in identifying this woman may be due to the angelic interpreter's failure to provide much detail; outside of her fate (17:16) and her designation as "the great city, the one reigning over the kings of the earth" (ἡ πόλις ἡ μεγάλη ἡ ἔχουσα βασιλείαν ἐπὶ τῶν βασιλέων τῆς γῆς, 17:18), the internal allegorical interpretation in 17:8-18 is concerned far more with the Beast. Still, contemporary exegetes have probed these symbols from several angles: historical-critical scholars identify the Prostitute as a symbol of Rome[6] or

---

interpretation is largely a story of tragic misinterpretation, resulting from a fundamental misapprehension of the work's literary form and purpose. Insofar as its arcane symbols have fed the treasury of prayer and poetry, its influence has been benign. More often, these same symbols have nurtured delusionary systems, both private and public, to the destruction of their fashioners and to the discredit of the writing." L.T. JOHNSON, *The Writings of the New Testament* (Minneapolis: Fortress Press, 1999) 573. Even a century after it was written, Irenaeus seems to agree that certain interpreters of Revelation's symbolic imagery—particularly names of the Antichrist derived from a corrupted edition of the number of the beast (616)—should be condemned since they break the charge of adding or subtracting to the text (Rev 22:19) and also lead themselves and others astray (*Against Heresies* V, 30, 1).

5. E.F. LUPIERI, *A Commentary on the Apocalypse of John*, trans. M. POGGI JOHNSON – A. KAMESAR (Grand Rapids: Eerdmans, 2006) 13.

6. Although several authors have covered this position at length, Eugene Boring, David Aune, and Craig Koester's work serve as fine exemplars of this dominant position. Cf. E. BORING, *Revelation* (Louisville: John Knox, 1989); D.E. AUNE, *Revelation 17-22* (Nashville: Thomas Nelson Publishers, 1998); C.R. KOESTER, *Revelation* (New Haven: Yale University Press, 2014). Koester goes on to expand the Roman designation to apply to a variety of imperial powers, arguing that "[John's] vision is not about the timeless quality of evil but summons readers to resist the ruinous yet seductive forces of imperial society ... The whore is Rome, yet more than Rome ... The vision speaks to the imperial context in which Revelation was composed, with images that go beyond that context, depicting the powers at work in the world in ways that have subsequently engaged readers." C.R. KOESTER, *Revelation* (New Haven: Yale University Press, 2014) 683-684.

Jerusalem,[7] literary approaches compare her to the other female figures in the text,[8] and more theological approaches have understood her as a more general symbol of imperial or worldly power.[9]

Because she has evoked such a vast range of meanings, identities, and significances, there are significant hurdles for any argument attempting

---

7. Whereas a Roman designation projects the author's work into the future, those interpreting the Prostitute as Jerusalem instead seek to explain the fall of Jerusalem by critiquing her economic and religious pacts with Rome in the same way as the prophetic literature of the Hebrew Bible. Cf. J. MASSYNGBERDE FORD, *Revelation* (Garden City: Doubleday, 1975); E. CORSINI, *The Apocalypse: The Perennial Revelation of Jesus Christ*, trans. F.J. MOLONEY (Wilmington, DE: Glazier, 1983); E.F. LUPIERI, *A Commentary on the Apocalypse of John*, trans. M. POGGI JOHNSON – A. KAMESAR (Grand Rapids: Eerdmans, 2006); B.J. MALINA – J.J. PILCH, *Social-Science Commentary on the Book of Revelation* (Minneapolis: Fortress Press, 2000). For further research and argument on the Prostitute as Jerusalem, see the other contributions to this volume.

8. Paul Duff argues that she is the quintessential female character whom all other female characters in the text (Jezebel [Rev 2], the unnamed woman in the desert [Rev 12], and Jerusalem the bride [Rev 21]) are compared against. Duff also argues that "Jezebel" serves as the author's prophetic opponent, so the text is rhetorically composed to link Jezebel with Babylon so that audiences will be persuaded against her "liberal stance toward the larger pagan society." P.B. DUFF, *Who Rides the Beast?* (Oxford: Oxford University Press, 2001) 14-15.

9. Focusing on the Great Prostitute's enduring significance, both Hans Lilje and Robert Mounce treat her as a timeless symbol of earthly political power. Cf. H. LILJE, *The Last Book of the Bible*, trans. O. WYON (Philadelphia: Fortress Press, 1957); R. MOUNCE, *The Book of Revelation* (Grand Rapids: Eerdmans, 1988). This approach helps explain interpretations that understand the Prostitute as a world power in the contemporary world of the exegete: for example, Wolfgang Aytinger's *Commentary on Methodius* interprets the Prostitute as Turkey, the Ottoman Empire of his contemporary world, while the Morgan Beatus illustrated manuscript depicts the Prostitute as wearing a crown inset with a crescent moon seated atop a throne of cushions rather than a beast, a jab at the Islamic Iberian empire. Cf. L. SEIDEL, "Apocalypse and Apocalypticism in Western Medieval Art," in B. MCGINN, ed., *The Encyclopedia of Apocalypticism: Apocalypticism in Western History and Culture*, vol. 2 (New York: Continuum, 2000) 474-475. This approach may also explain the rise in certain anti-ecumenical and anti-Catholic readings: similar to Dante's *Inferno*, exegetes like Pierre de Jean Olivi and a cadre of Post-Reformation Protestants like Thomas Brightman, Henry More, and Benjamin Keach viewed the Church (or the Church of *Rome*) as a machine of significant political power and thus an easy analogue to the corrupt, collusive Prostitute. Cf. J. KOVACS – C. ROWLAND, *Revelation* (Malden: Blackwell, 2004) 18-19; H. MORE, *Apocalypsis Apocalypseos* (London, 1680); T. BRIGHTMAN, *Revelation of the Revelation* (Imprinted at Amsterdam, 1615). The example of Anne Wentworth is also instructive on this point: having been kicked out of her home by an abusive husband, Wentworth's interpretation of Babylon and Jerusalem/Zion "finds Babylon in a society based on patriarchy in which a woman who rebels against harsh treatment finds herself socially destitute." J. KOVACS – C. ROWLAND, *Revelation* (Malden: Blackwell, 2004) 7.

to decisively establish the referent of this woman. However, if a different question is posed—*how has this symbol been transmitted, received, and interpreted?*—perhaps we can shift our attention from who she *is* to what she *means*. This study offers a reception-critical approach to Babylon the Great that aims to focus not only on how early Christians of the second – seventh centuries CE understood the Prostitute, but how she functions as instructive for and indicative of their hermeneutics, theology, and worldview. In what follows, I will focus on those who present themselves "within" the reception history of the text: early Christians who explicitly connected their work with the text and imagery of Revelation's Babylon the Great. This representative survey includes the patristic writings of Irenaeus and Tertullian, as well as the early commentary tradition on Revelation provided by authors such as Victorinus, Tyconius, Oecumenius, and Andrew of Caesarea. However, before examining these explicit receptions, I will discuss the contours of reception history, as well as probe the implicit dimension of reception seen in Revelation's contemporary Jewish and early Christian apocalypses.

## 2. The "Ins" and "Outs" of Reception History: Implicit and Explicit Dimensions of Reception

The dominant trend in contemporary scholarship on Revelation has been to approach the text in a historical-critical manner in an attempt "to specify the referents of apocalyptic imagery in as unambiguous a manner as possible."[10] This should not be surprising since the historical-critical task, in tandem with the work of text criticism, is to make determinative arguments about the interpretation of a constructed text that, based on the evidence available, fits into a hypothesized original context. The study of apocalyptic literature, having also considered literary-critical arguments to distinguish the genre of apocalyptic,[11] also mirrors this process. John Collins presents a brief *Wissenschaftsgeschichte* that traces two separate trajectories or "tendencies" in the study of apocalyptic literature, pitting R.H. Charles's emphasis on the "sources of apocalyptic language primarily in Old Testament prophecy" against Hermann Gunkel's emphasis on Near East and Greco-Roman mythological allusions, "motifs and patterns

10. J.J. Collins, *The Apocalyptic Imagination: An Introduction to Jewish Apocalyptic Literature* (Grand Rapids: Eerdmans, 1998) 16.

11. J.J. Collins, ed., *Apocalypse: The Morphology of a Genre* (Semeia 14; Atlanta: Society of Biblical Literature, 1979). For a more recent attempt at constructing the genre of apocalyptic literature using prototype theory, see J.J. Collins, "The Genre Apocalypse Reconsidered," *Zeitschrift für antikes Christentum* 20 (2016) 21-40.

that are ultimately derived" from traditional religious stories of these ancient cultures.[12] Collins emphasizes that the relationship between context and interpretation is key,[13] and the example of the Great Prostitute is especially instructive here: if the text is conceived of in a Greco-Roman mythological (or historical) context, Babylon is clearly an allusion to the hopeful downfall of Rome; on the other hand, if the text is conceived of against the backdrop of Jewish prophecy and traditions from the Hebrew Bible, Babylon is a figure explaining the recent destruction of Jerusalem. Again, the hypothesized "original context" is determinative of the resulting interpretation—and meaning—of the text.

Recently, however, reception critics have problematized the notion of an "original" text and context. While contexts are determinative for interpretation and meaning, Brennan Breed argues that contexts are also *determined*, constructed by those who engage with the text, and complex from the very inception of a text:

> Biblical texts are, from the very moment of their initial inscription, already sedimented with various semantic, literary, and historical contexts. In addition, contexts themselves are not given, predetermined and predelineated units that automatically clarify the referential structure of texts. On the contrary, contexts initially provide the raw materials for an active determination (or construction) that then bears the title of "the context." Contexts are, from the very start, capable of signifying very different things to different people. While some construals are *wrong*, there is no particular construal of a context that is *right* in any universal sense. Contexts, like texts, can mean many things.[14]

Texts are not limited to their original contexts—they would be lost to history if they were—but are sustained by being transmitted into new contexts.[15] By pointing out the complicated nature of texts and their contexts, Breed argues that we should understand the transmission and reception of

---

12. J.J. Collins, *The Apocalyptic Imagination: An Introduction to Jewish Apocalyptic Literature* (Grand Rapids: Eerdmans, 1998) 15-18.

13. "Mythological allusions, like biblical allusions, are not simple copies of the original source. Rather, they transfer motifs from one context to another. By so doing they build associations and analogies and so enrich the communicative power of the language" (J.J. Collins, *The Apocalyptic Imagination: An Introduction to Jewish Apocalyptic Literature* [Grand Rapids: Eerdmans, 1998] 19).

14. B. Breed, *Nomadic Text: A Theory of Biblical Reception History* (Bloomington: Indiana University Press, 2014) 204.

15. Some reception critics point out that the very experience of a text directly relies upon its reception because, in the words of James E. Harding, "[t]ext and reception are inseparable" (J.E. Harding, "What is Reception History, and What Happens to You if You Do It?," in E. England – W.J. Lyons, eds., *Reception History and Biblical Studies: Theory and Practice* [London: Bloomsbury T&T Clark, 2015] 38).

biblical texts as "a series of processes—text, reading, transmutations, and nonsemantic impact—whose nature it is to change over time."[16] These processes not only focus on the text or context, but also include receptors—scribes, a listening audience, readers—as a key piece of the transmission process. Scholars must be attuned to the dynamics of this third party, creating a need for further understanding of the role that reception plays in the transmission of texts and traditions.

Reception history, as William John Lyons states, "aims to understand the interaction between a text, a context and an audience's response."[17] Working with ancient texts means that there are inherent limitations to all three components—text, context, response—but that does not prohibit a reception historian from probing the plausibility and potential of these components. Rather than working to "decode" the text itself, reception critics attempt "to understand the responses of a contextually situated audience to their texts."[18] Whether approaching the history of a text in an archival sense or attempting to theorize and explain the reason for a particular interpretive tradition, the task is not to argue how the text *should be* understood, but how it *has been* understood.[19]

Perhaps the two most difficult aspects of tracing the reception of a text are dealing with the inherent selectivity in telling its history and articulating what it means for a text to be received. First, because the task of reception history is selective, scholars are left to decide the metrics by which texts and traditions are included or excluded in the archive of receptions.[20]

---

16. B. BREED, *Nomadic Text: A Theory of Biblical Reception History* (Bloomington: Indiana University Press, 2014) 205.

17. W.J. LYONS, "Hope for a Troubled Discipline? Contributions to New Testament Studies from Reception History," *Journal for the Study of the New Testament* 32 (2010) 213.

18. W.J. LYONS, "Hope for a Troubled Discipline? Contributions to New Testament Studies from Reception History," *Journal for the Study of the New Testament* 32 (2010) 214. Judith Kovacs and Christopher Rowland discuss the matter of "decoding" versus "actualizing" in the following way: "Decoding involves presenting the meaning of the text in another, less allusive form, showing what the text really means, with great attention to the details. Actualizing means reading the Apocalypse in relation to new circumstances, seeking to convey the spirit of the text rather than being preoccupied with the plethora of detail. Such interpretation tends to regard the text as multivalent, having more than one meaning" (J. KOVACS – C. ROWLAND, *Revelation* [Malden: Blackwell, 2004] 8).

19. Markus Vinzent discusses this process as the act of "Retrospection" in which "instead of finding 'primary sources' I will end up dealing with constructions, editions, manuscripts ...in a retrospective approach I do not disregard the possibility that new small and even bigger narratives will appear" (M. VINZENT, *Writing the History of Early Christianity: From Reception to Retrospection* [Cambridge, U.K.: Cambridge University Press, 2019] 30).

20. This is not unlike the general task of history, which is by its very nature a selective enterprise (Cf. H. WHITE, *Tropics of Discourse: Essays in Cultural Criti-*

Second, the very act of "reception" typically implies that there is a relationship between two texts, but this has been understood in the field of biblical studies in a variety of ways. Terms like "literary dependence" and "parallelomania" have been used to convey a more direct literary relationship, while the language of "familiarity" and "use" offers a more neutral and nuanced view of the different media dynamics at play in the ancient world.[21] These two factors together contribute to what I am referring to as the "ins" and "outs" of reception history, the explicit and implicit dimensions of categorizing which texts and traditions are classed as "receptions." In some cases, an author makes direct reference to the text in question by quoting a passage or earnestly name-dropping the author, in our case John of Patmos. Because the connection is drawn within the text, such texts demonstrate an explicit approach to reception. In other cases, authors and texts make use of similar imagery or names, in our case the figure of a lavish prostitute or the named city Babylon. These instances demonstrate an implicit approach since scholars must draw out the designation of analogous material as "reception" while also accounting for the relationship between source and reception. For example, Revelation can be seen as a fairly popular implicit example of the reception of Daniel since the "mythological allusions to beasts in chap. 13 *draw on the imagery of Daniel*" rather than explicitly quote the text; still, we should not overlook the ability of an author to rework, or inadvertently stumble upon, similar and familiar concepts for their own purposes and referents.[22]

---

*cism* (Baltimore: John Hopkins University Press, 1978); E.H. CARR, *What Is History?* (New York: Vintage Books, 1961).

21. On literary dependence (particularly in the Synoptic Gospels): "Whatever the reasons, the synoptics are so close to one another that virtually all students of them have concluded that the relationship depends on direct literary copying from one gospel to another, or from common sources" (E.P. SANDERS – M. DAVIES, *Studying the Synoptic Gospels* [London: SCM Press, 1989] 51); On parallelomania: "We might for our purposes define parallelomania as that extravagance among scholars which first overdoes the supposed similarity in passages and then proceeds to describe source and derivation as if implying literary connection flowing in an inevitable or predetermined direction ... I am not denying that literary parallels and literary influence, in the form of source and derivation, exist ... However, I am speaking words of caution about exaggerations about the parallels and about source and derivation" (S. SANDMEL, "Parallelomania," *Journal of Biblical Literature* 81 [1962] 1); On familiarity: "It may be preferable, therefore, to move the terminology away from 'dependence' or 'independence' and instead to talk about 'familiarity,' 'knowledge' or 'use'" (M. GOODACRE, Thomas *and the Gospels: The Case for* Thomas's *Familiarity with the Synoptics* [Grand Rapids: Eerdmans, 2012] 7).

22. J.J. COLLINS, *The Apocalyptic Imagination: An Introduction to Jewish Apocalyptic Literature* (Grand Rapids: Eerdmans, 1998) 272-273 (emphasis added).

## 3. Jewish and Early Christian Apocalypses: An Implicit Approach

Although not directly referencing the text or author of Revelation, there are several contemporary Jewish and early Christian apocalypses that show a similar engagement with the figure or behavior of Revelation's portrait of Babylon.[23] One literary comparison is the Ethiopic (Akhmim) version of the *Apocalypse of Peter*, where adulterous women are tormented alongside and in association with adulterous men and murderers, and the text passes from the punishment of adultery to the punishment of murder (Apoc. Pet. 23-24). While Babylon the Great is not explicitly mentioned in the text, the intertwined themes of murder, punishment, and adulterous women are also present in Rev 17-18. This is more pronounced in the *First Apocalypse of James*, where Jerusalem performs several of the roles of Babylon the Great: the kings/archons dwell in her (cf. Rev 18:4) and she is in possession of a "cup of bitterness" (cf. Rev 17:3) which she gives to "sons of light" (Nag Hammadi Codex V 25:15-20). Additionally, while not directly related to the text of Revelation and thus not a reception of the *text*, there are other works of Jewish apocalyptic literature that use the same image of Babylon, thus demonstrating a reception of the *tradition* of using Babylon antagonistically.[24] *3 Baruch* includes an indictment against the Babylonians, which may be aimed at the Romans,[25] whereas Book 5 of the *Sibylline Oracles* uses the figure of Babylon as a means of "venting its outrage against the heathen power [Rome] that was responsible" for the destruction of the temple of Jerusalem (Sib. Or. 5:398-413).[26] While these may not be explicit receptions of the text of Revelation 17-18, they

23. Not all treatments or namings of Babylon are equal for the reception history constructed in this study. For instance, the Coptic Gnostic *Apocalypse of Paul* mentions the Babylonian Exile (NHC V 23: 13-17) but offers no personification of the city, the *Ascension of Isaiah* mentions the vision of Babylon in (4:19) as a reference to Isaiah 13, and the *Passio Simonis et Iudae* sets the scene of this work of apostolic acts in Babylon. While these can be conceived of as instances of the reception of Babylon in early Christian apocalypses, they seem to have a much different understanding of Babylon than Revelation 17-18, showing that not all early Christian understandings of Babylon were colored by Revelation's characterization.

24. Some of the later books of the Sibylline Oracles, especially book VIII and its condemnation of Rome, may have been responses to or influenced by Revelation; for more, see U. Treu, "Christian Sibyllines," in W. Schneemelcher, ed., *New Testament Apocrypha Vol. 2 Writings Related to the Apostles Apocalypses and Related Subjects*, trans. R.M. Wilson (Cambridge, UK: James Clarke & Co, 1992) 655.

25. J.J. Collins, *The Apocalyptic Imagination: An Introduction to Jewish Apocalyptic Literature* (Grand Rapids: Eerdmans, 1998) 250.

26. J.J. Collins, *The Apocalyptic Imagination: An Introduction to Jewish Apocalyptic Literature* (Grand Rapids: Eerdmans, 1998) 235; J.J. Collins, *The Sibylline Oracles of Egyptian Judaism* (Missoula: Society of Biblical Literature, 1972) 78-79.

demonstrate that the figure of Babylon, or her characteristic behavior in Revelation, was still an important and widespread symbol in both Jewish and early Christian apocalyptic literature and tied together with many of the same themes evident in Revelation 17-18.

## 4. Early Christian Reception of Babylon the Great: An Explicit Approach

On the other hand, several early Christians throughout the first few centuries CE made direct reference to the text, tradition, or author of Revelation. Even more, these early Christians interpreted the symbolic language of the Great Prostitute, offering a window into their theological worldview and understanding of the text's relevance to their lives. As early Christianity transformed from a small conglomerate of diverse Jewish-Christian groups at conflict with their contemporary imperial world to an imperial-backed state religion, the reception and subsequent use of Revelation shows the influence of the interlocking dynamics of text, context, and early Christian receptors.

### 4.1 Irenaeus[27]

One of the most significant church fathers in the second century CE was Irenaeus of Lyons, the "first great theologian" to set out a systematic argument against Gnostics in his *Against Heresies*.[28] Woven into this polemic are brief references to John's apocalyptic imagery and its significance for life in the Roman empire of the second century. While Rome plays an important role in Irenaeus's eschatological expectations, his views on the empire are complex. On the one hand, Irenaeus holds to a monotheistic ideal arguing that God has appointed the kingdoms of the world (*Against Heresies* V, 24, 1) and even comments on the benefits that the *pax Romana* offers for public safety and transportation (*Against Heresies* IV, 30, 1).[29] On the other

27. Latin citations from W.W. Harvey, ed., *Sancti Irenaei, episcopi lugdunensis. Libros quinque adversus haereses: textu Graeco in locis nonnullis locupletato, versione Latina cum Codicibus Claromontano ac Arundellano denuo collata, praemissa de placitis gnosticorum prolusione, fragmenta necnon, Graece, Syriace, Armeniace, commentatione perpetua et indicibus variis*. 2 vols, Cantabrigiae: Typis Academicis, 1857.

28. A. Hastings, "150-550," in A. Hastings, ed., *A World History of Christianity* (Grand Rapids: Eerdmans, 1999) 29. Cf. E. Thomassen, "Orthodoxy and Heresy in Second-Century Rome," *Harvard Theological Review* 97 (2004) 241.

29. Cf. W.C. Van Unnik, "Irenaeus and the Pax Romana," in C. Breytenbach – P.W. Van Der Horst, eds., *Sparsa Collecta: The Collected Essays of W.C. Van Unnik. Part Four: Neotestamentica – Flavius Josephus – Patristica*, trans. D.E. Orton (Leiden: Brill, 2014) 363-376.

hand, he claims that the Roman empire is the intended referent of John and Daniel's prophecies (*Quia Johannes et Daniel prædixerunt imperii Romani dissolutionem et desolationem*) and that Rome, as the empire of his contemporary world in which the "ten kings" currently reign (*decem regibus, in quos dividetur quod nunc regnat imperium*) will play a significant role in the "end times" (*novissimo tempore*) and the rise of the Antichrist (*Against Heresies* V, 26, 1). Babylon's identity is also similarly complex. It is clear that Irenaeus expects the city to be destroyed, leading the ten kings/horns to transfer their kingdom to the beast (*dabunt regnum suum bestiæ*, *Against Heresies* V, 26, 1), but it is not clear whom Irenaeus envisions. While Irenaeus may intend this passage to implicitly refer to Rome, the previous chapter also discusses the "earthly Jerusalem" (*terrena Hierusalem*) and how the Antichrist will be responsible for transferring his kingdom's power to it (*transferet regnum in eam*), thus linking together the earthly Jerusalem and Roman imperial power (*Against Heresies* V, 25, 4).

The ultimate aim of Irenaeus's work is to refute Gnostics who charge that the Creator is different than the Father, so it is beyond the scope of his argument to expect a systematic interpretation of Revelation's symbolic language. Still, despite his polemical aims, Irenaeus's work demonstrates an understanding of the prophecies of John and Daniel as open-ended allegories, interpreting symbols in light of Roman imperial power while also leaving room for prophetic symbols that may not yet have real-world referents in his contemporary world.[30]

### 4.2 Tertullian[31]

As the voice of "the new elite of North Africa," Tertullian's writings offer an interesting upper-class perspective on the events of Revelation 17-21 and their relevance in the early-third century CE.[32] Tertullian directly men-

30. Irenaeus shows the tendency to leave Revelation's symbols unaccounted for elsewhere. In his discourse on the possible names of the Antichrist, he floats certain names (ΕΥΑΝΘΑΣ, ΛΑΤΕΙΝΟΣ, ΤΕΙΤΑΝ) to demonstrate that there are many names that fit the numerological parameters. Rather than pointing to a particular referent, he supposes that the prophecy is not yet fulfilled, and the figure does not yet exist, which may help to explain why he expects this Antichrist to take up residence in the (currently destroyed) Jerusalem temple. Cf. *Against Heresies* V, 30, 1-4.

31. For Latin citations, cf. M. TURCAN, ed., *Tertullien. La toilette des femmes (De Cultu Feminarum)* (Paris: Les Éditions du Cerf, 1971), and T.R. GLOVE – G.H. RENDALL, eds., *Tertullian: Apology. De Spectaculis. Minucius Felix: Octavius*, with an English trans. (Cambridge: Harvard University Press, 1931).

32. Ferguson also puts Tertullian's personal social relationship with Rome into perspective, claiming he "prospered under Roman rule," since he was not a member of either the "Roman colonizers nor the poorer indigenous population," and "[h]e addressed those of the same social class, whether Christian or non-Christian." E. FERGUSON, "Tertullian," *The Expository Times* 120 (2009) 314.

tions the Prostitute on a few occasions (*The Apparel of Women* 2.12.2; *Scorpiace* 12), but she is not an overarching figure in his works nor is she typically the main object of focus. In fact, when Tertullian does address the Prostitute, as he does in *The Apparel of Women*, he spends more time fixated on her extravagant "appellation" (for instance, her clothing and adornments, *The Apparel of Women* 2.12.2-3) than the significance of her symbolic details and behaviors. Still, some have argued that he directly interprets her in this passage as Rome.[33] This interpretation is not clear; he refers to her as "that strong city who presides over the seven mountains and many waters" (*Illa ciuitas ualida quae super montes septem et plurimas aquas praesidet*, *The Apparel of Women* 2.12) that, while conceivably intended to be Rome, may also simply refer to the *civitas magna* of Rev 17:18 that shares the same features. Tertullian's most direct reference to Rome's role in Revelation occurs in an excursus on the symbolic meaning of certain geographic names used in biblical prophecy. To argue that Isa 7:13-14 is fulfilled by Christ, Tertullian turns to allegory: in the same way that Egypt can be understood as a synecdoche for the whole earth, Samaria should be taken in this passage to refer to idolatry. As an aside and a further example, he claims Babylon "is a figure of the city Rome" (*Romae urbis figura*, *Against the Jews* 9.15). While still not referring to her role as the Great Prostitute, he explicitly references both John's apocalypse and the general behaviors and demeanor Babylon displays in Revelation 17-18. Furthermore, Tertullian's *Apology* gives a reason for why this understanding of Rome is significant for his contemporary world by arguing that Christian piety and prayer is a boon for the entire empire. In praying for not only the emperor, but also "every rank in the empire and the affairs of the Romans" (*etiam pro omni statu imperii rebusque Romanis*), Christians take an active role in delaying the "imminent end of the age" (*imminentem ... clausulam saeculi*) and the destruction of the world (*Apology* 32). This is a fitting progression for Tertullian's interpretation: even though he never offers a systematic explanation or commentary on the symbols, his identification of "Babylon" as Rome has led him to link the downfall of the contemporary Roman empire to the eschatological expectations he has drawn from Revelation and the fall of Babylon the Great.

### 4.3 Victorinus[34]

A third century bishop of Pettau and martyr, Victorinus is not only the first to author a full-length commentary on Revelation but is also one

33. Cf. E. Ferguson, "Tertullian," *The Expository Times* 120 (2009) 321.

34. Cf. J. Haussleiter, ed., *Victorini Episcopi Petavionensis Opera* (Vienna: F. Tempsky, 1916; New York: Johnson Reprint, 1965).

of the first in the commentary tradition to write in Latin. Jerome (*On Illustrious Men* LXXIV) notes that his knowledge of Latin was inferior to his knowledge of Greek, but his familiarity with the language is perhaps masked by his extensive bibliography: though only his *Commentary on the Apocalypse* remains, he authored over a half-dozen commentaries on biblical texts, including Genesis, Leviticus, Ezekiel, Isaiah, and Habakkuk. Regardless of his perceived lack of eloquence, Jerome remarks that what he suffered in style, he made up for in the "excellent" content of his works.[35]

As the oldest Latin commentary on Revelation, Victorinus's hermeneutical approach shows a tendency toward allegory as well as a desire to situate the apocalyptic imagery within the context of first century Roman imperialism. In the midst of identifying the angel of Rev 7:2 as Elijah (Elias) the prophet, he mentions the "ruin of Babylon, that is, the city of Rome" (*ruina Babylonis, id est ciuitatis Romanae*) as one possible outcome of the plagues associated with the blowing of trumpets and pouring out of phials.[36] Elsewhere, his comments on Rev 17:10 urge that the imagery must be understood in the text's historical context of first century Rome.[37] His extended comments on chapters 12 and 17 show the tendency to allegorize accordingly: the seven heads of the beast in 12:3 and 17:3 are Roman kings (*reges Romanos*), and when the angelic interpreter later identifies them as seven hills (17:9), Victorinus quickly identifies these as the hills as Rome (*id est ciuitas Romana*), listing out seven associated emperors.[38]

When Victorinus turns his attention toward the Great Prostitute of chapter 17, his allegories become slightly more pointed, but his interpretation of the symbolic woman is ambivalent at best. His comments on verses 1-6 offer another implicit allusion to Rome by recalling "the decrees of *that* Senate" (*ex decreto senatus illius*). This remark aligns with the aforementioned discussion of how the heads, hills, and horns symbolize Rome in different capacities, and his further explicit contextualization of the authorship of the text again makes it obvious that he is envisioning Rome. His interpretation of these symbols is clear and pointed, a stark contrast from the unclear interpretation of the woman. One of the first complicating factors is that the woman is linked with the beast, and his treatment of this beast differs slightly from before in chapter 12. The "red dragon"

---

35. JEROME, *On Illustrious Men*, trans. T.P. HALTON (Washington, DC: Catholic University of America Press, 1999) 105-106.

36. J. HAUSSLEITER, ed., *Victorini Episcopi Petavionensis Opera* (Vienna: F. Tempsky, 1916; New York: Johnson Reprint, 1965) 86.

37. *intellegi igitur oportet <tempus>, quo scribitur apocalypsis* (J. HAUSSLEITER, ed., *Victorini Episcopi Petavionensis Opera* [Vienna: F. Tempsky, 1916; New York: Johnson Reprint, 1965] 118).

38. Victorinus lists Domitian, Titus, Vespasian, Otho, Vitellius, Galba, Nerva, and Nero, whom he links to the mortally wounded head of the beast (13:3).

[*Draco ...rufus*] of 12:4 is interpreted as the Devil (*diabol*[*us*]), characterized as a murderous "runaway angel" (*angelus refuga*) to serve as the antagonist and foil to the woman clothed in the sun, "the ancient Church of fathers, and prophets, and saint apostles" (*antiqua ecclesia est patrum et prophetarum et sanctorum apostolorum*). Although Victorinus finds a natural connection between this symbol and the red beast (*bestiam rossam*) of 17:3, he remarks that it is the woman—and not the beast itself—that is now described as a murderer (*actricem homicidiorum*) and as the one having the "image of the Devil" (*zabuli habet imaginem*). Taken on its own, this would suggest Victorinus is arguing that the imagery of the prostitute colluding with the beast is symbolic of the Devil's control of Rome. However, his interpretation of this passage gets more complicated when he addresses verse 16, where he inserts an aside in quoting the text to clarify that the hated prostitute is not the Devil, but the city (*hi odient meretricem—urbem scilicet dicit*). It is safe to presume he means the city of Rome since that has been in view in his comments elsewhere in the passage and a frequent target throughout the work. He again passes from referent to referent when he transitions to a discussion of *Nero Redivivus* and the role that Nero plays as both a head of the beast and as Antichrist, and this discussion further complicates the target of apocalyptic imagery. On one level, Victorinus offers a thorough political critique of the city of Rome, but on the other hand he argues that there are evil spiritual forces behind the corruption and impending damnation of the city and its rulers.

### 4.4 Tyconius[39]

Tyconius, a late-fourth century Donatist in the North African church, is well-known for his influence on Augustine's doctrine of the "two cities."[40] Although he was an influential thinker for subsequent Latin exegetes in the first millennium, most of his writings, including his commentary on Revelation, remain only in fragments of later interpreters like Bede or Beatus of Liebana due to the condemnation of Donatism.[41] In those frag-

39. Citations from TYCONIUS, *Exposition of the Apocalypse*, trans. F.X. GUMERLOCK (Washington, DC: The Catholic University of America Press, 2017).

40. Johannes van Oort argues that while there certainly may have been a chain of influence from Tyconius to Augustine, the pronounced differences between the two and the prevalence of the tradition of two cities elsewhere means that "[t]he most one can say is that Tyconius, in his explanation of John's Apocalypse, stood in this broad tradition of Jewish-Christian testimonies of a doctrine of two *civitates*" (J. VAN OORT, "Tyconius' Apocalypse Commentary, Its Reconstruction, and Its Significance for Augustine's Doctrine of the Two Cities," *Vigiliae Christianae* 72 [2018] 532).

41. Some of the other successors and witnesses to Tyconius's work include: Gennadius of Marseilles, Caesarius of Arles, Primasius of Hadrumetum, and Cassiodorus. Cf. J. VAN OORT, "Tyconius' Apocalypse Commentary, Its Reconstruction,

ments, however, Tyconius's work offers an interesting juxtaposition to the foundation set by Victorinus. Whereas Victorinus approached the text as a historical allegory, Tyconius saw the text as a spiritual trove in which was stored a narrative of the church and its purpose in the story of God. Tyconius did not shy away from allegory; like Victorinus and others, his passages are still full of symbolic interpretation, but his allegories look less to a contextualized physical world and more to the spiritual circumstances of the life of the church, including the threat posed by the Devil's influence and agency in the world. These core concepts, also part of his larger "seven rules" for interpreting scripture, permeate the entirety of his commentary on Revelation and are best seen in his treatment of Babylon.

Tyconius's interpretation and understanding of the Great Prostitute in chapter 17 relies heavily on what he has already said about Babylon earlier in the commentary. In his remarks on 14:8, he interprets Babylon as "the city of the Devil," which he further clarifies as "the people consenting to [the Devil] and every corruption."[42] The logical move from discussing Babylon as a city to a group of people displays his penchant for drawing connections between symbols or interpretations of symbols.[43] Regarding 16:19, he takes a more generalizing approach to Babylon, claiming "Babylon, generally speaking, is evil."[44] These two exegetical tendencies—drawing connections and interpreting generally—are informative for his treatment of the Great Prostitute. First, she is linked together as the symbolic equivalent of the beast and the desert.[45] Then, having linked the Prostitute with the beast, the beast is subsequently linked more generally as one with "those dwelling on the earth."[46] When she is finally revealed

---

and Its Significance for Augustine's Doctrine of the Two Cities," *Vigiliae Christianae* 72 (2018) 514-515; cf. J. Kovacs – C. Rowland, *Revelation* (Malden: Blackwell, 2004) xvi.

42. Tyconius, *Exposition of the Apocalypse*, trans. F.X. Gumerlock (Washington, DC: The Catholic University of America Press, 2017) 142.

43. For instance, in his comments on 13:1, Tyconius makes a similar exegetical move by linking the beast from the sea and the beast from the abyss together: "[t]he sea and the abyss, from which he said that the beast came up, are one. What the sea is, that is the abyss, and that is the beast." (Tyconius, *Exposition of the Apocalypse*, trans. F.X. Gumerlock [Washington, DC: The Catholic University of America Press, 2017] 130).

44. Tyconius, *Exposition of the Apocalypse*, trans. F.X. Gumerlock (Washington, DC: The Catholic University of America Press, 2017) 158.

45. "The harlot, the beast, and the desert are one ... This body should be interpreted sometimes as the Devil, sometimes as the 'head as if slain,' and sometimes as the people, because Babylon is all this" (Tyconius, *Exposition of the Apocalypse*, trans. F.X. Gumerlock [Washington, DC: The Catholic University of America Press, 2017] 160).

46. Tyconius, *Exposition of the Apocalypse*, trans. F.X. Gumerlock (Washington, DC: The Catholic University of America Press, 2017) 162.

as a ruling city in 17:18, Tyconius draws out his famous exposition on the dual natures of the two cities. The Prostitute is not a particular geographic location found on a map but rather a more spiritual statement of good and evil embodied by the language of cities, "[f]or there are two cities in the world, one of God and one of the Devil, one originating from the abyss, the other from heaven."[47] The connections that Tyconius draws between symbols and across the text's revelatory unveiling demonstrates how he understands the Great Prostitute not only as a part of a satanic machinery linked to beasts, ruinous cities, and general rulers of the earth, but also as the symbol of the wickedness of Satan that rules over the multitudes of the damned. By interpreting Revelation through the concerns of the church, Tyconius's ecclesial approach "explores the battle of good and evil, order and chaos, which reaches even into the heart of the Church," which is part of what made it so influential to the host of witnesses to this fragmentary text.[48]

### 4.5 Oecumenius[49]

Because Revelation was initially met with hesitation in the Eastern church, the Greek commentary tradition was outpaced by the West.[50] Therefore, it is easy to mistake Oecumenius's (Oikoumenios) late-sixth century commentary as merely another medieval commentary following in the footsteps of the earlier Latin tradition. However, as the earliest full-length extant Greek commentary on Revelation, Oecumenius's commentary offers significant insight into Eastern exegetical methods and attention to allegory and symbolism which set forth a new trajectory for Greek commentaries in the East.[51]

---

47. TYCONIUS, *Exposition of the Apocalypse*, trans. F.X. GUMERLOCK (Washington, DC: The Catholic University of America Press, 2017) 166.

48. I. BOXALL, "The Apocalypse Unveiled: Reflections on the Reception History of Revelation," *The Expository Times* 125 (2014) 265.

49. Greek citations of Oecumenius given for the page and line number from H.C. HOSKIER, *The Complete Commentary of Oecumenius on the Apocalypse* (Ann Arbor: University of Michigan Press, 1928).

50. For more on early Greek church fathers and their hesitation in accepting Revelation, see L. BAYNES, "Revelation 5:1 and 10:2a,8-10 in the Earliest Greek Tradition: A Response to Richard Bauckham," *Journal of Biblical Literature* 129 (2010) 810-811.

51. Upon its discovery, it was argued to predate Andrew of Caesarea's commentary, with Diekamp setting forth an argument of Andrew's use of Oecumenius. Cf. C. DUROUSSEAU, "The Commentary of Oecumenius on the Apocalypse of John: A Lost Chapter in the History of Interpretation," *Biblical Research* 29 (1984) 22; L. BAYNES, "Revelation 5:1 and 10:2a,8-10 in the Earliest Greek Tradition: A Response to Richard Bauckham," *Journal of Biblical Literature* 129 (2010) 811-812.

Oecumenius's penchant for symbolism can be seen by the differing ways he treats Babylon. In reference to the angelic announcement of the fall of Babylon the great (14:8), Oecumenius first interprets Babylon in a philological sense. Because the name means "confusion," he argues that the angelic interpreter is referencing "the confusion of the present life and its vain temptations" (τὴν τοῦ παρόντος βίου σύγχυσιν καὶ τὸν εἰκαῖον πειρασμόν, 162.7-10). In essence, Oecumenius takes this first appearance of Babylon the Great to be a comment on idolatry in his contemporary context ("the stupidity of idolaters," τὴν τῶν εἰδωλομανούντων ἐμπληξίαν, 162.9-10). His later comments on 16:19 emphasize that a different Babylon is in view than 14:8. He supposes that this Babylon—the Great Prostitute—should be understood as Rome (καὶ οἶμαι περὶ τῆς Ῥώμης φησὶ, 182.11). This interpretation situates his discussion of chapter 17, where he relates the behavior of Rome and its constituent nations to the "fornication and idol-madness" (τῇ πορνείᾳ αὐτῆς καὶ τῇ εἰδωλομανίᾳ κεκοινωνήκασι, 184.12-13) of the Great Prostitute and her co-conspirators. He further identifies the Great Prostitute as Rome explicitly when interpreting the seven mountains (ἑπτὰ ὄρη, 17:9) as "seven hills" (ἑπτὰ μόνους), and his closing remarks on the chapter claim that the text itself offers a clear understanding of this designation at verse 18.

By still treating the Prostitute as Rome, Oecumenius fits alongside the early Latin commentators in his views of the city.[52] It is not immediately clear why he chooses to focus on Rome, particularly when the Roman Empire of his contemporary world looked very different than that of the preceding centuries, a concept that informs the approach in Andrew's later work. Perhaps the most sufficient reasoning for the Roman allegory is found in his introduction to the commentary, where Oecumenius asks a similar question:

> But what does he mean by adding *what must soon take place*, since those things which were going to happen have not yet been fulfilled, although a very long time, more than five hundred years, has elapsed since this was said? The reason is that all the ages are reckoned as nothing in the eyes of the infinite, eternal God ... On this account, therefore, he added *soon*, looking not to the actual time of the fulfillment of future events, but to the power and eternity of God (προσέθηκεν οὐ πρὸς τὸ μέτρον ἀπιδὼν τῶν χρόνων τῆς τῶν γενησομένων συμπληρώσεως, ἀλλὰ πρὸς τὴν ἰσχὺν καὶ τὸ αἰώνιον τοῦ Θεοῦ).[53]

---

52. It is important to note that Oecumenius considers the "great city" split into three parts (16:19) to be Jerusalem, although his specific understanding of Jerusalem and which iteration of the city he's referring to (e.g., a spiritual Jerusalem, the pre-70 CE, Jerusalem, the post-70 CE Jerusalem, the biblical Jerusalem, etc.) is not clear and becomes a point of clarification for Andrew's later commentary.

53. OECUMENIUS, *Commentary on the Apocalypse*, trans. J.N. SUGGITT (Washington, DC: The Catholic University of America Press, 2006), 22; H.C. HOSKIER,

Because Oecumenius is not concerned with tracing a timeline of events down to a particular day or time, and because he recognizes the spiritual nature of prophecy and the prophetic nature of scripture, his treatment of Rome's downfall is not limited to allegorizing the text to align with historical events. Instead, he focuses on the broader reasonings behind the downfall—idolatry—and, in his comments on chapter 18, brings the two Babylons together, discussing the prophetic events as foretelling the sufferings of "the rational Babylon" (τῆς νοητῆς Βαβυλῶνος, 198.15). When these threads are pulled together, Oecumenius's understanding of the Great Prostitute is not solely to critique the sins of Rome,[54] but to serve as a spiritual warning to any who would find themselves accused of the same charges of idolatry.

## 4.6 Andrew of Caesarea

While Oecumenius's commentary attracted interest in the Apocalypse, his influence and significance must be paired with Andrew of Caesarea, a seventh century bishop and successor in the limited Greek commentary tradition of the first millennium. Although he did not author the first Greek commentary on the text, Eugenia Scarvelis Constantinou offers lofty praise by claiming that Andrew "entirely eclipsed" Oecumenius "in importance and influence."[55] Regardless of their rank, both Andrew and Oecumenius significantly offer a glimpse into the reception history of the text in the East: by looking to Greek patristics rather than the commentaries of their Latin predecessors, Andrew and Oecumenius "shaped and preserved the Eastern ecclesiastical tradition," especially in setting the groundwork for the acceptance of Revelation that would continue to gain steam over the centuries following their works.[56]

Andrew's ingenuity and divergence from the Latin commentary tradition, as well as his Greek predecessor, can be seen in his treatment of the Great Prostitute. He begins his comments on chapter 17 with a reference to

---

*The Complete Commentary of Oecumenius on the Apocalypse* (Ann Arbor: University of Michigan Press, 1928) 33.5-7.

54. Significantly, the scarlet beast of chapter 17 is identified as the Devil, who is guilty of spilling the blood of the martyrs, thus linking Rome's actions to greater evil forces in a manner reminiscent of Victorinus.

55. Andrew of Caesarea, *Commentary on the Apocalypse*, trans. E.S. Constantinou (Washington, DC: The Catholic University of America Press, 2011) 8.

56. Andrew of Caesarea, *Commentary on the Apocalypse*, trans. E.S. Constantinou (Washington, DC: The Catholic University of America Press, 2011) 8. DuRousseau also links the acceptance of Revelation as scripture in the East during the Third Council of Constantinople in 680 CE to the influence of the commentaries of Oecumenius and Andreas. Cf. C. DuRousseau, "The Commentary of Oecumenius on the Apocalypse of John: A Lost Chapter in the History of Interpretation," *Biblical Research* 29 (1984) 23.

those who have understood her as Old Rome, likely referencing Oecumenius. Following this line of thought, Andrew points out how this designation cannot be true: the city must still have ruling dominion (Rev 17:18), but "ancient Rome from long ago lost the power of its kingdom, unless we suppose the ancient rank were to return to her."[57] In requiring the allegory of the Prostitute to remain relevant to his contemporary world, he discards the Roman understanding since Rome's reputation as a reigning world power faltered significantly after the events of the early fifth century. Rather than substituting Rome for another city or state of dominant power, Andrew's treatment reconsiders the entire allegory and identifies her as a more general "earthly kingdom" or "ruling city" that works in tandem with the Devil (the scarlet beast) to spread apostasy, idolatry, blasphemy, and murder. Whereas Oecumenius saw the "seven hills" as a smoking gun for Rome, Andrew continues to take a general approach and allegorizes the seven heads/mountains as "seven places standing out from the rest in worldly prominence and power ...the kingdoms of the world," which he lists as the Assyrians, Medes, Chaldeans, Persians, Macedonians, Old Romans, who reign up until the establishment of Christian ("New") Rome under Constantine.[58] Once again, he discusses the Great Prostitute as a ruling city and understands this passage as a foretelling of "the sufferings of those holding ruling power" in an irresponsible and idolatrous manner in the coming age. Although he rejects the earlier allegory of Rome, Andrew's understanding of the passage remains steeped in the historical and political circumstances of his contemporary (and forthcoming) world while also staying rooted in a concern for the spiritual (and allegorical) meaning of the text and its symbols.

### 4.7 Summary of Early Christian Receptors

The first millennium of Christianity demonstrates a variety of exegetical approaches and allegorical activity regarding Babylon, the Great Prostitute. Many in the early Latin tradition understood her as a veiled political critique of Rome. On the other hand, Tyconius's ecclesial approach sought a spiritual meaning in the text that linked the Prostitute with other apocalyptic symbols and attempted to understand her more generally in the overall battle between good and evil, a battle reflected in the history and mission of his contemporary church.[59] Like the early Latin tradition,

57. ANDREW OF CAESAREA, *Commentary on the Apocalypse*, trans. E.S. CONSTANTINOU (Washington, DC: The Catholic University of America Press, 2011) 181.

58. ANDREW OF CAESAREA, *Commentary on the Apocalypse*, trans. E.S. CONSTANTINOU (Washington, DC: The Catholic University of America Press, 2011) 185.

59. Although the treatise *On the Antichrist* by Hippolytus (or pseudo-Hippolytus, since his works are contested) focuses on the significance, timing, and details of the Antichrist in his contemporary Roman world, it offers a similar understanding

Oecumenius brought a similar interpretive approach to the East, focusing on the political and ethical failings of Rome. However, Andrew of Caesarea raised critical questions that urged the reevaluation of the relevancy of the Prostitute, arguing instead that she is a general symbol for any ruling and powerful entity in the world, a position that would serve as a springboard for later critiques of other global empires and even the Roman Catholic Church.[60]

## 5. Concluding Remarks

Exploring the reception of a text opens further interdisciplinary possibilities and offers a fuller understanding of a text's effective history.[61] For biblical scholars, it is an opportunity, perhaps even a requirement, "to explain *why* and *how* [the biblical text] remains relevant" across a variety of cultural worlds.[62] This is a task at the heart of studying apocalyptic literature since one of the key features of apocalyptic literature is its relevance: by using symbolic language, apocalyptic authors infuse traditional imagery, whether biblical prophecy or the mythology of nearby cultures, with con-

---

of the Prostitute that attempts to understand her, as well as the prophetic identification of Jerusalem, as a "clear" portent of the destruction and judgment of God that has been woven through the scriptural and prophetic narrative of the Church in Isaiah, Daniel, and Revelation 17-18. Cf. Hippolytus, *On Christ and Antichrist* 29-43.

60. For the adaptation of the Great Prostitute to fit contemporary ruling world empires, see n. 9. The more long-lasting effect of this trajectory can be seen in the work of Peter Olivi's treatment of the Great Prostitute as a worldly Church, which, in addition to Joachim of Fiore's work, served either as a foundation for or a demonstration of anti-ecumenical sentiments that would permeate readings throughout the late Middle Ages and Reformation period. Cf. J. Kovacs – C. Rowland, *Revelation* (Malden: Blackwell, 2004) 19; Dante, *Inferno*, 19.106-109.

61. "[W]e must realize that any one determination of a text, context, or meaning is a limited and impoverished viewpoint on the given objectile. A single determination of a text reveals merely a fraction of that text's contour" (B. Breed, *Nomadic Text: A Theory of Biblical Reception History* [Bloomington: Indiana University Press, 2014] 206).

62. J.G. Crossley, "An Immodest Proposal for Biblical Studies," *Relegere: Studies in Religion and Reception* 2 (2012) 177. Harding argues that reception also allows scholars to highlight the ethics of interpretation, claiming, "[t]here are good ethical reasons, however, for an approach to Biblical Studies that accounts, in as much detail as possible, for how biblical texts shape the ways in which particular cultures have come to think" (J.E. Harding, "What is Reception History, and What Happens to You if You Do It?," in E. England – W.J. Lyons, eds., *Reception History and Biblical Studies: Theory and Practice* [London: Bloomsbury T&T Clark, 2015] 44).

temporary relevance.[63] Scholars should not merely rush to identify the referent of these symbols and neglect looking at how these texts and traditions were received and made relevant for new audiences. As Collins, drawing on Ricœur, puts it, it is important for scholars to not miss the "effect" of the text "through the element of uncertainty," nor the "allusive and evocative power of apocalyptic symbolism."[64]

While the Great Prostitute is an enduring "mystery" for exegetes of the text of Revelation, perhaps she is something more. Her context is determinative, but her context is also *constructed*. Exegetes must choose the backdrop against which to view her: does she exist solely within the literary and visionary world of the text, or does she have a historical, physical referent? Should she be understood in line with the Roman Empire of the first century CE, or should she be understood against the backdrop of the prophetic tradition in the Hebrew Bible? Is she a projection of the future or a flicker of the past? These contextual markers are each indicative of how the Prostitute will be interpreted, and although the commentary tradition may treat her as such, she is not solely an allegory. Rather, she is a reflection of the exegete's task, representative of "*the dynamic tension between spiritual and political readings of Scripture*."[65] It is this tension that has kept her relevant for the past two millennia and, no matter the identification or allegorization, allows her to remain as an enduring symbol of apocalyptic imagery.

---

63. "Ultimately the meaning of any given work is constituted not by the sources from which it draws but by the way in which they are combined" (J.J. COLLINS, *The Apocalyptic Imagination: An Introduction to Jewish Apocalyptic Literature* [Grand Rapids: Eerdmans, 1998] 20).

64. J.J. COLLINS, *The Apocalyptic Imagination: An Introduction to Jewish Apocalyptic Literature* (Grand Rapids: Eerdmans, 1998) 16.

65. M. GORMAN, "What Has the Spirit Been Saying? Theological and Hermeneutical Reflections on the Reception/Impact History of the Book of Revelation," in R. HAYS – S. ALKIER, eds., *Revelation and the Politics of Apocalyptic Interpretation* (Waco: Baylor University Press, 2012) 26 (emphasis original).

# BLAKE'S REVELATION: FROM JEZEBEL TO THE NEW JERUSALEM?

**Megan Wines**
*Loyola University Chicago*

Résumé

Dans son œuvre illustrée *Jerusalem the Emanation of the Giant Albion*, le poète et artiste anglais William Blake caractérise le personnage de Jérusalem d'une manière dichotomique et paradoxale, comme une « chaste putain » qui peut servir de modèle pour lire les figures féminines dans l'Apocalypse. Ce chapitre explore cette dichotomie et la manière dont sa caractérisation comme une « chaste putain » peut permettre d'utiliser *Jerusalem* comme modèle pour réexaminer les femmes de l'Apocalypse. Il reprend l'approche du théâtre visionnaire appliquée par Suzanne Sklar à l'œuvre de Blake, qui encourage l'engagement créatif non seulement avec *Jerusalem*, mais aussi avec d'autres textes (dont l'Apocalypse). Pour Blake, et peut-être aussi pour l'Apocalypse, les personnages peuvent simultanément représenter une multiplicité de choses. Puisque le théâtre visionnaire permet (et peut-être nécessite) la suspension des notions acceptées de temps, d'espace, de soi, et de la réalité concrète, en l'utilisant comme méthode, on peut plus facilement retracer les façons dont Blake, dans la création de son personnage de Jérusalem, semble avoir lu les femmes de l'Apocalypse comme une seule et même femme passant par des étapes de développement successives. Ainsi, ce chapitre examine la transformation de cette femme depuis son apparition comme Jézabel, en passant par la femme enveloppée de soleil et la prostituée, jusqu'à ce que finalement elle soit révélée comme la Nouvelle Jérusalem.

Abstract

In his illustrated work *Jerusalem the Emanation of the Giant Albion*, English poet and artist William Blake presents a dichotomic and paradoxical characterization of his Jerusalem as a "chaste whore" that can serve as a model for reading the female figures in the Book of Revelation. This chapter explores that dichotomy and how the characterization of a "chaste whore" can let one use *Jerusalem* as a model to re-examine the women of Revelation. It takes up Suzanne Sklar's use of visionary theatre as she encourages creative engagement not only with *Jerusalem*, but with other texts as well (including Revelation). For Blake, and perhaps for Revelation as well, the characters themselves can simultaneously be representative of a multiplicity of things. Since visionary theatre allows (and perhaps necessitates) the suspension of accepted notions of

*"Who is Sitting on Which Beast?" Interpretative Issues in the Book of Revelation. Proceedings of the International Conference held at Loyola University, Chicago, March 30-31, 2017*, ed. by Edmondo Lupieri and Louis Painchaud, JAOC 29 (Turnhout, 2023), pp. 287–308

DOI 10.1484/M.JAOC-EB.5.131937

time, space, self, and concrete reality, by using it as a method it becomes easier to trace the ways in which Blake seems to have read the women of Revelation as one woman going through stages of character development in the creation of his character Jerusalem. Thus, this chapter examines her transformation along with the women of Revelation from her appearance as Jezebel, to the Woman Wrapped in the Sun, to the Harlot, until finally she is revealed as the New Jerusalem.

## 1. Introduction

This chapter is a foray into the world and women of William Blake as presented in his epic illustrated work *Jerusalem: The Emanation of the Giant Albion.*[1] As his final, and longest, illuminated book, it is a culmination of his interests in the politics of his day, eccentric and marginal religious teachings, artwork, and poetry, and as such presents a compelling hybrid of his own creative mythology and Christian biblical history. Blake's *Jerusalem* has been the subject of much study and speculation throughout its history. A highly visionary and esoteric text, it has been said to occupy the space between Revelation and Genesis, where something that seems like destruction can actually be creation.[2] The conflation of seemingly opposite poles of existence is embodied in the title character, Jerusalem herself. While often understood as the pristine, chaste bride of Christ, in *Jerusalem* she is instead transformed into an all-loving consort of Jesus whose openness to love leads other characters in the book to repeatedly call her a whore or a harlot. This chapter seeks to delve into that dichotomy and how the characterization of a "chaste whore" allows us to use *Jerusalem* as a lens to re-examine the women of the Book of Revelation. *Jerusalem* is a one-hundred plate illustrated book that Blake created between 1804 (the date on the title page) and 1820. There are ten known extant copies of it, Copies A-F were printed in Blake's lifetime and Copies H-J were printed posthumously. Only two copies are fully colored; Copy E, which is the one referenced for the purposes of this study, and Copy B.[3]

1. I am indebted to S. Sklar, *Blake's Jerusalem as Visionary Theatre: Entering the Divine Body* (Oxford: Oxford University Press, 2011) as I use her arguments as a road map in my examination of *Jerusalem* and explore how reading the Book of Revelation in conversation with *Jerusalem*'s world works to reveal new ideas about the identity of the figure of Jerusalem, the woman-city in Revelation.

2. S. Sklar, *Blake's Jerusalem as Visionary Theatre: Entering the Divine Body* (Oxford: Oxford University Press, 2011) 29.

3. While the comparative study across different versions of Blake's works is common and an insightful practice, Jerusalem references ("J") in this chapter (unless otherwise noted) will refer to the text and artwork coloration as it appears in Copy

## 2. *Jerusalem*, an Overview: Its Characters and Plot

It will be important to have a foundation about the major players and plotlines within *Jerusalem* before delving into a conversation about its relationship to Revelation. As this chapter progresses, one must keep in mind that within the narrative world of *Jerusalem* the human and the divine can coexist and overlap, there is less of a hard line found between the two than may usually be expected of narrative media. This section will first briefly cover the major characters of import to the examination of the women of Revelation and as such, is by no means an exhaustive list of all characters and players found in the poem.[4] Then, the section will conclude with a short overview of the principal parts of the plot and structure of the poem.

### 2.1 Albion

At the center of the narrative stands Albion, the representative of humanity itself. While there is certainly relevancy to the fact that Albion is the ancient mythic name of England, it is instead the Adam-like resonances of the character that take the forefront in this narrative. His "fall" in Chapter 1 aligns him with the biblical Adam as it helps to illustrate Albion as this central symbol of humanity.[5] His "fall" is not due to any actions that could be considered malicious, or evil (though some of his actions may be considered so), and unlike the biblical Adam's relationship with Eve, Albion's fall is not instigated by Jerusalem who is his emanation (or female counterpart). Instead, the cause (and result) of this fall is that Albion is referred to throughout the poem as being sick or diseased. This illness is also described as somehow contagious, aligning more with a disease in how it spread, then with specific malicious intent. The driving crisis of the narrative is the need to save Albion from this sickness, but it becomes clear throughout the narrative that this illness can be healed by "Jesus alone," much to the dismay of the poem's hero, Los (see below).[6] Both Los and Jerusalem spend the narrative seeking to save Albion from his fallen, diseased state.

---

E as reproduced in W. Blake, *Jerusalem: The Emanation of the Giant Albion*, M.D. Paley, ed. (Princeton: Princeton University Press, 1991).

4. Largely left out of this chapter's exploration are the poem's extensive cast of male/masculine characters who serve as representatives of biblical characters or persons from English history (or both simultaneously).

5. Albion is a common poetic name used for England, and it is in this sense that Blake initially uses it. With mythical connections to "the name of the aboriginal giant who conquered the island and named it for himself" (D.S. Foster, *A Blake Dictionary: The Ideas and Symbols of William Blake*, 2nd ed. [Hanover, NH: Dartmouth College Press, 2013] 9; for a full overview of how Albion reoccurs as a figure in Blake's work, see pp. 9-16).

6. S. Sklar, *Blake's Jerusalem as Visionary Theatre: Entering the Divine Body* (Oxford: Oxford University Press, 2011) 114.

### 2.2 Los

Although the hero, Los is a fallible hero, and he is considered the artist's placement of himself into the narrative.[7] In images he is associated with a hammer and his main action of the narrative is his constant work on building the city of Golgonooza, in hopes that he is creating a temple-city that will save Albion. This proves to be an unfruitful endeavor, since even as Los is constantly constructing it, Golgonooza is conversely constantly decaying. In her work, *Blake's Jerusalem as Visionary Theatre*, Suzanne Sklar emphasizes that this city is something that Blake has opted not to draw. Through Blake's work in printing and engraving he would have been more than capable of providing readers with a map, yet he does not.[8] Los is also a Christic figure; he is Christ and Christ is him. Yet I want to be clear that this does not make Los *the* Jesus character encountered in the narrative, for Jesus himself is a separate character. Instead, their overlap serves to illustrate how Jesus exists in everyone and everything.

### 2.3 Spectre, Hand, and Luvuh

Connected to Los is the shadowy figure of Spectre, a bat-like oppressive figure, who works in conjunction with Vala in the chaotic repression of Jerusalem. Also a part of the group characters who aid in Albion's fall and continued falling is Hand, who is usually identified with Robert Hunt, whose devastating reviews of Blake in 1808 and 1809 functionally ruined Blake's reputation.[9] Sklar however identifies him with the magistrate presiding over the sedition trial of 1804. In this same vein of antagonistic characters, we encounter Luvuh, the Emana-

7. Sklar sees this conflation in Los' relation to the first-person narrator, who in turn is related to Blake's authorial voice in her character breakdown (S. Sklar, *Blake's Jerusalem as Visionary Theatre: Entering the Divine Body* [Oxford: Oxford University Press, 2011] 63-66).

8. S. Sklar, *Blake's Jerusalem as Visionary Theatre: Entering the Divine Body* (Oxford: Oxford University Press, 2011) 136.

9. There is a significant amount of scholarly debate about the identification of Hand with Robert Hunt, with disagreements about if he was inspiration for Hand or if he merely informed the continued presentation of the character after the fact. For a brief overview of the scholarly conflict see: S. Sklar, *Blake's Jerusalem as Visionary Theatre: Entering the Divine Body* (Oxford: Oxford University Press, 2011) 50-52. For scholars who engage with the identification of Hand see: D. Erdman, "Blake's Nest of Villains," *Keats-Shelley Journal* 2 (1953) 60-71; D. Paley, *The Continuing City: William Blake's Jerusalem* (Oxford: Clarendon, 1983) 218-219; G.E. Bentley, *The Stranger From Paradise: A Biography of William Blake* (New Haven: Yale University Press, 2001) 313; J. Mee, *Romanticism, Enthusiasm, and Regulation* (Oxford: Oxford University Press, 2003) 273-275.

tion of France who is often related to fury. It is with Luvuh that Vala is said to begin forming the dragon-harlot of war.[10]

## 2.4 Vala

Vala is the dark, negative aspect of the feminine presented in *Jerusalem*. In the beginning, she is paired with Jerusalem in creation, she is responsible for overseeing the formation of the outward expression of bodies, while Jerusalem works on the inward expression of souls.[11] When Vala is separated from Jerusalem, she encourages the worship of that which is outward, or material, and is painted by Blake as a cold, ruthless virgin. She is depicted as being veiled, and throughout the poem is illustrated with at least seven different veils.[12] This veiling, as representative of her virginity, puts her in direct conflict with Jerusalem, who is called a harlot throughout the piece.

## 2.5 Jerusalem

Already mentioned as the positive feminine aspect, Jerusalem is not only a city, but also a woman in *Jerusalem*. She offers love, forgiveness, and peace to all, and is called a harlot throughout the work due to her unconditional loving acceptance.[13] This is Blake's reversal of a more traditional definition of harlotry, and this ability to reverse and reform concepts is central to how this work (and his works more broadly) functions. All humans are considered Jerusalem's "little ones" and thus when Albion—the representation of humanity—falls, he pulls Jerusalem with him. As in Revelation, she is the Bride of Christ, and this relationship between her and Jesus in *Jerusalem* is explicitly sexual.[14]

10. S. Sklar, *Blake's Jerusalem as Visionary Theatre: Entering the Divine Body* (Oxford: Oxford University Press, 2011) 204.

11. S. Sklar, *Blake's Jerusalem as Visionary Theatre: Entering the Divine Body* (Oxford: Oxford University Press, 2011) 178.

12. The importance of the number seven in apocalyptic literature will be explored further below.

13. This dichotomy is not an entirely new idea and can be seen in Christian tradition particularly in the concept of the *casta meretrix* which examines the Church as a "chaste whore," being both holy and fallen simultaneously. A concise history of the ways in which the *casta meretrix* has appeared can be found in H.U. von Balthazar, *Explorations in Theology. 2, Spouse of the Word* (San Francisco: Ignatius, 1961) 193-288. Balthazar dedicates an entire chapter to the history of the development of the *casta meretrix*, tracing it from the depictions of the woman-city of Jerusalem in the Hebrew Bible (especially as she is depicted in the prophets), through early Christian thinkers like Origen, Ambrose, and Augustine, up to contemporary (to him) reflections of the church as being one composed of sinners.

14. S. Sklar, *Blake's Jerusalem as Visionary Theatre: Entering the Divine Body* (Oxford: Oxford University Press, 2011) 73.

For Blake, sexuality and human lovemaking are a highly important part of spirituality, and sexual shame and fear severs humanity from the divine.[15] Although she is inextricably connected to Albion, Jerusalem is the consort of Jesus, even as she works to try to save humanity-Albion. It is asserted, even from the very beginning of the poem, that it is solely through Jesus that humanity can be pulled out of darkness. This sets up the ultimate necessity of the union of Albion, Jerusalem, and Jesus, with Jerusalem as the link between Albion, who is humanity, and Jesus, who is salvation.

### 2.6 Jesus

Jesus is a character within *Jerusalem*, and is integral to it, but he is not always apparently present. The idea that he exists within all (with an emphasis on his existence within Los being prominent) pervades the poem. There are only three visual images of him in the poem : the creation of Eve from Adam (J35), the resurrection of Lazarus (J37), and the depiction of Albion before the crucified Christ (J76). The hidden, or "backstage" nature of Jesus's character leads him to be described as the "cosmic stage manager" of *Jerusalem.*[16] The fourth plate, which features the beginning of the poem proper, features the words μονος ὁ Ιεςσυς[17] (J4), echoing biblical stories of the transfiguration, as found in Matt 17:8, which reads that the disciples "saw no one except Jesus himself."[18] Similarly, in Mark 9:8, "they saw no one with them anymore, but only Jesus,"[19] and Luke 9:36 reads that "when the voice had spoken, Jesus was found alone."[20] For Blake, highlighting the phrase "μονος ὁ Ιεςσυς," "Jesus alone," serves as a reminder from the very beginning of the poem that it is solely through Christ that humanity can be pulled out of darkness, but also in his usage of the Greek (a language most of his English-speaking contemporaries likely did not know) maintains the esoteric nature of the text (and Jesus himself).

---

15. See the exploration of Blake's influences regarding this idea in M.K. SCHUCHARD, *William Blake's Sexual Path to Spiritual Vision* (Rochester, VT : Inner Traditions 2008).

16. S. SKLAR, *Blake's Jerusalem as Visionary Theatre : Entering the Divine Body* (Oxford : Oxford University Press, 2011) 113.

17. While the Greek here is incorrect, it should read Ἰησοῦς, the sentiment is understandable.

18. ἐπάραντες δὲ τοὺς ὀφθαλμοὺς αὐτῶν οὐδένα εἶδον εἰ μὴ αὐτὸν Ἰησοῦν μόνον (Matt 17:8 ; Greek citations are from the NESTLE ALAND 28 and translations are my own, unless otherwise stated).

19. καὶ ἐξάπινα περιβλεψάμενοι οὐκέτι οὐδένα εἶδον ἀλλὰ τὸν Ἰησοῦν μόνον μεθ' ἑαυτῶν (Mark 9:8).

20. καὶ ἐν τῷ γενέσθαι τὴν φωνὴν εὑρέθη Ἰησοῦς μόνος. καὶ αὐτοὶ ἐσίγησαν καὶ οὐδενὶ ἀπήγγειλαν ἐν ἐκείναις ταῖς ἡμέραις οὐδὲν ὧν ἑώρακαν (Luke 9:36).

## 2.7 Plot Synopsis

*Jerusalem* is divided into four chapters, each having 25 plates and titled as being "to" a certain group: "To the Public," "To the Jews," "To the Deists," and finally "To the Christians." The first chapter, "To the Public," depicts Albion's "fall" as he descends into the worship of abstract reasoning power. The adherence to strict reason that comes from this worship of reasoning power in turn leads to the repression of the feminine as well as the divine imagination (and therefore of Jerusalem herself). Chapter two, "To the Jews," features Los's attempts at saving Albion and Jerusalem (a pair that is still united at this point in the narrative) from the Moral Law of the Israelite Druids.[21] However, it is revealed at this point that Albion does not want to be saved from the state of Selfhood he has fallen into, and that it is impossible to rescue him unless he also desires to be saved.[22] In his understanding of the plot structure, Northrop Frye categorizes this chapter as being representative of "the struggle of men in a fallen world which is what we usually think of as history."[23] Chapter three, "To the Deists," is arguably the most convoluted chapter of the poem, with constant character and location shifts, requiring an active visionary imagination to work through the chapter. In it, Los is infected by Albion's disease, and so while Los believes he is building a redemptive structure as he works on the construction of Golgonooza, he is actually building what is called "Religion Hid in War." Frye categorizes this chapter as the one in which the world is redeemed by a divine man (Jesus), and one in which "life and death achieve simultaneous triumph."[24] Chapter four, "To the Christians," serves as the final apocalyptic moment of the narrative and holds the final awakening of Albion. This final awakening is initiated by Jesus, for within the narrative he is the Breath Divine, and as previously mentioned, in the context of *Jerusalem* it is only through Jesus that one can be saved. In this final chapter, no one is left out of the Divine Body (the ideal state of being in *Jerusalem*) and, in sharp contrast to the Book of Revelation, all are forgiven, and no one is damned.

21. Druids will be explored in more depth below.

22. Words that are capitalized such as "Selfhood," "Moral Law," "Breath Divine," and "Divine Body," among others are capitalized within Blake's work and serve as technical terms for Blake. Many of these terms are used repeatedly across Blake's corpus and definitions and an overview can be found in D.S. Foster, *A Blake Dictionary: The Ideas and Symbols of William Blake*, 2nd ed. (Hanover, NH: Dartmouth College Press, 2013).

23. N. Frye, *Fearful Symmetry: A Study of William Blake*, ed. N. Halmi (Toronto: University of Toronto Press, 2004) 348.

24. N. Frye, *Fearful Symmetry: A Study of William Blake*, ed. N. Halmi (Toronto: University of Toronto Press, 2004) 348.

## 3. William Blake: Life and Influences

William Blake was an English poet, visionary, painter, engraver, and printmaker who lived from November 28th, 1757, to August 12th, 1827. In his lifetime, he was largely unrecognized by his contemporaries, many of whom considered him mad, but he is now regarded as a pivotal figure in Romantic and Pre-Romantic era poetry and art. In 1804, he was accused of and tried for sedition, a trial that greatly shaped his work on his epic masterpiece, *Jerusalem*, which he started in that same year. His work more broadly is influenced by his knowledge of the Bible and pseudepigraphal texts such as the books of Enoch and *4 Ezra*. He was highly skeptical of the Church of England, if not of all organized religion, but found himself drawn to the circles of experimental Christian-based organizations that were flourishing in London during the late eighteenth and early nineteenth centuries.

### 3.1 Revelation Watercolors

Between 1800 and 1806, Thomas Butts commissioned Blake to complete works that specifically depicted scenes from the Bible.[25] As a part of this commission, Blake produced around eighty watercolors, several of which included depictions of scenes from the Book of Revelation. Found within these watercolors are figures such as the slaughtered Lamb (Rev 5:5-6), the four and twenty elders (Rev 4:4), various depictions of the dragon and beasts (Rev 12:7ff; 13; 17:3), the binding of Satan (Rev 20:1-3), and of course, pertinent to this study, the various women, including the Woman Clothed in the Sun, the Whore of Babylon, and the new Jerusalem.[26] Blake also depicts the Whore upon the Beast in his illustrated edition of Edward Young's poem *Night Thoughts*, commissioned by Richard Edwards in 1795.[27]

The watercolors from the series commissioned by Thomas Butts that will be relevant for this study are the four that depict the women of Revelation: *The Great Red Dragon and the Woman Clothed with the Sun: "The Devil is Come Down"*, *The Great Red Dragon and the Woman*

---

25. Thomas Butts was Blake's first, and most consistent patron, for historical background on Butts see J. Viscomi, "A 'Green House' for Butts? New Information on Thomas Butts, His Residences and Family," *Blake: An Illustrated Quarterly* 30/1 (Summer 1996) 4-21.

26. For easy online access to the various watercolors of the Bible, see the William Blake Archive (http://www.blakearchive.org/work/biblicalwc), for a printed version of the full collection of Blake's paintings and drawings, see M. Butlin, *The Paintings and Drawings of William Blake* (New Haven: Yale University Press, 1981).

27. C. Rowland, *Blake and the Bible* (New Haven: Yale University Press, 2010) 226.

*Clothed in the Sun*, *The Whore of Babylon*, and finally his imagining of the New Jerusalem in *The River of Life*.[28] It is through the examination of these paintings that the visual connections between Blake's work on Revelation to his work on *Jerusalem* begin to crystallize.

That Blake's work on the Book of Revelation impacted his illustrations of *Jerusalem* is even more evident when his illustrations are looked at side by side with his watercolors. The clearest example can be seen in the examination of the visual overlaps between the depiction of Jerusalem (the character) and the central figures of Blake's Revelation paintings. The image of Jerusalem seen in plates J92 and J87 is strikingly similar to that of the Woman Clothed with the Sun from his *The Great Red Dragon and the Woman Clothed with the Sun: "The Devil is Come Down."* Physically both figures are in gold, flowing dresses, with matching golden hair, and in terms of their posturing both women feature expressive arms that seem to be mid-motion as they look elsewhere in the painting (up at the "Great Red Dragon" in the watercolor, and down at the fallen heads in *Jerusalem*).[29] This same golden hair is also used on the central figure of *The River of Life* who is ushering the "little ones" into the New Jerusalem. While some have read this figure to be that of Jesus, in this case there is an argument to be made that the overlap of physical similarity to Jerusalem could imply that instead this figure is Jerusalem herself, bringing humanity home to the city of New Jerusalem. What I am arguing is that Blake's illustrations show a consistency of image across his depictions of his major female figures throughout his works that does not seem accidental and reinforces the need to make connections between characters and concepts across the corpus of Blake's work.[30]

Blake's artwork is known for how his characters constantly seem to be in motion. As previously mentioned both the Woman Clothed with the Sun with her arms outstretched and Jerusalem's seeming shrug illustrate

---

28. N. O'Hear – A. O'Hear, *Picturing the Apocalypse* (Oxford: Oxford University Press, 2015) 36.

29. This similarity between the watercolors and *Jerusalem* is also noted in S. Sklar, "Blake's Jerusalem: Refiguring Revelation's Women," in C.E. Joynes – C. Rowland, eds., *From the Margins 2: Women of the New Testament and Their Afterlives* (Sheffield: Sheffield Phoenix Press, 2009) 300. Morton D. Paley identifies the heads she is sitting upon as the fallen heads of the four Zoas in W. Blake, *Jerusalem: The Emanation of the Giant Albion*, M.D. Paley, ed. (Princeton: Princeton University Press, 1991) 287.

30. The connection of characters and themes across the Blakean corpus is a regular feature of Blakean scholarship, as he frequently uses and re-uses and re-casts his characters, mythic and historical, and often the meanings they have held in previous works are drawn upon in further works. For a good resource that allows the reader to get an overview of how characters and concepts are used across the body of his works, see D.S. Foster, *A Blake Dictionary: The Ideas and Symbols of William Blake*, 2nd ed. (Hanover, NH: Dartmouth College Press, 2013).

the ability of Blake to show characters in action rather than just as stationary features on the page.[31] This ability to paint life onto a page does not end with physical gestures, and examples such as his painting of *The Whore of Babylon* as well as figures in *Jerusalem* (see the figures atop the chariot in J46) allows Blake to use facial expressions to give his characters emotions about the actions they are partaking in. In his drawing of a beast-drawn chariot in *Jerusalem* (J46), Blake gives his reader a pair of morose (or perhaps sleepy?) riders who, while pulled along by majestic beasts seem unbothered by their situation.[32] Through these expressive artistic depictions, Blake allows his readers to determine potential character motivation via reading the facial expressions of his subjects. With the figure of the Whore in *The Whore of Babylon*, Blake uses facial features to emphasize his interpretation of her: she looks unsure, wary of her position atop the Beast. The souls pouring into her cup (who in turn are all holding their own cups) are coming, not only out of the chaos below, but from a figure holding a matching cup at the bottom of the frame. In *Jerusalem*, Jerusalem is described as taking a cup from Vala as part of her larger work to save Albion, and thus humanity (J88). In a way that is not offered to us in Revelation, Blake's uncertain Whore could perhaps provide an alternate way of reading her not as this drunken, gleeful harlot but instead a tentative, unhappy prisoner. For Blake, it seems that the Whore's motivation for being atop the Beast is not one of maliciousness, and if we read her together with Jerusalem, can illustrate how this cup-bearing is a necessary step towards the New Jerusalem.[33]

### 3.2 Esoteric Religious Movements

In addition to being heavily influenced by his own works on the Book of Revelation, Blake's work on *Jerusalem* was also impacted by ideas propagated by several movements gaining traction in London during his formative years, including but not limited to the Freemasons, the school of Alchemy, Society of Antiquaries, an increased popular interest in Druids, and the Moravian Church. Sklar describes Masonic Lodges as "little visionary theatre companies," an apt description as the Freemasons, rather than solely relying on the written textual medium, required a theatrical embodiment of their mythic stories. It was thus not through reading, but

31. D. Piccitto, *Blake's Drama: Theatre, Performance, and Identity in the Illuminated Books* (London: Macmillan, 2014) 35.

32. The identification of the figures is yet another point of much scholarly debate, I identify the two as Albion and Jerusalem. For other identifications see W. Blake, *Jerusalem: The Emanation of the Giant Albion*, M.D. Paley, ed. (Princeton: Princeton University Press, 1991) 203-204.

33. Cf. Genesis 38, where Tamar is presented as a righteous woman taking on the appearance of a prostitute.

through theatrical rituals that masonic initiates were transformed. The goal was not to simply decode the symbolism found in their tradition, but to live *in* the allegory.[34] Further than these theatrical influences, which open space for us to read Blake's works performatively, the Freemasons also had an impact on the imagery in Blake's works. Blake consistently uses Masonic symbols such as the compass, temple building, pillars, architects, metalworkers, etc. in his works.[35] Like the Freemason use of theatrical metaphors, so too did alchemical writers lean into the idea that "all the world's a stage," an idea that, rather than simply being coined by Shakespeare actually served as part of the "mental furniture" of the general population.[36] The school of Alchemy's reliance on theatrical metaphors thus sought to transform not only metals, but also (in the case of spiritual alchemists) human souls and societies, and was influential as Blake created a space where characters/objects/buildings can and do shift constantly. In *Jerusalem*, as is found in alchemical schools, the macrocosmic dimension of the world and the cosmos intersects with the microcosmic of the mind.[37]

Blake would have been exposed to the ideas of the Antiquaries through his apprenticeship to James Basire, the master engraver to the Society of the Antiquaries in London.[38] The Antiquaries' idea that Britain was the "primitive seat of the patriarchal Israelite religion" features greatly in Blake's work, and the conflation of England and ancient Israel is prominent in *Jerusalem*.[39] This connection allows Blake to map the Israelite "chosenness" by God onto England, an imperial power who already seemed to believe it was "chosen" to conquer the world. This geopolitical overlapping of the cosmos, the ancient world, and the modern world allows the text

34. S. Sklar, *Blake's Jerusalem as Visionary Theatre: Entering the Divine Body* (Oxford: Oxford University Press, 2011) 40. In her discussion of this, she even mentions that in a conversation with a Freemason, "the text is not written; it is transmitted orally through dramatic enactment" (see her footnote 39 on page 40).

35. In the case of *Jerusalem*, Los is a particularly relevant example of Blake's use of this imagery as seen in Los's construction of Golgonooza and the blacksmith's hammer serving as defining prop of his character.

36. F. Yates, *The Rosicrucian Enlightenment*, 2nd ed. (London: Routledge Classics, 2000) 182.

37. S. Sklar, *Blake's Jerusalem as Visionary Theatre: Entering the Divine Body* (Oxford: Oxford University Press, 2011) 26. Sklar walks through a number of alchemical texts as examples of the types of visionary/complex literature that may have influenced Blake (or at minimum allows us to understand how Blake's work fits into the wider spectrum of literature during his time).

38. For an in-depth analysis of the types of work Blake would have been exposed to working under Basire see S. Sklar, *Blake's Jerusalem as Visionary Theatre: Entering the Divine Body* (Oxford: Oxford University Press, 2011) 126-127.

39. There was also an idea (held by Antiquarian Elias Ashmole and John Milton) that civilization began with British Druids before spreading down to Greece. S. Sklar, *Blake's Jerusalem as Visionary Theatre: Entering the Divine Body* (Oxford: Oxford University Press, 2011) 125, 171.

of the poem to cover more ground, as it requires the readers to expand their understanding of situations within the text as having the ability to apply to England, Israel, and the macrocosmic world presented in *Jerusalem*, often all at the same time. The rise in interest in Druids was to some extent connected to the synchronistic work of the Antiquaries. The use of Druids and their structures by Antiquarian William Stukeley to promote imperial domination (as he imagined England as a new Rome and New Jerusalem) sits in direct conflict to Blake's own vision.[40] In Blake's works then, Druids and their structures become negative images, and he leans on traditions of depicting Druids as bloodthirsty and regularly engaged in human sacrifice that Stukeley often downplayed. Additionally, Blake's Druids promote sexual repression and chastity (J63) in their emphasis on rationality and reason. As will be detailed further below, for Blake healthy human sexuality is not a negative aspect, and he is seeking to point to a humanity that does not worship reason. Both reason and natural law are, to Blake, aspects of study that cause the promotion of chastity, which in turn promotes Selfhood, and ultimately war.[41]

Finally, and perhaps most central to this project, the source of Blake's favorable outlook of sexuality as found in *Jerusalem* (as well as his larger body of work) is most likely the Moravian Church and its erotic spirituality. His mother had been a member of the congregation of the Moravian Church at Fetter Lane in the 1750s during her first marriage to Thomas Armitage and her exposure and experiences as a member of that congregation may have influenced the young Blake.[42] Blake's mother was involved with the Fetter Lane congregation of the Moravians during the "Sifting Time" (*c.* 1743-1753), which was one of the most tumultuous and creative periods for the Moravian church. The Fetter Lane congregation was known for its unconventional, esoteric, and often heretical participants, as they were exposed to a "theology of sex, wounds, and blood."[43] This theology was largely dependent on the work of Nicolaus Ludwig von Zinzendorf (1700-1760), who drew upon Christianized versions of Kabbalah to spiritualize sexuality in a way that sought to be emotionally and intellectu-

40. D.B. Haycock, *William Stukeley: Science, Religion, and Archaeology in Eighteenth Century England* (Woodbridge: Boydell, 2002) 120; S. Sklar, *Blake's Jerusalem as Visionary Theatre: Entering the Divine Body* (Oxford: Oxford University Press, 2011) 129.

41. S. Sklar, *Blake's Jerusalem as Visionary Theatre: Entering the Divine Body* (Oxford: Oxford University Press, 2011) 125.

42. K. Davies – M.K. Schuchard, "Recovering the Lost Moravian History of William Blake's Family," *Blake/An Illustrated Quarterly* 38/1 (Summer 2004) 39.

43. This tradition was heavily involved with reconfiguring the side wound of Christ as being akin to the vulvar opening. M.K. Schuchard, *William Blake's Sexual Path to Spiritual Vision* (Rochester, VT: Inner Traditions, 2006) 13, 29.

ally liberating as it sought to reintegrate the divine feminine.[44] Zinzendorf also composed erotic hymns which were sent to his various congregations in which the Hebrew "Mother *Ruach*" copulates with "Christ's *Logos*,"[45] while at the same time developing the importance of the mystical marriage in which sex between a married couple was viewed as a sacramental act. To fight against the more chaste-focused traditional Protestant views, Zinzendorf created "Married Choirs" in which couples were encouraged to serve as resources in a type of sex education and marriage guidance.[46] The instructions emphasized the importance of consent by both parties in marriage, properly informing young men and women before and after marriage about sex, and how and why their bodies and sexual organs were made holy by Jesus, the methods of sexual intercourse and how often it should be performed.[47] Thus, rather than sex being something negative, Zinzendorf highlights the blessedness of it ("bodies and sexual organs... made holy by Jesus").

This section has suggested that Blake's positive views of sexuality that largely define his character of Jerusalem and her relationship to the masculine characters around her are not solely inventions from the mind of a singular "madman." Rather, they find a home with the theologies and ideologies of not only the Moravian church (as has been mentioned here), but also those that are Swedenborgian, Kabbalistic, Tantric, and Hermetic.[48]

## 4. "Visionary Forms Dramatic" (J98): Visionary Theatre and *Jerusalem* as Performance

One of the tools that Sklar uses to dive into the world of *Jerusalem* is a practice called "visionary theatre." In visionary theatre, the "stage" is both the cosmos and the mind, and this dual nature is key to how the poem

44. M.K. Schuchard, *William Blake's Sexual Path to Spiritual Vision* (Rochester, VT: Inner Traditions, 2006) 17.

45. M.K. Schuchard, *William Blake's Sexual Path to Spiritual Vision* (Rochester, VT: Inner Traditions, 2006) 28.

46. Schuchard suggests that it is possible that a listed "Mr and Mrs Blake" and a "Mr Wright" (the pre-married name of Blake's mother) could have been Blake's grandparents, so his family members were likely involved with this community (M.K. Schuchard, *William Blake's Sexual Path to Spiritual Vision* [Rochester, VT: Inner Traditions, 2006] 27-29).

47. A. Fogleman, "Jesus is Female: The Moravian Challenge in the German Communities of British North America," *The William and Mary Quarterly* 60 (2003) 326.

48. Unfortunately, a full detailing of the wide range of influences on Blake's spiritualized sexuality is beyond the scope of this chapter, but for interested parties, see the detailed monograph on the subject by M.K. Schuchard, *William Blake's Sexual Path to Spiritual Vision* (Rochester, VT: Inner Traditions, 2006).

works. This more fluid reading of the text as a type of performance is a methodology frequently employed by performance studies scholars as they read various media "as" performance. This type of methodology works to bring new life into works like those of Blake.[49] This section will provide a brief exploration of the ways in which "visionary theatre" as a category has been used to understand not only the work of Blake, but also the Book of Revelation.

### 4.1 Visionary Theatre

In the opening of "Chapter 4: To the Christians," Blake asserts that Christianity and the Gospels give "the liberty to both body and mind to exercise the Divine Arts of Imagination" (J77). The reading of *Jerusalem* requires the strong use of imagination since nothing is being "staged" in the traditional sense of the word. Instead, the reader must step outside of the accepted notions of time, space, self, and concrete reality as Blake uses time and space merely as ingredients to be molded and created with. The text is inherently relational, so "to read *Jerusalem* we must enter it, using our imaginations to insert obliterated words, to read in reverse, to identify morphing characters."[50] Sklar likens the morphing nature of the characters to an animated cartoon where it isn't outside of the realm of possibility for a character to turn into a road, or a sign, and morph back.[51] This fluidity does not stop with just character concepts and topic presentations but is evident even in the way the text and artwork exists on the pages. In a number of plates there are words missing, and in others there are words written as if you were reading through a mirror, with everything backwards. Often blocks of text are interrupted by the illustrations, some with words within the images, causing the reader to stop and digest what they are seeing. Unlike a modern comic book, the artwork on the page regularly does not even seem to match what is happening in the text. These aspects all force a change of perspective for the reader, since to figure out what is happening, they must change physically how they read.

It is this shift in reading mode that drives the use of visionary theatre as an appropriate method when examining the works of Blake, but

---

49. That "visionary theatre" and performance are an appropriate category especially for Blake is seen in the way in which even scholars who are not directly engaging with the performative aspects of Blake's works have referenced them. See for instance N. FRYE, *Fearful Symmetry: A Study of William Blake*, ed. N. HALMI (Toronto: University of Toronto Press, 2004) 348, 360; J. FEKKES, "'His Bride Has Prepared Herself': Revelation 19-21 and Isaian Nuptial Imagery," *Journal of Biblical Literature* 109 (1990) 269.

50. S. SKLAR, *Blake's Jerusalem as Visionary Theatre: Entering the Divine Body* (Oxford: Oxford University Press, 2011) 64.

51. S. SKLAR, *Blake's Jerusalem as Visionary Theatre: Entering the Divine Body* (Oxford: Oxford University Press, 2011) 123.

it is not a concept that was created by Sklar and can be found elsewhere. Visionary theatre methodologies are first detectable in seventeenth century commentaries on the Book of Revelation. In his introduction to his analysis, David Pareus categorizes the text as a "Prophetical Drama:"

> but that which beginneth at the fourth Chapter (which is the first prophetical Vision) and the following unto the end, if you well observe them, have plainly a *Dramaticall* forme, hence the Revelation may truly be called a *Propheticall Drama*, show, or representation.[52]

Since Pareus's engagement with Revelation as a drama was to reinforce his Protestant ideals (he even goes so far as to rearrange the text to further his vision), it is unsurprising that he identifies the harlot with the papacy. Using Pareus's same visionary/dramatic methodology, Joseph Wittreich was the first to apply this method to *Jerusalem* and read similar anti-papal ideals in Blake's text. However, with anti-papal sentiments came Pareus's anti-artistic beliefs, so Sklar posits that while it is not outside the realm of possibility that Blake knew of and engaged with Pareus's commentary, it is more likely that Blake had access to Pareus's idea of "visionary theatre" via the work of Milton or Joseph Mede.[53] Mede was particularly known for his reading Revelation in both sequential and synchronistic ways, perhaps creating the model for reading that Blake envisioned his readers to follow as they interacted with his own work. This multi-media approach to understanding the works is an inherently "performative" method of reading, and Mede too understands there to be something particularly "theatrical" about Revelation, even referring to it as "Apocalyptick Theatre."[54] Diane Piccitto also draws forth the fact that the category of "performance" was far less rigid in popular understanding during Blake's time. Rather than only denoting a vocalized expression of a text (such as is found in poetry readings, theatrical productions, etc.), "performance" could also denote literary, artistic, or other creative works. In fact, "performance" is the word that Blake often uses to refer to his own works.[55]

---

52. D. Pareus, *Commentary Upon the Divine Revelation of the Apostle and Evangelist John ... translated out of the Latine into English, by Elias Arnold ...* (Amsterdam: C.P., 1644) 20 (stress added).

53. Sklar points particularly to the preface of *Samson Agonistes* and in *Reason of Church Government* where Milton specifically quotes Pareus in support of his understanding of his work as "divine visionary theatre" (S. Sklar, *Blake's Jerusalem as Visionary Theatre: Entering the Divine Body* [Oxford: Oxford University Press, 2011] 20-21).

54. S. Sklar, *Blake's Jerusalem as Visionary Theatre: Entering the Divine Body* (Oxford: Oxford University Press, 2011) 22-23.

55. D. Piccitto, *Blake's Drama: Theatre, Performance, and Identity in the Illuminated Books* (London: MacMillan, 2014) 14. This further openness of the category of "performance" is something that is currently being drawn out in modern scholarship by the work of Performance Studies scholars as they broaden the

### 4.2 *Jerusalem* and the Book of Revelation

The themes and images in *Jerusalem* are clearly influenced by the Book of Revelation and when read in conversation with each other Blake's characters and ideas can help to open new ways of interpreting Revelation. Much like *Jerusalem*, Revelation is full of shifting imagery: the slaughtered Lamb is introduced as a lion (Rev 5:5-6), the narrator-scribe is constantly being shifted from one visionary location to another (Rev 4:1-2). So, to make sense of Revelation as a similarly complex text, it is helpful to also apply the lens of visionary theatre to the reading of it. Likewise, it is important to keep in mind that characters can be interpreted as representative of a multiplicity of things simultaneously rather than simply choosing one thing or another for each player in the narrative, so for instance, the beast can be more than just Rome.

In reading Revelation, it is equally useful to step outside of conventional ideas of time, especially when encountering characters like the figure of the slaughtered Lamb who has been "slaughtered from the beginning of time" (Rev 13:8).[56] Edmondo Lupieri has helpfully pointed out that in apocalyptic texts more broadly (and in Revelation specifically), the heavens do not seem to be held to any sort of temporal or spatial laws. This flattening of time often makes it hard for an audience to follow the sequence of events.[57] Numerology also plays a critical role in both Revelation and *Jerusalem*. Frye has pointed out in his examination of the works of Blake the propensity of Blake to use number symbols as holding great weight. This is also true of Revelation, where numbers play feature roles throughout the text, from the ever-famous number of the beast (Rev 13:18), to the 24 elders (Rev 4:4,10, etc.), to the four living creatures, four horsemen, etc. Most clearly there is also the consistent and prominent use of the number seven.[58] Frye points out that while Revelation uses the number seven as the "sacred or imaginative number," Blake rather tends to focus on fours and threes, but in both numbers serve as particular symbols.[59]

The expanding of imaginations helps to create a more interesting dialogue within the piece, and that imaginative reading can allow the text to

---

horizons of what can be understood as "performance." For further reading on Performance Studies methodologies, see text and resources in: R. SCHECHNER, *Performance Studies: An Introduction* (Oxford: Routledge, 2013).

56. ... ἐν τῷ βιβλίῳ τῆς ζωῆς τοῦ ἀρνίου τοῦ ἐσφαγμένου ἀπὸ καταβολῆς κόσμου (Rev 13:8).

57. E.F. LUPIERI *A Commentary on the Apocalypse of John*, trans. M. POGGI JOHNSON – A. KAMESAR (Grand Rapids: Eerdmans, 2006) 189.

58. For 7's within Revelation: the 7 spirits (1:4), 7 churches (1:11), 7 lampstands (1:12), 7 stars in right hand (1:20), 7 torches of fire (4:5), 7 seals (5:1), 7 thunders (10:3-4), 7 angels, 7 plagues (15:1), among others.

59. N. FRYE, *Fearful Symmetry: A Study of William Blake*, ed. N. HALMI (Toronto: University of Toronto Press, 2004) 358.

be more easily read forward in time as a prophetic text. It was said that the Revelation seems to have directed Blake in his composition of *Jerusalem*, and the overlapping imagery lends a solid foundation to this theory. In both texts, there is an apocalyptic wine press, seen in Rev 14:18 and *Jerusalem* in plates J72 and J82. The twenty-four elders of Revelation are reflected in the four and twenty cathedral cities, the four Zoas are reminiscent of the four Living Creatures but are also likened to the four horsemen in ferocity.[60] The inability to map Golgonooza due to its shifting nature is reminiscent of the constantly shifting throne geography in Revelation. In both texts the author or narrator presents questions to a divine figure for explanations of what they are seeing, and like John is commanded to "write" in Rev 14:13, Blake, too, is commanded to his divine scribe role as he is told to "shudder not, but write" (J47). This insistence of not fearing/shuddering, etc. is a common trope within apocalyptic literature, as well as a feature of theophanic encounters with God throughout canonical and noncanonical texts. In *1 Enoch* 15:1, Enoch is told not to fear, throughout the biblical texts we get repeated insistences by angels for their dialogue partners not to be afraid (see for instance Dan 10:12 ; Luke 1:13, 30, 2:10-12 ; Matt 14:27 ; Mark 6:49-50, 16:6, Acts 18:9-10, etc.).

In *Jerusalem*, it is said that the poem is written to "suit the mouth of a true Orator" (J3) pointing to Blake's desire to have his poem interacted with as a typical piece of literature but also heightening its drama through the emphasis of necessity of its vocalization. This emphasis on spoken performance then also echoes Rev 1:3's implication that John intended his work to be read publicly when he calls those who read and hear "the words of the prophecy" blessed.[61] It is this blending of the genres of poetry and visual art that insists the audience interact with Blake's works differently than with poetry or art alone. Where Sklar points to the text of *Jerusalem*, Piccitto reads the theatricality of Blake's artwork as allowing one to read the texts as a performance in and of themselves. The motion of the characters illustrated in Blake's illuminated books mimics stage performance, with characters emoting and moving as if they would come to life as the book is read.[62] It is this combination of the text and the artwork that makes Blake's illuminated books so compelling.

---

60. The word "Zoa" itself is pulled from the Greek word ζῷα as found in places like Rev 4:6; 15:7, etc. Zoas are typically masculine entities, and they reoccur throughout Blake's work, taking a prominent place in his *The Four Zoas*. For an overview see : D.S. Foster, *A Blake Dictionary : The Ideas and Symbols of William Blake*, 2nd ed. (Hanover, NH, Dartmouth College Press, 2013) 458-460.

61. E.F. Lupieri *A Commentary on the Apocalypse of John*, trans. M. Poggi Johnson – A. Kamesar (Grand Rapids : Eerdmans, 2006) 100-101.

62. D. Piccitto, *Blake's Drama : Theatre, Performance, and Identity in the Illuminated Books* (London : MacMillan 2014) 34.

## 5. Revelation and Blakean Women

The positive imagery surrounding women is intrinsically important in Blake's work. Rather than let the male figures dominate his narrative, *Jerusalem*, as its name suggests, centers on his female characters, and how the male characters in turn relate to them. His work highlights not only the importance of the feminine (and how awry things can go if that feminine presence is missing), but also the critical nature of sexuality as a positive element in human life. As mentioned earlier, this positive view of sexuality more broadly and female sexuality specifically was likely developed due to the Moravian church's influence upon Blake's thinking. Within the Moravian church the love of Christ is made fully manifest in human lovemaking, and this is reflected throughout *Jerusalem*.[63] For Blake, virginity is a negative dimension, and human sexuality lived to its fullest is the proper way of spirituality.

It is through an examination of Jerusalem (the character), as well as the general characterization of women in *Jerusalem*, that the ways in which Blake interprets the female figures in Revelation becomes clearer. By aligning Jerusalem's character arc and shifting characterization with the transitions between the women in Revelation, it is possible to begin to see how the four women of Revelation (Jezebel, the Woman Clothed in the Sun, the Harlot, and the New Jerusalem) could perhaps be understood to be one Woman moving along a character arc rather than as four discrete women. However, to do that, one must reconcile the contrary natures of Revelation's female characters: Jezebel and the Harlot's negative connotations with the positive imagery of the Woman Clothed in the Sun, and the woman-city of the New Jerusalem.[64] This section will draw that arc and seek to draw parallels between the characters in *Jerusalem* (particularly Jerusalem and Vala) and in Revelation.

### 5.1 Jezebel

With a name pulled from the foreign wife of Ahab introduced in 1 Kings 16, the Jezebel of Revelation 2 is one of John's prophetic com-

---

63. S. Sklar, *Blake's Jerusalem as Visionary Theatre: Entering the Divine Body* (Oxford: Oxford University Press, 2011) 108. For a thorough exploration of the wide variety of influences on Blake's spiritual view of sexuality, see M.K. Schuchard, *William Blake's Sexual Path to Spiritual Vision* (Rochester, VT: Inner Traditions 2008).

64. Biblical scholars like Tina Pippin, Lynn Huber, and Elisabeth Schüssler Fiorenza all point to this binary depiction of women in the text (as they handle their own explorations of the women of Revelation). T. Pippin, *Death and Desire: The Rhetoric of Gender in the Apocalypse of John*, 1st ed. (Louisville: Westminster/John Knox, 1992); L.R. Huber, *Thinking and Seeing with Women in Revelation* (London: Bloomsbury, 2013); E. Schüssler Fiorenza, *Book of Revelation: Justice and Judgment*. 2nd ed. (Minneapolis, Fortress Press, 1998) 199.

petitors, and who meets a similarly grisly death by the end of her story. In being named after a foreign, and thus idolatrous by the standards of the Hebrew Bible, queen, the Jezebel figure in Revelation is already set up to be the one who (according to the book's author) leads her followers away from God (Rev 2:20). To connect Blake's Jerusalem to Jezebel, one can start with parallels between Jezebel and Jerusalem's counterpart Vala. Since Blake's characters exist within each other, this co-inherence can also be used to connect Jezebel and Jerusalem. Jezebel is found in Rev 2:20-21, described as "not willing to repent and depart from her prostitution" (Rev 2:21).[65] And so in *Jerusalem* J64:12-17, Vala's rousing anti-male pro-female speech sounds like it could also be placed in Jezebel's mouth as a retort to those in the church of Thyatira who have perhaps attempted to stop her prophesying:[66]

> She cries: The Human is but a Worm, & thou O Male: Thou art Thyself Female, a Male: a breeder of Seed: a Son & Husband: & Lo. The Human Divine is Womans Shadow, a Vapor in the summers heat. Go assume Papal dignity thou Spectre, thou Male Harlot! Arthur Divide into the Kings of Europe in times remote O Woman-born and Woman-nourished & Woman-educated & Woman-scorn'd. (J64:12-17)

Yet as has been mentioned, Vala is specifically painted as being chaste, a legacy that "Jezebel" definitively has not received. With the accusations of prostitution and the violent sexual imagery in Rev 2:22, the description of a woman as a "Jezebel" has consistently brought up negative and *sexual* terms.[67] Jerusalem thus works to reverse this imagery as it reframes and reworks the understanding of what strong female sexuality can mean in a positive light. A final parallel between Blake's Jerusalem and John's Jezebel can be seen in the descriptions of the followers of either as "little ones" or "children" respectively.

### 5.2 Woman Clothed in the Sun

The next woman we encounter in Revelation is the Woman Clothed in the Sun in chapter 12. Sklar draws out the extensive parallels between the Woman Clothed in the Sun and Jerusalem:

---

65. καὶ ἔδωκα αὐτῇ χρόνον ἵνα μετανοήσῃ, καὶ οὐ θέλει μετανοῆσαι ἐκ τῆς πορνείας αὐτῆς.

66. Lupieri indicates that John's repeated emphasis on Jezebel's femininity serves also to suggest that *femininity* itself is negative, a point that Blake is in direct conflict with. E.F. Lupieri *A Commentary on the Apocalypse of John*, trans. M. Poggi Johnson – A. Kamesar (Grand Rapids: Eerdmans, 2006) 122-123.

67. The history of the reception of the idea of the "Jezebel" is nicely laid out in T. Pippin, "Jezebel Revamped" Pages 32-42 in *Apocalyptic Bodies: The Biblical End of the World in Text and Image* (London: Routledge, 1999).

> Blake's heroine retreats to a wilderness (J49-50, 78-80, 83; Rev 12.6, 14), is devoured by a seven-headed dragon (J89), occasionally has wings (J2i, 14i, 86.1; Rev 12.14) and carries the sun, moon and the stars in them (J2i; Rev 12.1). When clearly labelled in Blake's illuminations (J26i and 92i) she wears the same dress and has what looks like the same face and hair as The Woman clothed in the Sun in the watercolours Blake painted in 1803 and 1805.[68]

So, Blake's Jerusalem, too, is faced with a dragon, and in *Jerusalem* she is actually consumed by her dragon adversary (J89), a departure from the escape/deliverance of the Woman Clothed in the Sun in Revelation, but one that will allow for her connection to the destruction of the Harlot. Following this consumption, Jerusalem is resurrected. This resurrection imagery allows her trajectory to mirror the death and resurrection of her consort, Christ. As has been drawn out both in the introduction to this chapter and the Sklar quote above, there are striking parallels in the physical depictions of the Woman Clothed in the Sun and the imagery of *Jerusalem*'s plate J87. The illustration depicts a female figure that has been banished to the deserts who, although is stated to be Enion, the mother figure of Los, is drawn with a striking resemblance to Jerusalem, specifically as she is depicted wearing Jerusalem's golden dress. This visual connection serves to show how Jerusalem, much like Christ, can be, and is, present in more than simply her explicitly manifest state, and will open up imaginative space to read the cross-feminine character arc.

### 5.3 Harlot

*Jerusalem* is a work in which Blake challenges the concept of biblical harlotry. In his work, Jerusalem is labeled a harlot not due to her wanton nature, but instead due to her loving, forgiving nature. This flips the typically negative biblical sense on its head, a move that is not too far of a stretch when considerations of figures from the Hebrew Bible like Tamar (Genesis 38) and Rahab (Josh 2-6) do allow for the prostitute character to be a positive one.[69] The depiction of Jerusalem as "the Harlot" appears in plate J61 where she self-identifies as being "Indeed a Harlot drunken with the Sacrifice of Idols" (J61).[70] Similarly, the Harlot of Revelation is also described as being "drunk on the blood of the saints and on the blood of

---

68. S. Sklar, "Blake's Jerusalem: Refiguring Revelation's Women," in C.E. Joynes – C.C. Rowland, eds., *From the Margins 2: Women of the New Testament and Their Afterlives* (Sheffield: Sheffield Phoenix Press, 2009) 300.

69. T. Pippin, *Death and Desire: The Rhetoric of Gender in the Apocalypse of John*, 1st ed. (Louisville: Westminster/John Knox, 1992) 65.

70. While the figure in Revelation is called a variety of names (Whore, Harlot, Babylon, etc.) I have chosen to go with "Harlot" because that is the language specifically used in *Jerusalem*.

the witnesses of Jesus" (Rev 17:6).[71] In plate J88, although Vala has antagonized her throughout the poem, "Jerusalem took the Cup which foamed in Vala's hand Like the red Sun upon the mountains in the bloody day Upon the Hermaphroditic Wine-presses of Love & Wrath" (J88:56-58). In this way, Jerusalem's loving nature causes her to put herself in harm's way, taking on the sins of others, especially those of her "little ones"—exemplified by Jerusalem taking the cup from Vala—and this in turn mirrors the taking on of sin by her consort Christ. The images of cups and winepresses seem to be pulled from Revelation: Jerusalem's cup mirrors the Harlot's "golden cup full of abominations and impurities of her fornication" (Rev 17:4),[72] yet unlike Babylon in Rev 14:8 who has "made all nations drink of the wine of the wrath of her fornication," the Harlot of Revelation 17 is the one drunken on the contents of her cup. Similarly, winepresses of wrath appear in Revelation 14, both in 14:10 where the "wine of God's wrath" is mentioned and then also later in 14:18-20 where the process of making that wrath-filled wine is dictated as the angels are harvesting the grapes of the earth which are then thrown into the "great winepress of the wrath of God" (Rev 14:19).

### 5.4 New Jerusalem

Like any good narrative character arc, the trials Jerusalem faces throughout the poem shape her into her final form: the city and the Bride of Christ. Much like how humanity is molded by their experiences, both downfalls and triumphs, so too is Jerusalem shaped by hers. The difference is her experiences are shaped by her love for all of humanity. She falls with Albion, takes the cup from Vala, and is personally affected by those around her to a degree that paints her as the mother of all. In this sense she is all encompassing, the pinnacle example of femininity, and so, it would make sense that, for Blake, she is all the women found in Revelation. The Woman begins as an image of false prophecy, then swings to the other end of the spectrum as a life-giving pregnant woman as the Woman Clothed in the Sun, who then must flee to the desert to save herself from the red dragon. The dragon does not prevail in Revelation 12, for she reappears emerging out of the desert, riding the scarlet beast in Revelation 17, a Harlot drinking the blood of the saints. She has seemingly fallen as far as she can, but her destruction (as the Harlot in v. 17) is a key part of her rising again as the new holy city of Jerusalem, coming from heaven prepared as a bride would be for her husband.

---

71. καὶ εἶδον τὴν γυναῖκα μεθύουσαν ἐκ τοῦ αἵματος τῶν ἁγίων καὶ ἐκ τοῦ αἵματος τῶν μαρτύρων Ἰησοῦ (Rev 17:6).

72. ... ἔχουσα ποτήριον χρυσοῦν ἐν τῇ χειρὶ αὐτῆς γέμον βδελυγμάτων καὶ τὰ ἀκάθαρτα τῆς πορνείας αὐτῆς (Rev 17:4).

## 6. Conclusions

William Blake is arguably one of the wildest authors and artists of all time, but his eccentrically visionary way of interacting with both the world around him and the biblical texts creates a world that is open for interpretation and questioning. Through the lens of visionary theatre, Suzanne Sklar encourages outside-the-box thinking not only in relation to *Jerusalem*, but the world and other texts as well. Her book is a fantastically written road map that gives even the newest of Blake scholars a key into his works, while presenting as many differing opinions on the interpretations of his text as she can in addition to her own thoughts. Visionary theatre is a powerful lens that allows readers of apocalyptic and visionary texts to remember that sometimes the important details are not what a reader would normally look for. It is not necessarily imperative to map out how Golgonooza is laid out in *Jerusalem* or decide definitively if Satan willingly went down to Earth or was thrown down in Revelation, but instead there is room for a multiplicity of scenarios all happening concurrently. For Blake, and perhaps for Revelation as well, the characters themselves can be representative of a multiplicity of things simultaneously. Without a certain degree of imagination and suspension of disbelief, apocalyptic literature—and to some extent, most scripture—falls apart. Blake puts it best in plate J77: "I know of no other Christianity and of no other Gospel than the liberty both of body & mind to exercise the Divine Arts of Imagination."

# INDEXES[1]

## 1. Names and Characters (JS)



1. By Fabio Caruso (FC) and Julian Sieber (JS).

## 2. Places[2] (FC)



2. Except: Asia/Asia Minor, Babylon, Israel, Jerusalem, Mediterranean, Near East, Rome.

## 3. Primary Sources

### 3.1 Old Testament (JS)

## 3.2 Ancient Near Eastern Texts (JS)



## 3.3 New Testament (JS)

## 3.4 Apocrypha and Pseudepigrapha (JS)

## 3.5 Dead Sea Scrolls (JS)



## 3.6 Nag Hammadi (JS)



## 3.7 Hellenistic-Roman Jewish Authors (JS)

### 3.8 Rabbinic Works (JS)



### 3.9 Ancient and Medieval Christian Texts and Authors (FC)

## **3.10 Classical Authors** (FC)

## 4. Modern Authors[3] (FC)



3. Except translators.

## Judaïsme ancien et origines du christianisme

1. Régis Burnet, *Les douze apôtres. Histoire de la réception des figures apostoliques dans le christianisme ancien* (2014)
2. Thierry Murcia, *Jésus dans le Talmud et la littérature rabbinique ancienne* (2014)
3. Christian Julien Robin (éd.), *Le judaïsme de l'Arabie antique. Actes du Colloque de Jérusalem (février 2006)* (2015)
4. Bernard Barc, *Siméon le Juste: l'auteur oublié de la Bible hébraïque* (2015)
5. Claire Clivaz, Simon Mimouni & Bernard Pouderon (éds), *Les judaïsmes dans tous leurs états aux Ier-IIIe siècles (les Judéens des synagogues, les chrétiens et les rabbins). Actes du colloque de Lausanne, 12-14 décembre 2012* (2015)
6. Simon Claude Mimouni & Madeleine Scopello (éds), *La mystique théorétique et théurgique dans l'Antiquité gréco-romaine* (2016)
7. Pierluigi Piovanelli, *Apocryphités. Études sur les textes et les traditions scripturaires du judaïsme et du christianisme anciens* (2016)
8. Marie-Anne Vannier (éd.), *Judaïsme et christianisme chez les Pères* (2015)
9. Simon Claude Mimouni & Louis Painchaud (éds), *La question de la « sacerdotalisation » dans le judaïsme synagogal, le christianisme et le rabbinisme* (2018)
10. Adriana Destro & Mauro Pesce (éds), *Texts, Practices, and Groups. Multidisciplinary approaches to the history of Jesus' followers in the first two centuries. First Annual Meeting of Bertinoro (2-5 October 2014)* (2017)
11. Eric Crégheur, Julio Cesar Dias Chaves & Steve Johnston (éds), *Christianisme des origines. Mélanges en l'honneur du Professeur Paul-Hubert Poirier* (2018)
12. Alessandro Capone (éd.), *Cristiani, ebrei e pagani: il dibattito sulla Sacra Scrittura tra III e VI secolo – Christians, Jews and Heathens: the debate on the Holy Scripture between the third and the sixth century* (2017)
13. Francisco del Río Sánchez (éd.), *Jewish Christianity and the Origins of Islam. Papers presented at the Colloquium held in Washington DC, October 29-31, 2015 (8th ASMEA Conference)* (2018)
14. Simon Claude Mimouni, *Origines du christianisme. Recherche et enseignement à la Section des sciences religieuses de l'École Pratique des Hautes Études, 1991-2017* (2018)
15. Steve Johnston, *Du créateur biblique au démiurge gnostique. Trajectoire et réception du motif du blasphème de l'Archonte* (2021)
16. Adriana Destro & Mauro Pesce (éds), *From Jesus to Christian Origins. Second Annual Meeting of Bertinoro (1-4 October, 2015)* (2019)
17. Marie-Anne Vannier (éd.), *Judaïsme et christianisme au Moyen Âge* (2019)
18. Pierre de Salis, *Autorité et mémoire. Pragmatique et réception de l'autorité épistolaire de Paul de Tarse du Ier au IIe siècle* (2019)
19. Frédéric Chapot (éd.), *Les récits de la destruction de Jérusalem (70 ap. J.-C.) : contextes, représentations et enjeux, entre Antiquité et Moyen Âge* (2020)
20. Simon Claude Mimouni, *Les baptistes du Codex manichéen de Cologne sont-ils des elkasaïtes ?* (2020)

21. Damien Labadie, *L'invention du protomartyr Étienne. Sainteté, pouvoir et controverse dans l'Antiquité (Ier-VIe s.)* (2020)
22. David Hamidović, Simon C. Mimouni & Louis Painchaud (éds), *La « sacerdotalisation » dans les premiers écrits mystiques juifs et chrétiens. Actes du colloque international tenu à l'Université de Lausanne du 26 au 28 octobre 2015* (2021)
23. Bernard Barc, *Du sens visible au sens caché de l'Écriture. Arpenteurs du temps. Essai sur l'histoire religieuse de la Judée à la période hellénistique. Nouvelle édition* (2021)
24. Isabelle Lemelin, *À l'origine des femmes martyres : la mère de 2 Maccabées 7* (2022)
25. Cambry G. Pardee & Jeffrey M. Tripp (éds), *Sacred Texts & Sacred Figures: The Reception and Use of Inherited Traditions in Early Christian Literature. A Festschrift in Honor of Edmondo F. Lupieri* (2022)
26. Dominique Côté, *Pseudo-Clément et Vrai Prophète. Itinéraire d'Athènes à Jérusalem* (2022)
27. David Hamidović, Eleonora Serra & Philippe Therrien (éds), *The Reception of Biblical Figures: Essays in Method* (2024)
28. Cristiana Facchini & Annelies Lannoy (éds), *The Many Lives of Jesus: Scholarship, Religion, and the Nineteenth Century Imagination* (2024)
29. Edmondo F. Lupieri & Louis Painchaud (éds), *"Who is Sitting on Which Beast?" Interpretative Issues in the Book of Revelation. Proceedings of the International Conference held at Loyola University, Chicago, March 30-31, 2017* (2023)